FAST CHEVYS

Alex Gabbard

&

Mary Gabbard

Published by Gabbard Publications, Inc.
Rt. 1, Box 76
Lenoir City, TN 37771
Copyright 1989, Gabbard Publications, Inc.
Printed in USA
1st Printing
by Viking Press

Distributed by:
Motorbooks International
729 Prospect Ave.
Osceola, Wisc. 54020

NOTICE: The information and historical accounts contained in this book are true and accurate to the best of our knowledge. The authors/publisher disclaim all liability incurred in connection with the use of the information contained in this work. However, should an error in historical accuracy appear, it is solely the responsibility of the authors and will be corrected in later editions of this book.

Library of Congress Cataloging-in-Publication Data
Gabbard, Alex & Mary
  Fast Chevys

  Includes index.
  1. Automobile racing - History - Pictorial works.
  2. Chevrolet, General Motors - Historical - Pictorial works.
  I. Title.
  1989
  ISBN 0-9622608-0-0

Cover photos and design by Alex Gabbard
Gallery of Fast Chevys photos and design by Alex Gabbard
Book layout and design by Alex Gabbard

This book is dedicated to Mary. Without her unending
assistance, it could never have happened.

CONTENTS

Acknowledgements:

The following is a listing of the organizations and people who have helped make this book possible. They have provided information, opened their files, supplied photography, provided computer assistance, provided special photo-processing or supplied their cars for photography by the author. This book would not have been possible without these people who have contributed so much in so many ways. It is to them that I owe a great debt of gratitude. I extend many thanks to all these people and hope that I haven't overlooked anyone. If so, my sincerest appologies. However, should any errors be found, they are mine alone.

Alex Gabbard
Lenoir City, TN
July 22, 1989

Chevrolet Division, General Motors:
Floyd Joliet, Dave Hedrick, Cynthia Reid, Herb Fishel, Wes Yocum, Jr., Gib Hufstader, Fred Frincke, Dr. Steve Bates, Don Rust, Ken Kayser, Ralph Kramer

Indianapolis Motor Speedway: Ron McQueeney

National Hot Rod Association: Wally Parks, Leslie Lovette, Steve Gibbs

International Hot Rod Association: Ted Jones, Butch McCall, Don Gillespie, Charles Carpenter, Danny Carr, Larry and Rick Green, Michael Martin, Bill Kuhlmann, Wally Stroupe, Ken Koretsky, Thurmer and Hously, Rob Vandergriff

International Motor Sports Association: John Bishop, Dic van der Feen

Charlotte Motor Speedway: Susan Russo

Darlington International Speedway: Tommy Britt

NASCAR: Daytona International Speedway: Bill France, Bob Mauk, Jonathan Mauk, Bob Costanzo, Chip Williams

Sebring International Grand Prix of Endurance:

Watkins Glen: J. J. O'Malley

Sportscar Vintage Racing Association: Alex Quattle-baum, Joe Pendergast, Bill Butler, Hans Huwyler, Bill Wonder, Dave Rex, John Baldwin, Jonathan Evans, Murray Smith, Don Orosco, John "Bat" Masterson, Ron Vanke, Bob Wechsler, Larry McKay, Robert Verhasselt, Bill Morrison, Jerry Cash, Lawrence Connelly, Larry Barcza, Garrett Waddell, Ignatius Russo, Curt Stucky, Russ Gilmore, James Heck, Leon Hurd, Ed DeLong, Miles Collier, Gene Shiavone, Dave Tom

Walter Mitty Challenge: Steve Simpson, Howard Turner

Car Owners: As noted in the color section and elsewhere throughout this book.

Photographers: Floyd Joliet, Tom Swabe, Bill Preston, Bob D'Olivo, Lionel Birmbom, Dr. Edgar B. Wycoff, D. Randy Riggs, Squire Gabbard, Wesley Gabbard, Mary Gabbard, Gold Dust Classics, NASCAR and Chevrolet photographers of old

Computer Wizards: Dr. Jim Rome, Dr. John Whitson.

Models: Mary Gabbard, LeahDorne Kennedy, Squire Gabbard, Wesley Gabbard

Special thanks to:

Smokey Yunick	Zora Arkus-Duntov
Dr. Dick Thompson	Augie Pabst
Harry Heuer	Bill Devin
Dick Keinath	Fred Frincke
Bill Howell	Paul Prior
Gib Hufstader	Junior Johnson
Hayden Proffitt	Bill "Grumpy" Jenkins
Bill Preston	John Greenwood
Geoff Bodine	Brian Redman
Ken Howes	Bill Kuhlmann
Wes Yocum, Jr.	Herb Fishel
Dr. Steve Bates	Jim Hall
Hap Sharp	Carroll Shelby
Don Rust	Ken Kayser
Tom Swabe	Dr. Jerry Winston
Brad Siqueiros	Don Griggs
Michaela Cox	Keith Kibbe

Introduction:

When the GIs returned to America following the end of World War II, they brought with them a new spirit. Thousands of these seasoned veterans went to college, many with their new wives. They were the source of a huge wave of highly capable men in the nation's work force. And they were all eager for new cars.

The first few years of the postwar era were rich with vitality born from a hunger for the "new". New cars, new household appliances, new everything. The youth movement brought by the returning GIs was taking hold, and the world would never be the same again.

Detroit's designers had been doing war machines, and new cars after the war looked like cars before the war. The GIs were not happy with the selection of new cars available to them. They had seen the spirited European cars, the small and exciting machines from England, France and Italy, and many service men brought their favorite examples back home with them. These men and their cars were the beginning of changes in the way automobiles were manufactured and marketed in this country. But, it took time.

Changes were slow in coming. It took several years for the major manufacturers to tool up to produce cars that looked entirely new. As a result, the first few postwar years offered widespread opportunities for enterprising sorts who could respond to the clamor created by this new force in the automobile market. Names such as Tucker, Kaiser-Frazer, King Midget and Muntz were among many new marques that sprang up alongside Studebaker, Ford, Chrysler and General Motors. Their cars didn't look like warmed-over 1941 and '42 models from the major manufacturers, and the public liked what they saw.

Major redesigns began with the 1947 Studebaker, the Virgil Exner design that was so new in theme that viewers had to look closely to determine which way the car was going. It was smooth in shape with integrated fenders, not even a hint of running boards. It featured curved glass and an aeronautic look so different from prewar designs it had to be all-new. The next year saw Hudson's entry with its equally radical design of smooth sides flush with fenders from front to rear.

Automotive design was rapidly changing. Cars were becoming lower and lower. Hoodlines had always been higher than fenderlines, and occupants sat high in the cars. Not any more. The trend was toward longer, lower, roomier cars with larger trunks - cars with bodies built around frames rather than on them.

Redesigning American-made cars during the three years following the end of WW-II culminated in 1949 when both General Motors and Ford Motor Co. introduced entirely new models that left prewar styling in the dust of the modern era. Fully integrated designs from tip to stern were seen in showrooms all across America, and buyers lined up to buy new cars by the millions.

Ford invested over $118,000,000 to design and tool up for its new-for-'49 model that sold a total of 841,170 units, over 300,000 more than the year before. Even though Ford's "flathead" V-8 engine was by far the fastest in the low price field, buyers flocked into Chevrolet showrooms to buy 1,031,466 cars, a new sales record.

The '49 Chevys were also all-new and very handsome cars of more rakish styling than Ford's rather boxy design. Although Buick, Oldsmobile and Cadillac had their own high compression V-8 engines that year, Chevrolet Division boss Thomas H. Keating did not recognize the rising youth market. He imposed his ultra-conservative ideas by retaining the "stovebolt" inline 6-cylinder whose ancient forebear debuted in 1928 with standardized 1/4-20 bolts common to stoves of the era. The name "stovebolt" stuck and became synonymous with staunch reliability.

While Ford was still offering only 4-cylinders back then, Chevrolet marketeers championed their smoother engine as, "A six for the price of a four". And for 1949, Chevrolet outsold Ford's well-proven V-8 by 23%, a remarkable testimony to the public's respect for the Chevrolet-6. In a few years, though, Chevrolet engineers were to invent a new overhead valve V-8 that would become a tremendous force in the future of American automobiles. It was an engine that remains so good today that millions are still being made each year, some thirty-five years after its introduction.

Buyers drove their new '49 model cars billions of miles, and manufacturers couldn't turn out cars in enough variety to meet demand. Each make sought an edge over its competitors and hawked their edge with advertising as it had never been seen before. Battle lines for new car sales were becoming more entrenched than ever. Automobiles had been a major part of the American economy for four decades, but the influence of the car-hungry postwar buying boom was at a fever pitch.

This period became a fertile time for innovation. Designers and engineers of each make eyed something new from their competitors and rushed back to their drawing boards to invent something newer. Buick dealers offered buyers the first torque converter type automatic transmission, the Dyna-Flow, in their 1948 models, then released the rakish convertible-like hardtop for 1949. Both Buick and Cadillac shared this styling advance with Oldsmobile and Chevrolet, but the top three introduced overhead valve V-8 engines that year. The high compression Olds Rocket-88 set buyers ablaze with performance never seen before in a car styled so handsomely, a higher priced car that shared some styling influence with Chevrolet.

Chrysler "copped" them all with a simple method of starting their car's engine with just an "ignition" key instead of key and a push button. GM returned in 1950 with Buicks featuring tinted glass. The next year, B. F. Goodrich stepped into the "new" market with "Puncture-sealing" tubeless tires for topline cars. Chevrolet introduced its 2-speed PowerGlide autoshifter with a reliable, if rather stodgy, 105 hp, 235 cid six.

With so many all-new cars, everything was indeed rapidly changing. Americans everywhere were caught up in the fascination with "new". Manufacturing methods were changing to produce more and better products of all types. Advertising shifted into high gear to attract more and more buyers who were spending increasing amounts of money on themselves, especially cars. And Americans were taking to the highways like never before. "See the USA in your Chevrolet" was soon to become a theme captured by Chevrolet marketing, and the nation was making it happen with an extensive interstate highway system resulting from the Federal Aid Highway Act of 1944.

For the young movers and shakers of the emerging car culture, cars were no longer simple utility vehicles, they were freedom machines of status and class. Buyers were willing to spend far more on their cars than in previous years, and along with the blossoming hot rod and street machine movement came a burgeoning aftermarket industry. Cars allowed Americans to move to the suburbs and commute to work. More and more homes were being built with integral garages and paved driveways. Car care products beyond gas, oil and grease were a growing part of the multitudes of service stations that sprang up across the horizon.

The population of this country was shifting to a progressively younger average age as the postwar vets became family men and women. Increasing numbers of families were also becoming 2-car families. Growing prosperity fostered optimism that spread confidence throughout this country and fueled a flamboyant era of two-tone paint, fins and chrome; an age of a growing love affair with cars, those that inflamed the "let's go" spirit of a time that has now become hallowed as "the good old days" of the "fabulous 50s".

Although the reality of the times were not nearly so good as we sometimes nostalgically recall, the mid-50s were a time when cars became the expression of America's predominately youth-oriented dream. Convertibles were the rage along with high style two-seaters for the masses, a new theme from Detroit in many ways.

Cars brought America's youth together for roadside gatherings at drive-in restaurants, an outgrowth of the '30s era "diners" that were usually made from surplus railway dining cars that gave the sandwich mills their generic name. Daytime shopping "strips" with angled parking slots in front catered to customers who drove from the suburbs to shop. In time, "shopping centers" would move to the suburbs where the cars were.

Cars also became inextricably entwined with courtship and were the pulse of nighttime "cruisin'". They were transport to the "drive-in" movies for an inexpensive evening of fun at 50-cents a car load, including all the jokesters in the trunk. Dull late-night drive-in often became passion pits for couples who could just as easily drive to the lust lairs of a secluded lover's lane, but "goin' to the movies" was more acceptable for mom and dad.

Countless after-dark arguments about whose car was fastest were settled with races staged between stop lights and on lightly traveled public highways. Hot rodding flourished, and to make it both legal and safe, the first drag strips were built during this time. Drag racing as a sport became formally organized in 1951 when Wally Parks established the National Hot Rod Association in California. Many other racing oriented organizations across America responded to the growing interest in all sorts of automotive competition from high speed record attempts on Muroc Dry Lake, now Edwards Air Force Base, to southern stock car racing. Bill France established NASCAR (National Association for Stock Car Auto Racing) in Daytona Beach, Florida in late 1947, and by 1950, big time stock car racing was underway when the first superspeedway opened, Darlington's 1.25-mile paved almost oval. Johnny Mantz won the first Southern 500 in a Plymouth followed by Herb Thomas' Hudson victory in '51. The Oldsmobiles of Fonty Flock and Buck Baker took the next two Southern 500 wins. Then Thomas repeated his trip to victory lane in '54, again in a Hudson.

The manufacturers in Detroit were slow to recognize the potentially huge market for high performance cars and products, but in a few short years, they were deep into racing on a factory sponsored level, all for the kids.

Traveling during the early 1950s with overnight stays was usually less than desirable and signaled another need generated by a growing and mobile economy. The first motel designed for motoring travelers, Holiday Inn, open its doors in Memphis, Tennessee in 1952.

Like the "Motor Inn", architects were quick to recognize that the "new" America was going to be centered around the automobile. They designed shopping centers as the focus of the new suburban life. This was where the new society was born, where America parked its cars.

The movement that ushered in the new America brought by the returning GIs was perhaps best displayed in the explosive growth of hot rods. They were the interplay of wrenches and dollars, the result of the yearning for more exciting cars, and the desire to do it yourself regardless of what could be bought in new car showrooms.

Although hot rodding was as old as the automobile, southern California with its drag strips and NHRA became the home of the hot rod movement. The dry climate with its year-round warmth was conducive for the stripped down, hot rod roadster. At the time, most of them were Fords.

The "flathead" Ford V-8 introduced in 1932 was a boon to hot rodders. By the late '40s, the flathead was in every conceivable type of hot rod and hot rodders were spending millions of dollars on their cars, and the man who would later become immortalized as "Mr. Corvette", Zora Arkus-Duntov, earned widespread acclaim for his cast aluminum, hemispherical combustion chamber head conversions for the flathead. Racing Detroit's iron was not a passing phase; it was here to stay.

Competition was a previously untapped market for Detroit. Loyal hot rodders were highly "make" conscious and mostly Ford addicts. A billion dollar aftermarket industry had sprung up in support of Ford hot rodders and racers, and anyone who wanted to go fast for low bucks thought "Ford". GM marketeers had pegged the reasonably affluent market with the Buick, Olds and Cadillac V-8s, but not Chevrolet. Keating held his division back a half-decade, but when the all-new Chevrolet V-8 was unveiled, Chevrolet placed in motion the most influential V-8 engine of all time. When introduced in 1954, there was a new mover and shaker. A new era in high performance had dawned.

It was called, Chevrolet.

"When I first saw the Corvette, I thought it was the most beautiful car I had ever seen."

Zora Arkus-Duntov

1
The American Dream

Corvette styling and fiberglass body material were revolutionary concepts for Chevrolet in 1953. Chevrolet photo.

The rise of Chevrolet to become the hot rodder's choice began in the early years of the 1950s. Division General Manager Thomas Keating might have been slow to recognize the emerging youth-oriented market segment around 1950, but what he was doing made his division the biggest seller in the GM fold. He was doing things right, though perhaps without an eye toward future needs. When his boss, General Motors President Charles E. Wilson - known more often as "Engine Charlie" for his foresight that pushed GM into the modern era of V-8 engines - told Keating to prepare a young man's car, the proven, respected but staid 6-cylinder Chevrolets of the working middle class were to receive two new concepts that pushed the make into the forefront of postwar American automobiles. Those two concepts were the Corvette and the "small-block" V-8 engine.

No longer would cars wearing the bowtie be those forever-reliable "old fogies". By 1955, they became a new generation of highly styled cars with exciting performance, and remained just as reliable as ever.

The image of Chevrolet automobiles changed so completely from 1950 to 1955 that little resemblance to previous outward concepts could be seen. The Corvette was a radical experi-

ment, a fiberglass bodied two-seater that launched a love affair so pervasive that it survives stronger today than ever before. The V-8 rose to such overwhelming proportions in the hot rodding market that it soon ousted Ford and continues to dominate the aftermarket industry today. And along with the Corvette and V-8 engine came an entire new generation of revitalized Chevrolets of such captivating styling that the cars have become universally regarded as "classics" even though millions were built.

Just ten years after their introduction, the 1955-'56-'57 model year Chevys were being referred to as classics. Today, more than thirty years afterwards, they remain some of the most sought-after cars ever made for no other reason than so many were built that just about everyone has either owned one or knew someone who did.

What was the inspiration for such changes? Perhaps it was learning that Ford was restyling again for 1952 and was working on an overhead valve V-8 engine for its 1954 models, the all-new and modern "Y-block", all just three years after the hugely successful '49 model line. Perhaps it was this country's growing prosperity and Chevrolet's succession of million seller years. Huge profits are big incentive to update styling and innovation by implementing new concepts. More probably, it was time for change. The public was captivated by "new", whatever it was.

GM had the people to make it happen, and Chevrolet's role as the General's low-price leader entered a new era of technonological innovation so extensive that it literally shaped

Top form of Chevrolet's inline 6-cylinder was the triple carburetor Corvette rated at 150 hp. This version was near the limit of the engine's potential in production form. Chevrolet photo.

For 1955, the Corvette engine changed to the small block V-8 but styling remained the same. Performance improved, and owners could try out their new V-8 'Vette during Speed Week and maybe make it to the "Century Club". Chevrolet photo.

much of the future of America's experience with automobiles.

Although 6-cylinder Chevy owners of the early-50s could brag about their "Road Race" engine, the big-6 with higher compression and lighter weight cast aluminum pistons rather than cast iron, the Chevy-6 was never able to compete on even terms with Ford's flathead V-8 and its highly developed racing fraternity. The predicted demise of Ford Motor Co. following WW-II had not happened, and Henry Ford II was leading his company into expanded prosperity by recognizing that the venerable flathead had reached the end of the line as the heart of fast Fords. Chevy's big-6 was not dead, but Ed Cole & Co. were about to introduce Chevrolet power as it had never been before.

The December 1951 meeting of GM's Engineering Policy Committee dealt with a central problem: although Chevrolets were selling well, they were associated more with older than younger buyers. The younger the first time-buyer, the more future repeat sales were possible because of make loyalty.

Chevrolet wasn't planning well. The public had come to expect year-to-year changes in styling. Facelifts no longer worked and Chevrolet entered its 1952 model year with cars that looked like '49s while the new-for-'52 Fords were stylish and very appealing.

Although the Korean War limited production and sales, Chevrolet's market share steadily declined while Ford's increased. Ford sales jumped by more than 406,000 cars in 1953, followed by another increase of more than 210,000 in '54. Chevrolet's market share slid from 22.8% in 1950 to 20.9% in '51 to 20.2% in '52.

Another growing influence on car sales that Chevrolet had little benefit from was the rapid growth of interest in racing. Ford Motor Co. shone brilliantly in the early '50s Mexican Road Races that spanned the length of Mexico. Although the winning stock class Lincolns ran GM HydraMatic transmissions that performed flawlessly, General Motors was not benefitting from the exposure, while Lincoln showroom traffic flourished. The interested public wanted to see what a road racing winner was like.

Along with the stock car racing in the south, these western U.S. races were creating the first volleys of the horsepower wars that suddenly matured in the mid-50s. It would take a new Chevrolet to become part of the glory of winning, and although Chevrolet produced its 30,000,000th car in 1953, it was due more to marketing blitzkrieg by Ford and Chevrolet than attracting buyers with superior products.

Following the end of Korean hostilities, Ford launched a sales campaign for 1953 that forced dealers to heavily discount cars. Buyers swarmed in by the droves, and both Chevrolet and Plymouth as low-price competitors had to follow suit or be left in the dust. Chevrolet's market share soared to 25.7% while Ford grabbed 25.3%, and Ford produced its 40,000,000th vehicle that year.

The sales war was on, and advertising was quick to pick up on any twist that brought in more buyers. While the major manufacturers were trying every conceivable trick to outsell their competitors, the public became witness to the beginning of the fabulous '50s, the glory days of one new and better product after another, along with dramatic styling changes year to year.

The turnaround at Chevrolet began in May, 1952 when Edward N. Cole arrived from the Cadillac Division. He was Chevrolet's new Chief Engineer and brought to his post the experience he had gained from enginemaster Harry F. Barr on the high compression Caddy V-8 introduced in 1949. That engine was not the basis of Cole's new Chevrolet V-8, but the experience gained from it laid the foundation for a simpler, smaller and lighter engine with vast designed-in potential, so much so that the original engine has evolved into many variations with millions built since the small block was introduced in the 1955 models.

Cole was the consummate engineer, a seasoned and dynamic leader with a strong creative bent. He had the foresight and strength of will to bring several innovations to Chevrolet, including his rear engine ideas that later materialized in the Corvair. During the years leading to his succession of Keating as Chevrolet General Manager in 1956, Cole was

The 1955 Chevrolet was so refreshingly new and exciting that buyers bought over a million of them. Chevrolet photo.

And they went racing, too. Not only were the new Chevys seen in southern style stock car racing, this Bel Air convertible paced the Indy 500 in 1955. Chevrolet photo.

to have a profound influence on the future of Chevrolet. At his new post, he made things happen with both the new V-8 and the Corvette, and he did so by more than tripling the number of engineers on the staff to nearly 3,000.

Although Cole is sometimes given credit for the Corvette, that project was more the product of GM stylist Harley Earl whose pre-war styling exercises laid the foundation for much of GM postwar themes, notably the hardtop coupe and smoothly integrated body/fender lines. Earl saw and helped make the market for an inexpensive two-seat roadster for the increasingly affluent young buyer. His imagination no doubt hung on the gorgeous but horribly unreliable Jaguar XK-120, a car that he particularly liked. He also knew that Jags, and especially Ferraris and Aston Martins, were expensive, temperamental, and largely non-servicable in hometown U.S.A. where a Chevrolet, even a classy looking two-seater, would be driven. His Corvette was to be everything the European cars were not, yet be just as exciting. The Corvette had to be far cheaper and maintain Chevrolet's reputation of proven dependability.

In the beginning, Earl pursued his pet project in secrecy. On his staff at GM's Art and Color group was a young sports car enthusiast named Robert McLean tapped by Earl to do the layout of the car. What resulted is history, a beautiful roadster in the European tradition but truly American in design and construction.

To keep costs within the projected window of public acceptance, the basic hardware and driveline had to come from existing Chevrolet production items; the engine, transmission, chassis and suspension. Therein lies the rub created

when the Corvette was launched in 1953. Engine: the "Blue Flame Special" 6-cylinder all grown up to 150 horsepower and behind it the PowerGlide 2-speed automatic. Body material: fiberglass reinforced plastic. This was a sports car? With an automatic? Would the body shatter on a cold day if hit?

Overall, the car was impressive and well done for its price. It was also a spirited performer capable of running with anything produced in this country but in a handsome package unlike any assembly line product. What the first Corvettes established was that Chevrolet was now in the business of personal luxury cars as defined by the "typical" American buyer, but there were many unanswered questions from the public that measured it by sports car standards.

Not only was the Corvette a radical break in Chevrolet's traditional product line, it was a risky experiment in new manufacturing methods. Here was the long awaited rejuvenation for Chevrolet, a thrilling showpiece that Cole championed as a gem for Chevrolet as a profit-maker. He wanted Chevrolet to produce the car and sold the concept to his bosses, Keating and Wilson, on the basis of public response to Earl's one-off showcar displayed first at the January, 1953 Motorama.

The Motorama was held in New York at the prestigious Waldorf-Astoria. The show drew an estimated 4 million spectators who gave the Corvette a resounding vote of approval. That was enough to set the project on-line. As credit to the thorough design and engineering job performed by Chevrolet, that first Corvette was one of very few cars in the history of America's big three manufacturers that went from showcar to production virtually unchanged. It took less than 12 months.

Earl and Cole were sure that a market existed for such a car, but sales from 1953 to '55 proved otherwise. It would take at least 10,000 buyers, if not 20,000, during each model year for the bean counters to justify production. During the first year, 1953, only 300 cars were built, each by hand to work out details of increased production when a new plant was com-

Chevrolet's small block V-8 changed the way Americans thought about engines and also changed the way hot rodders powered their cars. The engine soon dominated stock classes of drag racing, and by the '60s, Chevys were also a boon to homebuilt gas class cars. Ed Schartman of Ohio raced a '55 like this one and later became a top star with factory Mercurys.

Styling! The '56 Corvette and Le Sabre. Chevrolet photo.

pleted in St. Louis. Each of the first year Corvettes was selectively placed, rather than offered to the general public, and carried a suggested retail of $3498. That was expensive by 1953 standards, about twice what a family sedan cost.

Corvette production for 1954 rose to just 3,640, although the cars were offered in three colors rather than just one, the original '53 Polo White, Pennant Blue and Sportsman Red. Corvette market planners made the connection between America's national symbolism with the red, white and blue colors, but it didn't help sales. End of year dealer reports told that Corvette was a dud. Almost half the year's production

was unsold. Now there was talk of dropping the car, but Ford Motor Co. saved the Corvette.

When the Thunderbird was introduced in 1954, it came with a high quality all-steel body, roll-up windows, a steel hardtop and spirited V-8 engine with either a manual or automatic transmission. Corvette was outdone in every way. T-Bird sales took off and totalled over 16,000 units for the year. But Cole would not let the Corvette die, especially since he knew that 1955 would be the first year for his new V-8.

Both the Thunderbird and Corvette were expressions of the American dream, but Ford had embarrassingly beaten Chevrolet to the punch. Thus stung by Dearborn, battle lines were being drawn around the 1955 V-8s. A horsepower and cubic inch war would unfold in dramatic fashion and burst on the scene in the form of hotly contested stock car racing, sports car road racing, drag racing and cruisin'.

"The times" were optimistic and confidence spread throughout this country. It would soon become a flamboyant era of two-tone paint, fins, chrome and high performance. Convertibles were the rage, and although two-seaters for the masses was a new theme, it wasn't styling alone that buyers wanted. The public was becoming increasingly brand conscious and wanted their make to win.

The Chevrolet versus Ford battles were about to surge past Lincoln, Oldsmobile, Hudson and Chrysler, and Cole's small-block V-8 in the new Chevrolet made it happen.

The man most responsible for the "new" Chevrolet Division and two of its most significant products, the small block V-8 engine and the Corvette, Ed Cole, seated in one of the experimental "low fin" SR-2 Corvettes. June, 1956. Chevrolet photo.

The Time Was Right

By the early 1950s, auto racing was becoming a big time sport in America. More and more sports cars, mostly from Europe, were being sold in this country, and dealers were springing up all across the nation. Not only was Detroit the home of the U. S. automobile industry, it was also fast becoming the home of many import agencies.

From east coast to west coast, amateur organizations were putting on more and more events that put sports cars in the limelight of public awareness. The events were becoming progressively better organized and made a lot of big names in the sport. Three areas of the U.S. were hotbeds of road racing; the northeast, California and Florida. The time was right for an American sports car, but the best that could be achieved then were the hybrids made from stuffing a Cadillac, Olds, Buick or Chrysler V-8 into a European roadster.

In the northeast, the Bridgehampton Road Races had begun in 1948 and drew record crowds each year. The races were run over public roads and were supported by local officials and sponsored by some municipal organization such as the Lions Club. The Sports Car Club of America, SCCA, was a growing sanctioning body dedicated to amateur racing.

By 1952, spectators were enjoying heated battles between the "big" cars from Britisher Sydney Allard and Italy's Enzo Ferrari, along with a host of "specials" in all sorts of configurations.

Allards were one of those hybrids that actually went into production, though limited. They were mostly cobbled together from existing hardware and rebodied in open roadster form. Such cars were the fire-breathing, American V-8 powered ground pounders of the time. Carroll Shelby, later to become Chevrolet's archadversary, raced a variety of cars during his days as a driver and commented, "Back then, if you had an Allard, you really had something!"

No doubt the huge success of the Allards in the early '50s was a strong influence on Shelby's later Ford-powered Cobras. Shoe-horning a big V-8 into a strong but lightweight European chassis was a growing movement which came to fruition with Shelby's World Championship winning Cobras of 1965. Engine swaps in stripped down pre-war American cars were the theme of the rapidly expanding hot rodding segment where the Ford flathead V-8 dominated. With GM power, hybrids were the racer's edge, but Chevrolet was not yet a part of it.

Like Allard, other specialty manufacturers of road cars and racing cars were attracted to the latest edition American V-8s. They had strong and powerful engines with lots of spine-tingling low-end torque that could propel a slick roadster or coupe upwards of 150 mph. Detroit's engines were cheap when compared to the typical European small displacement varieties available. American V-8s were also thunderously noisy, an attribute of admiration to this day.

Although purists maintained that internal cam V-8s were

Two men who got the Corvette rolling, Bill Mitchell and Zora Arkus-Duntov, look over an early fuel injection system. Fuel injection was another "first" for Chevrolet and a boon to racers, but public acceptance fell short of expectations because it was "cold natured" and easy to flood. Drivers had to learn not to pat the gas pedal when starting a fuel injected car when cold. Chevrolet photo.

Behind the scenes, a factory technician performs an air flow analysis of FI manifold. Chevrolet photo.

unsophisticated and therefore of little interest, the engines had huge potential and continued to be a thorn in the side of "sophisticated" engines such as Ferrari's single overhead cam V-12. Siata offered its highly developed sports car chassis with a Chrysler hemi V-8 topped with dual carburetors. This chassis was shown in Italy's Turin Motor Show of 1952. Like Allard, Siata built cars to order and offered both the Chrysler mill or less hulking Cadillac V-8.

America's own Briggs Swift Cunningham, of the Swift foods dynasty, set out to prove that the American will to win was second to none. He was this country's top sportsman at the time and chose the task of beating the Europeans at their own game; long distance endurance racing, particularly the 24-Hours of Le Mans. Cunningham selected the Chrysler hemi for his line of all-American cars, the same that carried the U.S. official racing colors of white and blue to Le Mans and almost won the most prestigious race of them all.

The Cunningham cars were the outgrowth of Briggs' association with Phil Walters and Bill Frick that began in 1949 when they met at Watkins Glen, New York's fingerlakes area road course through town and country. Walters and Frick built the Cadillac powered Fords known as the Fordillacs. Given the "good times" enthusiasm shown by amateur racers at the time, the cars could just as well have been called Walfricks or more likely Frickters. In any event, Le Mans officials would not accept entry of the Fordillacs because there was no recognized manufacturer of the cars.

Cunningham solved that problem in 1950 by entering two Cadillacs, and thus began a remarkable escapade of racing history. One was a basically stock Coupe de Ville while the second was similar underneath but with a special streamlined body. It was dubbed "Le Monstre" by disbelieving Frenchmen. These huge cars were the subject of considerable

attention. Of sixty entrants, twenty-four different makes were represented including the first post-war entries from the U.S.A.

During the race, Briggs stuffed "Le Monstre" into a sand bank and lost time getting back on the track. In the other car, water leaks and transmission problems prevented the Coupe de Ville from finishing higher than 10th, which was, after all, an astounding display of survivability of an American luxury car amid highly prepared racing cars. "Le Monstre" was faster on the long Mulsanne Straight, clocking 134 mph, but finished 11th due to its earlier altercation with the sand bank.

Many spectators and officials alike went away still shaking their heads. American cars were not supposed to beat pure racing cars. The purpose of the exercise was to finish and get as much experience as possible for the upcoming Cunningham attack on the continentals at Le Mans the next year. His special built racing cars, the C-2R (R for Race), were offered to any buyer initially with either a Cadillac or the new Chrysler hemi engine. However, only the hemi saw production, and Chrysler engineering performed extensive engine development for Cunningham. Reportedly, a C-2R was clocked at 152 mph in tests preparing for Le Mans.

In the 1951 24-Hours, Walters and John Fitch ran as high as second behind the eventual winner, the C-type Jaguar, but failing brakes dropped the car to 18th overall to take the 8-liter class win. Lessons learned brought about the C-3R, but the decision was made to offer the rather heavy Cunningham to the public and to develop an improved racer. Thus was born the C-4R, a resounding success that became one of America's all-time winningest sports racers.

V-8 powered hybrids were proving to be formidable competition. In an early race with a C-4R, Walters was entered at

Smokey Yunick and Duntov chat with "big" Bill France while NASCAR flagman Frank Swain set the scene during Speed Week, February, 1956. This is the Corvette, Yunick's "mule" test car thought to be the first prepared specifically for competion and the first to actually race when Paul Goldsmith raced the car the week before. Smokey Yunick photo.

Bridgehampton '52, but dropped out on the 15th lap because of a loose exhaust pipe, but went on to win numerous other races.

Allard and Cunningham versus Ferrari battles were the top attraction of sports car racing of that era. Right out of the box with no modifications, a bone stock Cadillac engine in an Allard made a race winning combination. The cars racked up many victories.

By 1952, SCCA had well established regions all across America with amateur racers enjoying a rapidly expanding sport. New York's Bridgehampton was a big race in the northeast. The circuit was over public roads and drew thousands of spectators who saw another Ferrari-Allard shootout. Bill Spear in a 4.1-liter (250 cid) Ferrari "America" just nudged past Fred Wacker's 331 cid Cad-Allard to win. England's Tom Cole in another Cad-Allard had been the winner the previous two years, but was put out by a thrown rod on the second lap, a rare occurance for the strong Caddy.

Watkins Glen, also in New York, began its more than 4 decades of road racing on October 2, 1948. Its first "Grand Prix", a 6.6-mile course through the village of Watkins Glen and surrounding ups, downs and curves over outlying roads (some not even paved), brought together 49 entrants for two races. The cars were a mixture of postwar specials and pre-war European cars. In the first race, Cunningham was on the front row in his BuMerc, a Buick powered Mercedes, along with Mike Vaughn in a Lagonda. At the green, George Weaver shot his 1936 GP Maserati V-8RI from the second row into the lead but was out just a lap later. Cunningham rounded the course hot on the heels of Frank Griswold's

late-30s 2900B Alfa Romeo but could do no better than 2nd at the finish.

Through the next few years of racing at the Glen, the course changed several times, then found a permanent home in 1956 on the 550 acre site it is now on. Cad-Allards and Chrysler-Cunninghams were awesome during those years. Although Briggs raced at the Glen several times, his luck kept him from winning five times, each a 2nd place finish. What his cars and Allards did was to firmly prove that American V-8s certainly did have a winning place in sports car racing.

By the early '50s, Watkins Glen had emerged as a premier race and attracted growing numbers of entrants and racing fans. The 1952 race drew 200,000 spectators who jammed the narrow streets through the village and outlying road course. On the second lap of the Grand Prix, the feature of three races, a 7-year old boy was killed when Fred Wacker attempted to squeeze his Cad-Allard past the leading Cunninghams of Briggs and John Fitch just as the course made a right turn out of town. It was a tragic day. The race was stopped and never run through the village again.

Because America was a rich market, Enzo Ferrari produced continually larger displacement roadsters and coupes in his "America" series of cars, and they were seen in the hands of more and more prominent Americans. Jim Kimberly, grandson of the founder of Kimberly-Clark, drove a 4.1 to fifth overall at Bridgehampton '52. By the end of 1954, Kimberly was regarded as America's No. 1 driver, having won 17 of 20 races entered from California to Florida to New York that year, all in 4.9-liter Ferraris. His was a very professional racing organization known as Scuderia Kimberly, the

Sports car racer, Tom Carstens, had Vic Edelbrock fit this British-built H.W.M. with a tri-carb small block to make the first Chevy V-8 engine swap in a road racer.

forerunner of the completely equipped racing team of modern times.

Another up and coming driver was young Phil Hill from California. He also helped introduce the Ferrari 12-cylinder sound to this country and later became America's only World Driving Champion at the wheel of Ferrari factory backed Grand Prix machines. He and a number of sports car enthusiasts such as Kimberly and movie screen writer Ronald MacDougall, Texan Carroll Shelby and other notable drivers liked the Italian's overall approach to sports car design. And while the big bore V-8 sound intermingled with the shrill of 12 small pistons in full chat, an estimated 100,000 San Francisco spectators saw their first road race, yet another Ferrari versus Allard battle.

It took place in 1952. The San Francisco Region of SCCA hosted the event at Golden Gate Park. Unlike today's flourishing city street races, it was the first time in many years that a major road race had been held within the limits of a large American city. The event was a fund raiser sponsored by the Guardsmen, a local organization aiding under-privileged children. Local newspapers carried weeks of pre-race publicity and followed it with front page results. The Army sent a detachment of MP's to assist a large group of volunteers from the San Francisco Police Department who donated their day off for charity. It was a huge success.

Golden Gate was considered the best road race ever seen in the west up to then. Drawing a huge contingent of competitors and spectators, it was another example of the growing appeal of sports car racing. No doubt many spectators drove their Chevys to parking areas, for that was about all the make could do. The rumblings of change were taking shape in Detroit, but it would be another year before the Corvette would appear, and then to a market that didn't know just what to make of it.

The Cad-Allards that roared around Golden Gate's 3.1-mile course gave GM enthusiasts something to brag about. Bill Pollack, *AUTO Speed and Sport* magazine's advertising manager, attacked each of the 28 laps of the Guardsman Cup Race with his usual winning form. After completing 86.8 miles, his victory made it four in a row in four starts at the wheel of Thomas Carstens' Cad-Allard which was resplendent in wide whitewall tires all around, including its matching spare. Pollack was later to figure in Chevrolet racing when he drove the car Carstens commissioned hot rodder Vic Edelbrock to build. Edelbrock modified and installed a Chevy V-8 in Carstens' H.W.M. Grand Prix chassis in 1955. This was the first Chevrolet V-8 engine swap in a sports-racing car.

The under 3-liter Ferrari 212 of Phil Hill fell behind during the race, but closed with a vengeance toward the end by cutting Pollack's lead about 4 seconds a lap. Hill drove his 2.56-liter car to 2nd overall a scant four seconds behind Pollack. With that impressive duel, Hill was invited to co-drive one of the Ferrari factory cars with Tom Cole in the upcoming 24-Hours of Le Mans. His driving career was about to take off.

California sports car racing was also taking off. Its year-round good climate encouraged racing, and road races with

11

The great American dream machine, the '56 Corvette, was beginning to evlove from the previous styling and lackluster image of no performance into a refined sports car with teeth. This was a street car with winning potential as Dr. Dick Thompson proved when he won the SCCA C/Production National Championship in a factory prepared Corvette handled through Barney Clark of Campbell-Ewald. Chevrolet photo.

the names Golden Gate, Palm Springs, Torrey Pines and Pebble Beach were replaced by permanent race courses named Riverside, Laguna Seca and Sears Point.

Other names in the sport became nationally recognized, names like Edelbrock, Clay Smith cams, S.Co.T. superchargers and Chet Herbert, the cam and roller lifter supplier for Pollack's winning Cad-Allard. These men and others would have a strong influence on the future of hot rodding and racing in many forms.

Florida was another locale of growing interest in racing. It was centered at Sebring, a huge, flat WW-II bomber training airbase known as Hendrick Field. The 12-Hours of Sebring, located in Florida's orange growing region, was and remains a beautiful spring time race. It has been described as the world's largest outdoor party.

The first race on the bumpy Florida circuit was a 6-hour affair based on a handicap system that declared the tiny 1.1-liter (67 cid) Crosley of Fritz Koster and Ralph Deshon the winner, hardly a great American triumph. That was December 31, 1950.

Alec Ulmann was the man behind Sebring. He formulated his plans around a 12-hour enduro the next year that would attract professional teams. He wanted America to have an international caliber race. Since SCCA was an organization for amateurs, the club's directors were aghast at the thought of sanctioning a professional race. It was heresy! The next thing would be paying travel expenses, and - Oh, Lordy! - prize money.

Ulmann's continual efforts to make Sebring more than just another race brought great acclaim to the sport. In time, his

foresight was to prove to be the direction road racing evolved, prize money. By 1953, Sebring was an established international event with FIA credentials as a world championship point carrying race. Europe's top teams came to Florida, but the 12-Hours that year belonged to the C-4R Cunningham.

Briggs' works located in West Palm Beach, Florida was the hub of activity for many of the European teams, and it was his car driven by John Fitch and Phil Walters that made its way to the winner's circle. The spectators and competitors went home with a new respect for American V-8 power.

Clearly, the market was there for a high performance sports car, but racing involved only a few cars while Detroit's thinking was in tens of thousands. Such a car had to be a road car for the average person, not a racing driver. It had to be one that offered buyers both the image of exclusivity and those creature comforts necessary for day-to-day motoring. But being a road car meant certain compromises as a racer. The Corvette was Chevrolet's answer to the market, a compromise that had a very difficult start only to be saved by Ed Cole's V-8 and Ford's Thunderbird.

The Small Block

The now famous 265 cubic inch Chevrolet overhead valve V-8 introduced in 1955 completely changed the automotive market for most Americans. Not only did it strongly influence Chevrolet sales, it also made a significant impact on the

12

The legendary small block V-8 has been built in 10 different displacements and 6 basic induction systems. Over 60 million have been built!

performance car image that Ford had won since the introduction of Henry's flathead V-8 in 1932. The variety of all-new cars introduced made 1955 a boom year. It also became the norm for succeeding years noted by significant styling changes. New equipment emerged from the manufacturers at a faster rate than at any other time in the industry's past. Things automotive were happening fast.

Because of Ed Cole's masterpiece, Chevrolet and Ford quickly became locked in a struggle that had not existed before. Chevrolet had never been able to compete with Ford on even terms regarding top speed, nor did Chevrolet make much more than an underdog's impact on the hot rodder market. But with the new V-8, Chevrolet moved into the high performance league and pushed Ford aside to claim a fast growing share of both markets.

Not only were the rival firms still competing for showroom sales, they were thrust into escalating engineering, design and manufacturing battles resulting in the "horsepower" and "cubic inch" wars of the mid-50s. Ford returned to racing in a big way in 1955, largely because of the advertising hype given based on several successes claimed by Chevy's new V-8. And for the first time, Chevrolet went nose-to-nose with Ford, both with factory teams. Advertising took a dramatic turn. Publicly brandishing racing wins and high speed records was a new attention-getter that greatly heightened the public's consciousness. Simply put, racing victories not only fueled

rivalries, it sold cars.

It didn't take long for manufacturers to learn that a few well-placed emblems showing engine size or induction method or model type sharpened the interests of prospective buyers. Such emblems became bragging rights that contributed to the aura of being special whether the cars really were or not.

Modern movie themes cast fast cars, girls and outlaw racing as well entrenched in America's social structure of the fabulous '50s. It is usually exaggerated when looked back upon with a nostalgic eye. We've forgotten that those were also days of compromise. Nash and Hudson lost some of their former identities when they merged in May, 1954 to become American Motors. And a merger between Studebaker and Packard loomed as difficult times for both those time honored makes. The men behind Kaiser-Willys chose to end production of their cars. 1954 was not a banner year. That changed with the '55 models when Detroit exploded with new models, new everything. Passenger car production soared to almost 8,000,000. GM had put well over $1 billion into its new models, and Chevrolet got $300 million to finance all-new cars with an all-new engine. Chevrolet produced 1,830,038 passenger cars that year, a sales record that stood until 1960. 43% of those Chevys received Cole's new V-8. Thus, more than 780,000 small-blocks came onto the automotive scene in 1955 alone. V-8 powered Chevys exceeded the production totals from each of GM's other divisions. Chevrolet had hit the jackpot with its most handsome models since the war. The new look was "Show Car Styling at its Beautiful Best!" as proclaimed in advertising brochures.

Chevy's new engine was the evolution of concepts shown in GM's first V-8s of the late '40s. It took seven years after Cadillac, Olds and Buick for Chevrolet to get its own V-8, but when the "bowtie" engine emerged, it proved to be a far bigger success. Being small, compact and lightweight - about 37 pounds less than Chevrolet's current inline six - Cole's V-8 was a remarkable achievement of technical innovation.

The selection of 8-cylinders in a V configuration offered a strong crankcase layout with five main bearings. Crankshaft linebore axis to top of the block was several inches less than the current 6-cylinder. Choosing an over-square bore and stroke, (3.75-inch bore, 3.0-inch stroke) produced a quick revving mill with huge potential. In standard 2-bbl form, the engine turned out 162 hp @ 4400 rpm, 12 more than the most powerful six Chevrolet offered, the three 1-bbl Corvette. The

A factory technician dynos an FI 283 in 1956. Fuel injection was a bold move for Chevrolet and caused the development of a number of new high performance pieces like better heads and larger displacement that produced 1 horsepower per cubic inch. Note the "rams horn" exhaust manifold, another HiPo piece. Chevrolet photo.

compared to the 6's 4200 rpm of 551.6 inches per second, a reduction of 9.4%. All this indicates that the V-8 was able to make more power and more torque and did it easier. An added advantage from the more efficient V-8 design was increased fuel economy.

Cole and Harry Barr designed many features into the V-8. The engine's lower piston speed and shorter stroke from its over-square concept and large bearing journal area gave it a number of further advantages such as higher rpm potential, lower bearing loads and a lighter crankcase with a lower center of gravity. Although higher rpm implies greater piston acceleration and therefore increased loads on wristpins and crankshaft journals, the V-8 in fact had slightly less than 10% greater piston acceleration which was compensated for by using steel crankshafts (rather than cast iron) and stronger rods which actually reduced reciprocating mass by being shorter than the 6-cylinder rod.

Another feature designed into the engine that had profound impact on its future was the selection of bore spacing that allowed progressively greater displacement simply by boring cylinders. This feature alone assured the survival of the engine for many years because identical block castings could be built into a variety of engines for a variety of applications not limited only to cars.

An engine's rotational speed can be severely limited by its ability to efficiently exchange each cylinder volume during intake and exhaust strokes. Breathing was and remains the bottleneck of top engine performance. Cole's selection of valve size and wedge shaped combustion chamber with valves arranged in line produced a compact and direct flow-through path that simplified intake and exhaust gas transfer considerably. His selection was excellent, as can be seen in any small block head from 1955 or 1985. They are interchangeable. After more than thirty years, improvement has been little more than increased valve size, slightly reshaped combustion chambers and a few heads with angled spark plugs.

Cole established another break from older designs with the elimination of the rocker arm shaft that spanned all valve stems on each bank. Instead, each valve was given its own rocker arm on a ball fulcrum pivoting on a pressed-in stud and lock nut making each one entirely independent of other valve operation and more easily adjustable whether hydraulic or mechanical. Eliminating the rocker arm shaft also saved

most powerful V-8, again the Corvette engine, was rated at 195 hp @ 5000 rpm, giving a 33 hp gain over the base V-8 and 45 more than the 6.

Comparing the 6-cylinder and V-8 shows significant design differences. Piston area of the V-8 was 88.36 square inches while the 6 was 79.63, an 11% increase for the V-8. But cylinder output of the V-8 was lower, 24.38 hp versus 25 hp, showing that the V-8 had much more potential. Specific output of 0.276 hp per unit piston area versus 0.314 for the 6-cylinder was a 12% reduction which indicates that stresses on the 6 were considerably greater than the V-8 at peak power. The V-8's torque was also improved by 16.5%, and it was delivered more smoothly at higher rpm (3000 rpm for the V-8 versus 2400 for the 6). More impulses delivered to the crankshaft per rotation meant smoother operation because of two more cylinders. Piston speed at peak power was also in favor of the V-8 because of its 24% shorter stroke. At 5,000 rpm, reciprocating piston speed was 499.8 inches per second weight. Reduced manufacturing time and fewer parts to inventory and control lowered costs. Further simplification was achieved by making the heads interchangeable.

Effective lubrication of the rocker arms and valve stems was made possible by hollow push rods that provided the path of oil flow to the rocker arm assemblies. This technique, again very simple for the time, eliminated the need for external oil

speed automatic and excess weight.

If the Corvette was to be a sports car, it had to have, among other things, a manual transmission in the floor. Two or three key people at Chevrolet were listening, but four-on-the-floor was a thing of the future. However, late in the model year, a few 'Vettes received a new close-ratio three-speed manual. It was a step in the right direction, but while things were really

Styling of the '55 Chevrolets was a dramatic break from earlier models. Like most styling of the time, the front end was given a "leaning forward" stance to accentuate the visual appeal of motion. Chrome accents on the sides, especially the "arrow" on the rear flanks, produced a fleet image. This was also the days of hood ornaments, note the airplane. Chevrolet photo.

feeder lines. That reduced weight, lowered fabrication labor and materials costs.

Because the engine block was shorter, the path of water flow was reduced from the typical 6-cylinder, and that improved heat removal. Thus, the radiator and its volume of water could be smaller, a further reduction of weight and materials in any Chevrolet with the V-8.

Thus, Cole's engine was a benchmark of design and manufacturing simplicity. However, all of the clever ideas were rolled into it with one thing in mind; Chevrolets were the low priced leader, and its new V-8 had to be as CHEAP as possible to manufacture. By the numbers, it has proven to be the most successful engine ever produced.

The impact of the V-8 on Corvette was very pronounced. Road testers of the time praised the V-8's smooth and effortless performance. The car's rapid acceleration, 0-60 mph in 8.5 seconds, was 2.5 seconds quicker than the 6-cylinder Corvette in a virtually identical car.

Road & Track gave the V-8 Corvette many favorable comments and commended switching to more modern 12-volt electrics. They cited the car's stability and excellent ride, but lamented the car's overall "failure" as a sports for its two-

taking off at Chevrolet overall, Corvette sales took a nosedive.

Even at $2934 base, few people wanted one. All but six of the 674 Corvettes built in 1955 were V-8 powered. Sales were only 18.5% of the year before. The Corvette was almost dead. Almost.

While racing results of the V-8 Chevys prompted Ford to go racing, Ford's trend-setting Thunderbird was the main reason that Corvette production was not dropped. Thunderbirds sold 16,155 that year, and Harley Earl steadfastly defended the Corvette saying that presence of the Thunderbird made keeping the Corvette essential.

Even though Chevrolet had been thoroughly embarrassed by the T-Bird, Earl had seen the future with new styling. Re-tooling costs for the mainline passenger cars had prevented Corvette from getting a facelift in 1955. But Earl was ready. Hidden away back at Bill Mitchell's Art and Colour section was another all-fiberglass body that would keep tooling costs at a minimum.

If the Corvette was to continue in production, it had to succeed on its own. The man that made it happen was Zora Arkus-Duntov.

15

Churning up the dust on an empty stretch of Pikes Peak. Duntov sets a new record for stock cars on the climb to 14,110 ft. September 9, 1955. Chevrolet photo.

idea of a better sports car. His fertile mind produced innovation after innovation that sat on shelves collecting dust while factory bean counters pursued cheaper but better door handles, dashboard control knobs and hubcaps.

What Duntov saw in the Corvette was a dual-pronged attack on the world two-seater market. One was an uncompromising racing car; the other a very good road car. Being well steeped in European thought, Duntov believed that racing cars were for racing and road cars were for the road, each a different application where each could benefit the other while remaining separate. There was no conflict.

Racing in Europe was big business. The factories built a few special cars to race with, hired team managers and crews, contracted drivers and set out to prove in public competition that their cars were superior to the competition. It was the way the Continentals did things, win or lose. Not only was it good business to race, it was almost a necessity derived from a long legacy of rivalries between marques and nations. Not only were major racing events of national importance, spectators could judge the worth of cars for themselves. Why not America?

Duntov was to find his first few years with Chevrolet very productive. But when it came time to get serious about racing, not just building a few design studies, he was to find the American frame of mind quite different. Racing was and always had been of lowest priority. Maximum sales were the bottom line. Maximum profits were the goal. Unlike European manufacturers, engineers did not lead the American automotive industry; accountants did.

"Keep Duntov"

During the 1953 Motorama show, Chevrolet began an era of product development that has kept automotive journalists and enthusiasts on the edges of their seats ever since. The man who was to become largely responsible for making it happen stood looking at the gleaming white showcar. Zora Arkus-Duntov was not yet employed by GM, but he let his creative engineering mind mold the Corvette into a race winning roadster comparable to anything European.

This was a car that many people believed could compete with Jaguar and Ferrari. Although it was built on a passenger car chassis shortened 13 inches and powered by an ancient 150 hp inline 6-cylinder, it still had lots of promise. No doubt, Duntov thought that Chevrolet Division of GM was the place where it would happen, a place where his own prolific talent could expand into all sorts of creations.

The two, man and machine, made a striking contrast. The man stood before the latest machine from the capitalist world's largest corporation as a emigrant seeking freedom. He was from Belgium, of Russian parents, and lived all but the first year of his early life in Moscow, but left his native country for Germany in 1927. His arrival in the United States was to achieve that quest for freedom, but his ensuing decades with GM were to prove frustrating. He was not allowed to use his creations the way he intended, to create his

The Early Years

Of his early life, Duntov once remarked, "I was interested in anything that moved, any motorized propulsion ship. At home in Moscow when I was a boy, that meant rail cars, then motorcycles, anything." Inspired by things mechanical, Duntov was one of the few people whose curiosity fueled his interests, that something often called genius. His was a natural talent bred from an understanding of fundamental principles of machinery.

After settling in Berlin, he began formal studies in electromechanics at Charlotenburg but switched to mechanical engineering. His own competitive urge materialized in a motorcycle he tinkered with and raced. Because of objections from his parents, he traded the two-wheeler for a car, a racing car.

As a result of his interest in high performance engines and his formal education, Duntov wrote a technical treatise on supercharging internal combustion engines to 30 psi rather than the conventional 7 or 8 psi. Duntov's theory of supercharged engines brought him to the attention of a Mr. Zoller who was designing a blown 2-stroke racing engine with 12-cylinders.

Supercharging had been around since the FIAT Grand Prix cars of the late 'teens. Those highly successful cars established the principles that dominated GP racing engines for the next thirty years, including two-stage supercharging to around 40 psi. The inline 8-cylinder Italian Alfa Romeo Grand Prix cars, along with the German Mercedes-Benz and Auto Union machines of V-12 and V-16 configurations, had fully exploited such high inlet pressures before the second world war. What Duntov did was to spark renewed interest in engines with similar volumetric efficiencies.

Zoller was so impressed by Duntov that he hired him for a time as assistant. Duntov was just 23 years old and still a student. Clearly, his acumen for the mechanical arts was extraordinary. A year and half later, he graduated as an accomplished engineer well ahead of the norm.

"Depsite a broken back sustained in a Proving Ground accident, the introduction of the 1957 cars with Fuel Injection was on time." Z. Arkus-Duntov.

Afterwards, Duntov traveled Germany and later France, where he became engaged in a number of projects from machine tool design to diesel locomotives. The latter came about during his stay in France. There was increasing talk of war with Germany, but France was using German diesel engines, a situation with dire consequences should trade sanctions precede war. To remedy that situation, three companies got together and hired Duntov as lead engineer to produce French diesel engines.

During this time, he designed and built a twin cam engine for the MG he was racing. Its four cylinders were fed by four Ford Stromberg 97 carburetors. Two superchargers and a water pump were driven from the engine's camshafts. In an ingenious but unconventional method, the water pump shot a spray of water onto the exhaust valves for additional cooling. Duntov's engine was a potent and excellent test bed of new ideas.

Also during this time, Duntov made a discovery about the Ford flathead V-8 he was racing. He noted that the car was fastest down hill by a considerable margin and calculated that at top speed, the engine must be turning around 6,000 rpm. Although its redline was just 4900, it wasn't throwing rods. That told him that internals such as the rods and crank were strong enough to handle racing rpms, but its valve-in-block design and "flat" type heads restricted breathing so much that

considerably more potential lay untapped. He made a mental note to do something about that engine.

The Second World War intervened. Duntov joined the French Air Force and came briefly to the U.S. to consult on torsional vibration dampening, one of his specialties. It was an eye-opening experience to earn $100 a day while working just two or three days a week. He chose America's land of opportunity as the place to go into business as the war ended. After locating a site in New York, he and his brother Yura set up shop to produce the ARkus-DUNtov, or ARDUN heads for the flathead Ford engine.

These free-breathing cast aluminum heads were designed around hemispherical combustion chambers that bolted directly to the engine block. Valve actuation was by pushrod and rocker arm similar to the Chrysler Hemispherical head design introduced several years later. Also pre-dating many big valve heads, the ARDUN received 2-inch diameter valves feeding cylinders of a 3.375-inch bore diameter.

Now with free flowing heads and its strong bottom end, the ARDUN-Ford proved to be a formidable, although expensive, racing engine. In the post-war years, it was THE engine for top speed whether drag racing or record setting. From the original 85 horsepower, the 239 cubic inch "flathead" Ford suitably modified and equipped with ARDUN heads, a supercharger and three Strombergs was reportedly capable of over 500 hp on gasoline! That was an astounding achievement that brought the Duntov name instant credibility.

By 1950, Duntov had sold off his ARDUN works and moved to England as assistant to Sydney Allard who produced those ferocious American V-8 powered cars seen earlier in this chapter. But after two years, he and his wife became restless to return to America. Although *AutoSport* Magazine editor, Gregory Grant, launched a movement to "Keep Zora in England", his mind was made. Late 1952 saw him back in the U.S. with a new employer, Fairchild.

Following a lead that he was reluctant to follow, Duntov sent a letter to General Motors that reached Ed Cole. Cole responded that Duntov should drop in sometime. He did not intend to.

Corvette Magnetism

Then came the 1953 Motorama. "The Corvette was the most beautiful car I had ever seen. Not yet a good car, but a good start," recalls Zora.

He sent a letter of compliments on the car to Cole, along with a copy of a technical paper that had been published in a British journal. That resulted in an invitation to visit GM, and the third visit was sufficient to receive an offer that Duntov accepted. He joined Chevrolet in May, 1953.

When the new man with a strong foreign accent arrived at Chevrolet, no doubt few of his fellow employees recognized that his interests were to become both revolutionary for Chevrolet products and a constant source of aggravation for top management. They were later to squelch many of his personal interests that could have made the Chevrolet mar-

1956 styling changes were minor and tended to be more chrome and accents on the fleet image. Power that year included the new-for-'56 dual-quad intake on the 265 that boosted output 30 hp from the top rated '55 model. Chevrolet photo.

que foremost in the world of racing.

A little more than six months later, Duntov's influence began to unfold in a memo entitled, "Thoughts Pertaining to Youth, Hot Rodders and Chevrolet". In this memo sent to his boss, Maurice Olley, Duntov outlined his awareness of markets that Chevrolet management had apparently never given much priority, if they had even thought about them. It was so different from the usual sort of memo, and so far reaching, that if a single document can be cited as the beginning of Chevrolet's entry into high performance, this is it.

What Duntov outlined was the growing hot rodder movement, almost all of it Ford. He noted that a young man who bought his first hot rod magazine was immediately introduced to Ford, and as he progressed through life, he was more likely to think Ford because of the excitement hot rods gave him during his youth. Duntov wanted to make American youth Chevrolet-minded but noted that recent records were achieved by ARDUN-Fords and Chrysler's new Hemi V-8.

He went on to point out that it takes about three years for a new idea to catch on with hot rodders, and even though the new RPO V-8 Chevrolet was due out in less than a year, it would be the latter part of the decade before the consciousness of hot rodders could be raised to the potential of the Chevrolet V-8. With Ford's new overhead valve "Y-block" V-8 already on the market, Duntov proposed a plan to accelerate the learning curve and enhance the marketability of Chevrolets in the hot rod market sector by introducing well-developed, high output parts such as camshafts and manifolds.

He proposed the image of a true high performance Chev-

rolet, namely the Corvette, receiving regular production order (RPO) parts. Duntov pointed out that attempts to build 'Vettes with Cadillac engines replacing the six would occur, and the outcome was anticipated to be less than desirable. The disproportionately large amount of publicity generated by the few Corvettes seen in racing would be the image the public talked about.

The new Chevrolet V-8 was not, in itself, capable of producing a winning combination. To do so, Duntov proposed to help people racing Corvettes do a better job with all sorts of light alloy hardware and heavy duty parts from brakes to driveline equipment, all developed through extensive research and development to make any Corvette a complete racing package for those buyers who wanted to race.

Having a successful image was good for marketing, which means increased sales; the bottom line. Duntov was given the go-ahead, and his group began the quest that brought Chevrolet more sales than any marketing strategy before or since. His work is largely responsible for displacing Ford as the hot rodder's store, and ad man Barney Clark told the world about the new and exciting V-8 Corvette.

Clark was Duntov's outlet to the public. It was his advertising that introduced Chevrolet to the "win on Sunday, sell on Monday" market. The V-8 in its new and refreshing Chevrolet BelAir package had indeed become a young man's car, and Chevrolet's new image. When the car was selected as the official Indianapolis 500 Pace Car, the public was treated to a thrilling new Chevrolet, and Ford went away licking its wounds.

Dearborn's new line that year showed extensive redesign

Two-Ten two door sedans like this rolled off the assembly line in 1957 as cars to go racing with. However, a run of cheaper One-Fifty two door sedans were produced especially for stock car racing. These cars received rear flank accents like the '55 Bel Air rather than the '57 style extended wedge. Either model could be received with fuel injection and 4-speeds. Chevrolet photo.

with the Crown Victoria being Ford Division's showcase. Not only did the Chevrolet versus Ford battle come to Indianapolis in the selection of the Pace Car, it was to unfold as a heated battle on the race tracks in factory rivalries.

From 1955 through the next few years, the V-8 Chevy was to displace Ford as the hot rodder's engine just as Duntov had predicted. The high output parts he was instrumental in producing did just what he said they would do, but other events were to have a significant and recurring impact on his desire to make the Corvette into a real racing car of international proportions.

Chevy Comes Alive

Red Byron had driven his Ford to win NASCAR's first sanctioned race (held on the Daytona Beach course Feb. 15 1948), and Johnny Mantz won the inaugural Southern 500 at Darlington (Sept. 4, 1950) in a borrowed Plymouth. These wins showed that low priced cars had a place in stock car racing, but little was made of it. The favored cars were much bigger and more expensive, especially as was shown by the string of 66 Hudson wins from 1952-54 and the 49 wins by Carl Kiekhaefer's Chryslers in 1955 and '56. Herb Thomas was the Hudson big name, probably the biggest name in stock car racing at the time. Thomas and his mechanic, Smokey Yunick, were about to launch Chevrolet into a new era when they switched to the bowtie brand in 1955.

One thing learned during the 1955-56 period of racing is

that it makes no difference from a marketing standpoint how many races you win unless you tell everyone about it. Raising public awareness that the new Chevrolet was a high performer was Barney Clark's job. He was director of Campbell-Ewald's racing group.

Campbell-Ewald was Chevrolet's advertising agency, and with Ed Cole and Duntov behind rapidly expanding high performance interests, Clark made the most of it. During that time, though, neither Chevrolet nor Ford had the best cars for stock car racing. That distinction belonged to Kiekhaefer and his Chrysler 300s.

He was a millionaire that brought his Mercury outboard motor fortune into the sport and raced on a scale that far exceeded his competitors. His cars took the championship both years, totalling 27 wins in 1955 and 22 in '56. In the face of mounting factory-backed efforts from both Chevrolet and Ford, he was effectively forced out of racing and quit following the latter season.

The beginning of Chevrolet's rise as a stock car racing threat began when Jack Radtke entered his Chevy in the February '55 NASCAR Grand National at Daytona Beach. The beach race had, on occasion, been called when the tide came in and covered the course. It was 4.1-miles around with parallel straights connected at each end by turns through sand. Half the course was along the beach and half along the hard surface two-lane that ran adjacent to the beach. As a whole herd of stockers, usually around 100, came roaring down the hard surface at the start, many didn't make it past the ditch just off the south turn. Radtke started from back in the pack and drove a more cautious race. When he came in

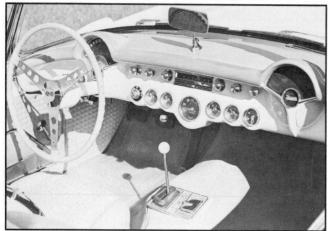
The handsome and sporty '56 Corvette interior was functional and spacious compared to many European cars.

In 1956, Corvettes invaded production sports car racing and cleaned house. Today's vintae racing revives that era.

Dual-quads and the legendary Duntov cam made the 240 horse '56 Corvette a no-nonsense high performer.

10th overall, a lot of people noticed.

From the first beach race in 1938 with its more than 20,000 spectators, stock car racing fans flocked to Daytona. Why Daytona drew such large numbers is still being debated. Perhaps is was simply that times were slow and here was something really exciting. Whatever the reason, spectators saw a lot to talk about.

Rules in those days were not nearly so refined as today, and officials were more interested in getting the cars and big name drivers to the race rather than dawdle over what might or might not be legal equipment. Although heated arguments erupted from time to time over what sort of fuel was being used, such as nitromethane or alcohol hidden in the windshield washer bottle, or special tires not generally available to other teams, or the ever-present banging and bashing on the course, stock car racing went on and grew by leaps and bounds.

What gave the sport its biggest push in the early days following WW-II was a track built in the cotton and tobacco fields of tiny Darlington, South Carolina. Daytona's large number of paying spectators spoke of big money to a small group of businessmen from that slow, dusty town in the middle of nowhere. During a poker game one night, Harold Brasington suggested that they should build a real hard surface race track right there. Darlington was as good a place as Daytona. Although more of a joke than serious business at first, it actually happened.

It made no difference that Route 151 was only a two-lane state highway going to the track. And so what if the average personal income of the area was hardly $2400 a year? People would find the money for a ticket somehow. It wasn't important that for miles in any direction there was not a single large metropolitan area with hotels and restaurants to support the anticipated crowds. And what about the state's law against races on Sunday and selling race tickets on Sunday? The first race at Darlington, the Labor Day Southern 500 of 1950, should have been a colossal failure. It was just the opposite;

a colossal success.

A big race track at Darlington was more than a dream, but stock car racing had never been done on asphalt before. Could a car last 500 miles on that sort of surface? No one knew, and both the leading sanctioning bodies, AAA and NASCAR, were hesitant to go much beyond sand and Saturday night fairground dirt.

All day Sunday and through the night prior to the Monday race, cars jammed the road leading to the track. But since officials couldn't sell tickets, what resulted was a huge traffic jam. They got together with local police and reached a compromise; they would let the crowd and their cars into the infield to spend the night, then set off a loud explosion to wake everyone up the next morning so the fans could drive out, buy a ticket and come back in. By sunrise, thousands of spectators not only faced getting their own tickets, they were also up against a horde of incoming traffic that snarled the single infield entrance for hours.

Outside, traffic was backed up for miles. But the big names were there; the cars were there; and Bill France watched 30,000 spectators nearly break the gates down to get in.

Big time stock car racing was definitely on the move up. That rather odd egg-shaped 1-1/4 mile "oval", later lengthened to 1-3/8 miles in 1953, was the first super speedway. In a few years of newspaper and radio coverage throughout the south, Darlington became the mecca of stock car racing. It inspired France to build the 2.5-mile tri-oval at Daytona. The first Daytona 500 was run in 1959. Then came the 1.5-mile Charlotte highbanks and similar 1.52-mile Atlanta oval in 1960, and later, Talladega. The big tracks helped stock car racing mature as a profession. But then as today, the more traditional 1/2-mile short tracks are the key to a NASCAR driver's points championship.

The reason Detroit factories became so interested in stock car racing was simply that they recognized the huge audience that sedan racing appealed to. Since most of the south leaned toward low cost cars out of economic necessity, here was a tremendous market for Ford and Chevrolet and Plymouth, not Chrysler and Oldsmobile.

Smokey Yunick and Herb Thomas, with Smokey's dog Herkimer, invite racing fans to Daytona Beach: Speed Week 1956, Feb 12-26. Smokey Yunick photo.

Even though the cars were true production cars modified for racing, there were many tricks from the moonshine trade that sly mechanics and drivers could use. Many of the better known drivers had learned how to drive fast while trying to outrun the "revenooers". Their cars had to be hopped up to outrun the law. Where the booze was made and sold was kept hidden from the Feds, but they knew it was being hauled over public highways. The white lightnin' business had grown out of southern hard times and had become a more or less accepted way of life for back woods folk who could not otherwise make much of an income. The "Bible Belt" region from Atlanta to Richmond, Raleigh to Knoxville had remained dry and consequently made an immense geographic market for bootleggers. And making corn squeezin's was a lot easier than farming the hill country where most fields tended toward vertical.

These same drivers and mechanics brought their abilities to Daytona and Darlington and became heros. The fans loved the rough and tumble style of stock car racing, and spectators began noticing whether or not drivers had put the "Darlington stripe" on their cars. If a man didn't drive fast enough to scrape the railing at the top of the banking, he wasn't driving. To get by drivers like Curtis Turner, Paul Goldsmith, Buck Baker, Lee Petty, the brothers Fonty and Tim Flock, Junior Johnson and Glenn "Fireball" Roberts required guts. Not only did they make you work for it, the rough track itself was rightly becoming known as "too tough to tame".

By 1955, stock car racing was paying real money to the men who weren't accustomed to getting it easy. Winning $250 on a dirt track was one thing, but to win $2,500 for driving as fast as you could without worrying about the Feds was different. Prior to 1955, only a few drivers such as Herb Thomas were professionals. He had been driving the factory's "Fabulous

Hudson Hornets" prepared by Smokey Yunick. When the men at Chevrolet wanted to go racing that year, they looked around for the best and chose Thomas. Smokey built a Chevy with parts and equipment supplied by the factory. If not the very first NASCAR Chevy V-8, it was certainly the first factory Chevrolet.

Three time Indianapolis 500 winner Mauri Rose was a Chevrolet engineer sent south by Ed Cole to organize Chevrolet's entry into racing. Yunick's "Best Damn Garage in Town" located just off the inland waterway at Daytona Beach was Rose's choice as a Chevrolet base of operations. Stock car rules were so limited that durability to win was all that was needed. Since the '55 Chevy was a good deal lighter than the Olds '88, the car regarded as best for stock car racing in 1954, it was clear that making a winning Chevrolet was the job of Chevrolet engineering. As parts broke, new heavy duty replacements were designed and placed in the parts catalogs.

Duntov's memo of 1953 had laid out the guidelines for what he thought it would take to make Chevrolet a winner, and with more and more heavy duty hardware also came high performance parts. But while both Chevrolet and Ford factory men suspiciously eyed each other on race day, the Chryslers cleaned house. Chevrolet and Ford won only two races apiece that year, and Oldsmobile was far ahead of Chevrolet with 10 victories. But Chevy was on the move.

Following the Daytona Speedweeks and two early season short track races, Clark put together an ad that appeared in the June 1955 issue of *Motor Trend*. "Don't argue with this baby!" he said, and ended the ad saying Chevrolet had been the "Sales Leader for 19 straight years". That was clearly a snipe at Ford. He told readers that the new V-8 Chevrolet had taken most of the top positions during NASCAR's standing start measured mile. He added that the cars took the first two places for straightaway top speed in the Under-$2500 class, and that Chevrolets took three of the top five slots on 2-way average straightaway speeds for cars powered by engines between 250 and 299 cubic inches.

Readers saw a different kind of Chevrolet. The old "stove bolt" that Dad would buy was now the fastest low priced V-8

born and were accompanied by Ford engineers when sent to Charlotte. Racer Buddy Shuman was put in charge of making the cars into 500 mile winners.

Yunick's shop in Daytona was Chevrolet racing headquarters. The car Thomas drove at Darlington carried Yunick's banner on the front fenders along with "Motoramic

Fans poured into Darlington for the Southern 500 of 1955 and saw a Chevrolet parade of winners. The Turbo-Fire V-8 wasn't the fastest, but it was fast enough in the lightweight '55 Chevy. The Chevys were not as rough on tires as the bigger cars, and fewer pit stops meant more time on the track and victory. Darlington Speedway photo.

on the road. Advertisement of racing and high speed results was a new pitch for people in 1955, but southern dealers loved it because it brought in droves of people wanting to see what a race winning car was like. All of a sudden, Chevrolet built exciting cars that were now described as "The Hot One".

Winning the 100-mile feature at Columbia, S.C. with no pit stops, then taking the 150 lap Late Model Event at Fayetteville, N.C., with a car driven only in second gear, was the stuff that changed Chevrolet marketing forever. Chevys were now cars that could win races, especially with the new 195-hp "Super Turbo-Fire V-8" that Clark told the world about. For around $2,000, and a few hundred more for special parts, anyone could have a basic car that could go the distance with the big boys. Such a Chevy might not outrun the far more expensive Chryslers on the big tracks but they could easily do them in on the short tracks.

Ford saw what was happening, too. Ford boss Robert Mc-Namara dispatched the Charlotte field service district manager, Bill Benton, to find out what it would take to make Ford a Southern 500 winner. Benton had racing connections and recommended that Ford engineering build cars to race. Two cars were built in Ford's experimental garage in Dear-

Chevrolet V-8" while the factory Fords were entered through Schwam Motors of Charlotte. Charlie Schwam had the cars painted purple with ferocious snorting hogs depicted on the sides along with his motto; "What we say it is, it is". Drivers for these 230 hp cars were Curtis Turner and Joe Weatherly, two of the best.

During qualifying, Weatherly set a sizzling 109 mph lap followed by Turner's similar lap, but Fireball Roberts' Buick was on the pole at 110.682 mph. Tim Flock set a new track record of 112.041 mph in one of Kiekhaefer's Chryslers. Thomas was further back.

The Ford Thunderbird 292 was larger in displacement and rated slightly more powerful than the Chevy V-8. It was powerful enough for Turner to quickly pull into the lead with Weatherly not far behind. It looked like a Ford day at Darlington, but Thomas was putting on the heat by running well up in the pack. About mid-way through the 364-lap feature, the front suspension of Turner's "Hog" let go and he crashed. Weatherly took the lead. It was now a Ford versus Chevrolet show. When Weatherly pitted on the 278th lap, Thomas roared into the lead. But with a new set of tires and a load of fuel, Weatherly's Ford showed a considerable level of supe-

22

riority over the Chevrolet when he regained the lead on the 304th lap and stretched to a full lap lead over Thomas.

Here was Chevrolet and Ford going at it hot and heavy, but most fans did not know of the factory's involvement. What they saw were production sedans out there racing, just what marketing men wanted the public to see. Suddenly, these low

racing days. The better balanced Chevys with softer compound rubber stuck better than the bigger cars that simply wore out their tires. The Chevys went by the Oldsmobiles, Buicks and Kiekhaefer's Chryslers during tire change pit stops.

The crowd saw a great race, but few recognized what really

Herb Thomas in Smokey's "Best Damn Garage in Town" Chevrolet gave the Southern 500 a new twist when he won the shootout in a '55 Chevy, his third Southern 500 victory in six years. Ad-man Barney Clark wrote advertising that told America about the '55s, "DON'T ARGUE WITH THIS BABY!" Darlington Speedway photo.

priced cars had a new image; they were race cars. The level of excitement at Darlington was astounding, and luck was on Thomas' side when the suspension of Weatherly's Ford collapsed and he crashed, too. Thomas once again led the roaring stockers on the Darlington oval. It was his third Southern 500 victory, but ironically, he did so at a slower pace than his 1954 victory in a Hudson, averaging 93.28 mph compared to 94.93 the year before.

At the flag, Thomas led a parade of seven Chevys across the line. It was a fabulous day for Chevrolet to win the granddaddy of them all finishing 1-2-4-7-8-9-10 in the face of very stiff competition. It was also a new day for tires. What gave the edge to the Chevys were their durable engines and several sets of special Firestone tires that Rose had located in Dayton, Ohio, leftovers from Briggs Cunningham's sport car

happened. It was the first race of the new age, the age of corporate commit to stock car racing. True, Hudson had earlier been behind Thomas, but with both GM and Ford now out there doing battle, and soon followed by the tire companies, NASCAR would never be the same. Manufacturers saw stock car racing as a marketing tool to increase sales. Bill France not only hooked Chevrolet, he snared Ford as well and got Firestone to boot.

More than three decades of the Chevrolet versus Ford war have unfolded on NASCAR's tracks, and today's fans that pull for Thunderbirds or Monte Carlos (or Luminas as of mid-1989) can look back to that first showdown at Darlington as the beginning of it all. What Cole saw as a new market and what Duntov predicted could happen in his memo of 1953 was for real when Chevrolet came alive in '55.

Smokey Yunick

Recalls The Early Days

Before the war started, I was a kid probably 15 years old. I didn't have much of a home. My dad died when I was 11, 12, 13, somewhere along in there, and I ended up in a little town called Pitcarin, Pennsylvania (near Pittsburgh).

I had a strong interest in motorcycles. I had a motorcycle then and I used to race'm. Around Pitcarin, there was a racer named Bob Hallowell who was U.S. champion. I knew him a little bit and went to races around 'till I could get somethin' of my own. I probably had thirty bucks in my racer. It smoked like hell, but I got it goin' enough to get noticed. The guy at the track couldn't remember "Henry Yunick", so he started callin' me "Smokey" and the guys at work picked up on it. That's how that got started.

I was working at a garage making my own way, and I thought I would like to be a pilot. There in Pitcarin, there was an inventor that had a pretty nice little factory. His name was Pitcarin. He was building autogyros, not an airplane, somethin' like a helicoptor. It had a rotor and a propeller, but the rotor wasn't geared to the engine. I went in there and got a job to train to be a welder on aircraft. Well, you had to take Army and Navy tests. To make a long story short, I got certified, then war broke out.

Before the war, Pitcarin had built a plane called the "Mailwing" that started all the airmail. He was a very wealthy man,

a nice guy and took real good care of the pilots. There were a lot of mail pilots around. They weren't really doing much of anything, but he paid'em anyhow just to hang around, maybe pilot an autogyro once in a while, tinker with things, fly some of the old planes. Looked like he'd decided to pay'em for life.

So I'd met all those guys, now very famous old pilots. Well, I got the aviation bug and they told me, "Why don't you get in the kadets?"

I said, "That's what I'm gonna do." So I went down to Philadelphia to get in the kadets, and the first thing they wanted was a birth certificate. I didn't have one. Mainly, I gave up on it 'cause I didn't have the foggiest idea where to get a birth certificate. I didn't know what my real name was. Some people said it was Henry, some said Howard, some said Gregory. And some said my name was spelled U-N-I-C. Then, some said Y-U-N-I-C-K. Since most people called me Henry, I kept it.

Anyway, Pitcarin said, "I can get you fixed up. Go to this address in Philadelphia." It was a Catholic church. There was a priest down there, such-and-such a name. "Take ten dollars with you," he said, "and get you a birth certificate."

I went and got a birth certificate, then I got concerned about the test because you had to be a college graduate to be in the kadets. I'd only had, what, ten grades. I started the eleventh grade, then dad died. I don't think I went but about a month before I had to leave. Eatin' got more important than going to school. Somehow or other I must have got started pretty early 'cause I was pretty young to be where I was. I thought, "Well, shit. Why not take the test?"

So, I took the test. It was a very complicated, extremely tough test. Kinda like a picture of a bulldozer, a jackass and an airplane. It said, "circle the airplane". That was the test. It might have been more complicated. Maybe it had four things to figure out.

When I got put in the kadets, well, you don't know these things when you are sixteen years old. They swear you in the regular army first, then they swear you in the kadets. So, if you don't make in the kadets, you're in the army!

The biggest part of the physical test was 20/20 eyesight, standard hearing, can't weigh over X number of pounds or be over so tall. And you weren't allowed to be queer. They probably checked you more on that stronger than anything else. The FBI checked, but it couldn't have been all that good 'cause here I was with a phony birth certificate.

Just a couple days before Christmas, I was doing some welding on an autogyro. They had a joke around there; you put some hydrogen in a tube, then some acetylene, 'bout the time you ended the weld, that tube would explode. Sounded somethin' like a .22 rifle. The welding goggles I had were danglin' down my nose, and when I was closing the weld, that thing popped. The molten metal went in this left eye and totally blinded it. They next day, they called from the kadets, and said, "We're ready for you."

Well, I go down there with one eye. They examined it and said, "That one's gone, you'll never see again" and sent my ass to the army to Miami for basic training, then Sioux Falls, South Dakota to be a radio operator. The guy that flew that bamboo bomber took us from ninety degrees in Miami up there to thirty below. That was the most miserable place I'd ever been. Some of the guys got spinal meningitis; and the pilot couldn't fly worth a damn; scared shitless; at night in that shitty weather. If he'd had to pay five dollars to land, he'd have had to pay twenty-five dollars every time he tried to land; hit and bounce two or three times.

I complained. I said I wanted to be assigned to another pilot. I didn't feel like gettin' killed by some idiot right here. So, he heard about it, he was a second lieutenant, and he chewed my ass out. But he said one remark, he said, "If you think it's so damn easy, why don't you fly one yourself?"

I guess three months had passed, and when I went up for a physical, the eye was doin' pretty good. The doctor asked me what the story on it was. I told him, and he said, "You might get her back."

"If I do," I said, "I'd like to get back in the kadets." He told me to come back in a month. The day that lieutenant said that "easy" remark, I went back to the doctor. He told me it couldn't be good enough yet, but after he checked it, he said, "You're close now. Why don't you wait another ten days or two weeks and we'll check her again." I did and he said he could OK'er now. So, I started in the kadets.

I got through, and like everybody else, I wanted to be a fighter pilot. But I didn't make that part. They made me a multi-engine bomber pilot and threw me in the B-17s. So, when I was in Dyersburg, Tennessee, just gettin' ready to go overseas, they had this thing called OTC, Operational Training. You did your gunnery and you worked with your crew and so forth. While I was there, about half way through it, I got appendicitis at the Memphis State Fair. When coming back, it was 60 or 80 miles, we were flying in high altitude formation, and my appendix broke. I didn't feel good, but you didn't go 'round saying you didn't feel good. I didn't know what to hell was wrong with me. I thought it was from the drinking.

After a while, we got back and they kept me on the ground as a test pilot until I recovered. Now, a test pilot is not what you see in the movies. You take an airplane that's got so many hours on it, take it in and major overhaul it. Then somebody's got to drive that sonofabitch around for six or eight hours; I forgot how long. You've got this big list here and every so many minutes at a certain power setting, you write down all the gauge readings. The flight engineer was doing all that. It was six or eight hours of nothing. The only thing I would ever do was take the thing off and climb, slow cruise, cruise and high cruise, all the sonofabitch would go.

Didn't have radar then, so I got so bored with the whole thing that I got to looking at maps and taking trips. I wanted to look Florida over, but I couldn't get past Daytona and get back in the allotted time. And the fuel, we probably didn't have thirty minutes reserve. When they loaded it up, they'd give you the time plus thirty minutes reserve.

This place looked so beautiful from the air, and Daytona was a beautiful place back then, about twenty-five miles of pure white beach and all these streets here were just covered with trees. You'd see a car go in a tunnel, he'd come out ten miles further. He'd go in the tunnel at Ormond and come out

at Port Orange. It looked like a small town, maybe thirty or forty thousand people. I was impressed. That's how I come down here.

So, then the war ended. I thought I was going to stay in for twenty years. Then I did something stupid; I met some woman when I come back home and got married. I bought a house trailer. It was snowing and sleeting, and after about a week of it, I said, "I've had enough of this shit" and went back, hooked up the trailer and told my new wife, "I'm going to Florida. You wanna go to Florida, crawl on the front seat. If you wanna stay here with your parents, get out." I was pissed. So she decided to go to Florida, and we got down here with about two hundard bucks. I started putterin' around with cars, and that's how I got started.

The first eight months here, I worked in the trailer park down south Daytona, then in a blacksmith shop where the Cadillac place is now. I wasn't here a year yet when I started building this place here, named it "The Best Damn Garage in Town". Been here ever since.

It was the way all garages went. You started off with a little two-stall thing. Then you got a couple of bucks and you added four more stalls, then you got some more bucks and you added eight more and pretty soon you had a mess like this place. Finally, you got back and admired your handiwork after twenty years; everything was leaning on everything else. The front part was rotten and about to fall over. Really, nothing was worth a shit, but that was the way it went.

Almost everybody in the garage business, including the car dealers, started off with a gas station and a one car garage, some old barn or somethin' like that. It wasn't nobody that just went to a bank and borrowed fifty thousand dollars and started a repair shop or dealership or somethin'. I'd say, back in them days, ninety percent of the dealers were us mechanics. We knew the cars.

There was a local guy here named Marshall Teague, big driver and good mechanic, a very rare combination. That was 'bout 1946. I'd met him a couple of times, and when he was gettin' ready for the Beach race, he was runnin' way late and asked me if I'd help him. I did, and it seemed like every time after that when he was gettin' ready to race, he'd ask me to help him. I helped him off and on for three or four years.

Then, in 1950 and '51, he made a deal with Hudson. Herb Thomas was goin' to drive one of 'em. He asked me to build and mechanic his second car. In the meantime, I'd worked on some modifieds with "Fireball". After working on that Hudson with Thomas for a while, gettin' next to nothing for pay, I decided to quit. Then the Hudson guys came down and told me they wanted me to keep working on the cars, and they'd pay me; $200 an engine! That was a dollar an hour. It took 200 hundard hours to build one. So, I said OK, and that's how the racin' got started.

Back then, Hudson was the best there was for stock car racing. But, you got to remember, back in them days, there couldn't o' been over a hundard guys involved in stock car racing, at most, in the whole United States. We'd crank the windows down on the driver's side, take a belt off and wrap it around the door post on that side and crank the windows back up to the belt. We'd take the muffler off and drive 'em to the race track. That was real stock car racing.

I started and quit in racin' about six or seven times. I guess you could say I drank too much. In the Air Force, I went all around the world and never came back. I had probably every battle star in every air campaign they had from Africa, Europe, China-India, Burma. I was in the Flying Tigers. When the war was over, I was in Okinawa. After the first tour of flying a bomber in Europe, I could have come back after twenty-five missions, but I was afraid, too, 'cause I thought they'd put me in B-24s and send me to the Pacific. To me, that was no way out. I decided I'd rather take my chances on a second tour in Europe. My plan was to stay alive.

You'd go in at six o'clock at night to eat and on the bulletin board you'd see the name of the pilot that would go tomorrow. You'd see your name there; you just had a mission today and you got another one tomorrow. I gotta be honest with you. There was a lot o' times in the beginning it just scared the shit out of me, so I'd get drunk. I didn't have nobody to help me. The co-pilot wanted to be a fighter pilot, and he'd set there all pissed off. I suppose that happened to many crews. But hell, I was an old man at seventeen years old. So the drinking started. I guess I was an alcoholic when I came back at twenty-one.

The racin' required so much time and paid so little. I got a kick out of it, but when I got drunk I couldn't work on a race car. I couldn't work on Marshall's race car, so I would quit. After the Hudson and Oldsmobile and Chrysler and Packard and all the shit that was in there, in '55 I was in a quit period.

Racing and Chevrolet

Well France come over here one day, I can't say we were ever good friends, but we sure spent a lot of time together. He came over here and said, "Smokey, I want to get Chevrolet in this thing and you already got some experience. I heard you built an engine for one that won a race." So, he said, "I met this guy Ed Cole and he wants to get in racin' but he wants you to do it and nobody else."

I said, "Yeah, I know. He's already called here two or three times in the last couple of months. But I told him I was retired from racin'. I was tired of workin' twenty-four hours a day, seven days a week for nothin'. When I got caught up with my drinkin', call me later, maybe next year." So, I turned France down, too.

About a month later he come over here pleadin'. He said, "That guy Cole won't go for any body else. If you'd just do that one time, one race and get him hooked. I can take him from there."

I must have been half drunk and finally agreed to it. Well, France had a tri-pacer, a little chicken-shit airplane, and he was a half-decent pilot, so we flew up to, well, I remember it as Oconeechee. I guess it's North Wilkesboro now.

I had run on it. The front straightaway went down hill and back straightaway went up hill. Down at the end of number one was a big cow pasture. Over in number three was a swamp and some trees. There was no grandstand. The fans sat on the side of the hill by the front straightaway. I'm pretty sure it's North Wilkesboro now.

Anyway, France landed in a cow pasture nearby, and we met on top of the hill looking over the track. It was Ed Cole, Mauri Rose, a guy named Russ Saunders who was assistant chief engineer, another guy, I think his name was McDonald, he was the money man. A very English type, a mustache and the whole thing, sports car cap, tweed suit, very business.

We talked on that hill for about a hour and a half. When Ed introduced me to Mauri, he ask me if I'd ever met Mauri Rose. I said, "No." I said, "I'd heard a hell-of-a-lot about him, though."

Mauri smoked a pipe and weetled it around in his mouth all the time. He asked, "What have you heard about me?"

I told him, "Everything I ever heard about you was that you was the most no good, rotten, dirty sonofabitch that's ever climbed in a race car."

He just looked at me and smiled. He said, "I used to be, but I ain't any more." I have never met but two or three guys in my whole life that liked that guy, but I had about a ten year day-to-day association with him, and there couldn't have been a finer man in all ways.

I finally made a deal with 'em to run one race, the Darlington race. They kept talkin' about how they will really pay me. So he offered ten thousand dollars. I said, "Well that is a lot of money." But I gotta build a car and run it through the race." He said, "I'm going to let Mauri get an apartment there in Daytona to stay with you, so if we need to do anything, we won't have a big time delay."

After about two weeks of that, I got Mauri to move in with me because we had trouble. Quitin' to go eat. Gettin' back on time. I only had one helper, and Mauri worked like a dog, too. He was just as good as a full-paid man with the wrenches or whatever. With him living with me, we came to work together, left together and it just smoothed the whole thing out.

I decided I wanted to go to one race first to check the car out, so we went to West Memphis. In the meantime, I had built a Buick just before I quit. Thomas took it up to Langhorn. I didn't even go to the track. He sat on the pole, led the race and got a big nail in it with two laps to go and ended up second. Then, when he called, I said, "Bring the car back 'cause that track was rough and the axles will be bad. Can't run it no more." It was really my car, but he thought it was his. I didn't really give a shit, and I said, "Herb, you ain't gonna bring that car back. You're gonna take it to the Charlotte fairgrounds. If you do, you're gonna bust your ass with that thing."

He did what I thought he was gonna do. He took it to the Charlotte race track, a half mile dirt track, if I remember right. Broke the right rear axle and broke his leg. It was the first time he'd gotten hurt, and he was prob'ly the best driver around. So, I didn't know what happened and the first race after he broke his leg was West Memphis. That was a bad ass track. Before it would tear up, that was the fastest track in the country. It was high bank dirt track made out of mud from the bottom of the Mississippi, and it wouldn't stay put.

Herb looked like an old lady drivin' that car, and Mauri looked at me and said, "Smokey, you said that guy was the best stock car driver there is. There's something wrong there."

I told him I guess that accident got to him 'cause drivers always went one way of another. Either an accident didn't mean a thing or else that was the end of it.

So, I said, "Boy are we in for a long hot summer at Darlington. Mauri, there ain't but one way we can win that sonofabitch. We're gonna have to do somethin' nobody else is doin'. We're gonna be about four mile an hour slow. What I want you to do, you know all the tire guys, get me some tires better'n what we got. The prayer we got of winning that sonofabitch is running wide open without changing tires. The others are gonna' tear their tires all to shit."

I told him before he left that the rules were all screwed up. They said the rims can't be over five inches wide but they didn't put any O.D. dimension. I told him I'd like to find a seventeen or eighteen inch tire. He was gone about a month, and one day he called and said, "I think I found the tire." He was in Akron in a junk yard, and said the guy had a hundard and sixty-five or seventy-nine tires or somethin', and Otto Wolfer said they would do the job.

Otto was the best tire man in the country. At the time, he was working for Pure Oil Company. They were building their own tires, and he'd quit Firestone and went to work over there.

I thought if he said they were good, they're OK. And we were out of time anyway, but they weren't but sixteen inches. I ask Mauri, "What's the deal?"

"Well," he said, "this guy is gettin' ready to burn 'em and he wants a buck a piece for'em."

I said, "Well, buy 'em", but Mauri said we got another problem. They're white wall on one side. I said, "If you think they're the best and Wolfer thinks they're the best, are they directional?"

"Nope," he said, "that's the good part. We can turn the white wall in." Mauri bought 'em and stayed there to get 'em shipped. He got a guy that agreed to drive right down here, so he come down here and we unloaded 'em. That's how the Super Sport got started."

What had happened was that Firestone had built the tires special for Briggs Cunningham to run in Le Mans in 1955. They built about two hundard of 'em and Briggs took about twenty-five of 'em to France to test with but decided that Dunlops were better. So therefore, the tires left in the States were still here, and since he wasn't goin' to run 'em, Firestone decided to scrap the project and paid a junk man to take 'em away. Rose tracked them down the day before the guy was gonna burn 'em.

The tires were good enough to hold the car as fast as it would run. If I remember right, the fastest the thing would run was 114, maybe 116.

I actually owned the car, but that's not the way Thomas sees it. Chevrolet gave it to me. I think I got it from a local dealer right here in Daytona Beach. In them days, the factory would build two door cars special without a back seat. They had a plywood floor that set where the back seat bottom sat and that went all the way to the back of the trunk. Then, where the back seat went up, they had another piece of plywood. I think it was called the Model 1812. I don't know why. The car cost

brand new, list, two thousand, eighty-two dollars. I think I bought it for around eighteen-fifty and Chevrolet reimbursed me. They said they would furnish all the parts that they built, and pay me ten thousand dollars, and furnish Mauri Rose and the engineer.

As soon as I got started on the thing, I didn't like the rocker arms, based on my previous experience. Part of the deal I had made on the hill with Cole, for one race, West Memphis got thrown in because it was my idea to test the car, Cole agreed that if I could prove that the rocker arms were a problem, that they would make a shaft type rocker setup for it on some kind of a different head assembly. But he said, "You got to promise me that you'll try real hard before we go to all that kind of money."

Back in them days, we degreed everything in and spent a lot of time setting the cam in. You couldn't degree the thing in, well you did it, then you re-did it and you got a different answer. The hysterisis in the valve gear was all over the place. So, I made a shaft setup for it. We busted our asses makin' it, and I knew it was goin' to make a hell-of-a difference. We had it on the dynamometer here, got it all degreed in, and it didn't make one damn bit of difference.

I called Cole up and told him I didn't like it, but when we went up to Darlington, everything happened just like I thought. We were four mile-an-hour short, or somewhere around there. The thing didn't fall apart, we didn't change a tire the whole race! Practiced, qualified and raced on one set of tires. We won the race. Then there was a hell-of-a rhubarb about the tires. France tried to make me give 'em to Keikhafer, but I wouldn't do it. Then he threatened to throw me out'a there.

I laughed and said, "Shit, why don't you quit bull shittin' me? You know this is all to get Chevy hooked. Why are you givin' me this shit that if I don't give you some tires, you're going to throw me out?"

Then, Cole came down here and he talked me into stayin' with him. The first thing he wanted me to do after Darlington was run a twenty-four hour record run at Darlington. And he'd pay fifteen thousand dollars for that one. Herb drove, Betty Skelton, I don't remember who all drove. He wanted an average of a hundard miles per hour for twenty-four hours. We did it.

Then he talked me into racing with him steady, and he'd pay me some ungodly salary, a thousand dollars a month. The next thing that happened, this was Chevy racing headquarters. This room would have forty new engines in it and forty rear axles and forty right front spindles and so on. This whole place was filled with Chevy parts and anybody that run a Chevy had to get their parts from here.

One time I had a job to give away two hundard cars, and he used to call me up every three days and chew my ass out 'cause I wasn't givin' 'em away fast enough, to sports writers. He wanted people to drive Chevys. He told me in the beginning, he said, "Smokey, we've got an old man's car with a straight-six and I ain't got twenty years to get the kids to catch on. I want to sell cars to people who are fifteen, sixteen, seventeen years old now. I want to get to the young people, and I think I can do it through racing."

That was his plan. He didn't give a shit about racin' although Cole used to drive sports cars, a Cadillac-Allard. One of the engineers was his mechanic. Cole and I got along good. He come down here all the time to this little Chevy racing headquarters.

Then he said, "I want to start a racing team."

I said, "Don't do that. You're on the right track." That didn't mean I was right, but I said, "What we need is to replace McDonald with somebody who knows something about racing. He's a pain in the ass. He's holding the thing up. And you got another guy that works for Campbell-Ewald that's screwing the thing up royally." The guy by the name Jim somethin' or other, who later became very famous with Pontiac. Mauri and I threw his ass out o' here when we threw McDonald out.

One day when we was getting a Corvette ready to run, Cole came in here about eight o'clock in the morning. He didn't know what was goin' on. I'd already been in jail for runnin' the car on the road testin' it. We'd been here all night, prob'ly the second night in a row. Cole comes in with his super Brookes Brothers suit on and said to Mauri, "Mauri, that car's filthy. That car's not fittin' to represent Chevrolet Motor Co."

Just before Cole got here, Mauri had got a can of polish, and he was startin' to clean it up. He had the lid off the polish can. I'm gatherin' up some shit, the race was that mornin' in New Smyrna and Paul Goldsmith was drivin'. Mauri had a temper, and when Cole said that car wasn't fit to represent Chevrolet, he said, "If you don't like the looks of the sonofabitch, polish it yourself!" And he threw the can at Cole, and Cole caught it upside down and that white polish went right down the front of that suit.

So, McDonald was standing there, hope I got his name right, Mc-Somethin', we called him Mac. He took Mauri outside and told him to go pack his bags and go back to Detroit. "I want you out of here by three o'clock," he said. He knew the airlines schedule.

He grabbed a rag and smeared that stuff all over Cole's suit, and I couldn't keep from laughin'. I said, "You dumb shit, before you go runnin' your mouth, you oughta know the story. Mauri ain't been to bed in forty-eight hours, he's been working like a dog and he was gettin' ready to clean it when you said what you said. You ain't got no idea what's been goin' on here in the last forty-eight hours and you're wrong. I don't think he should have thrown the polish on your fancy suit, but," I said, "I don't like the looks of it anyhow. An' let me tell you somethin'. If Mauri Rose leaves here, you can finish this car yourself. I quit."

"All right," he said. "Mauri can stay."

"Nope," I said. "We're goin' t'get somebody on that airplane and it's goin' to be McDonald. Either his ass is gone or I quit right now." Guess who went back to Detroit?

Cole asked me, "You don't want McDonald, who do you want?"

I said, "There's a guy up in Detroit out of work now that knows somethin' about stock car racing. Name's Vince Piggins. Hire him to run the thing on your end of it."

Piggins was the Hudson engineer. He was the guy we worked with at Hudson. The PR guy was Tom Rhoades.

Mac didn't want to hire him, put him down. I said, "Let me make it easy for you. Either hire 'im or this deal is through. I quit." They hired 'im.

The first thing Piggins wanted to do was start a racin' team. He went on and made a deal with McNally Chevrolet in Atlanta. Got some space and McNally was in the middle of it. By now everybody that was Chevrolet was jumpin' on the bandwagon. Jim Rathman and the whole nine yards went Chevy happy.

Red Vaught worked for me at the time and they made him an offer. I told him, "Red, take it. It's double what you're gettin' here and you won't have to work as hard, and you show them other guys what to do."

I objected to the thing. I told Cole, "You don't need me no more." He said, "Well, now, let's just go on and race."

"No," I said, "I ain't gonna do that."

"Well, just build engines for the race team."

They decided to go on and race, but I was undecided on what to do. We had an engine problem, and I wanted to make a major change. I'd already done the development on it and checked production on it. I wanted to move the spark plug on the cylinder head and found out they was made all the way down the assembly line except puttin' the plug hole in, and I figured we could do that here. I went up there to talk to Cole about actually doin' it. OK, I had a meeting set up at 7:30 Monday morning. I get up there Sunday night, fly half the night, and get there Monday and he's got a "fire", can't see me. I understand that, so I hung around all day Monday and nothin' happened. Next mornin', scheduled for 8:30, he's not there. They've called him to the GM building. This goes on through Tuesday and I'm really gettin' anxious 'cause I got a race Sunday. Two o'clock, still hadn't got to see 'im, and here come France. Says somethin' to the secretary, and 'bout thirty seconds later, he goes right in the office.

When he took France right in there after I'd been sittin' there a day and three-quarters, I got pissed. I got up and walked out of the office. The secretary come runnin' sayin', "Mr. Yunick, Mr. Cole will probably be ready to see you in about twenty minutes. Where can we locate you?"

I work for Ford now.

I said, "Over in Livonia at Ford Motor Comp'ny. Just tell Mr. Cole I don't need a meetin' any more."

This was early 1957 and Ford had been tryin' to get me to go to work for them. So I went over there and by four o'clock, I'd signed a contract with Ford for four times what Chevrolet paid me for two years. I came back down here, and the next mornin' 7:30, Cole called and said, "What to hell happened to you?"

"I told your secretary. I work for Ford now."

He said, "Now, wait a minute."

I told him, "The next time you go take a piss, take a look at yourself and you'll notice that you've got one head, two arms and two legs just like I have. You may be a hellofa lot smarter, but I don't think you'd like it if I did to you what you did to me. Now, I don't have to take any shit. I have signed with Ford, and I'm gonna work for 'em and do my damndest to blow your ass off. What's done is done. You got a lot of miles to go and lot of bridges to cross, and you need to think about it and figure out that we are all alike."

I said, "I've seen you stop and talk to a guy that was cleanin' the floor and told you an idea that would make your cars better that was so stupid it was ridiculus, but you took the five minutes to talk to him sayin' it was well worth checkin' and you'd have your engineers look into it when you knew damn well it was ridiculus. Something's happened to you and you think you are some sort of god or somethin' and you ain't. The only difference is you are a lot smarter and you make a lot more money."

Then everything moved to SEDCO, Southern Engineering Development Company, in Atlanta. McNally was the guy that rented the space and Piggins was the Chevrolet engineer that run the whole thing. They prob'ly had a hundard employees.

I had forty engines sittin' here and asked Cole what he wanted done with 'em. He didn't care what I did with 'em, so I gave 'em away. Some went to maybe Tiny Lund, Fred Lorensen, whoever was runnin' a Chevy. We kept handin' 'em out 'til they were all gone.

I got a hellofa deal with Ford, four or five times better'n what GM was. The deal was, do anything you want. So, the first time we run it, a '57 Ford, we went up to Langhorn. Back in them days, Chevy had twin four-barrels and Ford had pieces of shit called superchargers. We got that thing pretty well herded up and went to Langhorn and took about a second or more off the track record. It was the first stock car to run a hundard miles an hour around Langhorn.

And I'll be damned, about three months later, the manufacturer's organization got together and decided to get out of racin'. Ford called me three months in advance and told me they were gettin' out in June or July. They told me, "You got a two year contract. We'll pay you in full. Keep all your stuff. If you want to race, fine. If you don't, that's fine, too."

I said, "You ain't all gettin' out?"

"That's what we're all supposed to do. I'll guarantee you we are getting out."

Ford was so fair about it, we just decided to race the season out in the car. We didn't win a hellofa lot of races, but we sure did give the Chevys a lot of anxious moments.

Goldsmith and Turner had a pair of '57 Fords at Darlington, and we were way gone from 'em. 'Course, it didn't end up too good. That went on all year. We slap run the shit out of the Chevys. I think I finished the year, then shut her down. I told Goldie to go with Holman.

I don't know where I came back to Chevy, prob'ly '63. I was workin' for Pontiac. That was the next maneuver, '58, '59, '60, '61 and '62 for Bunkie Knudsen at Pontiac. He made a deal with me. It was durin' one of my "quit" periods. He wanted me to run the beach, and he talked me into it.

When we got the car, the whole thing was painted silver. Got Goldie to drive it, and we won the race. I knew that Knudsen was gonna want me to run some more races, so I drove the car back here and got about halfway in the door, and here come Cotten Owens. He knew it was a one race deal,

and he asked me, "Say, what are you going to do with the car?"

I said, "I'm gonna sell the sonofabitch."

"I'd like to buy it. What do you want for it?" he said.

I said, "You got two deals. One for ten dollars if you get it out of here in ten minutes. If you don't get out o' here in ten minutes, it ain't for sale. I got the title right in there, and if you give me ten dollars and you get it past that traffic light in ten minutes, it's yours."

He said to let him run back to the motel, and I said, "You can run back to the motel if you want to, but you ain't gonna make it back in ten minutes. Two minutes are already gone." He woke up that I was serious.

He didn't get out o' here thirty seconds and here come Knudsen and 'bout four carloads of Pontiac people. He said, "I want to see the car."

"It's gone. I sold it."

"Whatayamean it's gone?"

"I told you, I sold it. We had a one race deal. It was my car, and I sold it, ten dollars to Cotten Owens. I figured that you'd try talkin' me into runnin' it the rest of the year."

He talked me into it, and we stayed with him 'til '62. He left and went to Chevy. He was General Manager at Chevy, and he wanted me to go over there. Estes was runnin' Pontiac, and I didn't feel like changin'. I kept thinkin' Pontiac would get a belly full pretty quick and quit.

It never really paid me that much. You worked your ass off. Me? It was seven days a week, at least eighty hours a week, three hundard and sixty-five days a year. Every year you'd get ten or fifteen all-nighters, sometimes two of 'em. It just didn't make no sense. You work that hard and don't get nothin' for it, it ain't much fun.

All the racin' I did with Herb Thomas, all I ever got out of it was two hundard dollars an engine. Chevy deal, I got the ten thousand, but he ended up with the cars and all the parts and all that shit. Herb was a nice guy, but he was a very poor man. He was scrapin' and clawin' for every nickel and dime he could get. Even share croppin', and I can't blame him for tryin' to better himself, but I finally got tired of it. He never came over sayin', "We made pretty good today. Here's five hundard dollars," whether I'd earned it or not.

Back to Chevrolet

When Knudsen got over at Chevy, I was turbocharging Pontiacs. It was a pain in the ass, and ol' Pete Estes was gettin' kinda hard to get along with. John Delorean was Chief Engineer and Estes was General Manager after Knudsen went to Chevy. Knudsen called me a couple of times and asked me about transferrin' from Pontiac to Chevrolet. I always said, "No, I'm not interested."

One day he called me and wanted to know when the next time I was comin' to Detroit. I said, "Tomorrow."

"Good," he said. "Could you stop by here in the morning before you have your meeting?"

"No," I said. "The meetin' I got is real early."

After Knudsen got through talkin' to me, Estes called and moved the meetin' up one day. So, I called Knudsen back and told him, "I could go up there tonight and spend the day with you." That was on Monday. He said, "OK."

The next thing that happened, Estes called. He'd changed his mind and he wanted to have the meetin' in the afternoon of that Monday instead of Tuesday mornin'. That didn't screw up what I'd told Knudsen, so I went over there, and he took me down to the engine room where they had this engine all scattered out. The engineers had already run it on the dyno and had it all apart like they do prototype engines. It was totally disassembled with reports on everything, regular engineering reports.

Cole had called me up there on a couple of other jobs, the 348 and the 409. I considered them junk. So, when I seen this engine laying there.... Chief Engineer then at Chevy was Harry Barr. He was at the meetin', Duntov, Ed Cole, I don't know who else, but there was a young burrhead guy with bullfrog type necktie and pants two inches too short, white socks, black shoes - you know, the stereotype young Chevy engineer. I looked the engine over for two, three hours, and Knudsen said, "What do you think?"

"This sonofabitch looks better'n anything I've seen yet. This is a nice engine. Who designed this engine?" I wasn't gettin' too many answers, but when I said that, that burrhead guy said, "I DID" so loud you could o' heard him a quartermile away. He hadn't said a word all the time I was lookin' over the engine. That was the only peep that came out of him. Name was Dick Keinath.

I said, "I like this engine. If you build this sonofabitch, there's gonna be big trouble for everybody." That was the Mystery engine. 427 cubic inches, looked good, best I'd seen in Detroit up to that point.

So, I left and when I got to Pontiac, went in to Pete's office, he said, "Well, you double crossing sonofabitch. You been down there with Knudsen again." Estes had a terrible temper.

Well, that started a fight. Every one of 'em had a hatchet man, a male secretary, big sombitch. He come in and stopped the fight. 'Course, I quit, and I went over to engineering to try to decide what I was gonna do with the turbocharger program. Delorean was just gettin' ready to start up a weird engine they had built for the Tempest. It was a overhead, hydraulic lifter thing, belt drive cam. It had a big brother, a V-8, same valve gear, belt drives and everything that they were thinkin' about usin' for a race engine the next year. It was very big, very heavy and in my view a very poor design. I was unhappy with 'em pushin' that engine.

While I was there, they cranked the V-8 up and it blew it all to shit in a few minutes like I figured it would, its maiden voyage. It was prob'ly 'bout a three hundred thousand dollar engine, just destroyed it. Estes come over and apologized, and I stayed with 'em a little bit longer, but the damage was done.

A couple of months later, Knudsen said, "I've got to do something with this engine. I like for you to consider transferring over here, and I'll pay you double what Pontiac's paying you."

Meantime, Fireball was drivin' Pontiacs, and I sensed he was havin' some problems 'bout like Thomas. So after we run out here at Daytona, he won the pole and the race. When the race was over, I told him, "You need to quit. You got somethin' wrong with you. You're drivin' scared now."

Shortly after that, I made a deal with him and Banjo, and I gave the Pontiac to Banjo, and I quit Pontiac. I thought Fireball needed to get out of racin'. Knudsen heard about it and called sayin' he wanted me to develop the Mystery engine. I accepted.

I guess we started callin' it the Mystery engine because they were half-assed in racin'. They wouldn't admit it, and what I remember, I'm an old man now and its a little hard for my memory to work just right, is that I had all of 'em right here. I've always remembered 42 sets of parts for 42 complete engines. Every engine that got raced got raced out of here to whoever run a Chevrolet.

We finally got it runnin' pretty good, but the decision at the top was that we ain't gonna put this in production. The bean counters are goin' to go through this thing. And finally, before the race, I knew that that engine would never be built the way it was. The bean counters pulled two head bolts out of each side and that screwed up the ports. Two of 'em went the right way, two the wrong way. They reduced the bore and increased the stroke which was exactly backwards to what we should have done. I knew that engine was not gonna be built, but I never talked to anybody about it 'cause I was told it was confidential.

Finally we went to race it, a '63 Chevy we stuck it in, and I went an got a young driver named Johnny Rutherford to drive it. He'd never drove a stock car in his life, but I'd seen him drive on the dirt and I was lookin' for somebody I could teach to drive the car the way I wanted him to, and I figured Rutherford was the guy. Knudsen objected to it, but he finally decided he shouldn't be stickin' his nose into it. When things started shapin' up, we took it and tried it out on the track. It was a joke. We were just way faster than anything else.

I had a long talk with him 'bout ten days or two weeks before the race, and I tried to get Knudsen to withdraw the cars. Don't run 'em 'cause it was a phony deal. I finally got him to agree with me. Then, when he presented it to NASCAR, they didn't want him to pull 'em out. So, Knudsen and France argued about it for a week. Now we're down to about three days before the race, we're all qualified and Knudsen agrees. "We are withdrawing the cars."

I couldn't see it. You had to get your parts from me. I had a limited amount of parts, and we would only give 'em to famous race drivers, or famous mechanics or wealthy car owners, and I couldn't see that bein' fair 'cause they had no intentions of producing any more. It was gonna be a totally different engine.

We were workin' around the clock; didn't know if we were in or out. Rex White, I think, had engine trouble, and we were puttin' them in and out of the dynamometer tryin' to patch up problems. Finally at five o'clock in the mornin', Knudsen calls and said, "Smokey, listen. I don't want you to say a thing 'til I get through. I've been up all night with this thing, arguing back and forth with France. Number 1, we are going to race the cars. Number 2, we are going to take two engines down to the

Chevy dealer for Ford to pick up, and they are to be there at eight o'clock in the morning. You are to keep the thing going, and try as hard as you can to win. Now, we've talked about this many times. I'm not asking you, I'm telling you."

I said, "OK, boss. I'll do what you say but I will not take the engines down to the dealer." He started to get pissed, but I said, "We got an engineer sittin' here ain't doin' a damn thing. He's sleepin' over in the motel, name of Vince Piggins, that works for you. He can take 'em down there. I'll have 'em loaded on the truck by six o'clock, and I'll call him and tell him to take the engines over there. If he don't take 'em over there, don't call me back and ask me why they were not there by eight o'clock. If it means quittin' if I won't take 'em there personally, then I just quit."

We went on and raced, but we didn't win. We won a hundard and twenty-five mile qualifier, and I guess it was expectin' too much of Johnny to win the first time, but what I did like about him was the way he run in and out of the pit and some of the decisions he made on the race track.

That's about all there was to the Mystery engine. After Keinath designed it, it went through its teething problems here. I didn't do all that good a job and some of the mechanics weren't the world's best, no different than today. If we had kept running the thing, a little bit of development time to fix the things that kept breaking, the things we were tryin' to get changed, then finally when the bean counters changed the whole thing, you had a hopeless case.

Now, you're talkin' about Chevrolet yesterday and today. Those guys at Chevrolet have had memory failure. You know this guy Herb Fischel? I got him his job at Chevrolet. One day I was workin' away here and this young guy walked in here, introduced himself, and told me he had just graduated from North Carolina State University and he wanted to work for me as an engineer. He wanted to be in racin'. He was about in tears because just north of here, a cop had got 'im and give him a speedin' ticket in his new Corvette, and he was really pissed. Wanted to know if I could do anthing about it. He hung around here all day, and he wanted to be a racer so bad. I was working for Chevrolet, so I said, "I don't need an engineer. Fact is, you're just out of college, you don't know anything and it will take you three or four years to figure out which end is up. But you want it so bad, Chevrolet needs some guys like you." So, I called Piggins and arranged for Fischel to have an interview.

I don't know how it all went from there on, but he got hired by Chevrolet and he got stuck in the drafting department. I didn't know they had hired him, but once when I was up there on a visit, I went to the drafting department and there he was. He still weren't where he wanted to be, so shortly after that, a little more conversation with Piggins and whoever it was runnin' the deal at the time, prob'ly Knudsen, he got transferred into Piggins' office, and I'm sure he don't remember any of that.

Every time Chevrolet got involved in stock car racing durin' that time, it was always through me and it was always a back door deal. The first Chevelle I ever remember gettin' involved with was in '63. Knudsen called me and asked me to come up and look at a new car they were thinkin' about puttin' out.

Went up there, and they had one car built, silver grey. At that time, Harry Barr was gone and Chevrolet had a new engineer name of Jim Primo. Jim Primo was the best car body builder in the world, but as far as running gear and engines, he didn't know much. Primo wasn't the easiest cat in the world to handle. We didn't get along worth a shit.

Chevelles

So, Knudsen took me down to R&D and showed me this Chevelle, and asked me what I thought. I had the car put on scales, with front sheet metal off, and the second day, after I got through looking it over and measuring, I said, "I don't like it worth a shit. The engine's too far forward and too high and so on." Primo said, "Just what I thought. Why don't we fire all these engineers and hire you to design the thing!"

Knudsen said, "Are you sure?"

"Yeah, dead positive. It'll push like mad. Way too heavy on the front."

Knudsen said, "Move her back and move her down" and gave 'em about a week to do it. Primo never forgive me. Knudsen wanted to take it to the Firestone proving grounds, so I told him to send it to Daytona and we'll move it, and they had a new transistor ignition they wanted to test at the same time.

I got it down here and moved the engine down and back, wasn't all that bad. 'Course from Primo's point of view, it was quite a bit of work. The car hadn't got in production yet, didn't even have the prototypes, you know, when they build the first two hundard. It was a handbuilt car. So, we went to the Firestone proving grounds. It was cold weather and they were slow. We took a Chevy engineer name of Doug Roe to do the test drivin'.

Doug could drive a car pretty good, just run around in a circle on the highbank Firestone test track. One thing wrong with it was it was rough. Another thing wrong with it was if you run off the track, it had boulders big as this room. Firestone laid everybody off, 'bout three hundard people, just gave us the test track. Well, after we was there one day, ol' car run pretty good, 'bout hundard and eighty, the transistor ignition just quit 'bout five o'clock at night. Really nasty weather.

I called Chevy for another transitor ignition, for someone to hand carry one down there. I called Knudsen first and he said call Primo. It was 'bout nine o'clock at night. Primo wasn't there, so I called Knudsen back and told him, "I don't need Primo, I need a distributor."

Finally got ahold of Primo, told him I needed a new ignition right away. "What're you bothering me for?"

"'Cause there's three hundard men over there at Firestone that were give a day off for us to run the car. They was nice enough to do that for us, damn sure don't have no right to just piss away a day."

I called Knudsen back and he had some guy to come up from Mesa, Arizona. He got there about three or four at night. He knew this ignition, but he had no spare. He was a pretty good man, worked his ass off. He took the thing apart piece by piece and laid it all out. Every piece checked out good. He couldn't find anything wrong with it. He put it back together, and that thing cranked up and run, and we went out and finished the test. That's how the Chevelle was born. All I did with it was move the engine and some of the initial testing.

We run that car. Andretti was gonna drive it in the Daytona 500. He'd never driven a stock car on a fast track before, and he run it into the ass end of a parked car out there and bent it up so bad we couldn't fix it, so we couldn't enter it.

That was the '64 Chevelle. Then there was the one we raced in '67. From the performance point of view, the chassis on the Chevys were horrible. The brakes were horrible. The transmissions were bad. The cars were really ill handling cars. So, we finally got a deal where they agreed that we would try to do it right and give us enough latitude to do it. I got them to build the chassis up there in Chevy R&D under Frank Winchell and Jim Musser. They were the two head knockers in Chevy R&D. After they wasted about a half a million dollars and run us out of time, we finally had to bring the car down here with about ten of their guys. We finally got the thing finished up and run it in the race. Turner drove it.

It was gettin' towards the end of the race, the beach race here, the 500, and we come in for a pit stop. It was a bad pit stop. Turner got from about a lap ahead to about three quarters of lap down. Just before he left, I hollered at Turner, "Don't try to get it all back in one lap!" We'd agreed that he wouldn't turn it over sixty-six hundard or sixty-eight hundard, and I knew that it would turn about four hundard more. But I was afraid he'd forget so I just warned him again. Just what I was afraid of happened. He turned it loose, and if you'd go over there and look at that lap speed, it would probably be about 184 mile an hour. Broke a rod, and that took care of that one.

The next year, '68, I decided I'd build one from what I'd learned in '67 but we'd do it here. And examinin' the rule book, I went by what they said, and anything they didn't say, I assumed I could do. The way I always handled it. Built my own frame, so on and so forth. 'Bout six weeks before the race, I'm runnin' late, I get France to come over here. I was sick, had a cold, just come back from the doctor and he said I had pneumonia. I said, "France, here's my car. I'm 'way behind and I'm considerin' stoppin' and not runnin' in the beach race. I've heard that Ford and Chrysler got together, and no matter what I do, the car ain't goin' to run this year. I'm not goin' to make it through inspection."

He denied it, but I told him, "We been through this shit many times. The information I've got, I think is accurate. So, man to man, I want you to tell me. If you have, I got nothin' to say to the newspapers. I'm just goin' to back off and try to get this damn cold under control. Then I'll finish it after the race and come back in the circuit some time later."

The '67 race just shocked everybody. We stuck her on the pole so easy. Chrysler and Ford were spendin' money ass over head and General Motors ain't spendin' a dime. Had to do with their racing programs. That's how they were puttin' money into NASCAR through some hellacious charges in their racing programs, and they were just goin' to cancel their race programs. France denied it. So, I told him I still didn't believe him, so I told him, "I'm not even goin' out there for the pole. I'll just come in the last day of qualifyin' and try for fast time and try to win the race." I got Johncock to drive it.

We get over there the last day, and I'd underestimated the shit they were gonna put me through. Next thing I know, they got it up to 'bout two o'clock. Well that was the last day you could practice and qualify. I was plannin' on bein' on the race track by 'bout 'leven or 'leven-thirty, give Johncock some practice and then qualify right at the end of the day at four o'clock. We finally get through inspection and push it to Union to get fueled up to go out and practice and qualify, and come to find out when the guys come back and say they won't give me any gas 'cause the chief inspector hadn't signed off. So, I go roarin' up to him, he's sittin' in there readin' Superman or Spiderman or somethin' - he was a comic book nut I said, "Sign this thing. We ain't got but a few minutes left here, and I ain't been on the track yet. We got to qualify today."

He laid his comic book down and said, "I got to inspect that car myself." So, he went and inspected it and made a list of ten or twelve things. Number one on the list was "Remove homemade frame and replace with stock." Well, that would take two months. The car was a throw-away car built to win the beach race. If we wrecked it, it would take six, seven weeks to fix it. I wanted to win the beach race, and I didn't give a damn about what happened at the next race. Either you win it or you don't. "If you mean what's on this list," I said, "I'm gone."

"You got to do what's on that list."

"Fine". Goin' back to the car, I sent a guy that worked for me to go get two or three gallons of gas 'cause I'd decided I was goin' to drive it out o' there, then hook it up and tow it home. Had a big ol' rope. Told one of the guys to put the rope on it, and I went back to break the seal on the empty gas tank. One of the inspectors grabbed me and pushed me and said, "If you break that seal, you've gotta take that tank out o' there again." I got him straightened out right quick, and at least two hundard people seen the whole thing. Then I went down to Union and told 'em I needed three or four gallons of gas, "And I don't need no horse shit. Either give it to me or I'll go buy it some place."

He finally told 'em to put some gas in the can, two gallons or four gallons or three gallons, and I went back to the car and put that gas can up there and everybody seen me. There was a hellofa crowd there. Now, I could'a prob'ly cranked it up and drove it home without puttin' any gas in it 'cause I had about a inch and half fuel line, held five gallons, but I didn't know. I assumed that all drained out. I didn't know if it did or didn't.

As I drove out of the tunnel, Len Cooper who was the No. 2 man at NASCAR, come running out. Somebody must have called 'em and told 'em I was leavin'. He stopped me and told me, "Smokey, if you take that car out there in the road, you'll have to go completely through inspection again and there ain't time for that. France wants to talk to you."

I said, "You see this list? Look at number one. Your inspector said that's it."

He said, "Well, how long does it take to change the frame?"

"If France wants to see me, he can go to the garage." I put that thing in gear, red light and all, went roarin' across there draggin' that rope and came on home. When France got over here, well, I'm not gonna tell you what happened then.

In 'bout a month, Firestone called me and said they wanted to run a tire test down there in June, like to use your car. I said, "Fine, it's sittin' here ready to go." 'Bout a week later they called and said, "Sorry, we can't use your car. NASCAR won't let it run on that track."

Then I sold it to a guy that never paid for it, and he took it back as a modified the next year. After he was in inspection a half a day, they discovered it was the same car; they threw him and the car out. So, that's the story on that car, the '68 Chevelle. I don't know whether it would have been a very fast car or not, it never run.

One day 'bout two, three months ago, *Circle Track* made some kind of arrangements with me to run it around a lap. I wouldn't even go out there. I wanted to run it in '68, not 1988.

I had a Camaro we were goin' to run out there in the 24-Hours. Jim Hall, Bruce McLaren and Dennis Hulme was goin' to be the drivers. We got out there and got in a hellofa argument in inspection. Again, it was so much that it wasn't do-able. I think I got pissed off and didn't want to do anything. Maybe I could have got it changed around. McLaren got mad. Jim Hall got all puckered up. I don't think they appreciated what was goin' on either. I don't know about Hulme. He'd just flown over here from New Zealand. We didn't run the car.

I had Bobby Unser to drive it in one race, the Paul Revere 250, the midnight race. They had them Mustangs tearin' up the whole world. We run late with the car and never got no practice. So, I don't think we got a qualifying lap. The way they did that thing, they ran through the infield like the 24-Hours. We started in the back of the field, and in the first lap, Bobby Unser was goin' into the number three turn and the number two car was comin' off number two. He'd passed the whole field and got down into number three runnin' about a hundred eighty-five mile an hour, and just as he was hittin' the bump, the battery terminal got up against the block on the engine and shorted out the battery and all the wires went up in smoke. Unser was in three with no lights. Blackest night you've ever seen. Boy that sonofabitch would run.

Then I took it to a bunch of tracks to try to start in the back of the Grand Nationals and run for first place or nothin' but they never would let me do it. We took it to Charlotte and we out-qualified all the Grand Nationals, in the Camaro. American Motors had something they were runnin' at Charlotte and they were really pissed about the car. I decided that since I couldn't run it in the Grand National there, I wasn't interested in runnin' that Baby Grand. I was just goin' to bring it on home and quit foolin' with it. They got to pissin' and moanin' about it, is it legal, I said, "Tell you what I'll do. You give me thirty-two hundred dollars right now and it's your car. At the end of the race, I get the purse and you get the car in whatever shape it's in. Then you can find all the cheatin' you want to. You can prove it." But they wouldn't take me up on it.

Overall, I think the small block Chevy is the greatest single engine that Detroit's ever come up with. From day one to today. The reason that thing happened was Ed Cole. That engine in '55 cost $85.60 runnin'. A set of five tires was $10. Spark plugs, four cents a piece. Carburetors, $6.25. Warranty on 'em was around $26, $27 a car. Advertising was around $28 a car. All that was figured out in advance. They'd say they were gonna sell so many cars and amortize everything. Everything was aimed at ten percent net profit. Hell, if I wanted a change to an engine that cost a quarter, I could never get it through.

There was the time when we were goin' to have an aluminum block, magnesium block. Shit, we got magnesium main bearings. Magnesium main bearing bolts, too. There's a box of them around here somewhere. For sports car racin', Jim Hall needed lighter engines. What I tried to get 'em to do from day one and even today was not use aluminum but get a light weight iron casting. A cast iron block is a series of holes knit together with iron. Aluminum is half as strong as iron. Then you have to ask yourself, which metal makes the best block? Why don't you make a cast iron block with walls half as thick and they'll both be the same strength and the same weight. As simple as it sounds, that is the truth. About three years ago, I got somebody at General Motors to cast a small block Chevy the right way, in Japan. They got it back and tested it. It weighed one pound less than the aluminum block, and it was thirty percent better because the third equation is, what's its coefficient of expansion? Aluminum expands and contracts at twice what iron does, so the candidate metal is iron.

To cast a light weight cast iron block, you'd have to centrifugal cast it, prob'ly in a vacuum, to get the density up so you can get the thin sections that won't crack and have the strength. Unfortunately, it costs more to do that than it does to cast aluminum. That's what all this aluminum shit is all about, cost. Same way with racin' pistons. If they made racin' pistons correctly, they'd be made out of steel, not aluminum. Then you wouldn't burn no more pistons.

I worked direct for Cole and Knudsen and Estes and Delorean, and when I worked for Chevrolet, I wanted to take the small block up to 427 inches. I built two prototypes and brought Cole down here and showed 'em to him. He turned 'em down. When they come off the Mystery engine and went to the 427, I didn't like it. I said, "Let's go back to the small block and open it up." But, I couldn't pull it off. The Mystery engine was a very good engine, and by the time they went to the 427, the decision had been made to go to 500 cubic inches. As time passed, they were goin' to put more bore and more stroke in it.

Bruce McLaren had sense enough to know. See, when you look at the McLaren engine, the bore and stroke is the Mystery engine. He used that combination. He shortened the stroke and increased the bore, but he was stuck with the heads with two backwards ports in each head. Bruce was like Marshall Teague and Jack McGrath, he could drive the shit out of a car, but he was also one of the best mechanics I ever seen. Bruce knew his car and he knew his engine.

Jim Hall is another smart guy, engineering-wise. Anybody that doubts that is crazy. That guy is a hellofa engineer. On chassis and aerodynamics, he's as good as anybody in this country.

No safety barriers. No corner workers. No emergency crews nearby. Just dirt and a constant uphill grind to the top of Pikes Peak. Chevrolet photo.

Duntov Takes The Peak

One of the hot rodder's favorite hills to climb was Pikes Peak. From the start, the climb rose to 14,110 feet in the Colorado Rockies. In all sorts of cars, drivers could pit their skill against the clock. The challenge was a 12.42-mile grind of hairpins, precipitous cliffs, dirt and bumps to the top.The curvy trek was a dangerous high speed blast up the side of a mountain, just the sort of thing that hot rodders did for the thrill of conquering the peak. But one mistake and it was a long way to the bottom in some places. There were no barriers and no safety crews at every turn, and no cheering crowds lined the route along the way. It was man and machine against the mountain.

Following 1955's year of many successes, mostly unexpected and encouraging, Barney Clark and Duntov launched the '56 marketing campaign early with a run for a record up the peak. The annual early September run had drawn competitors since the 'teens, and up until 1956, the Pikes Peak Hillclimb was an AAA Contest Board sanctioned event. Influenced strongly by the Le Mans disaster that killed 81 people in 1955, and the following disaster during the Tourist Trophy in Ulster, Ireland, AAA discontinued all association with racing. That left sanctioning open to other organizations and NASCAR stepped in. Later, it became a USAC function.

Since the early days of the hillclimb, the event was divided into two classes, Stock Car Class and Special Car Class. Duntov's run was held on September 9, 1955, in pre-production model '56 Chevrolets. It had been some twenty years since a stock car record had been established, so setting a new record seemed quite possible. And that equalled hype - another advertising blitz of Chevrolet performance. Duntov took two cars to the summit, and both set new records. One was a two-door, the other a four-door. The cars were equipped with the new 205 hp "Super Turbo-Fire V8" and had "get-up-and-go" wrote Clark. The two-door model got up and

At the top, NASCAR officials and Duntov's wife Elfi greet the new record holder. This 4-door '56 model Chevrolet was camouflaged to hide the new styling. Chevrolet photo.

Chevy's "Ball-Race steering for pinpoint steering accuracy" and "Glide-Ride front suspension".

"Chevrolet has unique outrigger rear springs that give superior cornering qualities," he proclaimed.

went faster than the four-door and established the new overall record for stock cars.

At 7:17 in the morning, the first run was made. Fifty minutes later, Duntov was in the second car setting another record. The cars were camouflaged to prevent premature exposure of 1956 styling to the press, and when Duntov raised the dust with the two-door Chevy, he took the peak in record time, 17:24:05 minutes. The four-door was actually a show car prepared for press showings and a good deal heavier. AAA had been the official timing body for the hillclimb, but NASCAR sanctioned Duntov's climbs under the direction of Bill France and witnessed by ace cross country record setter Erwin "Cannonball" Baker.

At the top, Duntov's wife Elfi was among the NASCAR officials that cheered his new success. In a letter dated September 14, 1955, addressed to Thomas Keating of General Motors, France documented the new record for American stock sedans. The new record was more than two minutes quicker than the previous mark, Bus Hammond's Stock Car Class record of 1934, 19:25.70 minutes in a Ford, and Clark put together an advertising "newspaper" proclaiming,

"HERE'S THE GREATEST SAFETY STORY OF ALL".

"No other car has ever gone so high, so fast, so safely...and taken so many turns at high speed as the 1956 Chevrolet did on Pikes Peak."

That statement wasn't strictly true, however. Many other Pikes Peak specials had reached the top in less time than the Chevy, but this was advertising. Clark went on to mention

The Hot one's even HOTTER!

In fact, the '56 models were little changed mechanically from the '55s and were rather typical of American made suspensions of the time.

Victories in competition were fast becoming a strong advertising theme throughout the U.S., but it wasn't advertising alone that made fast Chevys more appealing to the young buyer, it was winning. Ads appearing during 1955 spotlighted Chevrolet's new entry, and Clark made the most of Chevrolet's few wins with full page ads in auto magazines circulated nationwide:

It's easy to see why the 180-horsepower "Super Turbo-Fire" version (with four-barrel carburetor, big manifold and dual exhausts) is setting the drag strips on fire. And when you consider the potential in that ultra-light, ultra-compact powerplant ....

"Potential" was indeed the mark of the new V-8 Chevrolet, and America loved it. The end of 1955 saw Chevrolet production at 1,830,038 U.S. passenger cars to Ford's 1,764,524. The two divisions of their parent companies had a multi-billion dollar year, and such revenue showed that the market for new cars was soaring. But such high sales figures for '55 meant

remarkable that essentially stock Corvettes of 1956 could reach those speeds over thirty years ago.

Duntov planned a three car team with drivers John Fitch, Betty Skelton and himself. He determined what it would take to break 150 on a two-way average. He knew that a car on sand would be slower than on asphalt because the beach sand

Duntov, Smokey Yunick, Paul Goldsmith and other people drove this Corvette on the Beach at Daytona in February, 1956. Zora Arkus-Duntov photo.

reduced sales of '56 models. The next year, sales dropped off dramatically.

Corvettes on the Beach

Having recognized the potential sales benefits of exploiting the high speed achievements at Pikes Peak, Duntov proposed to Ed Cole that he take the new V-8 Corvette to Daytona Beach for the Speed Week in January 1956. As usual, all the automotive press would be there, and it would be a prime opportunity to show the world that the Corvette was no longer the "dog" that sports car and racing buffs had come to consider the 6-cylinder version. Cole was reluctant but emphasized that such a run was secondary to working out details of the new fuel injection system.

With that charter, Duntov undertook to show the public that a V-8 Corvette was a 150 mph car. The publicity that such an accomplishment would bring would be considerable, another advertising angle. Looking over the burgeoning hype surrounding 150+ mph cars in the late 1980s, it was indeed

had more rolling resistance than a hard surface. He calculated that he needed more speed on a hard surface, perhaps 165 mph, to make 150+ on sand. If he used the new-for-1956 dual Carter 4-barrel induction setup, as much as 225 horsepower was on tap, but that was calculated to come up short in a stripped-down Corvette roadster without a windshield or bumpers and with a tonneau cover over the passenger's side. He needed a little more power, maybe 20 more horses, to insure success on the beach.

New engine equipment for '56 included the "ram's horn" exhaust manifolds that were good for 5 more horsepower at 5000 rpm and a dual point distributor that gave reliable performance when revved that high, but the high performance cam introduced in 1955 was deemed insufficient for the task. Duntov designed another stick, a high lift cam that subsequently became the famous "Duntov" cam. Its origin was from the ARDUN-Ford engine.

"One day," relates Fred Frincke, Duntov's personal draftsman, "Zora handed me a sheet of paper with numbers listed in metric and wanted them converted to English. I did that and he took it to drafting. It became the Duntov cam."

Inside, the stock appearing Corvette that ran over 150 mph received lateral supports for the driver, a tach and a set of guages. NASCAR photo.

NASCAR Performance Trials attracted the best cars and drivers of the time. Smokey Yunick and "Fireball" Roberts lived around Daytona Beach and soon became great names in racing. Here, Duntov is away on a flying mile record attempt. Zora Arkus-Duntov photo.

It proved to be the right match and bumped the output of the top Corvette option to 240 hp at almost 6000 rpm. It also proved to be an excellent street cam and was fitted to a number of high performance production engines in 1957 which gave the owners considerable bragging rights about running the "Duntov Cam".

In testing, Duntov reached over 160 mph at GM's Mesa Proving Grounds where the Duntov cam was born. Later, at Daytona Beach, drivers had two miles to get up to speed, then the timed flying mile, then two more miles to slow down. Duntov posted a new sports car record at 150.533 mph. Fitch, Skelton and Duntov raced up and down the sand easily exceeding 140 mph. The Corvettes ran in the modified stock class, and both Fitch and Skelton claimed new records, Fitch setting a two-pass average of 145.543 mph.

Along with Herb Thomas' 1955 win at Darlington, the Mecca of stock car racing, the foundation was laid for Chevrolet's huge success in racing. Originally, the small block was conceived as a strong and simple engine that would be cheap to manufacture, yet be reliable and rugged even when used in high performance applications. In such fundamentally sound design concepts, those that steered away from complexity, were planted the seeds of greatness that matured over the years to become the most successful all-around engine ever produced.

The New Hot Rodder's V-8

It wasn't long until the 265 was yanked out of normal duty and given muscles for racing. That was part of the original plan in its conception, to be hot rodded, just as Cole and Barr had planned. Duntov was quick to follow its introduction with heavy duty, high performance parts in support of racing and hot rodding.

Fifties era hot rodders instantly found Chevy's new engine ideal for almost any racing application. Edelbrock produced 230 dynoed horsepower from a small block early in 1955, and

that brought a lot of attention to the engine. He produced a three-carb manifold for the engine by mid-year that bumped the 265 to around 225 horsepower. He subsequently became famous for his Edelbrock performance parts that made the new Chevy a winner in any application.

Early in 1956, he was commissioned to build a racing engine for Tom Carstens, owner of the British built H.W.M. that had been used in the movie, "The Racers". When the cars were sold off after filming, Carstens purchased the car for a new project to replace his nearly invincible Cad-Allard, the famed and feared black number 14 that had terrorized the tracks of the West Coast in the early '50s. The wealthy Tacoma, Washington, sportsman had the original 2-liter Alta engine yanked in favor of a much-warmed-over Edelbrock prepared Chevy with 10.5:1 compression ratio and a full-race cam. The Wilson Preselector transmission was replaced in favor of a much lighter Jaguar unit.

Edelbrock increased the bore and stroke of the Chevy engine to 3.875 x 3.20 inches to produce 301.9 cubic inches (4949 cc), just a bit under the 5-liter top for Class C racing. He milled the heads to increase compression, and enlarged and polished the ports to improve breathing. No changes were made to the valve gear except some lightening of the valves. Edelbrock installed one of his racing cams and special tappets.

The result? A formidable 300 hp roadster weighing in at around 1850 pounds, a car that easily spun its rear tires in 3rd gear. The H.W.M.-Chevy was first raced by Bill Pollack at Pebble Beach on April 22, 1956, the site of the first Corvette race. That was a landmark date, the beginning of Chevrolet in road racing and precurser of great things to come.

Pollack proved the car in its inaugural run at Pebble Beach when he won the pole position in the main event and simply walked away from the pack at the starter's flag. Some tough foreigners were in the pack; Ernie McAfee in a 4.4-liter

And back with a new record. Bill France looks over the official scorer's notes. Duntov beats the Thunderbird to the standing mile record. Smokey Yunick photo.

Jim Reed of Peekskill, N.Y., won three consecutive NASCAR Short Track titles, then made his debut in the Convertible Division race at Daytona Beach driving a '56 Chevrolet but bowed out early. Darlington Speedway photo.

Ferrari (he crashed on the narrow course and was killed 33 laps later); Phil Hill in a 3.5-liter Ferrari, the Sebring 12-hour winner; Carroll Shelby at the wheel of a Ferrari Monza, the previous year's main event winner. Shelby drove his Italian to a second victory while the H.W.M.- Chevy fishtailed around the course to finish down field. Tires that would stick under such power were yet to come.

The H.W.M.- Chevy, the first Chevrolet V-8 engine swap in a foreign racing car, began a landslide of attention that quickly shifted toward the new Chevrolet V-8. Why put up with expensive and hard-to-find foreign engines and parts when this American mill was cheaper, stronger, easily more powerful and was proving to be better?

The H.W.M.-Chevy became known as the "Stovebolt Special" and went on to a long and illustrious career of racing in many hands, notably those of John "Bat" Masterson of Ventura, California, who owned the car for many years. It has survived to be raced in vintage races today, still wearing black, number 14 (usually), and three carburetors on a small block. And it's still a handful to race.

Building specials was a growing trend. The "Morgensen Special", later to become dubbed "Old Yaller", was a genuine cobbled-up heap of going machine. This very successful racing car was lashed up from a homemade tube chassis, 6-cylinder Plymouth engine (later replaced by a multi-carbed Buick), a '38 Ford front end, a '49 Ford rear end, and back fenders from a '47 Chevy pickup. Built and raced first by Dick Morgensen in 1953, the car went through several years of racing in his hands, as well as those of Eric Hauser and Max Balchowsky, and tallied wins as late as 1960. The car's most impressive victories were against Ferraris and Maseratis among many other top line imports during the 1957-58 season. Hauser put "Old Yaller" across the finish line at Santa Barbara in front of Phil Hill's 4.9-liter Ferrari, the same that had not lost a race in this country!

Back yard specials were often highly competitive and proved to be training grounds for a lot of great names in racing. The Dick Troutman and Tom Barnes built Mercury special that Chuck Daigh drove to 2nd in the Santa Barbara

Road Races (Modified Over-1500cc race) of '55 led to big things later on with the small block Chevy. Troutman and Barnes were to figure strongly in Chevrolet sports racing of the late '50s and early '60s with the Reventlow Scarabs and Chaparral-1 sports racers. The small block was soon to become a giant.

In short order, other cars received Chevy engines, an A6GCS Maserati, a Ferrari or two, some Allards and a D-Type Jaguar, for instance, and many other backyard specials became Chevy powered. But one thing kept those early Chevy pioneers from getting the most from their cars, a suitable transmission. Then, Chevrolet Division came to their rescue with a strong 4-speed. It was first offered in May, 1957 as a Corvette option and became a boon to racers. Hot on the heels of this offering came fuel injection served up to entice Chevy racers with a complete performance package; engine, transmission and sophisticated fuel injection. Along with the new equipment, Chevrolet had to change the image of the Corvette to convince the growing numbers of sports car enthusiasts that the 'Vette was indeed a sports car.

When the '55 Corvette received the small block, it didn't make waves. At Daytona for the Pure Oil Trials that year, the V-8 Corvette was less than sensational. In '56, Duntov & Co. went back to the beach at Daytona and made history with world records. And by the end of the year, Dr. Dick Thompson had earned Corvette's first SCCA National Championship (C/Production). By 1957, Corvette was bumped up to B/Production. Their main adversary was the much more expensive Mercedes 300SL, and in the hands of the "flying dentist", Dr. Thompson's Corvette was once again an all-conquering winner, this time in B/Production.

Jim Massey and crew show off the sort of 225 hp Chevy that took NASCAR's Convertibvle Division championship in '56. Bob Welborn won the title with 3 wins and 40 top ten finishes against the 22 wins of Curtis Turner's Ford with 29 top tens. Jim Reed won the Short Track Division with 14 wins while Chevy tallied 25 victories to Ford's 11. Darlington Speedway photo.

It was in 1957 that Chevrolet introduced fuel injection delivering 283 horsepower from 283 cubic inches, a rarely-achieved accomplishment in a production car. The Chrysler 300 reached the same goal that year. That much power from an engine with the same outward dimensions as the 265, still with incredible durability, pushed Chevrolet into an arena the small block alone occupied. The flathead Ford was fast dying as the hot rodder's choice, and Ford's new overhead valve engines were not catching on.

Ford's new-for-1954 "Y-block" V-8 was the low-priced leader that year at 239 cubic inches. It became a tough customer in stock car racing during 1955 and '56, but hot rodders tended to lean more in favor of the Chevy. The Y-block was increased to 272 and 292 inch versions for '56, and Ford's hottest factory equipment in '55 was the 292 Police Interceptor that saw duty as a stock car racer. With a 4-barrel, solid lifters and dual exhausts, this engine claimed more cubic inches than the Chevrolet, and more power, 198 compared to Chevy's 195. Ford was winning the "wars", or so it seemed.

The battle lines were clearly drawn in 1955. Instead of Hudson Hornets and Chrysler 300s, Oldsmobiles and Buicks that the racing enthusiast either didn't want or couldn't afford, it was now Ford against Chevrolet, and both makes were emerging as giant killers. It was Ford and Chevy going nose-to-nose during NASCAR's Speed Week in '55, but facing off against Tom McCahill's *Mechanix Illustrated* magazine sponsored Thunderbird in the hands of Joe Ferguson, 'Vettes's came up short in '56, Chuck Daigh tried to steal the show in a high speed prepared T-Bird but lost to Duntov, who posted 87.74 mph in the standing mile. In '57, his slightly modified 'Bird was again prepared by Pete DePaolo and received some

racy improvements. Outwardly, what the fans and press saw was a T-Bird without a standard windshield and fitted with "moon" disc wheel covers. Otherwise, it appeared stock. Painted on the sides of the car, in large letters, read **FORD Thunderbird**, the sort of thing a factory would do. Daigh sailed along the sand at better than 93.31 mph for the standing mile, then blazed a flying mile at over 138 mph while another 'Bird posted 146 mph, but both were off Duntov's record of '56, 150.533 mph. Chevrolet was proving to be a truly "hot one" with that "something" that attracted hot rodders.

That "something" was happening at a grass roots level. Drag racing was the medium, and soon the high-revving Chevy small block was cleaning up in stock class strip shots. The factory unveiled new high performance equipment in '56, dual 4-barrels and high lift cam that dropped 0-60 under 10 seconds for the first time. By now, a stock Chevrolet so equipped was almost a 120 mph car and could lay down quartermiles in 16 seconds.

However exciting drag racing was for the participants, at the time it was widely regarded by the adult public as little more than outlaw racing. Unlike sports car "real" racing with well known drivers and expensive machinery, drag racers encountered stiff and continuous difficulties in their attempts to raise the image of their sport. The factories were not interested in the mid-50s, but in just five years they were rolling out big inch heavy hitters that pushed drag racing into the era of factory sponsored super stocks.

But 1955 was just the beginning. Clearly, though, the battle on the dirt and emerging asphalt ovals of the south was the main front of competition. There were, of course, enumerable "street fights" to see whose car was fastest, and

Speedy Thompson wins the 1957 Southern 500 while setting the fastest stock car race in history. He was the first driver to average over-100 mph for a 500 mile race when he averaged 100.10 mph. Darlington Speedway photo.

Accepting NASCAR's premier trophy, the Southern 500, Speedy Thompson's was the first of 3 consecutive '57 Chevy Southern 500 victories. Darlington Speedway photo.

that didn't help the image of drag racing.

For 1955, Ford had the advertising edge on Chevrolet; more cubic inches, more horsepower, and the fastest factory-built cars of the low priced three. But Chevrolet won races, like Herb Thomas taking the win at Darlington in Smokey Yunick's 210 post Chevy. The next year, Curtis Turner was the victor, but for the next three years, it was a trio of '57

Chevys that made their way to the winner's circle at Darlington; Speedy Thompson, Fireball Roberts and Jim Reed in that order.

Although Ford maintained the horsepower and cubic inch lead over Chevrolet with the new 312 cid Y-block in '56, both top Ford and Chevy engines were similarly rated, 225 hp. But Ford's biggest problem was that they didn't have a Duntov making all sorts of high performance equipment. In quick succession, Duntov served up a variety of parts that made Chevys faster and faster. To counter Chevrolet's twin 4-barrel carbs and hot cam, Ford introduced its own dual-4 induction setup for '57 rated at 285 hp. Still, Ford was winning both the cubic inch and horsepower war.

Even though Chevrolet's highly touted fuel injection system was well received by the press and racers alike, Ford put the needle to Chevrolet advertising with 300 horsepower "Racing Kit" dual-4 engines and followed that with the 340 horse Daytona-NASCAR engine. This was a huge power increase over Chevrolet's best, but Dearborn had to go to optional supercharging to do it. Supercharging was really an add-on rather than a thorough designed-in features like Chevrolet's fuel injection and clearly was not in the realm of the hot rodder. Although Edelbrock produced a 3-carb intake for the Ford engine and offered it and other equipment for the Ford hot rodder, the factory was gradually being left behind in high performance equipment development. The Ford engine was larger and heavier than the Chevrolet small block, and in a few years the engine was gone, replaced by a newer series of engines while the small block remained in production con-

Fairgrounds dust bowls were the home of mid-50s stock cars, and they came in all forms. Buck Baker was the NASCAR Grand National champion with 9 of Chrylser's 22 victories of the '56 season to Chevy's 3 wins. Ford won 14. Baker repeated in '57 during the controversial 1957 season with its AMA ban. Baker won 10 of Chevy's 18 victories. Bob Welborn took the Convertible Division title again with 8 of Chevy's 12 wins. Darlington Speedway photo.

tinuously.

Zora Arkus-Duntov is due great credit for making Chevrolet the hot rodder's store. He had pointed out Ford's overwhelming lead in his December 13, 1953, memo, and little had changed by 1955. But the seeds of greatness had been sown. It took about five more years for Chevrolet's small block V-8 to push aside more than thirty years of V-8 Ford domination.

By 1957, a rapidly expanding aftermarket industry was producing all sorts of power producing equipment to extract the designed-in potential of the small block. Far fewer parts were being made available for the Ford. For the hot rodder, there wasn't much needed in the way of modification. New engines right out of the box made a sports racer immediately competitive and many times taught car builders some important lessons; like, a bent chassis from not strengthening the platform the Chevy V-8 was mounted in. Things were changing, and the craftsmen who built and modified the "specials" were the men that made it happen.

What looked good in 1955 was expected to improve in '56, but sales dropped significantly. In 1956, Chevrolet production was down by almost 11.3%. Ford production also slid, by nearly 391,000 cars in the U.S. alone. Overall, GM sales were down over 23%. Ford Motor Company was down 25.5%.

The Detroit manufacturers lost over a billion dollars in potential sales in 1956. There were, however, thousands of small block V-8s pouring out of the factories, and they were beginning to show up in junk yards frequented by hot rodders in their never-ending quest for more speed.

Power of the 265 was upped in 1956 to 225 with twin 4-barrels on a dual plane cast aluminum intake. With that equipment in cars prepared under Duntov's direction, the first real racing of the Corvette began when he took a team

to Sebring that year. The Chevrolet engines had the power. Though the cars did extremely well, chassis development needed attention. Duntov and his team were at the long and rough Florida course with three 'Vettes, one with a special 4-speed transmission. That car was entered as a Corvette Special with John Fitch and Walt Hansgen driving. At the end of the 12-hours, 26 of the starters were sidelined including 4 Ferraris, 6 Jaguars and 2 Aston Martins. Twenty-four cars finished the grueling enduro, among them all three of the Corvettes. Fitch and Hansgen finished 9th overall, averaging 76.27 mph for 915.2 miles. The Crawford and Goldman Corvette finished 15th, 19 laps back, and the Davis/Gatz Corvette rolled in 23rd, 40 laps down. Among the cars that the Corvette Special beat were a Ferrari and a Jaguar. It was a good day!

Since the small block would fit about any engine bay and was forty pounds lighter than the inline-6 (532 lbs compared to 572), it was an obvious choice for racing, especially the Carter 4-barrel and dual exhaust "Power Pack" version. Three levels of output power became available from the factory at racer's prices; 162, 180 and 195 hp in the Corvette. With the hot rodder's art of engine building, a 4-barrel carb or Edelbrock's tri-power setup with an over-the-counter Duntov cam (also known as the SR cam - part number 3763097) made for a fast machine. Generally speaking, the Ford flathead was the dominant V-8 in the hot rodding movement into the early '60s. It would take some time for the small block to become a similarly economical junk yard piece for the typical low-bucks hot rodder.

Although the "Turbo-Fire" V-8 proved to be an excellent engine, production Chevys in hottest form were not the fastest cars. Their 0-60 mph times were still over 10 seconds. Chryslers, Buicks, Oldsmobiles and Fords, particularly the Thunderbird, were stiff competition, some under 10 seconds

"Fireball" Roberts became a favorite of stock car racing fans and capped off a fabulous season by winning the Southern 500 of '57 when he set a new race record of 102.59 mph. Darlington Speedway photo.

Veteran southeastern stock car racer Larry Frank always gave stiff competition as an independent. He later won the Southern 500 of 1962 in a Ford. Darlington Speedway photo.

from 0 to 60 mph. What made the Chevrolet a desirable car for stock car racing was its low cost and light weight which translated into less tire wear and better gas mileage. The cars didn't have the speed to compete in the long races like the Daytona 500 over the narrow 4.1-mile sand and asphalt beach course, but they didn't need as many pit stops, either. However, on the short tracks, Chevys were tough to beat. Peekskill, New Jersy's Jim Reed raced his 150 two-door sedan to take the NASCAR Short Track Division by storm. Reed won the title in 1955 and repeated in '56 with 14 of Chevrolet's 25 wins, then switched to Ford in 1957 and won the title again.

When NASCAR debuted the Convertible Division, another exciting series began. Ford drivers Curtis Turner and Joe Weatherly finished 1st and 2nd 14 times in the 48 race series, and Fords won 27 races. At season's end, though, it was Chevrolet driver Bob Welborn who emerged as Convertible Division Champion. His three victories were supported by 40 top ten finishes. It had been a season-long shootout between Ford and Chevrolet, and what won the manufacturer's title was durability. More and more Chevys were showing up at stock car races, making it increasingly tough on the Fords. Other makes won only 11 of the 1956 Convertible Division races; Dodge-10, Buick-1. The Ford versus Chevrolet war was on for real.

At first, when a Chevy won, hardly anybody noticed. Ad man Barney Clark beat the drums and Chevrolet engineering went back to the drawing boards to make more durable parts, but it took time. When Herb Thomas and Jim Reed led Tim Flock's Chrysler 300 across the finish line at Darlington in front of some 50,000 spectators, Chevrolet was on the move.

In the northern states where AAA sanctioning ruled, Jim Rathman and Marshall Teague went heads up against the Kiekhaefer Chryslers and managed a win apiece out of the 13 race schedule. 1955 was the last year of AAA sanctioning, and

USAC (United States Auto Club) stepped in to continue the series from then until now.

The factories came to race, and the fans came back in 1956. New that year was the 225 hp Super Turbo Fire V-8 making the Chevy 210 post sedan a stock car natural. The horsepower race and cubic inch war was on, and, except for Plymouth, Chevrolet was at the bottom of both. Even with dual 4-barrels, a Corvette option, the small block was small at 265 cubic inches. Ford touted its new 312, and Kiekhaefer was back with a team of Chrysler 300B cars replacing the 300, now with massive 354 inch hemis rated at an astounding 340 horses. The Chryslers were the cream of NASCAR stock car racing taking 22 victories and powering Buck Baker to the driver's championship. Chevrolet could only muster 3 wins in NASCAR's Grand National Division, but in USAC, Chevrolet came into its own by taking the first six races and totalling 11 wins in the 1956 season to Ford's 4. Johnny Mantz was overall champion.

Back to Pikes Peak under USAC sanctioning, the Ford versus Chevrolet duel heated up. Jerry Unser of the famed Unser family from Albuquerque, NM, pushed his Chevrolet up the snake path in 16:07 minutes to beat runner-up Chuck Stevenson's Ford by 20 seconds. Note that both of these times were more than a minute quicker than Duntov's record setting time of 1955.

The best examples of the Chevrolet and Ford product lines were the Corvette and Thunderbird. Proponents lined up on each side. Corvette buffs called the Thunderbird a heavy, ill-handling boulevard cruiser while claiming their 'Vettes to be America's only true sports car. 'Bird afficiondos championed better styling and speed records. When the cars were actually compared in stock form, they were remarkably similar. *Motor Trend* in June 1956 concluded their test with: "Which one for you? Within $2.60, you can have your choice.

Each performs a slightly different function, and each does right well for itself."

Corvette 0-60:	11.6 seconds	
Thunderbird 0-60:	11.5 seconds	
Corvette 1/4-mile:	17.9 seconds @ 77.5 mph	
Thunderbird 1/4-mile:	18.0 seconds @ 76.5 mph	
Corvette economy:	12.8 mpg	
Thunderbird economy:	12.7 mpg	
Corvette weight:	3,020 pounds	
Thunderbird weight:	3,600 pounds	
Corvette weight distribution:	53.3 front/46.7 rear	
Thunderbird weight distribution:	49.4 front/50.6 rear	

The testers gave the nod of better handling to the Corvette and picked the Thunderbird for better ride. Either way, it was a tossup and everyone looked forward to 1957.

The Corvette versus Thunderbird duel continued on the hard packed beach sand, and, to further the cause of the Corvette, Bill Mitchell brought his high fin SR-2 Corvette to run the flying mile. This car was fitted with an aerodynamic bubble cockpit over the driver. The car's gleaming red exterior was accented by high style side inserts of polished aluminum. White flashings from the head lights back, red and white stripes on the fin (like the American flag), and attention to minute detail showed that this beautiful car was serious. With an essentially stock fuel injected 283, the SR-2 turned in a flying mile of 152.866 mph. The 312 inch Thunderbirds didn't fare well. But Ford garnered the glory in the heavy weight division with streamlined 'Birds from the Holman & Moody stable in Charlotte. These cars were fitted with 430 cubic inch Lincoln engines that were optional in the Thunderbird. At better than 160 mph, the T-Birds chalked up a new flying mile record for production cars.

Complaints about the Corvette's imprecise handling from auto magazines and racing enthusiasts brought about the RPO-684 heavy duty racing suspension. For $725, a Corvette so equipped and with the RPO 579 fuel injected engine could be taken to the track and be competitive in the production class racing right out of the box. Corvette performancen was shown at Sebring in the spring of 1957 when Dr. Dick Thompson and Gaston Andrey finished the 12-hours in 12th overall position to lead all production cars. It was a momentous victory for Corvette. From the starting field of 65 entries, there were 27 retirements including four Ferraris, five Maseratis, four Jaguars and three Porsches. Each of the three Corvettes entered completed the race. The Duncan/Kilborn/Jeffords entry finished 15th overall, and the SR-2 of O'Shea/Lovely/Eager was 16th. The lead Corvette completed 899.6 miles averaging 74.97 mph.

Although the production Corvettes and the SR-2 ran superbly, the main quest at Sebring was the debut of the Corvette SS. This car was, by all estimates, a Chevrolet factory entry capable of beating everything from anywhere. Duntov and his team had been at Sebring testing for several weeks to refine two cars. Both SS cars were actually at Sebring on race day. First there was the "mule" that was extensively used for test-

Duntov's pet project, the Corvette SS was a world class racing machine to showcase Chevrolet engineering and performance. Chevrolet photo.

ing. This car was also a very light weight, tubular frame pure race car not at all similar to production Corvettes. The body of the car had gone through extensive wind tunnel testing and had been refined. There was no question that the SS was capable of overall victory against the finest cars in the world. Duntov put 2,000 miles on this car in preparation for the race.

The SS was the culmination of five months of work from drawing board to a running car at the track. Some fifteen people manned Duntov's shop at the Chevrolet Engineering Center in Detroit. There were four major groups - electricians, stylists, draftsmen and mechanics - that contributed to the creation of the chrome-moly tubular chassis car, all working under the direction of Duntov. Although officially secret to the outside world, the project fell under the watchful eye of Chief Engineer Harry Barr, who stayed abreast of progress made on the car. Excitement built as word of the SS project leaked out. Internally, the SS was an experimental vehicle for the purpose of testing a number of engineering ideas for possible future use on production cars.

The body of the SS was of hand formed magnesium over a custom interior fitted with heat shielding on the floorboards. The steering column was adjustable. A dash panel of four gauges and a tachometer in front of the driver kept track of engine vital signs, along with an auxiliary dual gauge package off to the right, and a 4-speed shifter was there for the right hand. The gearbox was an aluminum case close ratio unit that weighed a total of 65 pounds.

The front suspension of the SS was coil-over spring/shock absorber assemblies while the rear was a de Dion with inboard brakes of cast iron with aluminum finned muffs. Each

Fuel injected 283 and equal length tubular headers. The roar of the SS was all-American. Chevrolet photo.

Duntov tested this SS, the "Mule" car, for 2,000 miles in preparation for the 12-Hours of Sebring. Chevrolet photo.

Overall craftsmanship of the SS was far better than most European cars of the time. Note the heat shield blankets and lightweight construction. Chevrolet photo.

Duntov & Co. weigh the SS. At around 1740 pounds, it promised overall victory. Chevrolet photo.

Magnesium was used to lighten overall weight. Note the oil pan and tubular chassis. Chevrolet photo.

spindle assembly had its own internal fan for brake heat dissipation. A dual hydraulic brake system provided excellent stopping power, even with the skinny tires of the day. Cast alloy Halibrand wheels were functional racing equipment and accented the handsome exterior of the car. Its gleaming light blue and silver exterior finish rivaled show quality cars and exceeded the norm for racing cars by a considerable margin.

Power was provided by a standard 293 cubic inch (3.875-inch bore and 3.0-inch stroke) with fuel injection, solid lifters and Duntov cam. Compression ratio was a modest 9:1. the

most impressive visual feature of the engine were those magnificent equal length stainless steel tubular exhaust headers that arched upward over the inner wheel wells, then down

On the "brick yard" at GM's Tech Center, the SS was reviewed before shipment to Sebring where John Fitch and Piero Taruffi were the drivers. Chevrolet photo.

World Champion Juan Manuel Fangio set a Sebring record in the SS during practice. Later at Daytona for the opening of the Speedway in 1959, Duntov attained 158 mph lap speed in the car. Marshall Teague had been killed in an attempt to set a new record at the track and gave the new speedway the reputation of being a "killer". Chevrolet photo.

and under the car.

Engine cooling was by the venturi effect. The radiator was laid over to allow a low frontal area, and air from the grill was ducted inward and through the radiator, then out louvered vents just in front of the hood. The entire front of the body was hinged in the front for total access to the engine bay. The rear section was similarly hinged and enclosed a 43 gallon lightweight fuel tank. The fuel system used dual fuel pumps. Total dry weight at the factory, with a driver, topped out at around 1520 pounds, but race weight was listed as 1850.

During testing of the SS, four time world champion Juan Fangio put the car through some paces and set a new track record at Sebring. This was with the mule, missing its driver's door and rear hatch cover. But Fangio brought the car back into the pits having dropped the lap record a few seconds. Fangio lapped Sebring's 5.2-miles in 3 minutes, 27 seconds and lowered Mike Hawthorn's D-Type Jaguar record by 2.4 seconds. By the end of the year, Fangio had earned his fifth world championship title.

Following Fangio's drive, Stirling Moss took the SS for a spin and similarly proclaimed it to be an outstanding car with lap times under the previous record. Duntov and his men had clearly done a superior job. Unfortunately, the intended car for the race didn't arrive from Detroit until the evening before the race. Duntov was enraged to learn that the car had been held at the factory for final details, the victim of the mandate of "standard of appearance for GM cars".

"My foot," he scoffed. "The car was designed to win, not for concourse d'elegance."

As the race unfolded, just 23 laps from the start, a rear suspension bushing gave way and the Super Sport Corvette was sidelined. After starting from the pole with the SS favored to win, what could have been a victory and a history-making occasion for Duntov & Co. became, instead, an embarrassment for certain people at Chevrolet. Some more development would surely make the Corvette Super Sport a world contender, and Duntov had big plans.

Then things changed. NASCAR banned both fuel injection and supercharging to help control the soaring cost of racing, and at the end of the February meeting of the Automobile Manufacturer's Association, GM's Harlow "Red" Curtice pulled out a deft bit of deception when he proposed that the factories really should not be racing against their customers. Robert McNamara, who was new at being CEO of Ford and unaware of the implications, did not object to the proceedings. From the bean counter standpoint, eliminating racing simply meant reducing costs.

At that time, no other firms had racing activities of any consequence, so a ban on racing benefitted their positions considerably if Ford and Chevrolet did not race. The AMA ban on factory racing took effect in June, 1957. Its purpose was to eliminate factory involvement in racing, eliminate high performance parts development and eliminate such parts from catalogs.

The results: McNamara stopped ALL Ford high performance and heavy duty parts development. In a few months, the "money saving" effort made it impossible to find anything for the Ford enthusiast from the factory. At a time when hot rodding was flourishing, McNamara removed Ford from the picture. On the other hand, Chevrolet and the other divisions of GM in performance continued to design, develop and offer the good stuff.

Before the ban, there were 21 NASCAR Grand National races and Fords won 15 of them against 5 for Chevys. Afterward, Chevrolets won 14 of the 32 remaining races with Ford dropping to 12 wins. The result of Curtice's maneuvering was to cut short Ford's racing program while boosting Chevrolet's. At the end of the season, Buck Baker won his second consecutive Grand National championship with ten victories, all in Chevys. He drove the #87 Valley Chevrolet Inc. '57 Two-Ten post to 30 top five finishes in 40 races.

In the Convertible Division before the ban, Fords and Mercurys had taken the first 17 races of the season as opposed to three for Chevrolet in 20 races. Afterwards, in the remaining 20 races, Fords won 10 and Chevrolet took 9. After all the points were totalled, Bob Welborn emerged the Convertible Division champion driving Chevrolets.

The SR-2 Corvette draws a crowd at Marlboro, Md. in its 1956 east coast debut. Chevrolet photo.

Taking the parade lap at Marlboro, Dr. Dick Thompson in Bill Mitchell's SR-2. Chevrolet photo.

The trend held in the Short Track Division. Ford won 14, Chevrolet 13, but point totals were in favor of Chevrolet because more people could get the parts to continue racing. After the ban, Chevrolets won 9 of the last 15 races, and Jim Reed won the title.

Curtice had dealt Ford a knock-out punch. In all three of NASCAR's divisions, Chevrolet was champion. There was glory in the victories, but it cost Chevrolet a lot of bad press from journalists who could see what was happening. Ford quit racing but Chevrolet didn't. Where there had been steadily increasing rivalries, there was now intense and often repeated accusations of cheating. Racers were no longer just competitors on the track, many became bitter enemies and occasionally confrontations erupted on and off the track.

From then on, there was continual back-peddling on the part of Chevrolet management to try and distance the factory from racing, but there were too many small block V-8s available and catalogs continued to carry the high performance parts wanted by racers and rodders. Ford was "done in" and Chevrolet was now the hot rodder's make.

At Sebring '57, Thompson and Andrey finished 12th overall and won the GT class in a B/P Corvette. This SR-2 finished 16th overall completing 863.2 miles to average 71.93 mph for the race. Chevrolet photo.

When the 283 inch '57 Chevys arrived, Ford had all but lost its 1/4-century dominance of hot rodding. Squire Gabbard photo.

Today's vintage racers continue the glory days of "old" Corvette racing as it was in the '50s and '60s.

The '57s have become highly sought-after classics and are regarded as one of Chevrolet's finest efforts.

Zora Arkus-Duntov

Looks back

I was born Belgium. At age of one, my parents took me to Russia. They were Russian. I stayed there until the age of eighteen. Then I joined my parents, they were already in Germany, and I studied in Germany, first at Darmstadt, then Berlin.

At the age of fourteen, I was in high school and I did well for a branch of the Russian air force, a school of pilots. I talked to them and get two engines. Hall Scott - that's American engine, six cylinder aircraft engine, and he gave me a man by the name of Niki Peroff to help. I attempt to put it in glider for to drive in the snow. I use for frame, I use double AVRO aircraft frame, British. By the time the sled was ready, was spring. Then, the man tell me to produce water glider. Never happened because timing was wrong. Air boat will be ready in winter! I work on many things.

Lot of things kept me busy - girls.

Throughout my formative years, I was a year ahead of my class in school. Therefore, when I arrive at graduation, I change my birth date and make myself one year older. That was for requisite entrance to Electrotechnical Institute. I was sixteen.

Difficult in Russia to get higher education, like hundred people apply to one place, but I got accepted, and the same year I get expulsion. But same year, I get reinstated because I was doing competitive skiing, cross country. Did not study, did not take too much time and neglected studies. I get infection in hand. Doctor says difficulty for using hand. It was subterfuge getting doctor certificate that I cannot do anything with my hand. Therefore, cannot draw. But, I ski very well! That was about 1926 or '27.

In fall of '27, I go to Germany, and enroll as extraordinary student. Not qualification of brilliance; you have to pass examination in German language, literature and history. I did not know. Higher education normally take about four years. I used five years to receive diploma engineering. One higher degree, doctor of engineering, research for older poeple in industry.

Before I finish my university, I have published an article, supercharging, to try to win graduation from university. As a result, a year later, in Germany everybody like to have supercharger. It helped like wild fire; everybody want supercharger. I did three designs, different displacement, because, at that time, cars have dumb irons in front. Therefore, logical to put compressor drive by crankshaft directly in front so you can match engine displacement for compressor displacement.

Then I work for Rinne and I design tractor. Max speed; four miles per hour. Therefore, everybody can drive this tractor, no need for license. Designed for use with bulky cargo. Berlin was very flat with a hundred bridges, but not long. I did some tuning work, motorcycles, in my garage in Berlin. Then I bought Bugatti, eight cylinder, built 1922. I know two young men, both of them motorcycle riders, and I spotted this Bugatti, not working. Not a race car, a two passenger sports car type. Money exchange with proprietor of Bugatti.

Then also upon graduation, I have a job with Zoller. Zoller was an inventor, particularly with supercharger. He want to build race car. He hired me, but I was far away from building race car. It was a twelve cylinder, two cycle, supercharged, fifteen hundred cc. This car he built to compete with Mercedes and Auto-Union but was not competitive. The reason was lack of Gleason gear cutting machine. Did not have bevel cutting, just straight gears.

OK, then I was in Belgium via Paris, France. In Belgium, I was to become chief of design for company building motorcycle engines and motorcycles, but no more build motorcycle just as I got there. So, company, Mondiale, from 1909 build machine tools, lathe. Well, I try my hand at it. Lathe very good, so I become chief of design of machine tools. They hire me chief of design motorcycle, but I wind up chief of design of machine tools and they hire another professor to help me. But soon they terminated this arrangement with him and I work alone.

At one time, after Belgium, in United States I see lathe. I think, "That is my design!" It was Chinese, copy of my lathe.

Coming back, Belgium now, there was a time of Spanish revolution, and my boss was planning to contract to build hand grenades. Machine tools continued but additional capacity for hand grenades. That was 1936 or '37 or '38. I designed, not much of design for hand grenades, but time of proof came. Designer should try it! Big steel plate, all people stand behind this plate, and I take this hand grenade and heave it. Like a roman candle, POOF! By simplifying design, using stamped metal instead of screw metal, they worked but all of a sudden, Germany, France, Belgium, England agreed not to supply to revolutionary forces.

Then, in Paris, I was hired to chief of design of diesel locomotives. Looked like there might be war, and French locomotives using German Deutz engines. I was hired to design French versions of the Deutz engines. This was 1939. Paris was where I met Elfi, my wife, and we were married that year.

My younger brother, seven years younger, was in England. Arrived in Paris. France was entering the war. He says he is going to join the fight against Hitler. My mother said, "That is very good. If Yuri is going, you should, too."

I said, "Really, when this is all over, we will embrace Germany and say, forget it. All war lead to nothing." But, I cannot sit and see my young brother go, and I enlisted also, but different time. He enlisted two months before me. This was with the French air force. The French, since Napoleon days, have a rule: no two brother have to serve together because one shot fired maybe hit two brothers. Therefore, separate. French bureaucracy, when they find that, OK, they transferred my brother. I was private second class stationed, Bordeaux. Yuri, my brother, picked up for officer training.

Two things happened. Paris was overrun. I did not know where my parents were or Elfi, my wife. Then I see Elfi's MG. She came to find me. She told me she lost track of my parents.

I was mechanic. Mechanic day start about seven o'clock. Shining of the aeroplane, including World War-1 Neuport.

Also bomber, light bomber in readiness. I remember going to bomber, lower seat and go to sleep. Typical day. One day I see the French naval aviation and two giant aeroplanes. Churchill was there. He was trying to get home.

I still did not know where I intend to go, still in air force. In Bayonne on border with Spain, I hear that the General De Gaulle was in England and invited all Frenchmen to join him. By all means, come to England to assemble fighting force of Frenchmen against the Germans. It was a ship with destination of England and requisitioned for Polish soldier. I thought for a moment, if I am on this ship, will I be held as Russian spy? That was in 1940 in June. I got demobilization papers in August. I find my parents and Elfi in Toulouse in the south of France. Very close to Mediterranean. My brother and myself got demobilized.

And then, while I am there, I get telegram. I have American visitor visa. I had not applied for. President Roosevelt issue five thousand visa for the people if their life will be danger, like scientists, and I was one of them. But exit visa from France, they didn't know. You signed for duration, but now is not peace. Therefore, you sit here and make ready to join your outfit.

In mid-August to beginning of December, take to get involve formality for myself, my brother, Elfi, my mother, my step-father. We boarded a train waving my paper, "Americana del Norte." Then, while staying in Spain, I pick up my friend Asja Orley, my racing mate. His parents in America long time, but he say, "I am very happy in Spain." I say, "Spain going to war and you will be climbing English fortress Gibralter!!!" Two months later he came, and three months later he was in the United States Army. It bothered him all the time that he did not participate in the war, so he stayed in the American army until, I think, 1951. This was very important. He was Russian, and they really wanted people like him in Intelligence.

I come to the United States on 4th December, 1940. My budget was $21 per week. Three weeks later I run into my friend and he tell me his friend, patent attorney, who cannot figure out with new invention from inventor. I say, "Maybe you introduce me to him, I can help figure out."

He introduced me, I figure it out, torsional damper primarily for ships, submarines, aircraft engines, and I get job that pay hundred dollars per day working for inventor. Yeah, hundred dollars per day for calculation of torsional dampening. In few weeks, I was happy be in United States. Twenty-one dollar per week, OK, but I did not feel content before. It was enough to move to nice apartment on Riverside Drive in New York.

Then, on December 7, '41, Japanese. Yuri and I started machine shop doing defense work. Started five men and five lathe shortly after Pearl Harbor. Did aircraft work. Government give machinery. Third of all propellers for bomber and fighter, I did front cone and rear cone, done in our shop, and breaker nut on center of propellers, and distributor valve for changing pitch of propeller. I get paid for that like ten dollars, I think. Three outfit doing this, one in New York and two in Michigan, Eaton and McKay. Eaton big outfit, still exists today.

I appear at Eaton and tell them following: "I know you get ten dollars for distributor valve. I give you distributor valve for five dollars and you package." My brother find low cost way of production, and I try to concentrate work in one place, but not the way government wanted to do work. I was drafted 1A. At that time, Navy was short of men, and I remember, they tell me I would be good for Navy. But I say I would like to be Air Force. Navy will be more difficult. That was one day. Following day, I cannot lift myself from my bed. I have old breakage of spine, like in mid-30s, but it was a moot question. Government decided I am more useful doing defense work than flying aeroplanes.

War was ended. I have maybe hundred people employed, at least. Ardun Mechanical Company. I have union. Then, I say, well I have place for twenty-five men and I have to select men. Therefore, seniority will not apply. That was a strong point. You have to lay off by seniority. They suspend their requirement, and I agree to reinstate union after I reorganize. Then did helicopter and Ardun engine. Ford.

I raced flathead Ford. My opinion was engine, was good engine, strong, did not break things but did not have good heads. In France, running between Brussels and Paris, two hours and twenty minutes from clock mounted in Rue Lafayette in Paris and railroad station clock in Brussels, including border examination. I did it at night going to Brussels, and same night departing to Paris. In the evening, kissing my mother good night, in half hour the house was asleep and I am in my car going to Brussels. Arriving in Brussels, dismantle something, and take trip back to Paris coming home when everyone still asleep. In the morning, my mother come, "Zora, time to wake up." She did not know I had been gone.

Going to Brussels to Paris and back in one night was because Prime Minister of France decreed: all gold transactions - frozen. Brussels continue like always. Therefore, wealthy people want to go put their gold Belgium. And I was running the gold in my Ford. With additional cross member in back, full of gold.

I noticed, running down hill, hundred miles per hour. I check rpms, five thousand. Then I got interested in Ford. For me, Henry Ford was the man. I don't know how anybody could do what he did. I admired Henry Ford immensely. Engine had connecting rod bearing turning in the rod and on crankshaft like floating bushing. How he make this connecting rod with integral bolts and floating bearing, in '37 I think, that is good engine to work on. In New York, I went back to engine. Actually, I designed head for engine during the war. Hemispherical combustion chambers, angled valves run off internal cam with pushrod and rocker assembly. Cast aluminum heat treated and pistons. Standard compression ratio was seven-to-one. Different pistons go to twelve-to-one. Three hundred, maybe three hundred-twenty horsepower. If use supercharger, maybe six hundred horsepower.

First *Popular Science* or something about engine, I get at least two thousand letters, like to buy engine. Then "New York Times" run story. In 1949, New York Automobile Show I strike a deal with Allard. At that time, we met Henry Ford

second, something had changed and I was force to sell out. We guaranteed loan with the shop and equipment that belonged to me, but my friend defaulted. I had enough of that, and I accepted employment with Allard.

For drab conditions prevailing in England, Elfi want to go back to America. Personally, I feel if I did not go back, I will be entirely forgotten. They did not want me to go, and Gregor Grant of *Autosport* wrote article to "Keep Duntov", but in fall of '52 I arrive in United States to be permanent.

I talked to Benson Ford about work because I thought he was instrumental with auto racing, but was wrong. I filed letter to him, letter to Ed Cole. Ford, came out nothing positive. Ed Cole said, "If you are in Detroit, stop and see us."

And I got job in aviation, Fairchild, in Long Island. My first job, atomic compressor for heavy water. Very pleasant. I think maybe be designer jet engine. Work on atomic compressor require traveling abroad, security. I have to delay, delay because my father was still living in Paris. My mother and step-father had already come to America. I was stalling.

In meantime, I see the Waldorf show, Motorama, see the Corvette, and I write a second letter to Ed Cole and congratulate him for the beautiful car. The best looking sports car ever I had seen before. Included in this letter, included article published in automotive magazine in Britain. He probably gave it to Maurice Olley.

Maurice Olley was in charge of research and development. He got very encouraged by that. Maybe three trip to Detroit followed because he did not meet my conditions at that time, fourteen thousand per year and no less because that was what Fairchild pay. Maurice Olley talked me into it because of bonuses and interesting work. Then, first of May of '53, I am assistant staff engineer in research and development to Maurice Olley.

Six weeks, maybe five weeks, I ask my boss Maurice Olley, "I like to have a leave of absence, ten days, for engagement to race in Le Mans." No chance he say. "I like to talk to your boss, Ed Cole." Ed Cole draws a rosy picture for my progression, you will be stepping in Olley's shoes when he retires. Model is not object. I say, "Engagement I have to do."

"Do it and come back, tell us about it." I departed for Le Mans. I bought myself one-way ticket. After talk with Ed Cole painting rosy picture of my progression if I stay here, but if I go away, I decided I was finished with Chevrolet.

Unfortunately, Le Mans was not good. I did not finish, and in Paris, I look for something. Sitting in cafe, friend from New York happened to pass by. I told him I was looking for something. He tell me I have to go back, but did not have ticket. He say, "OK. Wait a second. In a moment, I will be back," and he disappeared. Maybe five minutes he comes back holding ticket for Pan Am. "Take it and go back." He say it didn't make any sense. I have no prospects in Europe. That was not exactly true. I had few contacts.

Then in fall '53, I pen letter to Olley about hot rodder and Chevrolet. All hot rodder buying Ford. And I said, when we have a V-8, maybe it will be possible to enter hot rod market, but for this to happen, we have to have ready engineered parts. The letter was circulated and very positive, but nothing happened. Then, when '55 V-8 happened, I tried to raise power and did what I intend to do and did it. From that, then Pikes Peak in '55 with '56 model car. Then Daytona, I broke the record in December '56. By then I had developed the Duntov cam, two four barrels and three speed transmission. Then Sebring happened, and at Sebring, I had one 4-speed transmission, ZF. Briggs Cunningham ordered some gearboxes few years before. I selected one.

Give one car John Fitch and Walt Hansgen, and they were first in GT. That was the four-speed transmission, ZF. I was in contact with them since '53. I need four-speed transmission to replace PowerGlide and three-speed. Strangely enough, in early sixties, we have three-speed fully synchronized available in Corvette.

Fuel injection, in '55, Ed Cole called me and said, "Listen, I give you a job I myself would like to do if I were not General Manager. Super secret. John Dolza ask for you to come work with him in engineering staff." I was on loan to engineering staff. Fuel injection development was, Dolza directed, speed-density for fuel/air mixture. This did some horrible things to the engine. I didn't like it and came out with mass-flow injection. Mass-flow measure air and adds fuel as required to mix with air. Different than speed-density. And Dolza, in twenty-four hour, says, "You are right. Revise all this and we are on mass-flow system."

Mass-flow system, in '57, was in Corvette and was available for passenger car and passenger car NASCAR racing. We had fuel injection and Ford had supercharger. I wind up director of high performance vehicles and chassis, and we had SEDCO, Atlanta outfit because of proximity to racing. Very accessible to stock car racing. My responsibility included Atlanta. I intend to go visit my new acquisition, then - bam! - we are no longer in racing.

The AMA ban, did not affect me at all because I continue development high performance, and I still retained director of high performance except I have responsibility of police car and export car.

In '58, summer, I got telephone call from Rosenberger. He was assistant chief engineer for Chevrolet. I was on vacation. Ed Cole told him to contact me, and I should go to Trenton, meet Buck Baker. OK, I am in Trenton, go in grandstand, select a room upstairs, sitting alone. After while, racing uniformed man sat with me.

"May I have a light?" I give him light.

"You are Zora Duntov?"

"Yes."

"I am going. You look where I am going and follow me."

I did so. Through the grandstand, get outside, car waiting, get in the back seat. Car maybe travel three hundred yards, and Buck Baker get in. We arrange following modus operandi: he continue racing stock car and I supply everything, and he will supply me back with failing engine.

In 1958 I start to work with Buck Baker. In '59, two things happen: opening of speedway in Daytona, and two preliminary races, two heat, 125 miles each. Both races, three Chevrolet 1-2-3 and second race also 1-2-3. I think win second.

Then I decided engine good enough to go, 348 cubic inches, but not supposed to be racing, right? Cole devised following plan: sales department to buy five cars. I get $25,000, enough to buy cars and additional money to buy heavy duty equipment, suspension pieces to transform passenger car from showroom to race car. Sales department, engineering was not involved except myself.

I meet with Jim Rathman in Miami. He subsequently won Indy race in 1960, but he was employed in my SEDCO before. He buy all this heavy duty parts for nominal sum, and I am sitting in his shop in Miami with sales department man, Bob Lund (subsequently was General Manager of Chevrolet) and Fred Warner. Jim Rathman contact drivers on telephone and I have another telephone. If driver seems to me enthusiastic, then Jim tell them what it is all about.

OK, I disburse this money. Five Chevrolet bought. Jack Smith, stock car driver, he decided to buy a car, but he has no money. I arrange for him to buy at cost, a sixth car. That was the sixth car, 1-2-3, 1-2-3. At the time, we still not legally can race.

Jim Rathman ran 348 cubic inch displacement engines, part of my development. It became my development, and Dick Keinath came to my group and was instrumental in 348 and 409 and 427, but not Mk II. That was just Dick. The 427 exist only for drag racing, the Z-11. Identical block like 409 but 427 cubic inches. Other was Z-28. I think the "Z" was for "Zora."

Starting '63, Z-06 heavy duty suspension and Z-03 or something, some dress items also carry "Z" because specification man ask, "I am responsible?" OK, put Z.

Z-11, actually, the car was Vince Piggins' idea, I was responsible for engine. Or like Z-28, I did only engine. And ZL-1 was Corvette Group work. You see, Corvette Group in my time was responsible for engines. Not any more.

We had six cars that we had to support throughout the season, improvement, failing parts - all required money. Cole and Barr came up with idea - to establish Marine Division. Marine Division was, at that time, subterfuge. Marine Division was organized under me and provide means and engineering budget to funnel money, material and work for the racers. At that time, we did not realize that Marine engines grow to be 60% of all engines built in U.S.

348 Marine engine. I was director of high performance including Marine engine. But I will tell you, in 1960 eighty percent of the starters at Daytona were Chevrolets. And one failure was one car pick up debris and burst crank case. Mechanically, all cars were scot-free. That proved the 348, started out as a truck engine, was a very good racing engine also. Buck Baker, Jim Reed, Ned Jarrett, initially I think Joe Weatherly and Curtis Turner, Junior Johnson, Rex White and Jack Smith driving Chevrolet. In '60, Junior Johnson won Daytona 500 but Rex White was overall champion. Earlier, in '56 before we sign the agreement not to race, Corvette SS was a racing car. That was intentional. I proceeded to push program. I will tell you the high point was in Sebring. Fangio take the mule car around in record time. Moss did as well. You see, there were two cars. One mule I put two thousand miles on, and then real SS with magnesium body, lighter by a hundred pounds. The mule car was fiberglass body. Mule car

had engine with standard fuel injection. This car Fangio and Moss drove. SS arrive in Sebring day before the race, therefore, we try to put brakes from mule car to the SS.

John Fitch was bothered by heat. Piero Taruffi also, then bushing in rear suspension started to fail. Ed Cole and I decided to withdraw car, but with high hopes because when I came back, I get order for three more cars built and entered in Le Mans. I got Chevrolet money to enter these cars. I put name, Mr. St. Gill, for my name. (Pseudonym is accepted in Le Mans.) I enter three cars as Mr. St. Gill (for the locality of Belgium near Brussels where I come from). You see, Le Mans deadline to take entry is February. Therefore, Chev-rolet give me money and I entered these cars, but all of a sudden, scrap the whole thing. That was in June.

Second car, fiberglass body car, I give to Bill Mitchell with proforma explicit instructions: "After you finish your work, scrap the car." Car was scrapped and non-existent, but resurrection happened. Chassis was there and he put fiberglass body of the first Sting Ray. Only one built. I wash my hands of it, but I knew. One engineer, Jim Bedford, left me to work on car. That was car Dick Thompson won championship.

After try-out in proving ground, I lost interest in car - it was heavy lifter: example of styling get precedence to aerodynamics.

Through his efforts to race with world class Corvettes, however contrived, Zora gave a great legacy to America. The path he blazed laid the foundation of an enormously successful performance parts program for the sportsman racer. Chevrolet photo.

On the drag strips of America's home-grown sports, the performance engine equipment Zora produced has become a great legacy known throughout the world.

On the tracks of America's own stock car racing, no one knew that Zora was behind the 348 NASCAR engine. Rex White at the Southern 500, '58. Darlington Speedway photo.

3

The Road Racers

Chuck Daigh roars to victory at Riverside 1959. This was another big win for the Chevrolet powered Reventlow Scarab against the best drivers and cars in the world. Dr. Edgar B. Wycoff photo.

The New Age of Chevy Power

Bill Pollack's introduction of the H.W.M.-Chevy at Pebble Beach opened the gate to a vast array of Chevrolet small block powered sports-racing cars. Even today, IMSA GTO and GTPrototype cars, and SCCA Trans-Am racers still run descendants of Ed Cole's engine and are as competitive as ever.

One of the first cars designed specifically for the small block was Lance Reventlow's Scarab. Son of Woolworth heiress, Barbara Hutton, Reventlow undertook to set up his own factory in Los Angeles to build competition cars. He had just turned 21, and the cars he planned to build were to conquer the world.

The cars were financed by Reventlow and built by a team of expert racers like none seen before in this country. Ken Miles, well known builder, driver and editor of a series of articles on how to build a sports car, was commissioned to do the basic layout. Body man Dick Troutman, formerly the top body man at the Kurtis works, was assisted by Charles Pelly in the design of this ultra-modern roadster. Frame man Tom Barnes, also from Kurtis, worked under the direction of

Warren Olson, Reventlow's right hand man. Emil Deidt, a leading west coast body man who honed his talents with Harry Miller's famous Indy racers, was a key member. Driver for the team was Chuck Daigh, formerly of the Ford, Lincoln, Mercury and Chevrolet racing teams, who did double duty as engine man and pilot. Jim Travers was shop superintendent and Frank Coons' specialty was engines. They were later to team up to for Traco, Chevrolet engine wizards extraordinaire. The team's product was a stunningly beautiful metallic blue roadster, one that reached extraordinary levels of performance.

They started their project just after Labor Day, 1957, and on January 16th of the following year, the first Scarab was storming around the 2.5-mile Willow Springs circuit in its first tryouts, not yet with a body. Eight days later, the sleek roadster was out doing more laps, and drivers Daigh and Bruce Kessler proceeded to lower the track record by four seconds. On March 1 at the Beardsley Airport course at Phoenix, Arizona, the Scarab debuted as a full-fledged racing car. The prototype had cost around $25,000, a bargain for what it became. Kessler knocked several seconds off the existing record and so did Richie Ginther, who lowered the track record each successive lap to a best of 3-1/2 seconds under the record.

The Scarab name was from Egyptian lore that said the scarab beetle was good luck and a sign of immortality. As time

Things have changed in 30 years. Pit row, Riverside '59. The crowd is around Bill Pollack in the Dean Van Lines Lister-Chevy which qualified over 11 seconds off the pace of Daigh's Scarab. Dr. Edgar B. Wycoff photo.

Lance Reventlow handled his Scarab to a number of 1-2 wins with Daigh. At Riverside, Johnny von Neumann in his Ferrari 4.1 rammed the back of Reventlow's Scarab and split the car's fuel tank. Dr. Edgar B. Wycoff photo.

has proved, Reventlow was right. The Scarab forged a legacy unmatched in American racing cars of its era. All of the cars he built have survived to this day and remain the finest examples of American sports cars from the '50s.

Reventlow's crew designed and built three cars of the front engine/rear drive configuration in conformance with existing FIA regulations and later built a rear engine sports racer, also Chevrolet powered. The first Scarab was built as a left hand drive car to be used as the development vehicle for two more right hand drive cars that incorporated all improvements and updates learned in construction and racing.

Reventlow planned to continue where Briggs Cunningham left off, that is, putting the American needle to the Europeans. "I've got the chance of doing what most people only dream of doing," he once said. "I'm working toward the day when I can be in the same race with the top drivers of Europe, handling my own car and beating them all fair and square. If and when that day comes, I'll know it's all been worthwhile." He planned to campaign the cars in Europe on a full schedule, but the Continentals nixed any such plans when they lowered the maximum acceptable engine displacement to 3-liters. It has been speculated that if the FIA rules committee had known of the Scarabs, they might have left the old formula in place to have an American entry in international competition. If that had happened, the history of sports car racing might have been very different.

The Scarab's tubular chassis was equipped with de Dion tube rear suspension located by a Watt link and fitted with inboard 11-inch Mercury Turnpike Cruiser NASCAR type drum brakes. Brake swept area began at a very respectable 212 square inches, then was later increased to 336 square inches. The Scarab could stop! A quick change Halibrand rear end was fixed to the chassis, and each car was equipped with a twenty-five gallon fuel tank located at the rear of the chassis. Soon, fuel capacity was increased to sixty gallons. Front suspension was double A-arm using Ford uprights, and all four wheels were sprung with coil-over shocks. In the beginning, the cars were fitted with Hilborn fuel injected Corvette engines taken from 283 cubic inches to 302 cid cubic

inches. With 300 horsepower on tap, the 1750 pound Scarab was formidable. Once the cars were put on the track, engine displacement went up to 339 cubic inches. Tuned, equal length tubular headers joined 32 inches from exhaust ports into larger diameter side exhausts let the bellow of the Scarab be heard.

The engines were taken to 302 inches by boring to 4 inches with the stock 3 inch stroke retained. This gave 301.6 cubes, but a 3/8-inch stroke increase brought that up to 339.3 inches. A 10-quart baffled pan held the oil, and a Joe Hunt magneto fired the Hilborn fuel injection mixture. Head ports were enlarged, valve diameter increased, and an Engle .450 inch lift, 260-degree duration cam gave a wide torque range. With a hotter cam, power was brought up to 390 horses at 7,000 rpm, but the final choice was a 270-degree design giving 375 bhp at 6,500 rpm. The low profile Hilborn system, using special angled ram tubes, gave a low hood profile so that the Chuck Pelly penned lines of the roadster were not spoiled with humps or bumps that would have resulted with the use of Chevrolet's own Rochester fuel injection. Pelly's design was fabricated by Emil Diedt of .051-inch aluminum sheet into an appealing racing car of enduring shape.

With gearing for 0-100 mph in under 9 seconds and a top speed of over 160 mph, Scarabs simply laid waste to the opposition on American circuits in 1958 and converted many builders from the old faithful 210 cubic inch Jaguar inline-6 to the huge potential of the Chevrolet V-8.

Lance drew first blood at Palm Springs but spun the car in a preliminary race. He got back on the course and climbed to a credible 3rd overall. The first win was on June 1 at Santa Barbara during the CSCC formula libre race where Reventlow simply walked away with the win. It was no fluke, as was shown when the team came to the east and Daigh won the Montgomery Nationals. Later in September at USAC's impressive 3.3-mile Meadowdale circuit near Chicago, Daigh and Reventlow trounced the normally invincible Lister-Jaguars with a 1-2 sweep.

Then, at USAC's Riverside Grand Prix, nearly 100,000 spectators saw Daigh post the quickest qualifying time of

By 1959, Corvettes were invincible in production class racing. Skip Hudson won the production sports car race at Riverside '59 leading a Corvette 1-2-3 sweep. Dr. Edgar B. Wycoff photo.

2:04:03 minutes, two seconds under Phil Hill's 4.1-liter Ferrari followed by Reventlow's 3rd position at 2:08:14 and 41 other cars. As the race unfolded, Lance was put out of the race when his Scarab was rammed by a Ferrari that split the car's fuel tank. The third car had been sidelined in practice leaving Daigh to handle the howling pack. He drove his Scarab to a tremendous victory over local greats like Bill Pollack, Ken Miles, Richie Ginther, Dan Gurney and Carroll Shelby, along with international stars of the highest caliber; Phil Hill, Jean Behra, Roy Salvadori, Masten Gregory, Joakin Bonnier and rising Indy drivers Jerry and Bobby Unser. Two hours, seventeen minutes after the green flag fell, after averaging 88.8 mph for 203 miles, Daigh rolled in the winner of the first USAC-FIA race held on the West Coast.

More wins followed in a stellar 1958 season that culminated during the Nassau Speed Week where Lance won the Bahamas Cup race, and Daigh took the Nassau Trophy Race, a clean sweep. Throughout the '58 season, the Scarab's Corvette 4-speed transmissions gave no problems, proving the Chevrolet design capable of all-out racing. Building the Scarabs required considerable effort to scrounge the best parts, due to the lack of support from Chevrolet because of the 1957 AMA ban against factory racing. Inside, the 2-seater was spacious with full instrumentation behind the three spoke, wood rimmed steering wheel, but appointments were pure function for racing purposes. These were not GT cars for the street.

With a huge pile of victories over the best cars of the time, soon there were other Chevy V-8 powered specials; Bocar, Echidna, Sadler, and the Devin SS to name a few. Reventlow built his Scarabs intending them from the beginning to be full-bore racing cars, but the Devin became the first serious attempt at quantity manufacturing of Chevy-powered sports

cars for public sale.

There were also some very highly developed Corvettes around, as was shown by Skip Hudson who led a Corvette 1-2-3 sweep of the production sports car race at Riverside. His 81.7 mph average victory showed just what Chevrolet's sports car could do. Jim Jeffords of Milwaukee posted back-to-back SCCA national championships in B/Production in 1958 and '59. Whatever happened at Chevrolet was filtering down to the racers, and Corvette was proving to be king of the hill.

But by 1958, the AMA ban had returned to haunt Chevrolet. Duntov was still doing design and development work, but the chiefs on the 14th floor had handed down a strict "no racing" edict. Jobs were on the line. Later, a factory engineer summed it up in an often quoted quip, "Chevrolet doesn't race and win, 'cause racing is a mortal sin."

Although GM refused to allow factory involvement in racing, experimental and styling work went on in hidden recesses of the corporation. One such styling experiment was built on a Corvette SS "mule" chassis from 1957. The new car was ordered up by GM stylist Bill Mitchell and first ran during April, 1959. This was the first Sting Ray, so named by Mitchell. His fascination with deep sea creatures such as the Sting Ray and the Mako Shark explained the origin of the names of a number of his styling exercises.

Mitchell campaigned his Sting Ray as a private entry driven by Dr. Dick Thompson. The car won SCCA's C/Modified National championship, the same year that Bob Johnson won the B/Production National title in a Corvette. That Sting Ray was the car that inspired the production Corvette Sting Ray introduced in 1963, the body style of the split window coupe (and of course the roadster) that made the Corvette the great American dream machine.

GM stylist Bill Mitchell with two of his most significant creations, the C/Modified Sting Ray built from the 1957 SS "mule" chassis and the production Sting Ray Corvette of 1963 that evolved from the car. Chevrolet photo.

Mitchell's Sting Ray roadster, the car that Dr. Dick Thompson raced to the SCCA C/Modified National Championship in 1960. Chevrolet photo.

Four sports/racing Scarabs were built, three front engine cars and one with engine behind the driver. The lone left-hand drive car was converted to road service for Lance and became a *Road & Track* cover car as late as November 1963. This Scarab was among the Briggs Cunningham Automotive Museum collection, now the Collier Automotive Museum in Naples, Florida, but was sold before the museum moved. At this writing, it is owned by Don Orosco of Fresno, California. The Collier Museum currently owns Meister Brauser II.

Augie Pabst, SCCA national champion in the Scarabs still owns Meister Brauser I.

Although the Collier car no longer races, the other cars in the hands of Orosco and Pabst have proven to be the fastest '50s era sports cars on the vintage racing circuit today. The two of them have been known to put on sensational shows of vintage racing like days of old among arch-rival Lister-Corvettes. The Pabst and Meister Brauser story follows.

Lance Reventlow's Scarab was the most potent racing car

in the world in the late '50s, a magnificent machine of high style and tall performance, and when the two right-hand drive cars were sold, they became the invincible Meister Brausers in the hands of Harry Heuer and Augie Pabst.

Scarab, the premier sports racer of the '50s. They scored 8 wins in 15 starts in their first season. Four were big wins.

The Scarab was a superb showcase for the small block V-8. Hilborn FI with "horns" was for low hood profile; 375 hp.

This styling study is what the Sting Ray might have become. This is the Mako Shark II, another of Mitchell's styling projects that never made it to production. Chevrolet photo.

The last of the Scarabs, the 1962 rear engine car that Walt Hansgen drove to victory in the Bridgehampton Double 500 of 1964.

The engine behind the driver revolution had begun in 1959. This tube frame and aluminum body Scarab of '62 was two years ahead of the Chaparral.

56

Dr. Dick Thompson

Reflects on his many victories

I got started toward racing when I bought a Renault 4CV in '48 or '49. That got me into foreign cars. After that, I bought a Morris Minor from a local dealer. A friend of mine told me about a local rally where they raced such cars, and while there, I saw an MG-TD. The Morris dealer also handled MG, so I bought one. Another friend, Bill Kinchloe, told me about races with MGs at Watkins Glen, so we went. Someone told us about a race in Florida at Sebring in March, and Bill and I decided to go.

It was an AAA race and all you had to do to get a license was sign in. We signed up and we were in the race. We raced my MG-TD. Someone had told us that you couldn't race the whole thing on one set of tires and wheels so we took along a spare set from Bill's MG. This was 1952.

We won a trophy! We finished 8th overall, 6th on handicap and 3rd in the 1500cc class. (*AG - This was the first Sebring 12-Hour. Completed 129 laps, 670.8 miles. Averaged 55.9 mph*). I had only seen one race before and here we won the J. S. Inskip trophy for outstanding MG performance. Inskip was the MG importer in my area and awarded the trophy for the highest finishing stock MG.

It was the very first race for both of us. We only had one helmet. In practice, both of us were in the car where we critiqued each other's driving. I was a practicing dentist at the age of 32 and just a "weekend" warrior racer.

After Sebring, we towed the tired MG back to Washington DC where we rebuilt it. I started going to local races, mostly in Pennsylvania, the Reading Hill Climb, Giant's Despair, Watkins Glen and others. At Watkins Glen, Bill Spear was in an OSCA. Bob Fergus with his MG-TC and I had a great dice. Both of us finished. Bob won and received a trophy for the 1st place MG.

The course went through town and out around the countryside. Coming back into town, the course went down hill with a sharp left, then a hard right onto main street. Down hill, the car was turning 6500 rpm, much more than it was really capable of, but it held together. There were two OSCAs in the 1500cc class, but I finished 3rd or 4th in class with them.

In '53, I bought one of the 1500cc Porsches. In those days, they were mostly Volkswagens. By then, the MG wasn't very competitive and could only run for special trophies. Later, the Porsches became so popular that many of the events became virtually Porsche races.

That year, I was recalled into the Marines because of the Korean War. I had been in the Marines after graduating in 1944 and had been in the second world war. I was sent to Paris Island, South Carolina, as a dentist. I arranged with the Marines to be let off for racing, which they thought was a good idea for exposure. That let me race at Bridgehampton where I won the 1500cc class in the Porsche. What made that win so interesting was that I drove up, won the race against a special Glockler Porsche and drove back. Like most people back then, I always drove to and from races.

I got out of the Marines in early '54 and raced six or seven races and won the SCCA 1500cc National Championship (*AG - Tied with Art Bunker for the F/Production title.*) I did all my own work, but the Porsche didn't need a lot.

At the end of the '54 season, I drove to Florida and got on the boat to Nassau for the Speed Week. I raced five or six races and finished 3rd or 4th in class against Baron Von Hanstein who was there with a couple of factory Porsches. He was the factory's chief engineer. What made the Nassau thing so attractive was that I saw an ad that said "all expenses paid." All I had to do was get my car to Miami. That was the first time I had expenses paid to go racing.

The Baron was a lot of help when I rebuilt the Porsche. He recommended the good Porsche parts instead of Volkswagen pieces. Neither I nor anyone else knew the difference in those days. They didn't make any more power, but the car held together better.

I sold the Porsche in the spring of '55 and bought a Jaguar XK-140. I raced it first at Hagerstown, Md. That was a notable race because some guy spun in a 300SL Mercedes and crashed into Bill Spear's parked Bentley.

Chuck Wallace and I had a competitive year in our Jaguars. Chuck had a 120M. I was in contention for the championship throughout the season but Chuck won, his first of two in that car.

During the year, Paul O'Shea showed up with a factory 300SL. Back then, SCCA had a real "thing" about amateur racing. No factory and dealer support was allowed, so it was all done "under the table". We raced several races, and he asked me to co-drive with him at Sebring. That was the first time I had gotten paid for racing. We had one car to race and one car each for practice. Fangio's team of mechanics were our crew. Unfortunately, we never made the race.

The cars were fitted with a dry sump system with five gallons of oil. Sebring had five or six fast curves and oil came out the filler and spilled onto the track. That big disaster at Le Mans made people worry about cars sliding in the oil, and the engineers couldn't stop it within the rules. So they withdrew the car. We only practiced. After that, I went back to the Jaguar.

Sebring was the first time the Corvettes were raced. Zora Duntov and John Fitch and a big crew of people spent three months testing. Almost every day, an airplane came in bringing new parts or equipment and went out with something for the factory. O'Shea and John Fitch were friends. John and Zora wanted someone to race the Corvette, but since it was all supposed to be amateur, they asked me to buy the car. I was to send the car back to the factory after each race.

It was all arranged through Barney Clark. He was my "guru", my liaison with the factory. Without him, I wouldn't have been able to get anything done. I took delivery of the car in California because Chevrolet wanted the car in the first race of the year. That was Pebble Beach. I didn't expect much, but it turned out to be a lot better car than I expected. In practice, it had great handling but it had fuel starvation problems. The Chevrolet engineer assigned to the car, Frank Burrell, said he could fix it, and by the start of the race, the Corvette was really running well.

Pebble Beach was a course through woods so you didn't make mistakes. The car was entered in Class C for production cars along with seven or eight 300SLs as the fastest cars. Two or three of them were factory cars. I had a bomb under me. The Corvette was a very good car. It handled beautifully and went very well, but wouldn't stop well after six or seven laps. After getting off to a bad start, I was leading after the first lap and led most of the way until near the end when the brakes were gone entirely. Rudy Cleye's factory 300SL got by me, but I still finished first in class and second overall. That made Barney happy. At the end of the race, I had to stall the car in gear to stop in the pits. When the mechanics took the hubs off, brake pieces fell out on the asphalt. That was the Corvette's first race. I was thirty-six years old.

As far as Barney was concerned, the Corvette was competing against the 300SLs. Both were the fastest production sports cars in the world, and Barney wanted the Corvette to be THE fastest although the Mercedes-Benz cost a lot more. Barney was a great help with the politics with GM. He was a great politician.

The Californians didn't like the Corvette doing well. They favored foreign cars, especially the Mercedes-Benz in production cars. Ferrari was tops, but there were no production Ferraris at the time.

During the '57 season, we went all around the country: Cumberland, Maryland; Thompson, Connecticut; Bridgehampton and Watkins Glen in New York; Meadowdale and Elkhart Lake in Wisconsin; Sebring; Texas; California. We went to every national race that year. All I had to do was pay my air fare and the car would arrive complete with mechanics. Red Byron, who had won the 1948 Daytona Beach stock car race, was the crew chief.

After the races, the car went to Zora at Chevrolet or Red would take it to a local dealer for whatever work it needed. The car was an engineering exercise. I was, in effect, the factory's development driver although it was all under the table. Previously, GM had to stay officially out of it, but this year, it was overt factory backing. Still, we had just one car.

The car was basically a "blue printed" production Corvette with a 283 engine. It had two four-barrel carburetors and a four-speed transmission. What it didn't have was a limited slip. That was something it really could have used.

Sebring was the first race of the '57 season. Gaston Andrey co-drove with me. We had raced against each other many times. Foreign cars dominated the race, but we finished 12th.

The Ban

The Automobile Manufacturer's Association ban in the middle of '57 was the end of the Corvette deal. Chevrolet wouldn't touch racing with a ten foot pole after that. We continued on through the end of the season, and I won the B/Production National Championship with the Corvette the second year running. Although Barney was my connection with the factory until then, there was nothing after the factory clamped down on racing.

For 1958, I had a lot of different rides. I raced a Saab for the factory in the 12-hour sedan race at Lime Rock, and the owner of Manhattan Auto, a local Washington DC dealer, asked me to drive his Austin-Healey. That was a 6-cylinder car. We raced it for the entire season and won the D/Production National Championship that year.

In 1959, I raced the Sting Ray for Bill Mitchell. I had known Bill from my earlier Corvette days. He had the SR-2 with the big fin that I drove at Marlboro and won with in 1956. He decided he wanted a better car and built the first Sting Ray from the mule chassis of the SS. He was a very enthusiastic guy, very effervescent.

Some of the guys from his group at GM worked on the car. It was a totally volunteer effort. Larry Shinoda, one of his stylists, had been my mechanic on the SR-2, and he was my mechanic on the Sting Ray. Zora couldn't give us anything, engines, nothing. His hands were tied by GM management. Everything on the Sting Ray was strictly a Bill Mitchell effort, and, of course, being a Corvette, it had no brakes to speak of; no discs, nothing like the Scarab.

That Sting Ray had absolutely no help from GM. It was Bill Mitchell's creation to publicize the Sting Ray styling. And, I suppose, GM didn't like it much. They might have given him some grief over it, but he had his own little empire and there wasn't much they could do about it. The car had quite a potential even without factory support, but it was strictly amateur. It even had a production engine.

We won the 1960 C/Modified National Championship with that car, but the Sting Ray wasn't what it could have been if they had let Duntov do what he wanted. It could have been a lot of car if some of the CERV engineering were let loose and applied to the car. His group had all kinds of things, but he wasn't allowed to use anything.

That car didn't get light in the front, not like the later Grand Sports, but it didn't go as fast, either. To my knowledge, nobody checked it aerodynamically. Back then, nobody knew

sions, and every four or five laps, they would bring the car in and it would get a bucket of ice dumped on the engine. They didn't go very fast, but the car finished.

Fred Windridge was my co-driver, in car number two I think. The engine blew fifteen hours into the race. That was my first drive at Le Mans. It was very intriguing. Really, there is no race like it except maybe Indianapolis. The whole town

With Dr. Dick Thompson at the helm, the Sting Ray was the fastest through the back straight speed trap in the Road America 500 at Elkhart Lake in 1960, 145 mph, but failing brakes kept the car and Thompson from victory. *Chevrolet photo.*

anything about aerodynamics. I guess it would do, maybe 160. The earlier Corvette, the SR-2 in '56, was capable of around 140, I guess, and the Sting Ray was maybe 20 mph faster.

We took three stock Corvettes to Le Mans that year. Briggs Cunningham entered the cars, and we were very welcome at Le Mans. He was very well liked, and it was quite a big promotional deal. It was the first American production car effort since the Cunningham Cadillacs of the early '50s. Zora and a bunch of his people went over two months early for practice. It took two days to get the cars through scrutineering. Since they were production cars, every part on them had to be stamped.

During the race, we had brake problems as usual, head gasket problems because of the three mile long straightaway and gas problems. They had sent Briggs a sample of the gas that was going to be used during the race, but, of course, it wasn't the same gas at all. John Fitch and Bob Grossman finished, their's was the only Corvette that did, but it did so with a blown head gasket. The water had leaked out, and according to the rules, we couldn't add water or oil. With about three or four hours to go, Frank Burrell, who had been my mechanic with the SR-2, thought of packing the engine with ice. We bought all the ice we could find from conces-

becomes the race; thirteen kilometers of countryside with a couple of little towns. There was an awful lot of people. So many of the entries were factory teams with all sorts of members.

At Le Mans, we weren't running against anyone in particular. Maybe if you were leading, you might race against someone, but we were trying to do as well as we could and finish. It rained as it always rains at Le Mans. Fog. Night. Just keeping the car going required all our attention, so we didn't do much racing against other cars.

After Le Mans, I continued the SCCA season with Mitchell and the C/Modified Sting Ray. We raced against the Scarabs, BOCAR and Devin SS, mainly the Scarabs. I'd have to say that Augie Pabst was my fiercest competitor. The Scarab was a much better car, better brakes and a much more powerful engine. The reason I won the C/Modified Championship that year was that we went to more races. (*AG - Pabst won the B/Modified Championship in the Meister Brauser team Scarab.*) We raced ten or twelve races that year; Riverside, Laguna Seca, Meadowdale, Elkhart Lake, Watkins Glen, but no endurance races. They were too expensive. Remember, Bill Mitchell financed the whole thing. Nobody got paid. Everything was strictly volunteer.

The Sting Ray was a lot lighter than the Scarab. It would accelerate with the Scarab, but it wouldn't stop with it. We raced the Sting Ray a little in the 1961 season, but I'm not sure about that. It just got too expensive. Overall, racing hadn't changed much, but it was becoming more and more professional.

At the time, Don Yenko was driving for Grady Davis. Davis was Executive Vice President of Gulf Oil Company. I think it was after the third race that season that Yenko lost his license. His car was caught with a Sebring flywheel in a production Corvette. Grady called and wanted to know if I could finish out the season. To win the championship, I had to win every race remaining on the schedule. I started in the fourth race of the season. Bob Johnson had won the B/Production championship the year before and had won the first three races in a Corvette, as I recall.

Grady financed everything. The cars had Gulf logos on them, but there wasn't any Gulf money in the program. He just liked racing. We finished out the year with me winning the B/Production Championship that year. That was my eighth National Championship in eight years of racing.

The next year, he had two Corvettes. Yenko drove the B/Production car, and I drove A/Production. Don won the B/Production championship in his Corvette, and I won the A/Production championship. That was a good year of racing for Grady.

In '63, Grady ran a Grand Sport and an A/Production Corvette. Don drove the production car. The Grand Sport and A/Production Corvette were really no comparison. The Grand Sport was a thousand pounds lighter and had good brakes. It went fast enough that aerodynamics began playing a part. It got light in front.

Dr. Dick Thompson, SCCA National Championships:
1954 (tied)	F/Production	- Porsche
1956	C/Production	- Corvette
1957	B/Production	- Corvette
1958	D/Production	- Austin-Healey
1960	C/Modified	- Sting Ray
1961	B/Production	- Corvette
1962	A/Production	- Corvette

Meister Brausers

On the 3rd of March 1959, Nickey Chevrolet of Chicago became the owner of Scarab chassis #2, the first right hand drive Scarab built, for the handsome price of $17,000. Jim Jeffords, noted Milwaukee Corvette racer and winner of the SCCA B/P National Championship in 1958 and '59 and pilot of the SR-2, was the designated driver. Four months later, the Nickey team was disbanded and Jeffords purchased the car, then sold half interest to fellow Milwaukeean Bob Wilke who

The most potent racing car in America, the Chevrolet small block powered Scarab in the hands of Augie Pabst on his way to winning the Road America Nationals, 1960. Photo courtesy Augie Pabst.

sponsored the Leader Card midget and Rodger Ward Indy car. Later that year, in December, the car was sold to Peter Hand Brewing Co. It became Meister Brauser II and was usually driven by Harry Heuer, son of the company president, who was captain of the Meister Brauser team.

Meanwhile, on August 3rd, Scarab #3 was sold to Peter Hand for the same price. Local name and highly talented driver, Augie Pabst, of the Pabst Blue Ribbon family and Peter Hand rival, was hired as the #1 driver for the Meister Brauser team. The car was designated as Meister Brauser I with the purchase of the second Scarab, and once again, the cars were together as a team where they resumed their role of vanquishing all foes.

Heuer fashioned his team of Meister Brausers very professionally and molded cars, drivers and crew into a cohesive unit dedicated to professional racing at the highest levels. His purpose was, of course, to advertise Meister Brau beer, a label of Peter Hand. The dream that led Lance Reventlow to build the cars in the first place was adopted and carried on by Heuer. His was an all-American team of racers, cars, drivers and crew, dedicated to the cause of always being as competitive as they could be. These were the big bores, the top sports-racing cars of their time.

Scarab, chassis #1 - the left hand drive car - was kept by Reventlow and was converted for street use. It was the subject of several magazine articles and appeared on the cover of *Road & Track* magazine on at least two occasions. Even in the early '60s, the beautiful Scarab was the subject of great admiration.

The concept of the team approach is worth note because it allowed one car to be the rabbit to force competitors over their limit while the second car stayed in the hunt and won. That was proven by Reventlow and Daigh in the four "big" wins during the cars' earlier competitions; the Montgomery and Thompson SCCA nationals, the Riverside Grand Prix and the Nassau Trophy race of '58. During these races, there were four victories and four DNFs. As a team, the Scarabs

Formidable power from its fuel injected Corvette engine gave the Meister Brauser a tremendous power advantage over the typical sports racer of the time. Power slides and drifts were the norm on skinny tires. Photo courtesy Augie Pabst.

proved to be formidable opposition. In other races, the cars swept to victory with 1-2 finishes at Laguna Seca and the inaugural Meadowdale event.

While in the hands of Nickey Chevrolet, Meister Brauser I blew an engine at the Virginia International Raceway (in May '59) and was subsequently fitted with a special block of 339 cubic inches. Being one of Chevrolet's largest Chevy and Corvette dealerships, Nickey had the connections for the "right" parts. The much modified Corvette block of the Reventlow days had done well, but the new block made the car bullet-proof. Never again did the Nickey-raced Scarab have engine problems. Jeffords won three 104-mile heats for victory in the Memorial Day event at Meadowdale while beating Lloyd Ruby in a 4.5-liter Maserati and rising Grand Prix ace Ricardo Rodriguez in a Porsche RSK. Along the way, he lowered Daigh's lap record by 4 seconds.

In the June Sprints at Road America, Jeffords sat out the feature and watched Fred Windridge's Lister-Corvette take what was sure to be his win. The gear had let go and sidelined the car during practice. However, ace mechanic Ron Kaplan was dialing in the suspension and making the car a better handler. With more power and better handling, Jeffords was proving to be more formidable than ever, as was shown by his 3.9 second quicker lap times than the record.

With the Scarab marque having won every major event run at Meadowdale, the Nickey Nouse team took the 4th of July feature with Jeffords breaking his own record by lowering the quickest lap by 1.3 seconds to 2:07.7 minutes. A week later while on their way to Riverside, Jeffords & Co. lowered the record at Buckley Field in the Rockies during an SCCA National and took two back-to-back wins, both the preliminary and main events.

On to Riverside and misfortune after Jeffords qualified 2nd, just 2/10s of a second behind Richie Ginther's 4.5-liter Maserati. A brake line failure, then clutch problems sidelined the car.

Back home in Detroit, owners of Nickey Chevrolet, Ed and Jack Stephani, decided to quit racing. That's when Jeffords bought the car, and big time USAC promoter Wilke stepped into the Scarab picture as part owner. That pitted the Scarabs against each other at the Labor Day affair at Meadowdale where Augie Pabst handled Meister Brauser. The Leader Card entry experienced a collapsed rear suspension, a most unusual occurrence. Pabst went on to post a 2nd in the 1st heat behind Ruby's 4.5 Maserati, then both were outdragged by John Staver's awesome Echidna at the start of the 2nd heat. Pabst reeled Staver in and secured his second victory in as many attempts and sailed past one Zora Arkus-Duntov in a Formula 1 Maserati. Augie Pabst was not a name of national driving prominence. Among the vanquished were Jim Rathman in a Lister-Corvette and the three Echidnas, Paul O'-Shea and Rodger Ward, all names of recognition.

Both cars headed west where Pabst once again humbled the field, this time a USAC event at Vaca Valley that drew other big names such as Ginther and Billy Krause, Ferraris and Porsches. It was three for three as the 25-year old Pabst was quickly proving to be a driver of top rank and came within 1/100 of second of setting a new track record.

Then at Riverside, Jeffords once again experienced troubles, and Pabst was penalized a "long" lap while waiting for the last straggling starter. He had been held back for performing "mechanic work" on his car just before the restart following an early mishap that did not involve Pabst but that sidelined the Ferraris of Dan Gurney and Rodger Ward. He brought the car up to speed and went the distance against

The Heuer team learned a good deal from the Jeffords car, Kaplan's chassis work, and with these updates and a BOCAR, questions were being asked: Are the Meister Brausers America's top racing team?

In 1960, Pabst won more feature races than any other driver in America and set lap records at eight major tracks. He also won the Kimberly Cup, SCCA's most prestigious award as

Pabst leading Carroll Shelby in a Tipo 61 Maserati. The battle of the powerful Chevy powered American built sport racing Scarab against the European cars in the hands of top drivers proved to be a valuable lesson for Shelby. His later Cobra was equally overwhelming, although in production classes, rather than modified as the Scarabs. Augie Pabst photo.

Jeffords and Carroll Shelby in Tipo 61 Masers, Phil Hill in a 3-liter Ferrari and Dick Thompson in the Sting Ray, then beat them all while setting a racing lap record on the next to last lap. Pabst finished two seconds behind Bob Drake's Old Yaller B/Modified car and came in 9th overall.

Troubles on the Leader Card team saw Jeffords buying out Wilke and selling the car to Peter Hand with himself as driver. Now the Scarabs were back together again and promised to continue making believers out of the pro-European sports car crowd that Chevrolet power in the Scarabs was too hot to handle. Racing ace Red Byron had joined the Meister Brausers as team manager, making the team of professionals complete.

On the way to Nassau for a Meister Brauser 1-2 punch, the tow truck driver got mixed up going through a rainy Georgia. The trailer broke loose giving the car and trailer a trip into the underbrush. Pabst's car was beyond repair for the immediate contest, but he went on to take the lead in an XP-5 BOCAR, then just as quickly he was out with a clogged fuel line. Jeffords went on to a respectable finish, but an unspectacular off-course excursion bent some of the body requiring a pit stop. He finished 7th overall.

the most improved driver. By then Augie Pabst was SCCA National Champion and racing was his game full time. In the Scarab, he started 18 times in the 1960 season and collected 10 overall 1st place finishes followed by three 2nds, one 3rd, one 4th and only three DNFs. The previous year, he had taken the USAC crown as Road Racing Champion and was now SCCA's top competitor having raced eight types of cars all together in 28 starts.

Typically, lap times laid down by Augie were progressively quicker toward the end of the race. Clearly, his style was commanding. "This going faster and faster during a race and setting lap records is really peculiar to me," he related in a *Road & Track* interview. "It usually keeps me out of these opening lap drag races that break cars. I never go as fast as the car will go, particularly with the Scarab. I don't want to scare myself." For *Car&Driver,* he related, "I race because I feel I am accomplishing something myself."

That said a lot about the potential of the Scarab and the style of Augie as a driver; smooth, consistent and always avoiding incidents. He rarely put a wheel wrong. "The Scarab is extremely reliable, but you keep it reliable by the way you drive." And it "handles beautifully," related Augie, who still races Meister Brauser I in today's vintage racing. Pabst, who held the Road America record at 2:44.8, later qualified THREE(!) seconds a lap quicker, and once again proved the "man and machine" theory. This combination was the best in America. He aspired to be a racing driver. With the best machinery, one of the world's most beautiful cars and Red Byron's team preparation, Pabst became the best racing driver in this country. His record proved that, and his engaging smile won many fans. At one time, he had thoughts about trying to become World Champion, and of his three international races, Augie finished 7th and 4th at Sebring in two attempts and 7th at Le Mans in his first try.

And don't forget the name, Pabst. The fact that he was driving for Peter Hand was a story in itself. Harry Heuer contacted Augie in hopes of finding out how to get in touch with Paul O'Shea as a possible driver for the Meister Brauser Scarab. Pabst responded, "Why Paul? I know someone who would love to drive the car and his name is Pabst." Heuer was amazed that Augie would drive for the Peter Hand Brewery, but Augie was ready to win.

The saga of the Scarab continued as Meister Brauser II was kept and raced by Heuer to SCCA's 1961 B/Modified National Championship. Augie's Scarab was sold to Skip Lehmann in 1961, and the cars battled each other once more. At Meadowdale again, Lehmann put Augie back in the car and the crowd saw a fierce battle as Augie broke his two-year-old record. Beside Meister Brauser II sat another Troutman and Barnes creation, the Chaparral. Jim Hall was entering top level racing, and these front engine cars incorporated everything learned from the earlier Scarabs.

The cars were capable of 175 mph with the right gearing, but racing was changing to rear engines. Although capable of 0-60 mph in 4.2 seconds and 0-100 in 9 seconds flat, Scarabs were becoming old technology. Reventlow's single engine behind the driver effort was first powered by one of the Buick-Olds all-aluminum V-8s of the early '60s, but when the car went to the John Mecom team, a small block was installed instead. A. J. Foyt drove the car to several victories, then there was that Bridgehampton Double 500 win by Walt Hansgen.

While the last half of the '50s showed growing dominance of Chevy's remarkable small block, the '60s were its showcase.

Augie Pabst

Reviews his racing days

I started racing in 1956 in a Triumph TR-3. I had gone up to Road America in 1954 and saw my first race. They were racing around the lake, and boy, I just thought that was something else. Then I went to Janesville where they used to have races on the airport. Fred Wacker and Jim Kimberly were there. Kimberly had a Ferrari and Wacker had a Cad-Allard, and I got really carried away with it.

I thought, boy, I would really like to do that, and I talked a lot about what I wanted to do in racing when I turned 21, because in those days you had to be 21, not 18. When I turned 21, I thought, "My God, I am 21 and I have to put up or shut up." So, I bought a Triumph TR-3, joined SCCA and went racing.

At the time, some of the people thought that I was a "sissy". I did something that was not generally done in those days. I installed a "roll bar". I stepped back and looked at the car and said, "Jesus, if you go upside down, you are going to break your neck" because they made you wear a safety belt. I thought, "That is dumb. If you roll over, centrifugal force is going to pull your body out, and you are going to break your neck. So I am going to put a roll bar in." It was a great thing, because it also strengthened the car.

The next year, I bought a used AC Bristol and did the same thing to it. I was very lucky. The car was tremendously reliable, and we won a fair share of races. We raced the whole year and all we did was adjust valves and change the oil and filter and reline the brakes once. The car did not have disc brakes; that came a year or two later.

Then I bought a 1956 2.5-liter, four cylinder Ferrari Testa Rossa for $5,000, and again got very lucky. The car was very competitive. We could run very competitively with the Rodriguez brothers in their Porsches and Lloyd Ruby in the Masers and Jim Hall also in the 450 Maser, Roger Penske in his Porsche and others. Jim had some Lister-Jaguars, too. The little 2.5 just ran and ran and ran away from them.

I got started with Meister Brauser when Harry Heuer started the Meister Brauser racing team. He bought a Scarab from Lance Reventlow, and he called me up looking for Paul O'Shea to see if Paul would drive for them. Harry had a BOCAR that he was driving.

The BOCAR, at the best, was semi-competitive. It had, if I recall correctly, a Volkswagen front end, but it also had a Chevrolet engine. The car felt like the front end was inde-

Meadowdale, July 24, 1960, Pabst in Meister Brauser II squares off at the start against Dr. Dick Thompson in Bill Mitchell's Sting Ray. Photo courtesy Augie Pabst.

The Montgomery Nationals during August, 1960, Pabst leading two Ferraris and takes another win in the Meister Brauser Scarab. Photo courtesy Augie Pabst.

pendent from the rest of the car. But, it went like hell in a straight line.

Anyway, Harry called and asked if I knew where Paul was, and I said "yes, I did," but why did he want him? He said he wanted Paul to drive the Scarab for him. I told him he was committed to a man named Sadler in Canada. Then I said, "I know someone who would like to drive it and will drive it for you."

"Who is that?"

"Me!"

I don't know what got into me, but I did say that. So, he invited me down to test it at Meadowdale, and on my first lap the throttle stuck wide open. It about scared me to death because I didn't know how to shut it off. Finally, with dumb luck I found the ignition switch and brought the car back. The guys were quite upset because they could hear the engine winding, and all of a sudden, it shuts off. They thought, "Oh, my God. He has destroyed the car." From there we started racing,

We ran a SCCA national at Milwaukee State Fair Park the first time. The car was so much better than anything else there - we ran away with it. Then we started winning a bunch of races after that. The crew was extremely good, the cars are still reliable, predictable, and they were competitive from the time Lance built them in 1957. I think he started racing in early 1958, and he only kept them a year or so. We got them in late 1959. We bought one directly from Lance and the other from Bob Wilkie and Jim Jeffords who had previously bought the car from Lance and had mixed luck with it. The car broke quite often with Jeffords driving it. I'm not saying that he broke it, but the car broke. When the Meister Brau team got the car - I think the number of DNF's with both the cars over the years you could count on one hand.

One DNF that I recall was a USAC race up at Road America. That was a fun race. There were a number of really competitive cars there. Jeffords was in the "birdcage" Maserati Camorad. It had a long nose on it. Carroll Shelby had Old Yaller, and I just pipped him in qualifying.

At the start, Carroll took off like a scalded cat. I let him go and he broke. Then I am just cruising in first place. This would be a cake walk. Then, coming out of twelve, all of a sudden the input shaft on the transmission let go. That was the only DNF that we had when I was driving. No, we had a problem at Riverside. We broke a half shaft, which was my fault. I had forgotten that. It must have been 1959. But anyway, they were extremely reliable cars.

The Scarab, to me, was easy to drive. We ran a spool on the rear end, or locked rear end, so there was no differential and I steered the car with the throttle. I often drove the car in an oversteer situation bringing the rear end out pointing the car in the direction I wanted it to be when coming out of the corner. It seemed as though it exited the corner quicker this way.

But you have to remember, the Chevrolet engines in those days didn't put out much more than 375 horsepower, and we still had those narrow 6 inch wide tires. If we had more power, we couldn't have put it on the ground anyway because you could buzz the tires in third gear easily enough. The brakes were modified Lincoln drum brakes which were amazing. You could literally brake with, and sometimes out-brake, a "birdcage" Maserati; huge disc brakes on the Maser! The car had a four-speed Chevrolet transmission. I always double clutched that gearbox when I was going down 4, 3, 2, 1 in the Scarab for the reason that, if you used the synchros, the transmission began to heat up. We had problems at one time with the transmission getting very sticky, and it was due to the heat. The minute you started double clutching, you just lowered the temperature. The synchro works on the principle of friction.

We discovered some problems at Daytona. Any time we got on to a very fast track, the faster the car went, the less directional control we seemed to have. That was before we learned that the front of the car acted like a wing. We literally got lift. We fixed it just by pop-riveting a piece of sheet metal to the front about half way up the nose, and then bending it to swirl the air to break up that lift. Until we did that: we have

August 16, 1959 and victory in the Wisconsin Grand Prix. Photo courtesy Augie Pabst.

photos of the front tires off the ground half an inch or so. When we put the spoiler effect on the front end, it just dropped the car right back on the ground again. It made a big difference.

The transmission was a modified Muncie. The engine started out a 283, and I think they bored and stroked them to 333. Eventually, we used the 327 which was the same basic block. I think the 283, 327 and 350 blocks are basically the same.

One of my most satisfying wins, I guess, would be Vacaville in 1959, in California. Frankly, I was kind of nervous about it. It was the first time we were on the west coast, and I thought some of the guys were setting me up. We got to Vacaville and Ritchie Ginther was there and he couldn't have been nicer. He showed me around the track, and I think we got rained out the first weekend so we had a whole week in San Francisco. Then we won the race. How lucky can you get?

My most satisfying race in the car was one I did not win.

That was a twin one-hundred mile race at Laguna Seca. That would have been either 1960 or 1961. In the first heat, I lost the brakes. The brake line ruptured, and I had to start last in the second heat. Stirling was there and I think Jimmy Clark, Jack Brabham, Jim Hall, Roger Penske, and a lot of good European drivers were there. Stirling was in a Lotus 19. At the end I was second and catching Stirling at about 3 seconds a lap. In another lap or two, I might of had him. So that was my most satisfying race.

I think that Laguna is a real driver's course. It is a real equalizer. A little car can do extremely well there. I had this great big monster of a car in the Scarab compared to the little 2.5 liter Lotus and Coopers.

AG: By the early 60's when the rear engine cars were coming in, the Scarab was still competitive. At that time Harry Heuer bought a Chaparral-1. Did you ever drive that car?

Augie: Yes, but I did not drive a Chaparral when they owned it. The Chaparral was a refinement of the Scarab. It was also built by Troutman and Barnes, and it started out not as Jim Hall's Chaparral. He bought one and there was some kind of a contractual agreement were Jim bought one and Harry bought one. Jim went on to refine them into the cars that they became. He took over the whole project.

AG: In the races where both the Meister Brauser Scarab and the Meister Brauser Chaparral were entered, I think were you in the Scarab and Harry in a Chaparral, you won in the Scarab and Harry was second in a Chaparral. How did those cars compare?

Augie: That may have been Continental Divide, I am not sure where that was. I did beat him at Meadowdale when he was in the Chaparral. The cars were close. The Chaparral, I would say, was quicker as it should have been since it was an update built in 1959 or 1960, and lighter with better brakes. So it should have been quicker, but I don't think it was nearly as pretty. That was part of the fun of driving the Scarab; it was such a pretty car. There is something about driving a pretty car that makes it better and more fun.

"Meister Brau, the beer that made Pabst famous!"

Harry Heuer

Harry Heuer

Recalls his Meister Brauser Team

Owner of the team was the Peter Hand Brewing Co. and me, Harry Heuer. The original team manager was Red Byron whom , I met at Nassau 1959 with Jim Hall's team. Byron went with Meister Brauser and became team manager after Nassau. I wanted to put together an all-American team and had ambitions to eventually race in Europe. Red was to be the manager, but he suddenly died of a heart attack in 1960. Jack Sullivan was a mechanic and engine man for Augie but left to join Holman-Moody in early 1960, I think. Willy Weiss was crew chief and engine builder for Augie Pabst. Augie and I liked our engines built differently, so each of us had our own engine builder. Weiss became Meister Brauser team manager after Red Byron. Tom "Smokey" Yukawia, was my crew chief and engine man. We had a great team, and other members were Vince Vivirito, who was a mechanic and also worked on engines. Jack Baschieri and Pete Deprato were the body shop men, and Jack Choice was the vital statistics man who kept up with track specs and set up records for the cars. Then there was Richard "Richie" Ex who drove the rig so flamboyantly.

Nickey Chevrolet ran the Scarab for less than a season, but the team didn't get along. I had difficulty convincing the board at Peter Hand that we needed another car and during that time the Scarab was sold to Nickey. We bought the car for Nassau 1959 where we ran three cars, a BOCAR and two Scarabs.

There was no comparison between the BOCAR and the Scarab. The BOCAR was a compromise car for both racing and street driving but wasn't very good at either.

On the way to Nassau, one of the Scarabs, truck and all, rolled down a hill. Without that car, Augie drove the BOCAR. Jim Jeffords drove one Scarab, and I drove the second Scarab. Nassau was my second race. Some way to begin! After Nassau, we sold the BOCAR and set up the Meister Brauser team with a single big rig rather than the two smaller ones.

Roger Penske was at Nassau. His team and ours were the only ones with young people, so we unofficially formed the "26 and Under Racing Team."

The crew used to paint letters on the back of the Scarabs. One was "BBB" and when anyone asked, we never turned down the opportunity to tell them it meant, "Bye Bye, Birdcage".

Jim Hall and I teamed up on the Chaparrals, the Troutman and Barnes replacement for the Scarabs. Jim got the first one; I got the second. He was more interested in speed and power and went to bigger engines. I was more concerned with handling and stayed with smaller engines, 339 cid.

We tested them first at Riverside. They were scary to drive. At 185 mph, the front wheels would lift off the ground. We took our car back to Chicago and did more testing at Meadowdale where we improved the car's handling considerably. Then we went to Daytona during January and February for testing before the Speed Weeks of 1960. The car scared Augie to death. We finished 2nd, losing to Alan Connell in a Le Mans Birdcage. The reason was that the driver's door of the Chaparral kept popping open. We'd have to stop and close it, then go blasting by Connell until it popped open again. We set a new track record at Daytona and would have won except for that door.

From 1959 through 1964, the Meister Brauser team was the USAC and SCCA team champions each year. Augie won the USAC drivers championship in 1959 and the SCCA National

championship in 1960. I won the SCCA National championship in 1961 in B/Modified, and 1962 and '63 in C/Modified.

By then, I really wanted to take the team to Europe, an
all-American team to show the Europeans that American
cars and drivers were better on their own tracks. We had
beaten them in this country, but FIA changed the rules to limit
engines to 3-liters to keep the Meister Brausers out of
European racing.

The mechanics and engine builders we had were really the
unsung heros of the team. They were the guys who kept the
cars going with all-nighters while we were just the "stab and
steer" jocks.

When the Peter Hand Brewing Co. was sold in 1964, the
new owner wasn't interested in racing. The labels Meister
Brau and Lite were later sold by him to Miller. We sold the
cars and disbanded the team.

According to Jim Hall, there were six of the front engine
Chaparral-1 cars built. Other sources say five. These were
also of Troutman and Barnes construction and proved to be
the dominating evolution of the Scarab. They were lighter
than the Scarab and incorporated all the updates learned
during the Scarab's racing days. One was the fact that there
never was a chassis failure in the cars. That meant that their
design and fabrication was stronger than really needed and
consequently heavier than necessary.

Also, by European standards, the Scarabs were bigger cars
than the norm, and there were more modern rear suspension
systems than the de Dion incorporated in the Scarab design.
Thus, a new car would be small, lighter, have an improved
suspension and benefit from better tires and still be a formidable sports racer using the small block Chevy with advances made during several previous years of its development.

Toward the end of RAI (Reventlow Automobiles, Inc.),
Lance and his crew had made an indelible mark on sports car
racing in this country, but attempts to build a competitive
Formula 1 car came along when the rear engine revolution
was sweeping racing car design. The demise of RAI was
perhaps due largely to the failure of this car to be competitive,
but there was also the looming question of American tax laws
that did not favor "hobbies" such as racing, regardless of the
international prestige earned, if those who built and offered
their cars to the public did not make a profit. After the rear
engine Scarab and the front engine Formula 1 effort,
Reventlow's influence on racing was abruptly ended. There
is still controversy over the crash of a small plane that took
his life.

By that time, the early '60s, Troutman and Barnes were well
recognized as the premier fabricators of tubular frame and
aluminum body sports cars in this country. Later, they were
contracted by Ford Motor Co. to construct the first Mustang
prototype and also worked on the Cardinal, the line of cars
that Lee Iacocca killed when he became head of Ford
Division. At the end of the Scarab era, what Troutman and
Barnes needed was another millionaire. Enter Jim Hall.

This young Texan walked out the family oil fields with plenty
of drive and ambition - and lots of money. Enamored with
sports cars, Hall partnered with Carroll Shelby in a dealership. It never was a great success, but it kept Hall, Shelby and
many other sports car enthusiasts in close touch with the
latest in European equipment. When Hall sold Hap Sharp an
AC Ace, their long and fruitful relationship began. In short
order, Hall's own interest in driving matured. He was just 19,
but he was soon in the top cars of the world, but always
frustrated with the lack of the latest in European racing cars
and parts to keep the cars competitive throughout a racing
season.

The continentals had always maintained the protective pos-
ture of selling previous models to competitors and keeping
their latest "works" cars for themselves. This was their "unfair
advantage". Hall could always afford the best, but because the
best was frequently not available, he raced a variety of top
caliber cars in his early days, but rarely the latest.

Hall endeavored to solve that situation by designing, building and driving cars of his own. His fascination with the
hardware inspired him to seek a degree in mechanical engineering, resulting in graduation from Cal Tech. With his
own engineering knowledge and the desire to apply his own
ideas to racing, Hall moved into the position Reventlow had
previously occupied. He was now championing the cause of
American designed and built cars in the hands of American
drivers out to challenge the Europeans. His own driving skills
shone brilliantly in the U.S. Grand Prix at Riverside in 1960
when he worked his way up through an impressive field of the
best cars and drivers to run as high as a very visible 3rd overall.

Troutman and Barnes, having set up their own works, were
looking for another significant project. With Hall, it was an
ideal combination; their proven ability and Hall's engineering
backed up with dollars. Any car resulting from this combination was bound to be a formidable competitor, and the sports
car world followed the project closely.

The Chaparral, so named by Hall for the Texas road runner,
was designed around a four inch shorter wheelbase than the
Scarab. The cars were narrower by two inches and shorter by
fifteen inches. That translated into 300 pounds less weight!
At 1500 pounds, the Chaparral with the Chevrolet cast iron
small block promised to be a healthy machine. Many areas of
the cars were improved over the Scarab, resulting in lighter
but stronger components. The rear suspension was of the
latest design and showed a strong resemblance to Colin
Chapman's Lotus suspension. A new version of bolt on
Halibrand wheels were used instead of the Scarab knock-offs
which were sports car adaptations of Halibrand's sprint car
wheels. Unlike the Scarabs, the Chaparral received disc
brakes, and like the Scarab, the body was hand-formed
aluminum sheet.

Although not the beautiful Scarab, the Chaparral showed
its functional simplicity first in tests at Riverside in June, 1961.
The car was so well done that Hall immediately took it to
Laguna Seca and raced to a 2nd overall, to a "birdcage"
Maserati, in the marque's first competitive outing. A valve

train failure may have cost the car and Hall the distinction of a win on the first time out.

Even though the 327 and fuel injection was available, a 283 with three 2-bbl carbs was first used in the Chaparral. The objective was not more power but a better balanced car. Tires were not up to engine performance anyway, and more power tended to make a car less controllable at high speeds. In time, though, the lure of more power won over better balance because of the ease with which output of the Chevy could be increased.

The original idea for the Chaparral was to race the cars while building duplicates for sale to other racers. However, as Hall got deeper into competition, the plans became side-tracked. One car was built for Sharp and one was sold to a buyer in Europe. Harry Heuer of the Meister Brauser team bought one, so that accounts for just three. Where they are today, if they have survived, is not known for certain.

By the time Nassau rolled around, Hall and his Chaparral was there. But the feature was dominated by rear engine Coopers and Lotus XIX cars. Although the flyweight Brits proved to be fragile and tended to fall apart, they far outnumber the single Chaparral. Even Stirling Moss with his usual ability to keep cars together was having trouble. Had it not been for a similar Lotus on the mainland, he likely would have been in another car like Rodger Ward who moved from his broken Cooper-Buick to an Austin Sprite!

Among the front engine cars were a horde of Ferraris set to defend the Italian honor. Fred Gamble in Bob Publicker's Ol' Yaller with a huge 440 cid Buick was on the No. 1 spot at the Le Mans start, then wrenched the center out of the clutch in three laps. Of the 60 starters, Moss maintained his tradition of getting away first to lead the thundering herd.

Down Sassoon Straight on the first lap, Hall quickly dispatched the Ferraris of Pedro and Ricardo Rodriguez, and pressed the battle to Moss. He got by on the 5th lap to lead. Moss and Dan Gurney then had a heated battle with Moss seemingly setting a new record on every lap. Hall, meanwhile, was doing battle on seven cylinders. Then the engine let go. It was not a good day for the Chaparral.

During the June Sprints of 1962, Hall and Heuer faced off against the rear engine clan. The 38 laps of the 4-mile Road America course was the feature FIA race and had all the big boys. Front engine versus rear engine; technology was side-stepping the Chaparral-Chevys, but not before Hall and Heuer showed the way to victory lane. Roger Penske might have led for nine of the first ten laps, but his Cooper Monaco gave up along the way. At the finish, it was Hall and Heuer with a 1-2 sweep for the Chaparrals, but for FIA points, Porsche took the laurels. The Chevy specials were not among the cars recognized by FIA regulations because of engine capacity larger than 3-liters.

Heuer demonstrated the potential of the Chaparral-Chevy by taking SCCA's C/Modified National Championship in 1962 and '63. After that, the arrival of the rear engine cars in mass coincided with the sale of the Peter Hand Brewing Co. That was the end of the legendary Meister Brausers.

Devin SS

The story of Bill Devin and his sports cars is an intriguing

One of 15 of Bill Devin's SS roadsters. These cars showed considerable advances in the growing line of "homebuilt" Chevrolet V-8 powered sports cars of the late '50s. Devin's "kits" were on the market 30 years before today's "kit car" mania matured.

The Devin factory in El Monte, California, turned out fiberglass bodies and kits ranging from VW and Corvair powered cars to the awesome SS with Corvette power. Bill Devin photo.

look into the work of an idea man that made things happen. He was at the heart of the rise of sports cars and made his mark by offering a vast array of fun "kit cars" long before that term became widely recognized. With the stylish Devin SS, Bill moved into a new realm. Besides his many varieties of fiberglass bodies to fit anything under the sun, the Ferrari Monza-inspired SS was both beautiful and a well thought out sports car.

With a V-8 Chevy up front, this was truly a hot machine. Its tubular frame, de Dion rear suspension, disc brakes and general refinement made the SS a mechanical dream for enthusiasts. When fitted with the swoopy roadster body, the combination looked great and meant business, too.

Devin wanted to market a complete car under his own name. After a stint in the Navy during the war, then scraping together enough money as a tuner for local Chevrolet dealers, Bill moved from California to Iowa and set up business. A little later, with the proceeds of a healthy profit from selling his business, he was back in California (El Monte) doing sports cars again. The SS appeared first in kit form, although he designed and built many of his own pieces, he wasn't able to spend the time required to design a really good chassis. When a letter from Ireland arrived one day, the seeds of the true SS were planted.

Malcolm MacGregor of Belfast wanted to buy a Devin SS body to install on a chassis of his own design. He began with 3-inch diameter 14-gauge steel tubing, rack and pinion steering, fitted Girling disc brakes front and rear (inboard on the rear), a Jaguar type Salisbury differential, and de Dion rear suspension sprung by coil-over shocks. Powered by a Jaguar-6, such a car looked to be just the sort that Devin had been thinking about. A contract was struck whereby MacGregor built the chassis and once received in California, Devin installed the Chevrolet V-8, Corvette 4-speed transmission, driveshaft, electrics, body and interior.

Press coverage of the Devin SS brought a huge response. Here was a truly impressive sports car. With wire wheels, an open cockpit, Chevrolet power and rakish styling, the SS was impressive. Devin had something for every budget and said so in nationwide advertising.

"Whether your budget allows for a $295 fiberglass body, a $1495 bolt-on project, a $2950 finished roadster or a $10,000 custom SS capable of the most fantastic performance, Devin, and only Devin, can help you realize your goal. The...SS is available with up to 425 hp (dynamometer verified) modified Corvette engine for competition."

Although known for his roadster bodies that were very

With its advanced chassis, two 4-bbl Corvette power and 4-speed transmission, the Devin SS was an exciting and formidable roadster of its day. Bill Devin photo.

The SS was the car Bill Devin wanted to produce as a complete car under his own marque. Bill Devin photo.

Ireland's Malcolm MacGregor designed and built the SS chassis. Bill Devin with an early SS. Bill Devin photo.

popular, Devin produced a coupe he called the Devin GT. And since Chevrolet did not use Holley 4-bbls which he preferred, he designed one of his own - cast aluminum bearing the DEVIN logo. Now a Holley could be used on a Chevy. To add more of the DEVIN touch, he also produced finned aluminum valve covers that also displayed his logo.

Auto magazine advertising of the exciting SS attracted none other than Virgil Exner, Vice President of Styling at Chrysler Corporation who wrote and asked, "I would be interested to know if you would consider marketing the complete chassis except for engine and body." Perhaps Mr. Exner had plans of his own as did J. J. Carey of the Kaiser Jeep Corporation who wrote in May, 1964 inquiring about obtaining a Devin GT.

Devin Enterprises established outlets in several locations across America and one, Mr. Brian Waters of Imported Cars of Greenwich, Connecticut, ordered 60 Devin GT Coupes in one order, but such a big order made it difficult to meet schedules. Then came requests from American-La France for Devin to build fiberglass doors for their fire trucks.

The business left no time to race. That was left to enthusiasts who could easily build a B/Mod or C/Mod car. Stock performance was scintillating: 0-60 in 4.8 seconds; 0-100 mph in 12 seconds flat.

The SS was one of three basic models that Devin advertised. Most were for rear engine configurations while the SS could be fitted with any American V-8, particularly the new cast aluminum V-8s from GM. Ak Miller raced his Devin-Olds in all sorts of competitive events. Dean Moon's legendary "Moonbeam" sports racer was also a Devin SS. Clearly, Bill Devin had a good idea and created a rich legacy of sports cars although only 15 SS models were built. It is thought that as many as 8 have survived.

Bill Devin

Describes the Devin SS days

When they had the first sport car race in southern California, the first that I know of in Santa Ana, we went over. Phil Hill and some of the guys were running, and we got hooked on the sport car thing. I went back home and bought a new 1949 Crosley Hot Shot. I got Clay Smith to grind me a cam for it and fixed it up and started racing sport cars at Pebble Beach, Palm Springs, Torrey Pines and wherever we could race in those days.

From there, I bought four different types of Ferraris as well as other cars and ran them for a while. Then I decided that I could build sport cars. So, in 1954, I just started building sport cars. At that time, I bought out a Panhard distributor who had ten chassis, and I built those into sport racing cars. In some of them, we just modified the engine. On some of them, we installed a Roots blower, a French Roots blower made especially for the car. The "normal" car ran in the 750 class and the supercharged one ran in the 1100 class.

In 1955, I built the world's first belt driven overhead camshaft engine. Panhard cylinders were replaced with Norton Manx cylinders, pistons and heads, and nobody but me thought it could possibly work. In 1956, it was the national SCCA class champion. (*AG: Class H, 750 cc, Jimmy Orr*) Today, there are over 100 million cars with belt driven overhead camshafts.

Since the car was national class champion, a lot of people wanted to buy the bodies, but they were not adaptable to anything except front wheel drive, what I was using them on. So, we made the first one of the bodies that was similar to the SS. It was smaller, narrower, shorter and had a lower profile. We made that body and started selling them. I just sold the bodies and buyers put them on whatever they wanted to.

Right away, somebody wanted a different size. So then we cut and sectioned and did whatever was necessary to make a different size and had twenty-seven different ones before we were finished. We put out a brochure with all the dimensions and info so they could figure out which one fit what. We would recommend one that would fit a Triumph and one for an MG, one for a Crosley, and some for big American cars with a real big bubble in the hood to clear the carburetors.

The first D car we made had a Porsche engine. Porsche wanted to sell some 1600 cc engines you could buy in a box. It had a muffler, fuel pump, the fan and generator, everything. Just hook up the battery cable and the fuel line and it was ready to run. The only difference in it and the one in the cars was that it had cast iron barrels instead of chromed aluminum barrels, and it had a "plain vanilla" cam in it. We took the car to the public scales and weighed it. It weighed 1180 pounds on the street.

Then, right away, Porsche didn't want to sell any more engines. So then we bought ten sets of VW parts including engine and transaxle from a distributor in Texas. He was also buying cars from us, and he would send us ten sets at a time. One time, he was short three transaxles, so he asked the California distributor, a friend of mine, if they would send me the three transaxles, and he would either replace them or pay them or whatever. But, they didn't send them. Not only that, someone notified the factory or something. Anyway, the new parts supply disappeared. From then on, I had to go to a dealer and buy them, with just regular service station discounts, but we built a lot of them. They were a fun car.

I started on the SS in 1957. I was making the front wheel drive cars and all of those bodies and we were selling hundreds and hundreds of the bodies. We sold about 3,000 or so bodies, and about 300 cars, but only 15 of the SS. Most of the others were rear engine.

The SS was designed for the Chevrolet engine and transmission. That is another story. When we were making all those bodies and people were ordering them from all over and wanting to be our distributor and build them under license all around the world, we got a letter from a fellow in Belfast, North Ireland. He wanted to buy some bodies for a new chassis he had designed and built. He sent me the designs and specs. At the time, I was making a real crude tube frame chassis with '40 Ford cut down axles and other components for front engine cars, so I told him I would like to have some chassis like that, and maybe we could work out something. In 1957, I sent him a 1957 Corvette engine and transmission. I think I sent about three bodies, and when they got there I got on a plane and went over.

They had one chassis with a Jaguar engine in it. It had a 90 inch wheel base, and what looked like a tractor radiator on the front and a tractor gas tank on the back. We took it out

40 miles north of Belfast to an abandoned American WW-II Air Field. We chased the cows off the black top, I got my crack hat on, I fastened the seat belt and took off. It really worked, so we made a deal for them to build chassis for me, just the chassis, no engine or transmission. I wanted a 94 inch wheelbase instead of the 90 inch, so we compromised on that and made it a 92 inch wheelbase.

The first chassis with the Jaguar engine was built in 1957. It ran well, but it was a lot higher. A body like the SS wouldn't have fit on it, and it didn't run like the Chevrolet engine. It also cost a lot more.

We didn't complete the first SS until late 1958, and it seems to me we first advertised them for $5950. It was written up in the July 1959 issue of *Hot Rod* and *Road & Track*, *Sports Car Illustrated* which is now *Car and Driver*. I think they listed the price as $5950.

In response to your question about the Scarab, it all started in 1956 when Warren Olson, who was Reventlow's gofer or something, asked me if I could help them get an invitation to Nassau. I was going to Nassau, and I had three of my cars to take. I had a four car trailer built to haul our cars and, as we had room for one more car, I called the man that was in charge of invitations and helped Reventlow get an invitation to Nassau. I agreed to take his car, a Cooper Climax, to Miami and put it on the boat and then get it off the boat at Nassau and return it to Hollywood after the race for $300 before we left for Miami.

I asked for the money because I needed it for expenses and finally got them to give me half; they would give me the other $150 when we got there. But when we got there, I couldn't get the other $150. The people that owned the other cars didn't pay either.

I got a little upset with Olson and Reventlow and those people. I had previously talked to Olson about Reventlow to finance building the SS. Since Reventlow was only 20 years old, he couldn't do anything for a few months when he turned 21 and received his inheritance. At this time, Olson looked me up and wanted to talk about doing the SS. But by then, after my experience with them, I wasn't interested.

So they went away and hired a group of people including Chuck Daigh and others, some of the best race car builders and drivers in this country. They had all the money in the world. They built the race car but they didn't have any brakes. They made the brake drums bigger and bigger in diameter instead of wider and smaller in diameter which would have been the proper way for drum brakes.

Someone from the Reventlow group called our office and wanted to know if they could come out there that evening and look at our chassis. I said to some of my people, "Guys with that much balls, we ought to let the dumb bastards have a look." So, after dinner, we met them at our shop. Marshall Whitfield, who claimed to be the designer of the Scarab chassis, and others in his group looked our chassis over and told us what all was wrong with it. According to Whitfield, it was really horrible. They set up scales to check the torsional rigidity and figured it up. Then, one his people said, "What's the matter, Marsh?" He was scratching his head and everything. He said, "I must have made a mistake."

So, they did it over after they had put in an hour telling us what a bunch of crap we had. Everybody knows they had chrome-moly tube frames, like Lotus, and heliarc welded. It turned out that our frame had half again as much torsional rigidity as the Scarab frame. And our car weighed a couple of hundred pounds less. Our street machine weighed 200 pounds less than their racing car.

Some time after that, the person from the Reventlow group that called before called me again and said, "These poor guys have spent $30,000 on brakes and still don't have any brakes. Where can they get some brakes?" I told them to contact Girling in England and get a set of Devin SS brakes. I said, "They will come all in a box for $200 or $300. You will have all the calipers and discs and master cylinders and all the tubing and piping and everything."

I have read that at one time there was a movement to get my cars built so that Chevrolet would go for them. But not that I know anything about. At one time, I was coming back from Europe, and I stopped off in Detroit because I knew people there. I asked them to let me do something for them because I could use the money, and they said, "What could you do for us? We have over 31,000 engineers. What do we need with you?"

I thought, well, that made sense, so I came on back home. Later, I was over at *Road & Track* talking with John Bond, and he asked me how I was doing, and I said, "Not too good."

"Why don't you do something for Bunkie Knudsen?"

"I don't know Bunkie Knudsen."

"Well, he knows you. I was just back there and out to the Tech Center. They had one of your cars there jacked up and pulling it apart and measuring it."

But they didn't need my help. They didn't need my help to do the belt driven overhead cams. They didn't need my help when they were thinking about putting an independent rear end in the Corvette. I got a letter from an engineer there wanting me to send two complete sets of engineering drawings of my differential set up, suspension and everything. Naturally, I didn't send it. I sent him an 8x10 photo of it. I have never done anything for Chevrolet, and they have never done anything for me.

I did have a contract with GM one time to supply all of their racks and ladders for their GMC motor homes, and you couldn't get them to pay. On one invoice, they paid exactly four months from the time it was shipped. For a small company working out of a small shop, you can't wait that long. Then, as soon as they got the first set of our design constructed of premium material, they started shopping them all over and got someone to do it cheaper. Of course it was really crap and caused me trouble because people would buy that thing from General Motors and it would break. A Ford dealer bought a couple of the GMC coaches, and he wrote me a letter threatening to sue me because the step had broken and he had cut his hand or something. He called GM and asked them who had made that and they said that I had. Of course that was a lie! Because of the cheap copy available from GM, their dealers nationwide started buying from us direct.

When I was building the SS, Chevrolet wouldn't sell us

engines and transmissions direct so we bought them from a dealer. We used the fuel injected Corvette engine and just bolted it in the car. Chevrolet wouldn't sell you that. We didn't prepare the engines, either. Just bolt it in the car. It was a 283. I think it was rated 220 horsepower, just stock, right out of the box. As the Corvette fuel injection was no good, I wanted a low carburetor to fit under the hood, and the Holley was the best one. The only people that was using them then was Nash. They had a little four barrel Holley, so we got one and tried it and it worked, but it didn't fit the Chevrolet manifold. So, I wrote to Holley and asked them if they could supply me with a carburetor for the Chevy V-8 engine. I still have the letter from them that said they did not make Holley carburetors for Chevrolet.

Then, I made my own intake manifold. It worked good, and anything will fit on it because it is nice and flat. That's what we started running on the SS. It is just a stock four barrel carburetor.

Bob Carnes of Denver, Colorado was the man behind the BOCAR. This XP-5 is a superb example of his fast roadster.

BOCAR

Chevrolet powered specials flourished in the late '50s. The Corvette engine and transmission combination was so thoroughly developed that it was a natural to slip in any front engine chassis, then fit a body around it and you have a sports car. Bob Carnes of Denver, Colorado did just that.

His was another version of a triangulated tubular steel chassis, one of his own design, but in the selection of a suspension, Carnes relied on available VW/Porsche equipment. The Corvette live rear axle was fitted to the rear. With this combination, the BOCAR materialized as a road racing sports car but found the going tough against more fully developed machines like the Meister Brauser Scarabs.

Durable and effective brakes seemed to always be a problem until Carnes adapted Corvette Cerametallics.

By the time he had built three complete cars, Carnes had learned enough to go into limited production and did so with a new car designated the XP-4. Using the small block and 4-speed transmission, the BOCAR was a quick roadster, particularly in a straight line. The first five XP-4s found buyers rather quickly, and by the end of 1958, Carnes was into another limited production run with the updated XP-5. One source states that five of these were built and reportedly found buyers at $8,700 each.

Styling was reminiscent of the big Maserati, the 450. Body shape of the XP-5 was smooth and designed with aerodynamic principles in mind. But like all other sports car builders of the time, the concept of aerodynamic lift was not recognized to be a significant design principle. As top speed inched steadily higher, so did the front end of the cars.

Motor Trend writers drove an XP-5 some 1,300 miles including tests at Riverside. This car ran 3.70 gearing. "On the long straight, it tracked like an arrow and the engine seemed to rev without limit - 150 mph came in right now." Red line top speed was considered to be perhaps 155 and available 3.55 rear gearing was good for 160 mph. Then a wheel came off. Someone had mistakenly installed a right front hub on the left front and rotation was not tightening the lock nut but loosening. The car settled down to a stop with the hub doing sparking duty on the asphalt, and after scouring the surroundings, the wheel and spinner were located, reinstalled and the tests continued.

Considering that the XP-5 was the approximate size of a Porsche speedster of the time, the BOCAR was an efficient design. Carnes, being an aerodynamicist at heart, developed the car for balance in terms of flow of wind around the car and mechanical balance as well. He achieved that by offsetting the engine, transmission radiator and entire driveline to the right 1-3/4 inches. That meant side-to-side loading with only a driver was very nearly neutral. On a wheelbase of 90-inches and weighing just 1650 pounds dry, the XP-5 had considerable merit as a handsome and powerful road going machine.

When the BOCARs were raced, the compromises inherent in the choice of suspension used showed up most. Against the cars in its class, the BOCARs most often showed the need for further development to be competitive.

Carnes built a special car dubbed the XP-6, a one-off with a stretched wheelbase to 104 inches. To get more power, he installed a GMC Roots supercharger mounted in front of the engine and driven by a Potvin arrangement. This kept the hood low but made the car. The Porsche type front suspension was also changed. A new tubular front axle with double ball-joint trailing links and torsion bars was located by a Panhard rod for lateral positioning. The front of the body was stretched nearly a foot with a long, air penetrating snout. Rear wheel openings were covered, and painted brilliant red, the new road racing BOCAR was called the Stiletto.

Carnes demonstrated the enormous power of the last BOCAR, his Stiletto built on the XP-9, at a number of SCCA races, but achieved little success. One was at the Continental Divide raceway near Denver for the Labor Day classic in 1960. The Meister Brausers Scarabs were there, Augie Pabst and Harry Heuer driving, and the crowd was witness to an exhilarating race. Heuer held the track record on the 2.5-mile road course.

Continental Divide was located at the foot of Pikes Peak and drew the top racing teams in the business in several forms of racing. It was a complete racing facility; road course, 1/2-mile oval and drag strip. It was built in a small valley that gave spectators on the slopes a clear view of the entire race course.

Carnes put the Stiletto on the pole and lead away from Heuer at the flag. The BOCAR was a local favorite, and Carnes was cheered on for a few laps. Such things lost to racing as an announcer's voice are only memories, but the play by play announced by the famous tone of Ed "Twenty Grand" Steinback kept spectators informed. Heuer diced

BOCAR is thought to be the first supercharged small block powered road racer. XP-5 roadsers like this one were naturally aspirated.

with Carnes for a couple of laps then began braking deeper and put the superior handling of the Scarab to work to put the the blue Meister Brauser in front. Jim Hall and Hap Sharp had come up from Midland, Texas and raced a Cooper Monaco, but Heuer's 2:11 minute laps were never to be caught, and Heuer sailed to another 1st Overall. Unfortunately, the Stiletto made only a few laps.

The XP-6 led to the XP-7 series of BOCARs that were built without blowers. And along with the roadster, a strikingly handsome coupe was offered. Overall styling of the cars was similar. The improved suspension was carried over to all subsequent BOCARs, otherwise the XP-7 was identical to the XP-5. The last BOCAR was the XP-9, and the Stiletto body was also available. With supercharger, the price of such a car had exceeded $10,000 and there were a number of competitive cars at that price. After a fire destroyed the entire BOCAR facility, the remains were sold to another Denverite who attempted to bring about a similar car called the Gazelle. Little came of that effort and the BOCAR saga closed.

Lister-Corvettes were faster versions of the Lister-Jaguar due to Chevy's small block V-8 and 4-speed transmission.

Lister-Corvette

With the passing of the illustrious D-Type Jaguar and its

The "knobbly" bodied Lister-Corvette was the hottest British sports-racer of the '50s with Chevrolet power.

The small block was smaller and lighter but more powerful than the Jaguar inline-6. Note the tube frame chassis.

Costin-Lister, late '50s vintage sports-racing car with small block Chevy and Hilborn fuel injection.

three Le Mans 24-Hour victories, Coventry had little to say in racing. Proponents of the Jaguar marque championed a

number of specials built around the famed inline 6-cylinder and gearbox. Until the arrival of the E-Type in 1962, a number of builders adapted the Jaguar running gear to produce racing cars that were faster than the D-Types largely because of lighter weight and more development. In England, the Lister-Jags driven by Archie Scott-Brown burst into racing with record setting wins and Jaguar was suddenly back. Although not true factory cars, fans claimed Jaguar wins just the same.

Brian Lister was the semi-official contact for factory racing in the days of the late '50s. However promising his design was, the Lister-Jag followers enjoyed resounding disbelief when the cars made their American debut at Sebring and were out of the running in little more than an hour into the 12-hour enduro. The private entry D-Types soon followed and the days of winning production Jaguars were being replaced by Ferrari 250 GT cars.

Then, with the larger 3.8-liter engine, Jaguar dealer Walt Hansgen raced to victory at Marlboro in his Lister-Jag. The car proved to be a true handler on the twisty road course, and Jaguar was back in America, too. That car was prepared by Alfred Momo and was entered in every race conceivable. Hansgen had won the SCCA C/Modified National Championship in 1956, '57 and '58 in D-Types. Some of his wins during the '58 season were in Momo's Jag, and that carried over into the '59 season when Hansgen took that championship to make it four in a row.

The Lister-Jag's uncanny sticking power made the cars extraordinary handlers even in a time of tall, skinny tires. The way such powerful cars were driven was to power slide through every turn, set the back end out and hammer the thing coming out. Brakes were also highly integrated into the design making the Lister-Jaguar a very well balanced car capable of 10/10s from the best drivers.

In 1958 specifications, Lister offered an alternative drive line with the Chevrolet small block , an easy adaptation. This was essentially the Corvette 283 with fuel injection and a 4-speed transmission. The cars were known as the "knobbly" design because of the humps and bumps fashioned into the body to clear things underneath. Rated at 290 hp at 6200 rpm, the Lister-Corvette had 34 more horsepower and were actually lighter than the Jag version. Weight distribution was near ideal, 48/52 front/rear. The slight rear bias made for sensational acceleration without spinning the tires. Gear ratios offered ranged from 2.93 to 4.78 giving the cars enormous versatility. They could run successfully on any track.

The Listers were designed for English sprint type racing rather than long distance endurance events and that fit the American scene as well. Few races were longer than 6-hours.

Priced at $9,650, the Lister-Corvette was $700 cheaper than the Lister-Jag and offered more performance. Without an engine or transmission, buyers could acquire an otherwise complete Lister-Corvette for the attractive price of $6,604. For such an excellent racing car, that was a fair price indeed. The typical Ferrari was over $10,000 at the time and could not compete with either Jaguar or Corvette powered Listers.

The car's tubular chassis with independent front and de

The vintage cockpit. Looking back thirty years at one of the top road racers, the Lister-Corvette.

The Costin-Lister was more aerodynamic but did not prove to be much faster.

Dion tube rear suspension was at the leading edge of sports-racing car design of the time. When word got around that the Lister-Corvette was out, long time sports car racer Tom Carstens of Tacoma, Washington became a distributor in the northwest as did Carroll Shelby in Texas who handled the remainder of the west. Auto Engineering in Lexington, Mass was the eastern seaboard contact. Along with Shelby's own winning career as a driver, he was proving what he had long thought; rugged American V-8s were superior racing engines to the expensive European exotics. It could also be said that his own racing of Chevy powered racing cars, and the earlier Cad-Allard, was the foundation that made his later Ford powered Cobra possible.

When Carstens received his first Lister-Corvette, it won the first time out and went on to win the Northwest region championship. That car was later raced under the ownership of Al Dean of Dean Van Lines. Dean was a well known and respected competitor at Indianapolis. The Lister-Corvette was his first venture into sports car racing, and what he wanted was something with an American flavor. The Dean Van Lines Lister-Corvette did its first racing at Riverside in 1959. Drag racer Bruce Crower prepared the engine and the car for noted west coast hot shoe Bill Pollack. Being a drag racer, Crower fitted it with dragster style exhaust pipes sticking out the rocker panels! The car made an enormous racket. Pollack once described it as sounding like a WW-2 P-40 fighter plane.

With 352 cubic inches bellowing some 330 hp, Pollack took to the track only to discover considerable high speed front end lift although top speeds easily reached 160 mph with 3.31 final drive gearing. An off-track excursion gave him cause to ponder the brakes, then after climbing as high as 4th overall, the rear wheels locked up unexpectedly and put Pollack off the track a second time. This time, a cylinder also sprung a leak and vented water. He restarted the car and finished the race a credible 8th on seven cylinders.

In an attempt to give the cars more speed, aerodynamicist Mike Costin was brought on the Lister project and produced an all-new body. This rather bulbous design compared to the "knobbly" was expected to give the cars lower wind resistance

and consequently higher speeds. When actually raced, there was little difference although the Costin-Listers were about 200 pounds lighter. Wherever there was Formula Libre racing, you would find Listers of both types while the Lister-Corvette proved to be the superior.

By 1960, Chevy power dominated sports car racing in this country. The top levels were the big bores where Augie Pabst in the Meister Brauser Scarab won the SCCA B/Modified National Championship, Dr. Richard Thompson took the C/Modified title in Bill Mitchell's Sting Ray and Bob Johnson took B/Production in his Corvette.

The same followed in '61. This time, it was Thompson in a Corvette, Harry Heuer in the Meister Brauser Scarab and Atlanta's Peter Harrison taking the C/Modified championship in a Lister-Corvette. Of the 30 or so Lister specials built, they firmly established a strong racing legacy, but SCCA championships were denied the marque until the 1961 season.

Further down in D/Modified was a new name that year, a new champion by the name of Roger Penske who drove his Maserati and Cooper-Monaco to the season long points title. 1962 was another all-Chevy year. Don Yenko won the first of his back-to-back B/Production titles in Corvettes, Harry Heuer in the Meister Brauser Chaparral took the C/Modified title and there was Penske taking D/M again in his Cooper-Monaco, his 2nd in a string of three D/M championships.

The rear engine Cooper-Monaco was among the new movement. With the engine behind the driver, racing cars were better balanced and improved handling gave quicker times through turns. More development of the small block was giving racers higher top speed as well. Soon there would be new marques, Lola, McLaren and McKee to name a few, and the front engine Scarabs, Chaparrals and Listers slipped behind the scenes of top level championships.

However, in the last gasp, for the front engine genre of sports-racers, Joe Starkey of Dallas, Texas piloted his Chaparral-1 to SCCA's Southwest Division championship in 1965. SCCA honored each division champion rather than have an overall title winner. That was the last national title taken by a front engine sports-racer in modified classes.

Sadler

Just as Lance Reventlow, Jim Hall, Bob Carnes and Bill Devin had built cars before him, Canada's **Bill Sadler** made an indelible mark on sports car racing with his own specials. He also did it with Chevrolet power. Sadler was another of the designer-builder-driver types who was sure that his was a better idea, but bad luck seemed to plague his efforts.

Sadler's short wheelbase Mk I was Triumph 4-cylinder powered, but when that engine expired, he moved up a notch or two. Out came the 4-plug and in went a Corvette V-8! Some difference. The power was just a little different. His new special spun its wheels in every gear. Something had to be done. So, he designed his own chassis for the Corvette engine. Once the car was completed, he took it and his family to England temporarily and chanced upon a job with John Tojeiro at AC Cars where he designed a transmission and helped Tojeiro build one of his specials, the Tojeiro-Jaguar.

While in England, Sadler had an aluminum body hammered over the fiberglass shell he had built, and once back in the states, the car was now being called the Sadler Mk II. He and the car ventured to Nassau where Brian Naylor easily won a 5-lap preliminary heat race for the Governor's Cup Race, then pulled out to a long lead in the feature only to have a U-joint snap. After repairs, Naylor drove the car in the Nassau Memorial Trophy race and a stub axle broke. The Sadler luck. Bill and his car seemed to be jinxed as one thing or another sidelined the car almost every time.

During the Montgomery Nationals of '58, Sadler worked his way into the lead ahead of Reventlow and Daigh in the Scarabs, a couple of Lister-Jaguars and Fred Windridge in the Lister-Corvette. Among thundering cheers from the crowd who sensed an underdog victory, a U-joint let go. The jinx.

Earl Nisonger, a distributor of import car parts, decided to sponsor Sadler in the USAC pro series with Bob Said driving while Bill campaigned the car in amateur races. In the car's one jinx-free race, Sadler won his and the car's only major event, the Watkins Glen Classic on September, 20. The following day at Marlboro, Said finished 2nd to George Constantine's DBR-2 Aston Martin in a spectacular showing of a homebuilt Chevy special against one of the finest sports-racing cars in the world, the marque that won the 24-Hours of Le Mans in 1959 and the World Sports Car Championship.

Thus encouraged, Nisonger commissioned another car and Sadler produced the beautiful Mk III, an all-new car but still with Chevy power. With 326 cubic inches and Hilborn fuel injection, the car was a hot performer with around 345 hp. Now fitted with a Corvette 4-speed transmission rather than the previous car's ENV unit, Sadler had the right combination. The Mk III was competitive and could always run out front until the jinx returned. That seemed to be Bill Sadler's story. His was one with a lot of heart and a lot of ability to make things happen. Rarely did they happen his way.

Echidnas were Devin SS homebuilts and a huge success. John Staver drove his to the 1959 SCCA B/Modified National Championship.

Echidna

Australian Spiney Anteater, 1960, $7,500

Was that an exotic pet or what? 1960 was a wild time by some estimates, but in the frozen reaches of northern Minnesota? Maybe it was the long cold winters that tended to hatch plans centered around warmer things to do; or at least things to do when it was warmer. And in a way, the Echidna was a pet of sorts. A pet project to produce a car, three cars in fact, to go racing with.

The perpetrators of the Echidna saga were John Staver, Ed Grierson and Bill Larson. The three cars they built looked rather like Devin SS roadsters and in fact were fitted with Devin's fiberglass handiwork. Other than a Corvette power train, somewhat similar to Devin's in basic form, the similarity stops. This threesome designed the chassis and suspension of the cars, matched whatever it took and went racing. And all three cars won.

That's what makes this a "pet" story, because not only did the long cold nights up there near Canada's mid-west offer much time for thought and tinkering while the frigid winds blew, they produced another homebuilt Chevy that roared its way to SCCA's B/Modified National Championship in 1959.

John Staver of Virginia, Minnesota was the man who rode his Echidna to the title. The idea for the cars apparently stemmed from the desire to do something interesting while an otherwise boring winter confined activities to indoors. Corvettes were winning production class road races and with Devin's inexpensive kit body available, could it be that a half ton lighter car would be competitive with Corvette power? Such cars would race in the modified classes, C or B depending on engine displacement, and the going was tough. All sorts of Chevy specials made the ambitions of going racing with another version something to ponder.

By May, 1960, the facts were in. The Echidna team had notched 25 wins and were unknown, compliments of the Mesabi range habitat and its general lack of sports writers.

A sports-racer on a '56 Chevrolet frame? Many of the ideas that went into the Echida weren't supposed to work.

Three Echidnas were built and they all won races.

Two years of competition preceding the '59 season had brought the cars up to a state of refinement that made them fast, reliable and winners. Staver, a partner in an iron foundry, was the kingpin of the project. Optometrist Larson had some stock car racing experience, and Grierson's engineering ability became the key to designing and building the cars. All three were sports car racing drivers with honed ability. They were good, and they wanted to race something of their own creation.

So what do you start with to build a championship sports racer in the late '50s? A '56 Chevy frame? Now really!

There was a lot unconventional about what went into the Echidna. What worked, what was simple and what was available guided the designers of these cars. The Corvette engine, transmission and brakes were certainly well proven. And so were many more Chevrolet parts that came straight off junked sedans! Chevrolet built them by the millions, those ladder type frames with cross bracing. If they worked for cars weighing 3,500 pounds, shouldn't they work for a 2,000 pound race car? Why not!

Grierson sectioned, shortened and narrowed the frame, lightened it here and there, and the backbone of the Echidna took shape. A tripod roll-bar was installed to do double duty, increase safety and strengthen the chassis. Extra-thick wall tubing became an integral member of the car and helped produce a very rigid frame that actually weighed less than the production Corvette variety.

Front suspension? If it works for a 3,500 pound sedan, why won't it work on a 2,000 pound race car? Why not! Chevy's pressed steel A-arms, ball joints and everything familiar to so many Chevrolet mechanics made a good racing car. Then designer Grierson made his boldest move. Since most racing circuits close on themselves with more turns to the right than to the left, why not set the car up with lots more negative camber on the left front wheel compliments of a handful of Chevy's shims. That allowed faster right handers and a second or two a lap.

Rear suspension? If it works...Yes, indeed, a combination of Corvette and big Chevy components found at any local junk dealer. A live rear axle was positively NOT supposed to be effective in big bore racing, especially with a homemade Watt link and a couple of trailing arm radius rods cobbled up from more junk parts. Offsetting the driveline to the right wasn't supposed to be any benefit except for Indy cars, either. Then there were those standard Chevrolet pressed steel wheels, not wire wheels or cast aluminum knock-offs but plain-jane Detroit 15-inchers. They worked, too. Four really cheap wheels off a wreck.

The Echidnas were troubling machines for the purest sports car racer. They should never have worked. When Staver went to the larger displacement engine (339 cid, 340 hp) in 1959, all the supposed weaknesses and compromises in the design and fabrication of the cars should have made his #64 car less than competitive, or so the arm chair world champs mused jokingly. After the Echidnas were gridded in 35 SCCA regional, national and USAC races and secured 8 overall victories and 17 class wins backed up by finishing in the top four in all but 6 of those 35 starts, people still didn't believe the Echidnas would work. These cars were a lot of heart burn for the purists.

Echidnas were capable of over 145 mph top speeds and reached 100 mph from a standing start in 10 seconds flat. The cars worked as Dic Van der Feen, now of IMSA fame, reported in 1959. "No major component or fabrication has ever failed or given trouble in a race. What dumfounds observers, however, is that during their two seasons of racing, on no Echidna has it been necessary to tear down an engine or reline a brake." If it worked on a 3,500 pound car...

What does Echidna mean? If you were to name a sports-racing car, you probably would not choose the long-nose Australian spiney anteater. That just doesn't speak race car. A lot of things were strange about the cars, though, so why not the name. It is fitting, sort of, if you use a lot of imagination. It was offered by Grierson's wife and was probably a result of long, cold winters and lots of crossword puzzle time.

Echidna performance: 3.70:1 final drive ratio
1st - 2.20:1, 67.6 mph @ 6,500 rpm
2nd - 1.66:1, 89.7 mph
3rd - 1.31:1, 113.8 mph
4th - 1.00:1, 148.9 mph

4

'60s Road Racers

The roar of the '60s opened with Corvettes charging to the lead of production class racing. In the first three years, it was mainly Corvette versus Ferrari and Porsche. Bob Johnson, Dr. Dick Thompson and Don Yenko took the SCCA B/Production National Championship successively, 1960, '61 and '62. Chevrolet photo.

Duntov and his Corvette Group

As the decade of the '60s began, the horsepower and cubic inch war between GM, Ford and Chrysler really heated up. There were more high performance parts released by the factories during this decade than any other time in the history of motorsports. Each make had its own reasons to go racing, primarily as new car sales promotion tools, and the duels put on between the makes were what made that decade the sensational '60s.

The time was a mixture of inspired engineering entwined with political entanglements. At Ford, the commitment grew into "Total Performance" with top management publicly backing the company's will to race and win. GM's management, on the other hand, kept shooting its own efforts in the foot for no good reason other than the AMA agreement of 1957. The prestige that Ford gained was immense; a string of SCCA national championship Cobras; four consecutive GT-40 victories in the 24-Hours of Le Mans to rank equal to the achievements of Bentley, Alfa Romeo and Ferrari; and America's only World Manufacturer's Championship - Cobra.

Chevrolet? Certainly there was all the engineering ability and will to win necessary to beat Ford, but management's philosophy of "we don't race" kept getting in the way. Employees who wanted Chevrolet to be a world champion or a Le Mans winner or Indy 500 winner or Daytona 500 winner were continually getting into trouble rather than being encouraged by management to improve Chevrolet's products and image any way they could.

At Ford, management established the complete car concept to engineer the total racing machine while the Chevrolet men were constrained to develop pieces. As time has shown, though, those pieces such as engines were so well done that they have risen to dominate racing in classes where V-8 engines have been permitted. In the late '60s through to modern times, Chevrolet cars have become increasingly more aligned with the complete car concept. For example, there is no doubt that the modern Corvette is the most technically superior car built in this country in every way. How that has happened and who the were people that made it happen is another long story with some little known elements.

Who were the men who created the hardware that built the great legacy of Chevrolet power? Answering that question is one of the aims of this book. Having had the fortunate opportunity of locating many of the principle "hands on" men and compiling their stories has become a significant part of my effort to compile as much "people" history as I can for this book.

As outlined in the forgoing chapters, the small block V-8

Cal Wade, Zora Arkus-Duntov, Fred Frincke and Denny Davis; Chevrolet's inside men and their exotic engines. Photo courtesy Denny Davis.

The ultimate small block; 545 hp @ 6000 rpm in SOHC form with 11.45:1 compression ratio. If Chevy had let this one out... Photo courtesy Denny Davis.

was the inspiration of Ed Cole. But as a manager, it was his job to establish the guidelines and goals of what the engine should be, but others did the actual work. Who were they?

At the time the engine was being designed, the project engineer was Al Kolbe. His drafting group supervisor was Don McPherson who has related that Kolbe was, "an excellent engineer and the motivating force behind the small block. He really did a marvelous job on that engine but has not received credit for it."

"I spent most of my career in the engine department," continues McPherson. "I ran the engine group when the small block program was put together. That engine has always gone down in history as Ed Cole's engine. He was Chief Engineer at Chevrolet, but there were other people who were quite a bit more influential in its design."

"There was a tremendous effort put into developing the small block engine and chassis. Duntov was very active. We in the engine group did a tremendous amount of work making the engine a free-breathing engine. It was light weight, lighter than anything else we had.

"I can remember Ed Cole challenging me to make that engine into a 4-inch diameter bore. The bore centers on that engine were 4.4-inches, so that meant, between cylinders you had 4/10s of an inch to put some water and some iron. We had wall thicknesses down to an eighth of an inch, and I never thought it would work. It did, and worked very successfully. With a 4-inch bore, that was a pretty potent engine. That was the 327.

"Prior to 1955, I became an engineer in the motor department. Then shortly after that I was Assistant Staff Engineer, then Staff Engineer for motors. At the time I was Staff Engineer, we did the big block V-8. Dick Keinath was Assistant Staff Engineer to me on that project. That was my principle association with motorsports.

"We did a fair amount of work with engines down at Daytona, and after that, I became Assistant Chief Engineer for chassis, and then Chief Engineer for all the truck and passenger car group in 1970, and then finally Director of Engineering in 1975.

"The Camaro came along during the time I was Chief Engineer for passenger cars. That car was a sports passenger car. It was not conceived basically as a racing car. The Camaro was set to be a sports car, a better handling car than about anything else we had at the time except possibly the Corvette. It was designed to compete against the Mustang in the marketplace, and whatever work was done after that to put it on the race course was supplementary work.

"I don't think there is any doubt that the "no racing" policy took away a lot of the glamour that was associated with Chevrolet. There was a lot to be said for the image that Chevrolet picked up in the racing world, particularly with that small block engine. When you legally couldn't compete, legally by corporation standards, it took the wind out of a lot of sails."

As related by Zora in his interview, there was a lot more effort put into developing the 348 cubic inch engine into a race winner than has ever been recognized. Then came the cast aluminum engine program assigned to Dick Keinath. Then the 409 and Z-11 which were among the products of Duntov's high performance engine group. Competing with that engine was the famous Mk II "Mystery" engine designed by Keinath. Dick is now retired from Chevrolet but continues his association with Chevrolet with consulting work on racing engines for the Heartbeat of America.

About the time he left Duntov's group to take his aluminum design work into an abortive attempt at production, Denny Davis was brought on. Davis, now retired, joined Duntov's group in 1959 and became the cam man with responsibilities of valve train and power development including fuel injection and carburetor engines. One of his products is the famous "30-30" cam which was designed for the 409 but not used. It was later redesigned by Denny McKeller using the same profile for the small block.

The casting designer in Duntov's group was Fred Frincke who is still with Chevrolet and the main man behind the Mk IV big block becoming the Mk V. Fred was Duntov's personal draftsman and laid out overhead cam conversions for both the small block and big block engines. Ram tube fuel injec-

Chevrolet Engineering under Duntov produced these fully developed overhead cam heads for the small block in the early '60s. Photo courtesy Denny Davis.

And then came the SOHC big block! With 660 hp @ 6800 rpm, this engine produced 1.55 hp/cubic inch on 12.5:1 compression ratio. Photo courtesy Denny Davis.

tion, dual spark plug heads and all sorts of exotic hardware were penned by him. Gear drive train for the overhead cam heads were designed and patented by Harold Little.

Cal Wade, unfortunately deceased, was the reciprocating parts man in Duntov's group. His job was crankshafts, rods, pistons and the like. These were the men who created the CERV-I and CERV-II cars in addition to that fantastic array of super high performance engines proudly displayed by Duntov on the cover *of Hot Rod* magazine in December, 1967.

Davis has related that the engine design influence of Harry Barr, Chevrolet Chief Engineer, was the concept of big bore and short stroke to reduce piston velocity. Barr was also in favor of simplifying valve actuation which resulted in the pressed in stud, pressed steel rocker arm and ball pivot to lighten the enertial weight of the valve train.

A significant factor in the future of the small block was the "slipper" piston designed by Byron Ellis for Cadillac. It was later carried over to Chevrolet and was the key to the success of the engine.

A most important aspect of the small block was project engineer Al Kolbe pushing for casting of blocks and heads in green sand. That was both a time and cost saver. "It was his attention to detail that was the success of the design," confirms Davis.

Today, after more small block V-8s have been built than any other engine in history, approximately 60 million, history has seen the big block come and go as a passenger car engine. While the small block continues in production with no end in sight, the big block has not gone away but will continue to be Chevrolet's main line truck engine. Thus, both engines are alive and well.

The legacy and parentage of the big block can be traced to Dick Keinath's Mk II "mystery" engine. That was strictly a racing engine, and it proved itself in Daytona '63 when Junior Johnson and Johnny Rutherford won both of the 100 mile qualifying heats preceding the Daytona 500. Both were in mystery engine powered Chevys. (Johnson: 164.083 mph; Rutherford: 162.969 mph; previous record; Fireball Roberts

1962 Pontiac: 156.999 mph).

The mystery engine caused such a problem for Chevrolet's "we don't race" policy that management came down hard on employees. Not only did that engine solidify management's "no racing" position to the extent that jobs were on the line, the edict handed down following Daytona in 1963 hung heavy over the heads of Chevrolet R&D personnel for the next twenty years. Although the R&D group continued involvement with high performance vehicle dynamics with Jim Hall's Chaparral program, it was such a clandestine exercise that just at the time a thorough racing program could become a real engineering tool to help verify concepts, engineers had to back off.

The association of Hall and Chevrolet benefitted both sides. However, since engineering and racing see vehicle dynamics with different perspectives, it is probably reasonable to say that Chaparral Cars could have been much more competitive if Hall had developed his own racing cars, and Chevrolet would have been better off if management had allowed it engineers to do their jobs completely. The ban caused compromises to both sides of the same issue.

The proof of the engineer's ability was well proven in the engine room with test engineer Bill Howell working with the design engineers. For several years of the '60s, Howell was instrumental in development of a number of high performance engines that have since become legendary. If his work could produce all sorts of thoroughly de-bugged engines, why shouldn't chassis and suspension engineers have benefit of the same level of thoroughness? The difference is that a dyno can be hidden behind doors. There is no way to hide on a race track where photographers with long lenses can snap spy shots.

For decades, it has been repeatedly stated by racing oriented engineers that an hour at speed on a race track will show up problems that a year of normal driving would never expose. "Racing improves the breed" is the dictum of the racer, and the fruits of racing have indeed shown up as continual advances in automotive technology that become the

CERV-1

Profile reveals smooth lines of fiber glass body. Bullet-shape headrest is located beneath arched rollbar. Car is 172 inches long.

Louvers on hood exhaust warm air from radiator. Intakes on either side of nose feed air to oil coolers while vents behind front wheels supply air to cool engine and rear brakes. Driver has excellent visibility of road ahead and all tire treads.

Air enters scoop in nose cooling radiator. Unique warm air exhaust exit offsets a low pressure area that is built up over top of car and minimizes front end "lift" at high speeds.

Rear suspension is fully independent with fabricated steel radius arm, tubular lower link and axle shaft. Car has modified Corvette brakes.

Ten gallon rubber cell fuel tanks are mounted ➡ on each side of car. Magnesium wheels of 15, 16 or 18 inch diameter permit variety of tire sizes that can be used.

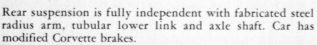

What you got from the factory was a little less exotic than cammer engines, but there is no doubt that the 375 hp fuelie 327 was one of the runningest engines ever built.

accepted norm. Disc brakes and active suspensions are just two of many racing car features adapted to road cars. Paul van Valkenburgh's STV (Suspension Test Vehicle) was as much a race car as many that actually raced, but what could be learned from such an R&D vehicle was limited without actually racing it to determine how competitive, and therefore how well designed, a concept incorporated in the car really is.

A lot of engineering experience was achieved through as-sociation with racers. If a part broke, that pointed out a weakness, and Chevrolet's engineers could use that data to improve the part. Vince Piggins' group had the responsibility of interfacing with the racers. In his group was Paul Prior who encouraged racers to use Chevrolet products. As the decade of the '60s unfolded, one reward of his efforts was the enormous increase of using Chevrolet hardware. Although it could be said that the aftermarket industry supporting Chevrolet hot rodders and racers was the primary fuel that led to Chevy's domination of road racing and drag racing, that could only have happened after the Chevrolet men had done their work and given the results to the world. Durable high performance equipment was what made Chevy's winners.

By far the largest percentage of drag racers and road racers were running the Chevrolet small block V-8 in the early '60s, but behind the scenes at Chevrolet, exciting work was going on with an all-new big block engine. And Chevrolet's engine men in Duntov's group produced all sorts of exotic equipment that never made it outside. Their game was developing complete conversions for both small block and big block V-8s such as overhead cam heads with hemispherical combustion chambers, ram tube fuel injection and all the associated pieces that made everything work properly.

These were factory people who were not allowed to race, but if management had changed its mind about "we don't race", Duntov, Wade, Frincke, Davis, Keinath & Co. were ready.

Bill Mitchell, wearing a "crew" badge, chats with Player's 200 driver Rodger Ward at Mosport Park, Ontario, June, 1962 while the mechanics prep the car. Chevrolet photo.

Corvettes lined up for the first Daytona Continental 3-Hour, February 11, 1962. Six deep on the production class grid were Don Yenko's #10 and Dr. Dick Thompson's #11 Corvette team cars. Thompson finished 13th overall and 3rd in GT class averaging 96.52 mph behind Stirling Moss and "Fireball" Roberts in 250 GT Ferraris. Yenko finished 19th overall and 7th in GT. Five Corvettes finished. Daytona Speedway photo.

Corvettes

Racing flourished in the early '60s and grew enormously throughout the decade. There were all sorts of cars from homebuilt specials to high-buck factory cars, mostly European in origin, but the production classes were to remain virtually all-American. Although Ford got heavy into both production class racing (Cobra) and prototype (GT-40) during and after 1963, Chevrolet wasn't allowed to race as a factory, and their end of the battle was upheld by independents. Chevrolet dealers were the main outlet for factory equipment, and Penske, Nickey, Baldwin, Yenko and a few others were to rise to the competition in some of the most exciting and memorable Chevrolet versus Ford battles every seen on the race tracks of America. Corvette drivers held the tide very well against rising corporate involvement. By 1962, the Europeans had been vanquished, and for the remainder of that decade, national champions in top production classes were either Chevrolet or Ford products.

No A/Production champion was crowned in 1960, and ex-

cept for 1961 when the Ferrari GTs took the title, Corvettes or Cobras captured the title each successive year. Dr. Dick Thompson was victor in 1962; John Martin won the Midwest Division title in 1965; Jerry Thompson raced a Corvette to the A/P championship in 1969.

B/Production was the domain of Corvette. For the ten years from 1960 through 1969, Corvettes won six years outright and shared 2 of 6 Divisional titles granted in 1965 when no overall champion was crowned. The much heralded Cobra with Ford's 289 cubic inch engine took only 1 title during that period, Don Roberts in 1968. Race prepared Shelby G.T.350 Mustangs won two overall titles and shared 4 of 6 Divisionals in '65. Thus, leaving out 1965, Corvette won more than half of the championships open to the cars during the decade. By the numbers, that says that Corvette as a marque held its own very well during the heady days of '60s road racing.

During the following decade, the '70s, it was all Corvette except for Sam Feinstein's Cobra victory in 1973 (A/P) and Bob Tullius winning the 1975 season in a Jaguar (B/P) followed by Howard Meister's Porsche victory in 1977 (B/P). SCCA dropped A/P class in 1979, and no champion was crowned in that class afterwards. John Greenwood opened the decade with his big block A/P Corvettes taking back-to-back national championships in 1970 and '71. Having won the 1969 B/P championship in a small block Corvette in B/P,

Final tuning before the 3-Hour. Car #0 is Harry Heuer's Meister Brauser Chaparral driven by Chicago's Dick Rathmann. The "door popper" Chaparral in its gleaming royal blue and white was in the Sports class won by Dan Gurney in a Lotus 19. Thompson's Corvette #11 was first in GT over 3-liter followed by Yenko's #11. Daytona Speedway photo.

Allan Barker was on a role that took him to four straight title years, 1969 through 1972, the latter being his fifth championship season. Present-day driver, Elliott Forbes-Robinson, got his introduction to big-time road racing with his first national title when he took his A/P Corvette to the run-offs and won in 1978, the last year of A/P. By then, there was no competition left for the Corvette, a recurring problem for the cars.

Then there is the absolutely phenomenal record established by Jerry Hansen. His 1980 championship year in an B/P Corvette is just one of 27 (!) overall SCCA National Championships he has taken. The nearest competitor is Bob Sharp with an impressive 6 national titles. Everyone else is a long way from Hansen's record which is likely to stand forever.

When totalling the victories available to Corvette during the 1970s decade (1970-1979), out of 18 season-long campaigns (both A/P and B/P) resulting in a national champions for each year, Corvettes and their drivers took 15. That accounts for a remarkable 83.3% win record.

What makes such numbers so convincing is the recognition that all Corvette wins were by independents with virtually no factory support. The factory engineers had done their work so effectively that the parts and equipment available to any racer anywhere were of the caliber to build a national championship Corvette.

During the '62 Daytona 3-Hour, Don Yenko leading NASCAR driving ace Joe Weatherly in a Lister-Corvette of the Costin style. Daytona Speedway photo.

In one of Corvette's finest showings, Dr. Dick Thompson raced the brand new production Sting Ray to 3rd overall in the Daytona Continental, the 3-Hour of '63, and led the nearest Cobra in 4th across the finish line by a full lap. Thompson avaraged 99.06 mph to beat Dave MacDonald's Cobra that averaged 97.79 mph. Here, he is about to blast by a Simca-Abarth. Johnny Allen brought his 'Vette in 6th overall to lead the next finishing Cobra that ended up 23rd. This was the first battle between Corvette and Cobra for internahtional points, and Corvette proved superior. Daytona Speedway photo.

The "Nickey Nouse" team from Nickey Chevrolet returned at Daytona '63. Unfortunately, neither Bob Johnson (#17) nor Jerry Grant (#7) finished. Daytona Speedway photo.

For 1964, the Daytona Continental went to 2,000-km in 12-hours and 40 minutes. Of 43 entrants, only 4 were Corvettes against 8 Cobras. Jack Moore's #3 Corvette Sting Ray shown here leading a 904 Porsche and a 250LM Ferrari was the highest finishing Corvette at 21st. Cobra domination had begun. Corvette driver Bob Johnson went over to the Cobra camp and teamed with Dan Gureny to finish 4th overall in a factory sponsored Cobra . Daytona Speedway photo.

One of the last long distance races for the Grand Sport Corvette was the February 4-5, 1967 Daytona Continental, now America's longest race at 24-hours. Jim White Chevrolet of Toledo, Ohio sponsored this car. Daytona Speedway photo.

Driven by Tony Denman and Bob Brown, this Grand Sport qualified for the race but completed only 82 laps. It was fitted with a 327 running a Trans-Am style cross-ram intake and dual 4-bbls. Daytona Speedway photo.

Oops! Yarborough in the rough. NASCAR highbank oval pilots G.C. Spencer and Cale Yarborough piloted this Corvette in the Daytona Continental of 1964, but did not finish. Daytona Speedway photo.

Leon Hurd in the ex-Grady Davis Gulf Oil Co. sponsored '63 Sting Ray. Don Yenko sold Hurd this car in December, '63, and he raced it for many years and came close to winning the 6-Hours of Marlboro in 1964. Leon Hurd photo.

The Roger Penske Grand Sport Corvette with its Traco engine saw battle in many races. Photo courtesy Bill Tower.

Photographer Bill Neale caught the Delmo Johnson GS in mid-flight at Green Valley Raceway in an SCCA Divisional race, Apr. 19, 1964. Photo courtesy Bill Tower.

Tuning the cross-flow Weber carburetor induction on the GS took a lot of skill but worked extremely well. Photo courtesy Bill Tower.

Inside the GS was Corvette only in form. Function was pure racing. Everything was light weight but carried Corvette Sting Ray styling.

Like many builders before him, Bill Thomas built the small block powered Cheetah in hopes of getting factory support to build these cars in quantity. If 100 or more had been built in one year, the Cheetah would have raced against Cobras.

Cheetah

The transition from '50s to '60s style sports car racing saw a vast variety of cars, some now famous while others have been forgotten. Also included in that period were a lot of advances in new sports car technology. The cars became increasingly faster, better handlers and used increasingly more scientific techniques to arrive at the proverbial "winning edge".

Bill Thomas' Cheetah illustrates the temper of the time but proved to be more of a last ditch effort at front engine cars rather than the vanguard of the new age. In concept, the Cheetah carried over the '50s style of racing car design - front engine - with its designer's intuitive "feel" for what the car should be. Thomas adapted many aspects of the new Sting Ray Corvette to produce one of the quickest sports-racing machines ever built. The Cheetah remains conclusive testimony to what a few clever people can do. The car's dramatic styling remains a striking image of the era, although the cars were rather rough around the edges racing machines rather than refined road cars you would take your lady for a drive in. Just getting in the cars was a challenge, and creature comforts were nonexistent.

The time was 1964, a year in the midst of radical changes in racing car design: the rear engine revolution had taken firm hold. Cars were built with increasingly larger engines and vast strides were being made toward implementing "the scientific method" in every area of racing car design. Little by little, how a design looked or felt was becoming increasingly less acceptable, and proving the worth of ideas both in theory and intensive testing were becoming the normal mode of racing car design. Designer/builders gradually became engineers with knowledge of aerodynamics, improved brakes, better suspensions and lighter but stronger materials. Tube frames were giving way to monocoques of riveted and glued sheet aluminum. Tire technology made great strides, and the age of computers had dawned.

The intuitive "feel" and experience from the old school of auto racing emphasized how features of a racing car "ought" to be. In the '60s for the first time, numbers, printouts and computer modeling were appearing as baseline data to design by. It was the beginning of the age of "scientific design" as the designer and his product became separated.

What began back then has matured today. For example, with a knowledge of the physics and mathematics of air flow, a computer aided designer can just as easily design the body of a car for least aerodynamic drag as design an induction system for maximum air flow. Both are governed by the same laws, both improve performance, and a designer need not actually know much about automotive design to know that his computer results are close to correct every time. Small refinements on a computer controlled dyno or in a wind tunnel can produce a component or a complete car of high potential before it is ever put on the track.

Things have definitely changed in the last twenty-five years, and in the transition period of the early 1960s stands the Cheetah. Although intended to be a production sports car to do battle against Carroll Shelby's Cobras, events confined the Cheetah to the rear engine revolution as prototype cars. Not enough Cheetahs were built to qualify as production cars, so they raced against rear engine prototypes that emerged from all quarters.

Thus, the Cheetah is an interesting look at one of America's most exciting "might-have-been" sports cars, one that had fantastic potential but is almost forgotten today. A few turn out for vintage races, about the extent of their exposure. In contrast, arch-rival Cobras were a huge success and are revered as one the world's all time greats. The 427 Cobra has been described as the most widely recognized car ever built.

Also in the shuffle are the Corvettes that gave rise, in some ways, to both cars. It was their many wins that prompted the Cobra and their failure to keep Cobras out of the winner's circle that brought about the Cheetah. The '50s decade special-builts like Scarabs and Lister-Corvettes, Echidnas and Chaparrals, all with Chevy V-8 engines, and all were among the fastest sports cars of their time. Their claim to "fastest" was due to ever more powerful engine swaps in increasingly lighter weight cars.

Most racing efforts in those days in either special or production classes were relatively small-time private entry sorts. There were a few factory sponsored teams and a few wealthy owners who ran teams, but most racers were out for the fun of racing on low bucks operations.

Bill Thomas was out racing and winning in A/Production Corvettes. He fielded one of the first successful V-8 Vettes in southern California sports car races and became known far and wide as "Mr. Corvette". He prepared cars that won over 100 races in five seasons in a row, and one took all but 2 of 56 races entered. Rochester fuel injection and Chevy small blocks were his game, and what he could do with them made other people, even GM, notice.

Up until 1963, the Corvette was king. Then Shelby came along that year with his AC Cobras that put a sudden and complete end to Corvette wins. Cobras won all three championships open to them, and Vette wins went dry. Thus, the challenge was laid for Chevy power to respond with something better, but several turns of events limited such efforts to frustrating failures.

On the corporate level, Duntov was at work inventing their Cobra killers, the Grand Sport Corvettes of Bill Mitchell Sting Ray styling. SCCA regulations said that 100 cars had to be built by a deadline to qualify for production class racing, but in February 1963, GM management handed down the edict that there would be no corporate sponsorship of racing. Only 5 Grand Sports were completed.

Although factory efforts came to naught, the time was right for another car to carry on the Chevy legend of racing. Thomas had done contract work with Chevrolet's Ed Cole on

Cheetah power was the small block taken to 377 inches and fueled by Rochester. At 520 hp, the 1510 pounds Cheetah was a real screamer capable of 200+ mph.

V-8 Chevy IIs and other development projects. Consequently, he had an inside track. Like Shelby and his Cobra, Thomas invented the Cheetah, but unlike Shelby, his offering to GM received no support while Ford backed Shelby with everything it took to produce both national and world champions.

Legend has it that Thomas struck a secret deal with Ed Cole to produce 100 Cheetahs. The car was configured as a front engine/rear drive two-seater on a 90 inch wheelbase, the same as the Cobra. But unlike the Cobra roadsters, Cheetahs were designed as coupes with gullwing doors.

Thomas and chassis man Don Edmunds laid out the Cheetah's tubular chassis as an all-independent, adjustable suspension of a very modern design for the time. The engine sat well back for a mid-ship location to enhance balance and handling. That located the cockpit over the rear wheels and produced a stunningly aggressive body design.

Their engines were Thomas' famous 327s with a 3.75-inch stroke for 377 cubic inches. Intended from the start for racing, the engines received Rochester fuel injection and tubular headers and side exhausts to the tune of 520 dynoed horsepower! A Corvette 4-speed transmission coupled directly to a '63 Vette rear end/suspension assembly with just one U-joint. The engine/trans assembly sat so far back that no drive shaft was needed. Most other components were Chevrolet like the big NASCAR Cerametallic drum brakes all around. Big car brakes should work well on a light sports car and did.

The body began as an aluminum structure formed by Don Broth from about 30 pieces into five major sections. The first two cars were of aluminum, but all later cars were built with fiberglass bodies. (One source says a total of 27 cars were built, another says 16, another says 13.) Considerable thought was given to making the cars as lightweight as possible.

Compared to Cobras, 385 horsepower at about 2000 pounds in racing form, Cheetahs came in at 520 hp and 1510 pounds. Thus, they clearly had a decisive advantage in both power and weight. Handling was much improved with Cheetahs showing 1.18g lateral acceleration which was also much superior to Cobras. These stats put the Cheetah in the performance league of the rear engine prototypes like the King Cobra. The Kings were well beyond the potential of production Cobras, even the later 427 Cobras.

The first Cheetah did its teething at Riverside but was crashed by a friend who wanted to take the car for a spin. Once rebuilt, Jerry Titus, editor of *Sports Car Graphic* magazine, tested the car and reported on it in his November '63 issue. That launched the Cheetah for real and hungry Chevy racers lined up for their Cheetah. Jerry Grant of Washington state, Ralph Salyer and Bud Clusserath of Indiana took their Cheetahs racing with astounding success. Development problems along the way had to be solved, and most were, but one problem continually plagued the cars. They were like ovens inside.

Driver position in the tight but functional interior placed the driver's feet and legs in a footbox that was surrounded by the engine and exhaust tubes on three sides. Overheating of drivers was the Cheetah's worst unsolved problem.

Other than that failing, Cheetahs were remarkable racing cars. At Daytona, Grant and Salyer drove fiberglass bodied Cheetahs and discovered that at speeds over 200 mph, the hood and doors simply exploded off the cars! Salyer shot the high banks reportedly at 215 mph. Salyer won the June Sprints at Elkhart Lake two years in a row in his Cheetah by posting top speeds of 185 mph. At Riverside, Grant turned better times than Shelby American's ace driver, Ken Miles in a King Cobra and reached top speeds of 198 mph. Against such cars in C/Modified, Cheetahs won 11 races in 1964. Frequent in-class high finishes were astounding accomplishments for a car designed and intended to be a Chevy powered all-American GT answer to the Cobra, not a prototype.

No Cobra in sight could touch a Cheetah's acceleration, handling or top speed yet Cobras became legendary winners known throughout the world while Cheetahs are only a memory. Why that happened is due to the lack of proper support. Little problems continually plagued the building of Cheetahs, and at one point, Thomas's shop burned. It had become clear that Chevrolet was not going to back Thomas in the way Ford backed Shelby, and without the necessary support to build and market at least 100 cars, the future of this very quick cat gradually slid into obscurity.

As a front engine racing car, technology out-stripped Cheetahs and numbered their days. By 1966, the cars were last seen drag racing. Nailing down 135 mph blasts through quartermile traps were easily within their ability, but since then, Cheetahs have quietly slipped from the racing scene.

Cooper Monaco-Chevrolet

John Cooper's works in Great Britain built cars that won World Championship titles in 1959 and '60. The later Monaco series of sports cars drew upon that technology as an enclosed wheel racer with aluminum bodywork. With the small block Chevrolet, these were one of the first Pro series sports-racing cars.

Rear engine sports-racers they were immediately faster around any track than a front engine car. The V-8 Cooper-Monaco of 1964 was on the leading edge of that trend.

Where a tiny 4-plug once sat, the small block Chevrolet with fuel injection tripled the power. These were not cars for the faint of heart!

Leading the engine-behind-the-driver concept was the mark of Cooper Cars of England. Charles and his son John were to put racing on a new course with their extremely successful cars. By 1959 when Jack Brabham won the World Drivers Championship in Cooper Formula-1 cars, and Cooper won the manufacturer's championship, front engine racing was dying a quick death. After that season, no front engine F-1 car was to win another world championship.

Eyeing the growing American market, John Cooper offered his Monaco. This line of cars was a spin-off of the impressive Cooper Formula-1 chassis and suspension but with all-enclosing bodies. Seat-of-the-pants aerodynamic concepts aided in shaping the body although extensive racing experience had shown that the lower and wider a car of this layout, the quicker it was around a race course.

In 1961 at Watkins Glen for the US Grand Prix, Walt Hansgen crashed Briggs Cunningham's T53 Formula-1 car. Young Roger Penske was there and immediately bought the car to rebuild and race. In his Newtown Square shop, his mechanic Roy Gaine straightened the car's bent chassis while Bob Webb and Harry Tidmarsh fabricated a new all-enclosing body for the center-seater. Penske was sponsored by DuPont and debuted the new car as the Zerex Special. At Riverside, Penske brought the 2.7-liter Coventry-Climax screamer its debut victory while edging out Bruce McLaren in a works car.

The Zerex Special and Penske went on to establish a memorable career. At 1100 pounds, the car was on the cutting edge of racing technology and proved that American ingenuity was as capable of developing winners as factory race car builders. However, questions arose as to whether or not the car was actually a sports car. Protests began to bring attention to the fact that as a center seater, it did not conform to regulations stating that sports-racing cars should have two seats located on either side of the longitudinal axis of the car.

Although Penske had won a number of races by the time the car was banned, it was nonetheless no longer allowed to compete. It was later sold to Texas millionaire oil man John Mecom who had it converted to true two-seat configuration, and the Zerex Special went racing again.

It is thought that the first Chevrolet V-8 conversion of a Cooper-Monaco was by Chris Summers in England during 1963. Soon afterwards, many specials were being fitted with V-8s from both Ford and Chevrolet, and Carroll Shelby's King Cobra Ford powered Coopers were to rise to a brief reign of supremacy until the Chevy brigade moved in. The Cooper-Monaco was an inexpensive car for what you got. Around $8,000 got you an engineless car with fittings for either a Ford or Chevy or Olds or Buick V-8 or Coventry-Climax 4, and each type won races at one time or another.

When the USRRC began with its first race at Daytona in February, 1963, Jim Hall and his Cooper rolled onto the winner's deck. Coopers were soon the dominate cars of the USRRC amid all sorts of tough competitors. The rear engine revolution had come to this country via the Brits, and their cars proved to be equal to the task. When fitted with small and lightweight Coventry-Climax DOHC 4-bangers, the cars taught American builders what up to date chassis and suspension technology was worth on the race track. But when American V-8s were fitted to Cooper and Lotus cars, the Yanks taught the Brits that top level racing was the domain of production based V-8s. In little more than a year, the durability and power of the small block Chevrolet was to rise to dominate pro series racing as the Cooper-Monaco faded away as Lola and McLaren moved into the front.

One by one the competition converted to Chevrolet power, and during the USRRC and future Can-Am racing, rarely did anything but a Chevrolet powered car win a race.

GALLERY of FAST CHEVYS

THE AMERICAN DREAM

This supercharged 454 Chevrolet powered street machine is a tire burning show winner and superb example of the heartbeat of today's hot rodding art and craft.
Owner: Vernon McLain

The 1955 V-8 Chevrolet started it all. Ed Cole's "young man's car" was a huge success and changed the course of automotive history world wide.

For 1957, the classic styling of the Bel Air was given the heart of a thoroughbred with dual 4-bbl carburetors or one horsepower per cubic inch fuel injection.
Owner: Alvin DeFord

Magnificent styling and the Impala marque were new in 1958 along with the W-series big block 348. This fabulous convertible Tri-Power 348 was made for cruisin'.
Restorers: Paul Rogers and Jeff Kennedy

The American Dream

Corvette styling and performance came of age in 1956. By 1958, Corvette had become the masterpiece of American sports cars. Archrival Thunderbird changed to 4-seats that year, and Corvette remained the only American roadster, a car of stunning beauty. Owner: Cliff Ernst

Gracious and elegant, the Imapala convertible of 1960. Owner: Jim Wyatt

Grace and very rapid pace in the Mk IV 427 powered Corvette roadster of 1967. This was the heart-throb of America. Big bores were the rage! Owner: Mark Flick

The mid-engine Corvette project became the Fiero, a unique automobile. By 1988, the Fiero GT was a very well developed road handler, but the marque was dropped from production.

The '50s Road Racers

This is the Tom Carstens commissioned H.W.M.-Chevy that Bill Pollack raced at Pebble Beach, April 22, 1956. That date was the beginning of Chevrolet V-8 powered specials in road racing.
Owner: Murray Smith

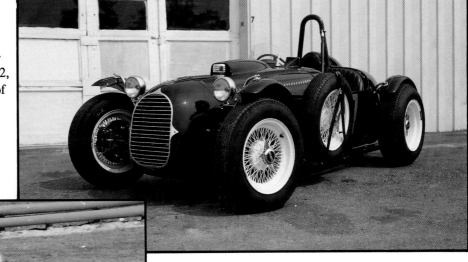

The first of Lance Reventlow's Scarabs. These were the cars heralded as America's finest sports cars of the time. Scarabs were potent racing machines that frequently beat the best cars in the world. Owner & driver: Don Orosco

The fabulous Meister Brauser I that Augie Pabst raced to victory and the B/Modified National Championship in 1960. The following year, team captain Harry Heuer captured the B/Mod title in Meister Brauser II. Between them, the Meister Brausers won 16 of 26 races entered. Owner: Augie Pabst

The Devin SS of 1957 offered sports car enthusiasts and sports-racers blinding performance in a superbly roadworthy roadster they could build or buy complete. With V-8 Chevrolet power, the Devin SS was a thrilling machine. Owner: Alex Quattlebaum

The '50s Road Racers

Modifieds were the big bore racers of the '50s, and as the decade of the '60s drew near, B/Mod and C/Mod Chevrolet V-8 powered specials were king.

Bob Carnes of Denver, Co. built and raced his BOCAR in a variety of forms such as this XP-5. With Corvette V-8 power, they were fast! Owner: Bill Butler

Corvette V-8 specials eclipsed the Lister-Jaguars, and Britain's Brian Lister built a series of Lister-Corvettes. Owner & driver: Joe Pendergast

To aerodynamically smooth the "knobbly" style Lister-Corvette, Frank Costin designed this Lister-Corvette, the Costin-Lister, one of three built. Owner & driver: Jonathan Evans

The '60s Road Racers

Jim Hall and Hap Sharp rewrote the book on Pro Series racing with the revolutionary Chaparral-2. This Sebring 12-Hour winner of 1965 was a "homebuilt" with the new decade's special feature, mid-engine. Still with the small block Chevrolet, the Chaparral-2 was to the '60s what the Scarab was to the '50s. Jim Hall still owns them all.

John Cooper's works in Great Britain also went the V-8 Chevrolet route with the Cooper-Monaco of 1963. Roger Penske's historic Zerex Special Cooper-Chevy started the trend. Although a few Ford, Olds and Buick powered sports-racers were campaigned, the '60s road racers were dominated by V-8 Chevys.

Owner & driver: Hans Huwyler

This was Lance Reventlow's last sports-racing Scarab. Walt Hansgen averaged 93.3 mph in this car to win the 1964 Bridgehampton Double 500. Owner: Augie Pabst

When Cobras laid waste to the A/P Corvettes in 1963 and '64, Bill Thomas countered with his fuel injected small block powered Cheetah. These cars were extremely fast and easily out-ran Cobras, but Cheetahs never went into production. They raced in Modified classes against Chaparrals, Coopers and the Scarab.

The '60s Road Racers

Bruce McLaren dropped Olds power and went to the small block Chevy in the Mk 2 series of McLaren Can-Am cars of 1966, then started winning. Owner & driver: Henry Wilkinson

In 1969, Jim Hall bought this M-12 McLaren, the only Chaparral-McLaren and the first M-12 to leave the factory. It was built by Barry Crow at Trojan who moved to Chaparral to wrench the car for John Surtees who drove for Hall that year. With 427 cubic inches and around 700 hp, this unique car was competitive with the Team McLaren M-8 works cars.
Owner & driver: Dr. Jerry Winston

The awesome M-8F! These Team McLarens were ZL-1 powered, 740 horse, 494 cubic inch rockets that shook the earth.
Owner: Bill Wonder

The most beautiful sports-racing car of all time, the Lola T-70 coupe, was updated to become the T-160 as shown here. Owner & driver: Steve Rees

Bill Mitchell's "high-fin" SR-2 Corvette was more than just styling. Dr. Dick Thompson drove this car to victory at it's Marlboro, Md. debut in 1956. Owner: Bill Tower

In 1956, Dr. Dick Thompson won the first of Corvette's 9 consecutive SCCA National Championships. In today's vintage racing, 'Vettes like this '57 are still favorites.

Allan Barker drove this '63 Corvette for V. V. Cooke and won the SCCA National Championship back-to-back, 1969 and '70.
Owner: John Baldwin leads Dave Rex at Road Atlanta

The Grand Sport Corvette roadster on race day. This Sunoco sponsored prototype was a Penske team car, one of five GS Corvettes built. Photo courtesy Bill Tower

Road Racing 'Vettes

427 big block Corvettes had it tough in SCCA A/Production road racing and earned the marque's 1st National Championship of the '60s in 1969.

The Penske 427 Corvette was prepared by Dick Gulstrand for Daytona but was secretly fitted with an L-88. It won GT class in the 24-Hours, then won at Sebring. Owner: Gene Shiavone

The Bandag Corvette was the first car SCCA allowed to race on recap tires, Bandag's of course. Their tires were recapped racing slicks. Owner: Dr. Jerry Winston

Like days of old, modern Corvettes have dominated production class racing for so long that the Corvette Challenge was established to give competitors a break. The cars have no equals in American production automobiles and few equals in the world.

Improved performance and styling marked the elegant 1958 Corvette. Sales for the first year of the quad headlight cars increased almost 3,000 over the '57s. This '59 model was one of 9,670 Corvettes produced that year. Owner Jim Wyatt

The 1961 and '62 Corvettes were slightly restyled, particularly in the rear, and each year brought record sales. This is one of 14,531 '62 models sold that year. The top 'Vette boasted stunning performance with the new 327 cid small block cranking out 360 hp on fuel injection. Owner: Ward Marsh

The Mk IV big block with 427 cubic inches and 435 horsepower in the Tri-Power option made the '67 Corvettes awesome road and strip performers. Owner: Kim Haynes

The best and fastest GT car built anywhere! The Callaway Twin Turbo Corvette gives today's superb Z51 or Z52 Corvette genuine 185+ mph potential. The special built but fully streetable Calloway Sledgehammer was clocked at 254.76 mph! *The fastest production based car in the world.*
Calloway Corvette Photo

Fast Camaros

Trans-Am racing of 1968 was the domain of Mark Donohue and the Penske team Camaros. Donohue won 10 of 13 races that year to dominate the series 222 points to George Folmer's 2nd place Javelin with 96 points. Donohue won 6 of the final 7 races of the '69 season and accumulated 156 points in that year's battle with factory backed Mustangs of Parnelli Jones who finished 2nd with 130 points. Jim McGhee photo

Thorough development of Chevrolet racing components has put big time racing within the reach of sportsmen racers at tracks such as Daytona, Sebring, Watkins Glen and Laguna Seca. This Whitiker/Cosby/Hudlett Camaro at Sebring is an example.

Buz McCall in the ex-Baldwin Camaro kept the Camaro marque alive in the last half of the '80s with the Skoal Bandit. Walt Bohen co-drove with McCall to four top five finishes in 9 races during 1986 and '87. The Bandit ran the twice around the clock Daytona 24-Hour of '88 to finish 2nd in GTO class and ran again in '89.

Camaro won the SCCA Trans-Am title in 1983 and the IMSA GTO championship in '84. Jack Baldwin in Peerless Racing's "most sophisticated Camaro on the planet" took 5 wins in '86 and finished 3rd in the GTO point race with big wins at Riverside, Charlotte and Watkins Glen. Shown here: the long, dark night of Sebring.

The '67 Yenko Camaro in its purest form, one of 54 built. 427 cid: 450 hp: 4-speed: 4.10 gear: This is muscle! Owner: Jim Parks

The '69 Z-28 Camaro with its 302 inch small block was rated at just 290 horses. They were thoroughbred horses! Owner: "Junior" Johnson

1970 was the greatest year for muscle, and from Chevrolet came the 396 Chevelle. With 350 hp and a 4-speed, this was a driver's car. Owner: Johnny Griffin

The Yenko package combined the best of the Z-28 and added the cast iron L-79 427 rated at 450 hp to produce the Yenko Super Camaro. This is the SUPER STOCK MAGAZINE test car of the July '69 issue. 11.94 @ 114.50 mph. Owner: Cliff Ernst

Don Yenko was a car enthusiast and Chevrolet dealer who put together a number of super performing packages. One of the rarest is the Yenko Deuce Nova. With the LT-1 small block, this was a tall running machine. Owner: Cliff Ernst

Charles Carpenter's world's fastest '55. This prostalgia sportsman/outlaw drag racer lays down 191 mph in 7.27 seconds with a 615 inch "mountain motor" cranking out 1,400 horsepower on "laughing gas".

Recalling more than twenty years ago when the 409s were king of the strip in A/Stock, a pair of fleet Chevys with W-power bring back the days when the first factory big bores were rated at 425 horspower.

The ultimate "shoebox", Rob Vandergriff's flying '57. Even with the aerodynamics of a brick, this awesome nitrous injected machine runs quarters in 7 seconds flat and touches 200 mph!

Hot rod big blocks dominate sportsman classes in drag racing today and make beautiful machines like this one. Billy DeWitt blasts his gorgeous IHRA Top Sportsman to 7.82 second, 171 mph quartermiles.

Drag Racers

In IHRA Top Sportsman, Chevys dominate the sport, and Michael Martin's All-Pro Corvette is a quick stripper that nails down 188 mph quartermiles in 7.35 seconds.

Builder and driver Wally Stroupe pilots this Pro Stock style Top Sportsman Camaro. Today's super-strong pro-built cars are what it takes to handle 1,400 hp big blocks of over 600 inches.

Rick Hendrick, motorsports enthusiast extraordinaire, fields several racing teams including this Pro Stock Baretta handled by 1985 IHRA Pro Stock World Champion Bruce Allen.

Two-time IHRA Top Sportsman World Champion Terry Housley has 7 national event wins. The Thurmer and Housley team Baretta is a 632 cubic inch rocket that blasts through the traps in 7.50 seconds at 185 mph.

Legendary driver and builder Junior Johnson launched the Monte Carlo legacy in NASCAR racing and taught stock car racers how to make Chevys win. The Monte Carlo was retired by GM in May, 1989 after the Montes became the winningest marque in NASCAR history, 95 wins in 183 races.

Three-time NASCAR champion Darrell Waltrip in the famous Tide Machine, one of three Hendricks Motorsports Monte Carlo Aerocoupes. He won the Daytona 500 of 1989.

Four-time NASCAR Winston Cup Champion Dale Earnhardt, always a threat to win anywhere, at Charlotte in NASCAR's longest race, the Coca-Cola World 600.

Geoff Bodine came south in search of his quest to race at Daytona and won the 500 in 1986 as the first driver in the Rick Hendrick NASCAR triad.

Open Wheels

Rick Mears set one lap and four lap qualifying records for the 72nd Indianapolis 500 with this Penske PC-17 Chevrolet. He set the fastest lap at 209.517 mph and led the final 250 miles making the 1987 Indy 500 victory his 3rd and Chevy's 1st. Indianapolis Motor Speedway photo.

Formula 5000 in the '70s was a fierce series of Chevy powered open wheel racing among the world's best drivers such as Al Unser, Sr. who raced this car. Owner & driver: Steve Simpson

The Formula-A Lola T-332 (5-liter) of 1974 was another home for the small block that pitted Chevy's 20 year old engine against the best Formula-1 engines in the world. The Chevys often beat them.

Owner & driver: Tom Shelton

Brian Redman won the prestigeous Formula 5000 championship three times, 1974, '75 and '76, in the Carl Haas Lolas similar to this Formula-A car.

GT Prototypes

This is the first of the IMSA GTPrototype cars. With ground effects applied to a full bodied car for the first time, veteran world class endurance racing driver Brian Redman set top level sports car racing on an overwhelmingly Chevrolet powered course. Redman put this fuel injected small block powered Lola T-600 in the winner's circle 5 times and backed the wins with 5 second place finishes. He ran 10 races out of the scheduled 17 races on IMSA's 1981 calendar and won the championship.

March chassis Prototypes with Chevy small block engines flourished in IMSA racing and soundly beat previously dominant Porsche. March cars won the GT Manufacturer's Championship in 1983, and Chevrolet engine cars won the championship in 1984. During the 1985 and '86 seasons, this Red Lobster sponsored March-Chevy was by far the most beautiful of the GTP cars, but those were Porsche years again.

Beginning with the great success of the Lola T-600, Chevrolet's High Perforrance Operations commissioned this Lola T-710 as a test bed of technology centered around the V-6. The Corvette GTP was a showcase of Chevrolet engineering in a highly competitive environment.

Results:
V-6: 775 hp
   turbocharged
V-8: 650 hp
   normal
   aspiration
1950 pounds
200+ mph
2.0+ g

"Big" Bill France confers with Chaparral drivers Jim Hall and Joakim Bonnier during practice for the Daytona Continental of 1966. This is an early version of the Chaparral 2D, it was sidelined after 318 laps and did not finish. Daytona Speedway photo.

Chaparral and Chevrolet

The Texas road runner gave its name to the cars with which Jim Hall established his reputation. Hall's efforts shown brilliantly as America's most innovative designer/builder/driver, but there is more to the story, more in terms of what observers of the time thought was a Chaparral connection deep in the heart of Chevrolet Research & Development.

With the Chaparral-2, Jim Hall and Hap Sharp engraved their names forever in the annals of America's top sports car racing. In the beginning, that car was totally Jim Hall and Co. Through many cars and a lifetime of racing, the Chaparral name still appears on world class racing machines today, particularly Indianapolis 500 type cars. As open wheelers, such modern cars are quite different in concept and execution than the full-bodied sports-racers Hall and Sharp drove to worldwide acclaim in the early-to-mid '60s. The Chaparral name came from the high speed ground-dwelling bird. It was appropriately chosen.

The evolution of Hall's 30 years of involvement in racing, first as a driver, then as builder/driver and today as team owner, is a fascinating success story. And although the beginning of his racing career predated the car shown here, the Chaparral-2, this car was the real beginning of a saga in prototype auto racing that placed the Chaparral team and Chevrolet in the forefront of racing car technology.

Historically, the Chaparral-2 was a very successful racing car, but aside from its record, there was an air of mystery surrounding the car. Intrigue and secrecy helped secure its place in history like no other car, and much of the mystery has long been debated, about whether or not the Chaparrals were actually back door Chevrolet engineering jobs. That aspect of the story has been well documented by Chevrolet engineer Paul van Valkenburgh in his book, CHEVROLET = RACING...?

Leading up to the Chaparral requires a look at what Chevrolet was doing and why they became involved with Chaparral Cars. Duntov was head of engines in the high performance development group, and thus Chevrolet was into a number of experimental high performance cars and engines. The Chevrolet Engineering Research Vehicles, CERV-1 of 1960 and the 4-wheel drive CERV-II of 1963, were by all outward descriptions racing cars but internally, they were research vehicles. There was a lot to learn about vehicles dynamics and Ford was putting a lot of pressure on Chevrolet with its "Total Performance" program to race the world's best engineering. Chevrolet couldn't be as visible because of its own management decree, but Duntov still had a Le Mans victory in mind.

That was with the CERV-II, a fully developed chassis that looked like a potential victor.

His earlier Grand Sport Corvette had proven to be an excellent melding of ideas into what a real racing Corvette could be, except for styling. The high front end was the source of aerodynamic lift that never was solved. After the GS program was canceled, Duntov had completed three engines with double overhead cam head conversions on the aluminum small block. These engines dynoed at 550 hp and were certain to give astounding performance in the Grand Sports, if they had actually been mated together. Two of the three cars built at the time had been sold while Duntov kept the third for development. With the restatement of GM's "we're not racing" policy, jobs were on the line and Duntov sold his development GS to Jim Hall who ran the car concurrently with his front engine Chaparral. With this tie-in, Hall's involvement with Chevrolet steadily grew into the advanced Chaparral programs that were Chevrolet R&D projects.

At Nassau in 1963, the Chevrolet gang was there in mass and everyone talked about the turnout of the "factory" Chevrolet team. It was, in fact, just the opposite regardless of what appeared obvious. The gathering of professional teams and drivers who happened to be racing with Chevrolet power was a coincidence of the time and was in no way a factory effort. There were Chevrolet people there, Duntov for one, who attended out of personal interest in the sport. For the record though, three Grand Sports, Roger Penske's Zerex Special, Heuer's Meister Brauser Chaparral-1 and Texan John Mecom's team of the rear engine Scarab and the first Lola GT, all with Chevrolet engines, did indeed appear too much of coincidence not to be a factory team. Many presumed such a gathering to "obviously" be a factory team regardless of the facts.

The facts? Well...When the differentials of the Corvettes began failing due to increased traction from 10-inch wide racing tires, a call to Detroit and subsequent conversation resulted in a fix requiring different gears and oil coolers for the rear ends. When a factory engineer suddenly took vacation to Nassau with heavy luggage, that could be construed and was construed as factory racing.

What had been previously thought to be a run-away week of racing for Carroll Shelby and his team of Cobras became a Chevrolet week. Augie Pabst took the Lola-Chevy to victory in two races. A. J. Foyt won two races in the Scarab-Chevy. Dr. Dick Thompson took the C/Modified class in one of the Grand Sports and could have done better had the aerodynamic lift problem of the Sting Ray styling been solved. What was truly a great week of racing for Chevrolet had been accomplished by independents.

To solve the problem of lift, Duntov proposed to Knudsen to sell off the remaining two Grand Sports and begin a new project as an all-out effort to win the 24-Hours of Le Mans. That was the origin of the CERV-II, and Duntov was convinced that a Chevrolet powered car of the proper design could win. Frank Winchell was head of Chevrolet R&D, and his quest to learn more about vehicle dynamics brought him in close contact with racing. His 2nd in command, Jim Musser, in association with Bill Mitchell's styling group, put together an exotic looking Corvair based sports coupe called the XP-777 and showed it at Road America in late 1962 to test public reaction.

Hall won the feature, the Road America 500, with Heuer in

The Chaparral 2G during the Edmonton Can-Am, Sept. 1968. The 2G was an advancement of the 2E derived from the 2C of 1965 that was built on an aluminum racing chassis. This is considered to be the best of the later Chaparrals although Hall flipped the car end over end several times at Las Vegas destroying the car and causing himself serious injury.

at second. Both were in Troutman and Barnes Chaparrals, and both had beaten the Europeans. Winchell, Musser and company were impressed, and Hall was impressed with the mid-engine XP-777. When he described the mid-engine Chaparral he was working on back in Midland, the Hall-Chevrolet association was born.

Bill Mitchell provided Hall with some aerodynamics advice on the current thought on aerodynamic shaping for the Chaparral that didn't work, so Hall contacted Winchell, and the car was sent over to GM's proving grounds and instrumented. It had enormous front end lift. Winchell had what would later be called an air dam installed and it too proved inadequate, but just the opposite effect. It forced the front of the car down so much that the front tires rubbed through the body. Nothing was really known analytically about automotive aerodynamics, and trimming the "plow" brought the right amount of down force rather than attempts to balance the car with down force on the rear. This work brought about an improved front end for the car that was laid up in Chevrolet R&D in time for the Chaparral-2 to run first in the Riverside Grand Prix where Hall put the car on the pole and lead until an electrical fire sidelined the car. In the next outing at Laguna Seca, Hall ran third and nobody noticed.

The Connection

Winchell began a project dubbed the Grand Sport II. This was a lightweight, mid engine sports car conceived for public consumption. It was built around the aluminum 327 and looked rather like Hall's Chaparral-2 in layout but was a coupe. Over in Mitchell's group, stylist Larry Shinoda had pinned a two-place design of true racing lines in GT form. (Years later, a car of remarkably similar styling, the Chevron B-8, appeared and established a new marque with 4-cylinder engines.)

When it came time to test the Corvette G.S. II, there was no place public that could be used without arousing interest, the embarrassing sort that would demand some answers and Winchell wasn't ready for that. It was the winter of '63 in Detroit, and he went to Hall about using his isolated west Texas tract with its 2-mile "Rattlesnake Raceway" and a 250-ft diameter skid pad. Hall and his experienced crew were just what Winchell needed to thoroughly test a car without nosy press people being the wiser.

A contractual arrangement was made whereby Hall was to be paid for the use of his facilities. Test driving was to be done by Hall, Sharp and Roger Penske who were paid on a per mile basis as driver/engineers. Winchell got the development he wanted, and while providing Chevrolet engineering and technical personnel his Chaparral Cars facilities, Hall gained a valuable inside track on Chevy's performance programs. Musser was the Chevrolet contact for the program.

The G.S. II project went along parallel with Hall's own racing efforts at Midland. Musser's car was mid-engine with

Webers and up-turned exhaust pipes and fitted with an automatic transaxle. Hall's cars were more conventional with available racing ware such as a Colotti transaxle. The single speed automatic had been fully developed by Chevrolet's Jerry Mrlik. Tooling and fabrication was charged under the G.S. II project. Drawings listed the equipment as "Future Corvette". This engine and transaxle was "loaned" to the Chaparral-2.

An automatic. Hmmmm... Why not try it in the Chaparral? So it came to pass that on the 3rd of May, 1964, the Chaparral-2 with the new, low front end without the plow was easily on the pole at Laguna Seca. That was a year after the Chaparral-2 had appeared at Riverside and Laguna Seca with the "ugly" front end. The car was fitted with an aluminum small block and automatic transmission. It was the car's first race in that configuration. Just as easily as Hall put the car on the pole, he just as easily won the race, and no one noticed the autoshifter. So far, so good.

The idea of mating a torque converter to a manual transmission was Mrlik's project, and by the time the new transmission replaced the Colotti in the Chaparrals, it was nearly bullet proof. The first type, a single speed with high gear only, was thought to match up well with the torque of the aluminum small block which put out less power than the iron block. However, a single gear ratio created some slow speed corner exiting problems and that meant a two-speed would be a better choice. Later, for the long distance Chaparral coupes conceived to contest the World Prototype Championship, a three-speed was needed. That was especially so since the more powerful 427 inch engines were used, and Mrlik produced the modified transaxles.

Making a two-speed was little more than making a longer case and adding another gear set, but careful shifting was required. These were really clutchless manuals, and the driver had to be very precise with shifts; back off the throttle and engage the next gear with precision. Each unit went back to Chevrolet R&D for inspection and updates under Mrlik's direction.

The engine/transmission match had been fully developed by Chevrolet R&D, and Hall was to use the equipment at will, but he couldn't talk about it. He was, however, doing development work for Chevrolet rather than racing for Chevrolet while he was also accomplishing his own objectives in advancing racing car technology. His organization was miles ahead of Winchell and Musser in what it took to race and win while the Chevy guys had a lot more engineers, the latest hardware and the instrumentation to determine what was going on. Both teams were interested in the same thing, vehicle dynamics, but for different reasons. While the Chevy guys had to stay quiet about what they were doing, Hall was out in the public eye. The automotive press began seeing more and more innovative racing hardware coming from Chaparral Cars, and that tended to raise public awareness of Hall's equipment, regardless of where it originated.

Then came the idea of rear down force. Hall experimented with a rear spoiler on the open 2C, but as a driver he also was aware of limiting visibility. So, he devised a hydraulically actuated rear "flipper" that could be lowered to produce a

Two versions of the endurance racing coupes were the 2F shown here and the 2D in the next photo. At Daytona 1967, this 2F handled by Phil Hill and Mike Spence dropped out early. Daytona Speedway photo.

The 2D was updated with the air intake scoop on the top and the rear spoiler for endurance races such as Daytona (shown here in '67) and the European championship events both the 2F and 2D raced in. This was the car that Jo Bonnier and Phil Hill raced to victory at Nurburgring in 1966, Chaparral's first (and only) European win in 1966. Daytona Speedway photo.

smoother rear surface on high speed straights and raised up in turns to increase rear adhesion. This control surface was actuated by a third pedal that was installed for driver control. Third pedal? All Chaparrals had automatics by then.

Van Valkenburgh relates that solving the problem of excessive down force was the subject of a Chevrolet bull session that took the idea of a rear spoiler to suspension mounted struts that held a wing over the car. When first seen in competition, it became known as the Chaparral wing. "...no one on the ad hoc committee was certain whose idea it was - so the patent was issued to Jim Hall and Frank Winchell and Jim Musser and Jerry Mrlik (who inherited the Chaparral project when Musser was promoted). Hall was most often lauded for the successful ideas, in spite of his careful but obscure, 'We did this...'."

The Wing

The concept of the wing was not new at that time. It had been demonstrated in competition during 1954 at Nurburgring on a private entry Porsche. The car was turning better lap times than the factory entries, and a protest by the factory had it removed "for safety reasons". The car was no longer competitive which proved the effectiveness of factory pressure. It also proved the effectiveness of the wing, but the device was not pursued until the Chaparral era.

Van Valkenburgh was a Chevrolet engineer and aerodynamicist in the R&D group. He was centrally involved in the technical development of the wing and states that its specifications were based on NACA Aerofoil Data. He had the first wing whittled out of a slab of pine and mounted on a Sting Ray coupe that he tested at GM's Tech Center in 1966. "It was not quite up to expectations, but it was good enough for Joe Kurleto to proceed on his superlightweight foam-filled monocoque racing wing."

Once on the new Chaparral 2E, the first race for the wing was Bridgehampton 1966. What began was a season of frustration with mechanical failures. There has been speculation that Jim Hall would have won more races without Chevrolet's help. So many new ideas showed up in completely new cars that Chaparral Cars was overwhelmed with the need to thoroughly develop something competitive. While on the track, Chaparrals were fast, but they rarely lasted the distance.

Kurleto continued to make improved wings, but mounting and actuation was left up to Chaparral. In time, growing complaints from competitors and increasing awareness of potentially severe failures caused the devices to be banned. If a wing or supporting strut should break while in a high speed load condition, the effect would be instantaneous and very likely disastrous.

Theory Versus Practice

Hall saw it coming and anted up the long, slender 2H. Recalling that his first Chaparral-2 had been the most successful of all the cars, Hall ventured into this one with autonomy. The beginning of the 2H appears to be with a set of drawings that van Valkenburgh sent to Hall in the summer of 1966. By early 1968, the car was in testing, but aerodynamic thinking had changed. No longer was long and slender the ideal, low and wide was "in". Comparison to the McLarens, whose development was more seat-of-the-pants, showed the latter effect empirically. If it works, its better. McLarens were low and wide and winners.

The 2H was a year late in appearing, and Hall ran the 2G during the '68 season. Development of the 2H necessarily slowed because Chaparral Cars was trying to be competitive with two different and frustratingly demanding cars. One was an older car needing development, the other was a new one needing development. Neither proved successful while Team McLaren cleaned house. They had wings, too, but theirs never gave any problems. Even year old McLarens were more competitive overall than Chaparrals. Then Hall crashed the 2G at Las Vegas and came away with serious injuries. His racing was over for a while and another driver was needed. John Surtees was brought on the team from England as development and racing driver for the 2H. A back-up car was needed, but there were no competitive Chaparrals. Surtees persuaded Hall to buy a McLaren. In due course, a white M-12 McLaren bearing the number 7 showed up racing for team Chaparral, a British car and British driver.

This McLaren was the first M-12 to leave the factory although it was chassis number 5 and 13th on the list of orders. The reason it was done so quickly was that Chaparral engine man, Gary Knutson, had talked ex-McLaren works fabricator Barry Crow into leaving John Surtees' works to join Chaparral and events had Crow back at McLaren building the car. Following Hall's crash in the 2G at Las Vegas and subsequent recovery, Surtees was hired as Chaparral development and competition driver for the 2H program. After testing the car, Surtees was not impressed and insisted through Chuck Hall that a McLaren back-up car be purchased. What he wanted was a year old works M-8, but McLaren would not sell one. Thus, Crow and Surtees were not parting ways after all, and John sent Barry to McLaren to construct the M-12 that Chaparral ordered.

Crow began work on the car in early 1969 and spent two months fabricating everything to complete the M-12 from Trojan's chassis. Trojan was the customer car builder of McLaren cars and offered buyers improved M-6 McLarens with some updates and what were essentially M-8 bodies. Crow arrived in Midland with the M-12 about a month before the first race of the '69 Can-Am season. He had set the car up for the aluminum Mk IV Chevrolet 427/430 engine. Chevrolet built similar engines with cross-over manifolds for the 2H and sent them to Chaparral. They also powered the M-12. The 430 could be taken to 494 cubic inches, and later was.

In testing, Surtees recalls that, "It was thought that the McLaren could have been made competitive at least for the early season races so that the Chaparral could possibly be used later in the year for places like Riverside where in theory it could have been extremely quick. While I do not know the full story of the politics which existed between GM and Jim Hall from the very outset the new car was in no way going to become a serious competitor for top honors inspite of having certain features which were certainly worthy of expansion and possible development. This immediately created a problem in that the McLaren was looked upon as being the reason why I did not want to drive the new development car and this was, of course, partly correct because the McLaren was both safer and faster and with the team playing a full part could have possibly brought the right sort of results which any racing programme must aim for i.e. to win. I would like to say...that the type of car like the McLaren and the Lolas which competed at the time in the Can-Am series were some of the most enjoyable and certainly most interesting sports racing cars of any period, and I had immense pleasure from driving in the Can-Am events. I feel that it was a great shame that the powers that be allowed the formula to get out of hand from its original concept, which in the end brought it to its downfall..."

Surtees ran the car in two races without the Chaparral wing, but then thought it would be an improvement. The struts, uprights and wing came off the crashed Chaparral 2G. During the season, another edge was developed, a larger engine, the first 494.

Barry Crow recalls, "The first 494 cubic inch engine that was ever built was built at Chaparral, and it was built for the M-12 McLaren to go to Riverside with, Riverside and Laguna. That was exciting because we saw more torque that we hadn't seen before. It was done in a discussion between Gary and I, and Surtees. Basically what happened was, Jim then decided that John had to drive the Chaparral, the 2H, and the M-12 was parked. Gary then sold the engine to Carl Haas. Chuck Parsons who was driving Haas' Lola was fastest down the chute at Riverside by about 4 or 5 miles per hour. So, you can imagine what would have happened if we had had it in the M-12 with Surtees behind the wheel. That was a very political year because, by that time, John and Jim were not talking. I was the gentleman in the middle passing messages back and forth. Soon after that, John and Jim severed their contract, and the following year, the 494 was all that was produced, the Chaparral engine."

A year later, the 2H was written off by Tom Dutton when he hit the wall at Texas International Speedway. The entire unit structure of the car was cracked.

The Chaparral Record

GM's corporate restatement of the AMA ban left little more than under the table racing out of Chevrolet. Unlike GM, Ford was mounting a massive program of racing. Ford's recovery from the AMA ban began when Robert McNamara left to become US Secretary of Defense for President John F. Kennedy, and Lee Iacocca took over with his policy of "Total Performance" - the most ambitious racing program any American manufacturer had ever undertaken. Dearborn's pride was the all-new GT-40 prototype to contest international racing at the highest levels as a showcase of Ford engineering.

It was in such a climate that the Chevrolet powered Chaparral-2 emerged as the dominate prototype car. While Ford was being open about its racing interests, GM was not. In that car, Jim Ellis Hall and James R."Hap" Sharp produced the pride of Texas in the form of another open road racer.

With downdraft fuel injection and without the Chaparral wing, Surtees in the M-12 pulls away from McLaren works drivers McLaren and Hulme at Mosport, 1969. The M-12 was a combination of M-6 chassis and M-8A and M-8B works cars. Lionel Birnbom photo courtesy Dr. Jerry Winston.

On the starting grid at Mosport 1969, Surtees looks over his drive. Like all the McLarens, the Chaparral M-12 displays the low and wide profile developed during the '60s but proven aerodynamically years later. Ford Motor Co. photo.

McLarens were the most illustrious home for road racing versions of Chevrolet's Mk IV big block V-8. Only on a rare occasion did a Ford powered Can-Am car even lead a Can-Am race. Wins were most often between Mclaren works drivers.

At the time, the Can-Am was the world's most competitive series for professional drivers in sprint style racing and was a Chevrolet showcase.

Equal length tubular headers were so common by the late '60s that "bundles of snakes" resided in the engine bays of all sports-racing cars. Kinsler fuel injection was run by the Chaparral team.

427 cid; 620 hp @ 7000 rpm
465 cid; 670 hp @ 7000 rpm
494 cid; 740 hp @ 6400 rpm

At Le Mans '67, the lap times of this Chaparral proved so convincing that the race organizers, in their normal fashion, banned off-the-body aerofoils. Automatic transmission problems sidelined this Phil Hill/Mike Spence driven entry. Ford Motor Co. photo.

Although Spence took 5 seconds off the sports-prototype record at Nurburgring while setting the first 100 mph sports car lap at the 'Ring, the finish was another DNF for Chaparral. The transmission failed again. Hill and Spence regained a portion of Chaparral's glory by winning the Brands Hatch 6-Hour with an average speed of 93.08 mph in the team's final race of the '67 season. That was Chaparral's second of two wins in Europe. Ford Motor Co. photo.

The Chaparral-2 received that designation because it was the second car Hall was involved in with that name. Hall described the first Chaparrals, the aluminum bodied and tubular frame front engine cars built by Dick Troutman and Tom Barnes in '61, as cars he thought could have been competitive against European entries. He relates that six of the first Chaparrals were built, two were raced by Hall and Sharp while the others were sold. The T&B Chaparrals were up against the new era of engines behind the driver.

Hall became an accomplished automotive engineer with these cars, and he says they became pretty good racing cars about the time they were obsolete. They had some problems that he undertook to solve with his Chaparral-2, the first cars Hall and Sharp built in their shop in the rather desolate oil town of Midland, Texas. These new cars were conceived, designed and built in the early '60s for the professional racing series of the time, the top rung of sports car racing in this country. The pro-series predated the much more acclaimed Canadian-American Challenge Cup Series that really got rolling in the latter part of the decade.

The new Chaparrals introduced many Chevy versus Ford controversies. When the Chaparral began winning in 1964, Ford was making its move into international endurance racing. In '65, a GT-40 took its first win, the Daytona 24-Hour. Then came the Chaparral win at Sebring, and few people really believed that a couple of guys, even Texans, could design and build their own race car and beat all the might of Dearborn in it. There was tremendous fan enthusiasm and admiration for the Chaparral team, and their support was rewarded when Hall and Sharp won at Sebring. It was time for the under-dogs to beat the big guys.

The AMA ban had been re-stated by GM in 1963, yet there were all sorts of behind-the-scenes ties with Chevrolet engineering and a few racing teams were running some pretty exotic stuff, the sort that average teams were not likely to have

unless they had either lots money and talent, as in oil man Jim Hall's case, or they had factory ties, which was also well known in Hall's case.

Ford was saying up front that they were going after victory at Le Mans, and consequently Ferrari, to prove Ford engineering was second to none in the heat of international racing. The epic struggle of the Chaparral-2/GT-40 controversy stemmed from the match-up of the tiny Hall & Sharp Chaparral effort with about 8 to 10 people against Ford's megabuck GT-40s. Chevy fans rejoiced with the Chaparral wins, and Ford fans claimed the cars were really Chevrolet-built cars spirited out the back-door to Hall.

"Not so," says the tall, quiet Texan. "My wife, Sandy, and I shaped the clay for the body of that car. We just decided what it should look like and did it! We assembled the car right there in Midland and tested it on the Rattlesnake Raceway. Andy Green of Fort Worth manufactured the fiberglass tub."

The use of fiberglass as a chassis structural material was very innovative and a highly unusual feature of the Chaparral-2; not steel as in the GT-40 or aluminum as in Lolas and McLarens. Hall simply used fiberglass with reinforcing lightweight metal alloy in strategic locations. It was a novel approach indeed, but proved to be both strong and durable. The body was also fiberglass, and the whole assembly produced a car weighing just 1,650 pounds compared to the GT-40's weight of over 2,000 pounds. A good deal of the engineering in the Chaparral-2 came from Hall himself, a mechanical engineer who earned his letters from the California Institute of Technology.

One highly controversial feature of the car was the famous and ultra-secret "automatic" transmission. Of the two-speed, it was said to have only two speeds, fast and faster. It was another item referred to as a Chevy back-door piece, and was in fact the product of Jerry Mrlik as related earlier.

The first single speed Chaparral "automatic" used a fluid torque converter with dog clutches. When the 2-speed came along, drivers made all shift changes by easing off the throttle to lessen the load on the dogs and shifted. With no requirement of operating a clutch pedal, drivers could "left foot brake" in turns which improved cornering times. At around 5,000 rpm the transmission locked-up mechanically to prevent further slippage. Thus, it was actually a clutchless manual using a fluid clutch for coupling.

A fascinating aspect of the story was that no one noticed the Chaparral was running an automatic until the fourth race of the season when a competitor happened to be alongside the car in a turn. A gear change was made, but Hall had both hands on the wheel. Something "funny" was going on, and once the word got out, attention of the entire motoring press turned toward the car and curiosity abounded. Hall and his Chaparral team were tight-lipped about it. Thus, the mystery.

Ford experimented with automatics but couldn't get them to work reliably while the Chaparrals ran simple but effective units, one of Hall's most satisfying achievements.

Another feature of the Chaparral-2 was its mid-mounted Chevy small block. It was an all-aluminum 327, just 327 cubic inches, producing about 420 horsepower at 7,000 rpm. When asked why he didn't use much more powerful versions of the engine, such as the 520 hp, 377 inch fuel injected engine Bill Thomas built, Hall says simply, "We didn't need it."

One reason was the nature of the automatic transmission. More power would have been tougher on it mechanically. Another reason was the engine itself, a pure racing variety rather than a converted production engine. These special powerplants came through Roger Penske who was a promising young driver and a dynamic salesman with the Aluminum Corporation of America. Earlier, Alcoa had done the castings for Duntov's ill-fated Grand Sport Corvette. That project was canned by the revival of the AMA ban, and the Grand Sports didn't get the engines. Winchell's Grand Sport II project was being developed at Chaparral Cars, and because of being under the same roof, Hall's race cars were presented with the opportunity of receiving a 110 pound lighter engine and an automatic transmission.

The Chaparral-2 raced three times late in the 1963 season. At Riverside in October, Hall went up against a star-studded field of drivers including Europeans Graham Hill, Jimmy Clark, Pedro Rodriguez and Roy Salvadori. America's own aces, Dan Gurney, John Surtees, A. J. Foyt, Parnelli Jones, Augie Pabst, Roger Penske and Richie Ginther were this country's top drivers. Hall qualified fastest and led from the flag to out-distance all challengers by a considerable margin until an electrical fire sidelined the car on the fourth lap.

In its second race, at Laguna Seca, Hall qualified a more conservative 4th and finished 3rd. Then the end-of-year Nassau Speed Week brought together the season finale where Hall ran strong but was put out by mechanical problems.

With further improvements, stronger suspension, wider wheels and the like, the Chaparral-2 came on strong in 1964 to take 7 victories (two of these were FIA international wins), 6 seconds and finished in the top three 15 times in 15 races. A two-car team ran for most of the season, although three cars existed at the time, and out of 24 starts the Chaparral-2 team made, only in 8 races did the cars not finish.

Still more improvements for the 1965 season brought huge success. In 34 starts, the cars won 15 races and retired only 3 times with 28 top three finishes in a 20 race schedule. Ten of those were FIA races, and the Chaparrals were 1st or 2nd in each one and took seven victories, an astounding record.

The Sebring 12-Hour of 1965 was flooded with torrential rains that hampered the performance of all the cars. The resulting average speed of the Hall and Sharp win of 84.72 mph was only a little faster overall than the Fangio/Castelotti win of 1956 in a Ferrari.

Looking back from today's vantage point makes the Sebring win all the more important. The reason is that most of the recent wins on that Florida circuit have gone to German cars, and you have to go back to the late 1960s to find another American winner. The GT-40 Fords won Sebring in 1969, '67 and '66. But before them was the Hall/Sharp victory of '65, and that was only the second time an American car had won! The first was in 1953 when Briggs Cunningham's Chrysler hemi powered C-4R won the first FIA sanctioned 12-Hours of Sebring. That puts the Chaparral victory into a very select group. Only three American marques have won Sebring; Cunningham, Chaparral and Ford.

Hap Sharp recalls, "I started racing in Corvettes in 1958 and was usually somewhere in the front of most races in our part of the country. An Ace-Bristol beat me in the rain once, and Jim and I got started when I bought one from his dealership. I later bought a 2-liter Maserati from him. When he moved to west Texas, he and I and some other guys built a race track out there (Rattlesnake Raceway), and after a few years of racing and trying to get spare parts from the Europeans, for the money we were spending, we decided we could build a car for ourselves. That's how it all got started. Jim admired the rear engine Cooper and Lotus Formula cars, and that inspired him.

Hall remembers Sebring as the great deluge. "We had a five lap lead during the rain when the fastest competitor was running 22 minutes a lap. In the pit, Hap and I had a big discussion about going back out. If the car sat there for an hour, we would still have had the lead, but Hap wanted to go back out. I gave in, and he jumped in the car. His first lap took 20 minutes. All the time, we were wondering if he was stuck in a puddle somewhere, but he finally came by at maybe 40 or 50 mph.

"Water was so deep in places, that it came in the radiator opening and up over the top of the car and filled up the cockpit. While Hap was out, it had gotten dark. When he came in, he was cold and wet and ready to get out, but I said I didn't know where the puddles were so he should continue driving. You should have seen the look on his face! But he did it and drove another hour and a half, three hours in the rain. I drove the last hour of the race (finishing 4 laps ahead of a

The Chaparral 2H was an aerodynamic wonder, but long and slender was good only for going fast in a straight line. Contrasting that theme, the McLaren cars were low and wide and winners. Speculation at the time was that Surtees would have been more competitive in this car, the M-12, than the 2H but Hall parked the car early in the season.

GT-40). So, Hap is the rain driver."

This victory was remarkable not only because it was largely a Jim Hall/Hap Sharp effort, it was also a thorough drubbing of Ford's massive GT-40 effort. The nearest GT-40 finished four laps behind the Chaparral-2.

Following the Chaparral-2 were the later 2C, an open Can-Am car, and 2D coupe for endurance racing. Then the open 2E Can-Am car which was the 2C with a new body and with the wing. Then came the 2F endurance coupes with the wing, open 2G Can-Am cars, the unsuccessful 2H and then the 2J ground effect "Sucker Car". In all, there were perhaps 20 Chaparrals, Hall estimates, not including the Troutman and Barnes cars. Some were built on chassis of earlier cars, but however many there were, he still has them all.

The 2J positioned Hall amid more controversy. Paul van Valkenburgh says the car originated with a crayon sketch an anonymous young fan sent to Hall of a "racing car held down with horizontal fans sucking the air out from below it. A few months worth of basic research with fans and sealing methods demonstrated that the idea was feasible, and I tested a crude device on the old Suspension Test Vehicle in November 1968. Charlie Simmons, the new head of R&D...gave Don Gates all the draftsmen, technicians and budget he needed to have it ready during the next racing season - in case Hall still had problems with the 2H".

The "Sucker Car" proved to be a big disappointment to Hall who shut the project down and closed up the Can-Am shop.

He was also running the Chaparral Camaros, so he turned his attention to those cars. Vic Elford won at Watkins Glen in the Camaro, and the team finished the season 3rd overall.

Still later, he and Carl Haas teamed to manage Formula 5000 cars that Brian Redman drove to the championship in 1974, '75 and '76. When full bodied Can-Am cars replaced F-5000 rules, Hall and his Chaparral Cars team won the championship in 1977 and '78. Then into Indy style cars for 1978, the team won all three USAC 500-mile races, Indianapolis, Pocono and Ontario. Then they won Indianapolis again in 1980 with the ground-effect Chaparral 2K and took both the USAC and CART National Championships!

With that sort of record, it is obvious that Jim Hall knows how to build winning cars. In fact, he frequently found himself with outlawed cars because some rules committee changed the rules. He simply adjusted his strategy and built other cars.

The Chaparral-2 started that trend. It was the first Jim Hall/Hap Sharp design, and as drivers, they won 21 of 41 races entered, including Sebring, where they beat the might of Ford and Ferrari combined. There were those who thought that Ford bit off a lot to go up against Ferrari, but then, for two guys to tackle both Ford and Ferrari, it was simply insane.

"The Chaparral-2 was one of the most successful cars we built," confirmed Hall. "There were big wins with later cars, the '66 Nurburgring 1000 Km in a 2D, the '67 BOAC 500 at Brands Hatch with a 2F and others, but for me as a driver, Sebring was the biggest."

The beautiful Lola T-70 was rewarded with major championships when John Surtees won the 1966 Can-Am season by edging out Chaparral in the last race of the season. The next year, Mark Donohue charged to the front of the USRRC series to take the title in 1967 driving this car, Roger Penske's Sunoco Special.

Lola's Racing Tradition

In 1975, Lola Cars, Ltd. produced their 1000th car. All 1000 were racing cars in one form or another. This figure alone should go a long way toward putting Lola at the top of the list of the winningest marque in modern racing history.

From the little 1.1-liter Mk I Lola-Climax of 1958, the Lola racing tradition evolved through the Lola GT of 1963 that became the world champion GT-40 Fords. After that came the T-70 Can-Am cars of 1966 that later became endurance racing coupes. There was also the Indianapolis T-90 of 1966, then the famed Jackie Stewart T-260 Can-Am car of '71. Later, the Formula-5000 T-330 of '74 and finally the IMSA GTP T-600 ground effect coupe conceived by Brian Redman and driven by him to the GTP championship in '81. Each of these cars is considered a Lola milestone design and counts for a quarter-century of race winning designs from Eric Broadley.

The tiny 4-banger Mk I proved capable of beating much more powerful cars in its day. Excellent handling combined with only about 900 pounds total weight gave the 95 hp Coventry-Climax powered cars a power-to-weight ratio of 0.11. The fastest cars of the time were likely the Lister-Corvettes with 265 hp and weighing 2010 pounds. Their ratio of

0.132 was almost twenty percent higher than the Lolas, but on tighter courses, the Lola's handling excelled. These were the cars that Broadley staked his future on when he gave up his engineering job to form Lola Cars.

With the successes of rear-engine cars around 1960, Broadley turned his attention in that direction and designed the Lola GT. Even though he was on a shoestring budget, the car ran rather successfully on Ford power at Le Mans '63 getting up to 8th after 10 hours. Then, after merging with Ford, the Lola GT became the awesome GT-40s that trounced all competition with a legend of high speed endurance. Disenchanted, Broadley broke from his Ford association to produce cars on his own again and introduced his Lola T-70.

The reliable GT-40s were his most fearsome competition until the Porsche 917s emerged even more fearsome in 1970-71. The T-70 was lighter and both quicker and faster than the GT-40, but it didn't have the long distance reliability of the Fords. That is probably not surprising in that the T-70 was aimed at Can-Am style racing rather than GT endurance events. Building on the successes earned by John Surtees who won the '66 Can-Am title in a Lola, Broadley found himself with a growing demand for his T-70.

Group-7 racing was flourishing in England, and Lola built 47 T-70/T-70 Mk II cars in the 1965-66 period. The '67 Can-Am rules for sports and GT racing were unclear and set no maximum on prototype engine capacity. That allowed Broadley to fit a aerodynamic GT coupe body to the normally open T-70 Can-Am cars which broadened the market for

The Lola T-70 was produced first in 1965 and originally intended to receive Ford's small V-8, but the small block Chevrolet proved superior.

A blur of speed was what Eric Broadley's Lola T-70 gave to racing. The Lola-Chevy was hard to beat in flat-out sprint style sports car competition.

Lola cars considerably. This venture into GT racing resulted in beefing up the Mk II suspension for added weight of the coupe body to increase durability for endurance racing. That car became the Mk IIIB.

The T-70 coupe remains one of the most beautiful racing cars ever conceived. Normally, these cars were fitted with Chevrolet's 5.4-liter, 460 horsepower V-8 engine, but there was also the Lola-Aston Martin coupe which received the new AM V-8 of the time. The Lola-Aston appeared first at the 1967 Le Mans test day where it was third fastest. But during the Nurburgring 1000 Km race, and Le Mans which followed, all Lola entrants did not finish because of mechanical failures. At the Reims 12-Hour which followed, four entrants held the top four positions after a few laps, but they were out after four hours. The Lolas were quite fast but lacked durability. Even though they were campaigned at Le Mans over the next four years, none finished a single race.

For the 1968 season, FIA limited prototype engine capacity to 3-liters and GTs to 5-liters. This was the year of the John Wyer-Gulf GT-40 and Mirage cars. Contrasting the Lolas, the light blue and orange Gulf-Fords were overwhelmingly reliable and won five FIA races to take the World Championship. One of those wins was the prestigious victory at Le Mans in 1968 followed by another victory in the famed 24-Hours the following year in the same car. Lola earned no points in the 1968 international championship series due to mechanical problems in most cases.

However, in shorter sprint type events, Lola took four victories with Brian Redman, Denny Hulme and Frank Gardner driving. Then for 1969, FIA dropped their minimum production requirements to just 25 units for GT cars. Instantly, the T-70s found themselves faced with two more fierce competitors. Factory car from Porsche, the 917, and Ferrari with its 512 came on the scene, and the T-70 was instantly obsolete. But they were not dead and even showed some long sought after durability when Mark Donohue brought the Penske/Sunoco T-70 in first overall for a Lola 1-2 finish in the Daytona 24-Hour enduro of 1969.

In lesser international events that year, Lola cars would again be strong in the hands of privateers. They won at

The Weber fueled small block was a tight fit in the T-70 Mk IIIB engine bay. It was the choice of Can-Am and USRRC racers. 460 hp @ 7500 rpm gave tall performance.

Silverstone, Snetterton, Thruxton, Monthlery twice, the Martini Trophy and the Tourist Trophy with drivers Redman, Hulme, Paul Hawkins, David Piper and Jo Bonnier showing that Lola GTs were excellent performers in short but fast races.

Lola couldn't compete with Porsche and Ferrari in the new FIA rules, and, of course, the Fords were still there. In '69, the GT-40 again won Le Mans, Ford's fourth victory in a row, and Porsche was chagrinned to be beaten by such an old car running a stock block 5-liter engine. Zuffenhausen gave up competing with John Wyer and hired him to manage their championship series 917 racing team. With Wyer's direction, the Gulf-Porsches brought Stuttgart into the golden era of Porsche dominance in international racing with two more world championships, 1970 and '71.

Against such competition, Lola returned to building Can-Am cars and brought out their T-160. A new series in the early '70s offered Broadley more opportunities and he ventured into the new open-wheel F-5000 racing with the T-150. Among the Can-Am cars, for instance, the T-165 for 1970 was fitted with a Chevy/Chaparral alloy engine with 437 cubic inches and Lucas-Kinsler fuel injection delivering about 700 horsepower. It showed lightening acceleration and top speeds around 200 mph. The car was a rocket on wheels with 0-60 times of 2.3 seconds. In the '71 season, the L&M team signed on Jackie Stewart to handle the Lola T-260 against the reigning McLarens, but even with his skill, the Lola was no match for the orange Kiwis.

Then Porsche invaded Can-Am racing. Again, Lola was well down in the field with cars that might have been world contenders with sufficient development. It was a case of the big guys moving in. Tiny Lola Cars, Ltd. was just Eric Broadley doing what he did best, but against the factories, it was tough going.

In typical form, the Lola T-70 series of cars were powered by Chevrolet V-8s displacing 4,990cc (304 cubic inches).

These small block engines produced around 430 bhp at 7,300 rpm with Webers and a compression ratio of 11:1. Such engines were conventional overhead valve cast iron Chevy derived from production based equipment.

A Hewland 5-speed LG500 or LG600 transaxle backed up the mid-mounted engine, and a healthy 12-inch Girling disc brake system all around gave the 1,940 pound cars excellent stopping power. Bodies were fiberglass over an aluminum monocoque chassis.

Fifteen years later, the small block powered T-600 of 1981 became another of Broadley's great cars. Then the later T-710 Corvette GTP carried on the tradition of Chevrolet powered Lola road racers. That legacy is a 1/4-century of race winning cars from the mind of one man; Eric Broadley.

As always, Bruce McLaren (#4) and Denny Hulme (#5) charge from the front row during the 1969 Can-Am season. These are M-8B works cars. Lionel Birmbom photo courtesy Dr. Jerry Winston.

Can-Am McLaren

Throughout motor racing history, there have been periods of domination by particular marques. Bugatti, Bentley, Alfa Romeo, BMW and Mercedes-Benz come immediately to mind as prewar marques that so overshadowed competitive events that they became legends in there own time.

As the postwar years unfolded, the competitive entanglements became so intense that it was rare for one marque to prevail over all others. Ferrari certainly ranks in that category as does Ford with the GT-40 endurance racing coupes.

Sports car racing has risen and fallen on good and bad times as available funds to support car building and racing have waxed and waned, but when the factories were involved, fans were sure that contests would be hard fought. Overall, the more competitive the series, the more fans it drew. Thus, larger purses could be offered and that drew better and better teams and drivers.

One of the all-time favorites throughout the world has been Formula-1 racing that has crowned both a constructor and driver world champion each year. The F-1 style of competition has always been flat-out, 10/10s from flag to flag. The thrill of such racing has drawn fans for decades, and all other events preceding an F-1 events were little more than warmups to get the crowds ready for the feature event.

In 1966, the price of a customer Mk 2 McLaren was $11,500 without engine. With a 333 cid Traco built small block Chevy cranking out 465 hp, they were very competitive.

And they are still competitive as was shown by Mike Murray who won the Central Florida Region A/Sports Racing championship of 1988 in this car.

In America, though, Formula-1 has never caught on the way it has in Europe. In this country, full-bodied cars have always been more popular, and out of that style of cars grew several professional series. First came the fall-of-the-year Pro Series of the early '60s. Then there was the United States Road Racing Championship (USRRC) followed the the Canadian-American Challenge Cup, the Can-Am.

Like Formula-1 racing, Can-Am was also flat-out, 10/10s all the way. The series flourished for about 10 years then languished during the austere '70s when the technically superior Porsche turbocharged cars ruled complete. What the fans liked was the ground pounding roar of American V-8s, and shake the ground they did. Imagine the flagman unleashing 35 cars to have a go at winning - with an accumulated roar of 22,000 hp.

The Can-Am was one of the most competitive road racing series ever fought on American soil. The potential of huge winnings was only part of the lure; corporate financial backing was growing, and racing was now more than an outlet for drivers who had the urge to win. It had become a lucrative profession entwined with personal aspirations of drivers whose lives became dominated by racing. Some lost their lives to the game.

To go ever faster and quicker was the goal of builders who made the cars that drivers could further their quest for glory. The man-and-machine symbiosis was as strong as ever. Can-Am produced great men and great cars still admired as among the best that racing has ever seen.

The most remarkable aspect of Can-Am racing in its first six years was the domination by Bruce McLaren's orange "Batmobiles" as they came to be called. McLaren was from New Zealand, the home of the flightless apteryx, better known as the kiwi bird. The symbol of the long beak kiwi was seen on a variety of McLaren racing cars, and they were frequent visitors to the winner's circle.

Bruce McLaren's own racing ability reached worldwide acclaim when he became a driver for Britain's Cooper Car Co. Formula-1 team with Jack Brabham who won the World

Driver's Championship in 1959 and '60. A few years later, McLaren moved on to designing, building and racing of his own cars, and one type was intended for Can-Am racing.

"We must have trained them well," confirms John Cooper. "Both our drivers went on to build their cars, and both won the World Championship with their own cars."

Attracted by the huge purses that grew to over $500,000, competition in the Can-Am was fierce and attracted many of the world's best teams and drivers. But, what is most astounding about that flat-out, sprint style of big-bore racing is that Bruce McLaren's cars dominated the series almost from the beginning and didn't relinquish that position until the coming of the turbocharged Porsches in 1972.

The first of the McLaren line was the 4.5-liter Oldsmobile powered M-1A of 1965. They ran in the four race schedule of the fall-of-the-year Pro Series put on in the western U.S., the forerunner of the Can-Am. The last of the line were the M-8F works McLarens that won the marque's fifth consecutive championship in 1971.

The first Can-Am Challenge Cup series was run in the fall of 1966. The six race schedule saw John Surtees take five wins and the championship in a Lola. Among the competition were Jim Hall's Chaparrals that were tremendously successful in USRRC racing in 1965 but didn't have the reliability for the Can-Am. The only 1966 Chaparral Can-Am win was by Dan Gurney, one out of six races. Back in the field were a number of high caliber drivers, among them were Bruce McLaren and Chris Amon in new M-6A McLarens. They earned three 2nd and three 3rd place finishes during that season to give McLaren as a marque a third overall finish in the standings.

For 1967, Britisher Robin Herd joined McLaren's works in Great Britain and designed the Formula McLarens, the M-2A and M-2B Formula-1 cars and the M-4A and M-4B Formula-2 cars. Next came the M-6 Chevrolet Can-Am car, a conventional monocoque chassis fitted with a 5.9-liter (359 cid) Chevy engine built by Al Bartz Engineering of Van Nuys, California. Bartz engines received McLaren's own dry-sump lubrication and his own fuel injection with Lucas nozzles and a Hilborn pump driven off the engine. McLaren's engine man, Gary Knutsen, did the tuning. These cast iron block engines (4.04 x 3.50 inch bore and stroke) proved phenomenally reliable.

M6 bodywork of an open fiberglass layout painted in Team McLaren orange soon evolved into sleek wedges that the line became noted for. Jim Hall's Chaparrals ran with a wing, one of several devices developed in association with Chevrolet, but few other cars including McLarens ran such equipment. Later, above-the-body aerofoils were ruled out and non-movable wings were incorporated into the rear body section of later cars. Generally, only Chaparral and McLaren ran with wings.

The 53,101 spectators on hand for the opening race of the 1967 Can-Am season at Road America, Elkhart Lake in Wisconsin, saw sudden mastery of the series unfolding for McLaren and his cars. Denny Hulme set a new qualifying record a full ten seconds a lap faster than Pete Revson's Lola had reached just a month before. Apparently, the wing was beneficial. Hulme set a new trap speed better than 180 mph, and the race average speed rose to over 104 mph for the first time. Although Bruce won the pole from team-mate Denny Hulme, it was Hulme who ran away with the race by averaging 104.454 mph and set a new lap record of 106.746 mph over the 4.0-mile Road America road course.

Elkhart Lake was the real beginning for McLaren and Hulme although McLaren's firm had been established in 1963. This twosome went on to win four of the next five races, Hulme taking Bridgehampton and Mosport after Elkhart Lake while McLaren won at Laguna Seca and Riverside. With two 2nds at Mosport and Bridgehampton, McLaren cars clinched the marques's first Can-Am championship, and Hulme became Driver of the Year. Bruce McLaren's cars proved to be the quickest thing on the road, and with greater than 1.2 G lateral acceleration, they were the fastest full bodied cars that ever went around a corner.

With growing success surrounding his cars, McLaren continued development of works entries while Trojan, McLaren's customer car builder, put the M-6 into production. Trojan built 20 M-6B Chevy powered cars for private entry Group 7 teams. The works M-6A cars led to the first M-8A for the 1968 Can-Am season. The M-8 was designed by Gordon Coppuck and Jo Marquart who replaced Herd upon his move to a 4-wheel-drive Cosworth GP car project. the M-8 was a little sleeker than the M6. Its main feature was an aluminum alloy 7-liter (427 cid) Chevrolet engine rather than the earlier cast iron, 350 cid Chevy small blocks.

Design features of the M-8 included 20 gage sheet aluminum with sheet magnesium for the undertray. Riveting and epoxy bonding of the sheet metal produced a monocoque structure that weighed only 80 pounds, 30 lighter than the M-6, and gave a torsional stiffness of 3000 ft-lb per degree. Bulkheads were fabricated steel with the engine being a stress member of the chassis. Bodies were built in four detachable pieces. Front and rear track was selected at 57.5/54.5 inches respectively on a wheelbase of 94 inches, and overall length reached 153 inches. Power was delivered via a triple plate dry

Charlie Hayes in the Smothers Brothers Mk 2 McLaren at Las Vegas, November 1967. The proof of the Mk 2 design had been proven by Chuck Parsons in 1966 when he won the USRRC in a McLaren-Chevrolet.

Denny Hulme signaling from his M-6 to enter the pits at Las Vegas. During the following year with updated cars, Bruce McLaren won the Time Grand Prix at Riverside in a similar works M-8A and finished 2nd in the Can-Am series.

clutch to a Hewland LG500 4-speed gearbox.

The 7-liter Chevrolet engine used for the first time in '68 was the ultra high performance, staggered valve ZL-1 that was similar in form to all other Mk IV Chevy engines. Although quite rare, engines of this type were available in production Corvettes and Camaros and found their way into other COPO factory built cars. These were the same engines that had become very popular among all sorts of racers.

Basically, the McLaren ZL-1 was a conventional push-rod powerplant with a McLaren developed dry sump lubrication similar to the M-6A. That let the engine sit lower in the chassis giving a lower center of gravity than an oil pan would allow. It was also fuel injected by a McLaren-Lucas system but with staggered velocity stacks which was found to increase power slightly over stacks of the same height. Brake horsepower was pegged at 620 bhp at 7,000 rpm with a compression ratio of

The new M-8A for 1968 showed considerably improved aerodynamics over the previous team M-6A. At 1450 lb and 630 hp, the McLarens were awesome.

In just the following season, the M-6A McLarens looked out of date when compared to the M-8A of 1968. Hulme was runner-up to Bruce McLaren in the '67 Can-Am.

11:1.

The M-8A was remarkable in that it was the first road racing car to exceed the power-to-weight ratio of 1,000 bhp per ton. Comparison has been made to the Formula Libre GP Mercedes-Benz W125 of 1937, long considered the yardstick in terms of sheer power. The W125 weighed 1,640 pounds and produced 646 bhp giving 0.394 hp per pound. They started 12 races winning 6 with 9 seconds. The M-8A weighed 1,450 pounds, produced 630 bhp by the end of the season, started 6 races, won four and placed second three times. Its 0.434 horsepower per pound was 10% greater than the W125.

Competition against the works McLarens during the '68 season included the Penske-Sunoco McLarens, Hall's 2H Chaparrals, the new Lola T-160 series of cars with the lightweight Chevrolet 427 engine, a Shelby entered McLaren with a Ford 427 engine driven by Pete Revson, Mario Andretti running a Lola T-70 with a 5-liter twin-ohc Ford V-8, a North American Racing Team 4.2-liter Ferrari driven by Pedro Rodriguez, and late in the season, Rodriguez was seen in a new 6.2-liter Ferrari 612. These teams were serious about the championship, and many back markers on each starting grid made for a lot of exciting racing.

In spite of their efforts, all 1968 Can-Am races were McLaren wins with the works drivers, McLaren and Hulme, taking four of those; Hulme at Road America, Edmonton and Las Vegas while McLaren took Riverside. Mark Donohue in the Penske M-6B won at Bridgehampton, and John Cannon surprisingly beat everyone in an old Mk 3 McLaren at Laguna Seca in rain. He had rain tires brought over by Barry Crow for the Hall McLaren M-12 and 2H Chaparral. But, as the season developed, the tires were not considered useful and discarded. Cannon ran the tires to victory in an ironic twist of racing fortunes.

For the '69 season, the team McLarens were the M-8B which differed little from the M-8A although a number of small design changes were made. The cars were lighter and had wider wheels. Their fiberglass bodies were aerodynamically smoother and were reinforced with carbon fibers for added strength. Such advanced construction materials also reduced weight slightly. Engines were again ZL-1s but were stroked to 7,101 cc (433 cid) producing 680 bhp at 6,800 rpm. These engines produced a better torque curve than earlier versions. The larger 454 cid Chevy engine was available but was used only once. Hulme's McLaren ran the engine in the Michigan race. Outwardly, the most visible change to the cars was the addition of a rear-mounted, stationary wing.

A dozen Trojan-built M-12 customer cars were made available in 1969. Their monocoque chassis were derived from the M-6 line and bodies were similar to the M-8A and M-8B. Works cars for '69 cars were built mainly from parts left over from the year before. They were equally successful. Out of 11 races on the Can-Am schedule that year, all were again won by McLarens.

Bruce McLaren himself took six; Mosport, Watkins Glen, Elkhart Lake, Michigan, Laguna Seca and the Texas International Speedway event. He was second at St. Jovite, Mid-Ohio and Bridgehampton. Hulme took five; St. Jovite, Edmonton, Mid-Ohio, Bridgehampton and Riverside with second place finishes to the boss at Mosport, Watkins Glen, Elkhart, Michigan and Laguna Seca. That rounded out 11 firsts and 8 seconds in 22 starts for McLaren works cars. That was a most astounding accomplishment by any comparison.

In 9 races, Hulme had the fastest laps with 6 setting new records. The orange cars led from flag-to-flag in 7 races with both the front two spots on the grid held by them in the first 10 events. Although Andretti was second fastest with the Ford-powered M-6B at Texas, only once throughout the season did a car not built by McLaren lead a Can-Am race! Although McLarens were clearly dominant, in truth it was because the 3-car team was far better organized than competitors. Part of that organization was race planning where one team car was the hare and set the pace by trying to run the wheels off other cars. Thus, Team McLaren had little real competition which showed that proper preparation and planning can provide the winning edge.

McLarens were built in Colnbrook, England, but for the '69

The M-8A in the hands of Denny Hulme on its way to winning the 1968 Edmonton Can-Am averaging 103.15 mph. It was another McLaren 1-2 finish.

The M-8F in later years. Many changes were made by 1971, and Peter Revson drove to victory in 5 races to lock up the title with 142 points to Hulme's 132. Squire Gabbard photo.

Can-Am season, the cars were prepared in a new facility in the Detroit, Michigan suburb of Livonia. This was also the home of McLaren Engines, Ltd. The team M-8D cars received larger displacement 7.6-liter (465 cid) versions of the Chevrolet aluminum 430-inch big block. These engines were prepared by works engine man Bolthoff and produced 670 bhp. Although other teams started the season with 494 cid engines producing from 710-740 bhp, Team McLarens ran the first race of the '70 season with the smaller engine. This race was less than two weeks after Bruce McLaren had been killed while testing a new generation car.

Chassis operated wings were banned that year, so McLaren responded with a rear mounted aerofoil built into the body as the most obvious change on the new M-8D. Except for wider front and rear tracks, dimensions were virtually the same as the earlier M-8B. Thinner sheet aluminum, .040-inch versus .048, gave a small reduction in weight. Fuel capacity was increased to 64 Imperial gallons to increase racing range because economy had decreased from 3.5 to 3 mpg.

On June 2, 1970, tragedy struck the McLaren works and to motor sports in general. Bruce McLaren was testing an M-8D at Goodwood. As he rounded a bend, his estimated speed was around 170 mph when the front of the rear body section became unfastened and lifted. With the sudden change of handling, the car veered out of control, then slammed into safety banking and took the life of its creator. In the wake of the disaster, just 12 days later, Team McLaren placed two cars on the front row of the Mosport Can-Am. This was the first race of the new season. Dan Gurney was the new member of the McLaren Can-Am and Grand Prix teams and was on the pole. Hulme was second although with bandaged hands, the result of an accident while testing at Indianapolis. Gurney won with Hulme third following Jackie Oliver in the Autocoast Ti22, apparently the only real McLaren competitor.

Gurney won next at St. Jovite, where the Autocoast was crashed, and the new season looked like another McLaren run-away. By Watkins Glen, won by Hulme, Hall introduced

The M-8F revealed! 9.1-liters of Chevrolet ZL-1 taken to 494 cubic inches and 740 hp. Squire Gabbard photo.

his very controversial ground-effect Chaparral 2J which left everything else in the shadow of its potential. Even though Can-Am was essentially modern Formula Libre racing with few regulations, the outbursts against the 2J resulted in it being banned.

At Edmonton, the fourth race, Hulme still ran the smaller 439 cid engine, but placed the car on the pole and won unchallenged. Gurney was forced to leave McLaren under pressure from Castrol who didn't like their driver winning for Gulf, McLaren's sponsor, and he was replaced by Peter

Bruce McLaren after winning at Mosport, 1969. At the right, Stirling Moss looks on, perhaps remembers his own racing days. Lionel Birnbom photo courtesy Dr. Jerry Winston.

Peter Revson, McLaren's 1971 Can-Am champion. Neither he nor Bruce McLaren survived their racing days. Lionel Birnbom photo courtesy Dr. Jerry Winston.

Gethin who finished 2nd at Edmonton. Both team cars carried the larger 7.6-liter (494 inch) engines at Mid-Ohio where Hulme won again. Gethin won next at Elkhart Lake which was Team McLaren's 19th consecutive victory in Can-Am racing. Road Atlanta was the end of the string, and for the first time since 1967, McLaren cars were not fastest.

Although they didn't win, it wasn't to the 2J or Revson's Lola, or Eaton's BRM, or any number of other cars. It was underdog Tony Dean who took the Road Atlanta Can-Am in his old 350 hp 908 Porsche spyder. Its superb handling, economy and fewer pit stops out-distanced several McLarens to a surprising win.

Two team McLarens, designated M-8F, were built for the '71 season. These cars were another step in the evolution of Can-Am McLarens and incorporated a number of improvements, most notably a 3-inch increase in wheelbase, wider track for wider tires, and inboard rear brakes. Otherwise, they looked like M-8Ds. Engines were still based on the ZL-1 Chevy but varied in capacity from 7.6- to 8.1-liters. Another engine was available, an alloy block from Reynolds Aluminum, co-sponsor of the cars, that could be taken up to 9-liters (549 cid). The cars normally ran 8.1-liter engines (494 cubes) rated at a conservative 740 bhp at 6,400 rpm. Torque was massive, 665 lb-ft at 5,600 rpm.

Pete Revson left the L&M Lola team to join Hulme as McLaren works driver. Although Hall's Chaparrals were gone with the banned 2J, the famed Scots driver and World Champion Jackie Stewart was at the wheel of a new L&M Lola, the T260. Porsche and Ferrari were still testing Can-Am cars. Porsche was gearing up for a tremendous factory-backed effort with turbocharged 917-10s for the next year. UOP Shadows and BRM were there, too, and it looked like McLaren had finally met its match. In the opening race at Mosport, Canada, Stewart was on the pole ahead of both Hulme and Revson. However, at the finish, McLarens took the top six finishing positions. Hulme and Revson lead the McLaren parade.

Stewart took Mt. Tremblant, the next Can-Am race, with McLarens 2 through 5. Hulme and Revson came in 2nd and 3rd. At Road Atlanta, the next race, Revson coasted across the finish line to win after a tremendous battle with Stewart who was sidelined by a flat. The drive pegs on one wheel of Revson's car had broken and the wheel was retained only by the retaining clip on the center lock nut! Hulme was 2nd some eight laps behind, and McLaren was back on top.

At Watkins Glen, Stewart was once again on the pole but was sidelined by another flat. Revson ran the big Reynolds aluminum engine with 510 cubic inches to win again. Mid-Ohio showed the Mclarens to have some deficiencies when suspension failures caused by the rough track took out both team cars, a very rare occurrence. Stewart led Jo Siffert's 917PA Porsche spyder, a factory car testing Can-Am waters, across the line.

Hulme's M-8F was fitted with outboard brakes for the next race, Elkhart Lake, where he placed on the pole but failed due to a broken crankshaft, another very rare occurrence. However, in a spectacular display of driving skill, Revson started from the back of the pack and worked his way through to win from Siffert. That showed just how superior the McLaren was to all other cars.

Next at Donnybrooke, McLarens were again dominant with cars in the top five spots. The Team McLarens of Revson and Hulme were 1-2. Hulme followed with a win at Edmonton beating Jackie Oliver's Shadow. However, Revson started 11 laps down due to having to remove a bolt that was discovered lying at the bottom of one injector stack. That dropped him to a 12th place finish, the lowest for the season.

Revson's fifth win was at Laguna Seca. Starting from the

The great years of Can-Am racing provided many north-of-the-border battles at Mosport, Edmonton and St. Jovite, Canada. It was always the same; #4 Bruce McLaren and #5 Denny Hulme out front. Lionel Birnbom photo courtesy Dr. Jerry Winston.

pole, he led all the way even though black-flagged a lap before the finish for smoking heavily due to a broken piston. Stewart was shown the checkered flag as victor, but later, Revson was fined for ignoring the flag and declared the winner.

At Riverside, the last race of the 1971 season, Hulme dominated to take his third successive victory there. Revson was second. Thus, McLaren cars won the Can-Am Challenge Cup for the fifth straight year, and Revson was champion over Hulme by 10 points, 142 to 132. Stewart was third with 76 points and Siffert placed fourth with 68. McLarens won 8 of 10 races, placed second 6 times and were third twice. During the season, McLarens set nine fastest laps. It was a good year.

The 1971 season was the last year a normally aspirated car won the Can-Am for while. It was McLaren again. Porsche was not able to campaign its 5-liter 917s in international races after '71, and following Siffert's lead in the 917PA spyder, Zuffenhausen developed the awesome 917-10 turbocharged Can-Am Porsche that eclipsed everything before them.

Can-Am racing was changing. When Mark Donohue and the Porsche panzers rolled into the Can-Am arena, everyone else was racing for 2nd place and that killed spectator appeal of the sport. Although the turbocharged cars were quicker, they didn't make the noise of the big American V-8s, and some measure of its attraction was lost.

Although the once dominate McLarens had built legends long remembered in the sport, normally aspirated engines could not compete with smaller displacement turbocharged engines. High technology had moved to the front of Can-Am. During the next few seasons and until the series was ended, Porsches won everything with their 1100+ hp cars. Unlike the huge effort of Porsche factory engineering that produced

THE most powerful racing engine ever seen in racing, the McLaren legacy of thorough chassis and suspension development, along with aerodynamics that worked, is a great tribute to the man who came from the land of the kiwi bird that could not fly.

McLaren Can-Am Record

The Can-Am grew out of the USRRC (United States Road Racing Championship) that featured unlimited Group 7 cars. The USRRC ran from 1963-68. The Can-Am ran its first race in 1966 and each following year until suspended in 1975 for two years to formulate a new set of regulations. The Cam-Am was again suspended in 1986.

From SCCA records of the Can-Am, the McLaren marque and McLaren drivers still hold the majority of entries with the following highlights:

Most career victories; Driver: Dennis Hulme - 22
Most career victories; Manufacturer: McLaren - 43
Most career victories; Engine: Chevrolet - 143
Most career victories; Engine type: Chev. (small block) - 95
Most consecutive career victories, team: McLaren - 19
Most consecutive season victories, team: McLaren - 11
Most consecutive career chassis victories: McLaren - 23
Closest margin of victory: McLaren, 0.01 seconds
  McLaren over Hulme at Road America 1971
Fastest race speed, over 200 miles: McLaren, Peter Revson 119.137 mph at Brainerd, 1971.

Early-day Can-Am small block: 465 hp on gasoline.

Early-day Corvette small block: 283 hp on gasoline.

Chevy Power

The Hardware

Modern-day Top Sportsman big block: 1400 hp on nitrous.

Modern-day sportsman big block: 900 hp on gasoline.

This chapter is devoted to the men who have contributed so much to the success of Chevrolet racing but who have gone unknown by the public that has admired their work for more than three decades. Their efforts at Chevrolet have been the day-to-day challenges of working out even the smallest engineering detail before a product goes into production and ultimately reaches the market. Their attention to detail and the quest to "get it right" is the major factor that has made Chevrolet hardware so easy for racers and hot rodders to work with and win.

The small block Chevrolet engine has been around for 35 years, and the first big block came along just three years later. That was the W-engine, the 348 and 409. When the big block Mk II and Mk IIS Mystery engines appeared in 1963 followed by the Mk IV in 1965, the Chevrolet stable of power was complete. Chevrolet cars with the small block and trucks with the big block still pound out millions of miles each year. It is to the credit of the men inside the giant that these engines have been so successful.

There have been other engines and still more are being developed within the confines of the GM Tech Center, but the small block and big block engines in their many variations are still the primary powerplants for most Chevrolets on the road, track and strip. The men who tell their side of the story in these pages were at the heart of it all.

In the beginning of Chapter 4, an overview of their work was introduced within the context of Chevrolet powered motorsport. This chapter is devoted to their own words.

Dick Keinath

With Chevrolet from 1950 to 1983
Chief Engine Engineer and Chief Drive Train Engineer

I think I've held almost every job available in the engine group starting in the drafting room and up to Chief Engine Engineer. From 1963 to 1967, I was Assistant Staff Engineer for all V-8 engines and then became Chief Engineer of engines in 1971. That job also included transmissions, axles and drive trains.

AG: What was your training that led you to General Motors?
Dick: I guess we would have to go back to the time before college. I have always worked with engines. I was reared on a farm in Michigan, and we did our own mechanical work back then. I was rebuilding engines when I was about fourteen or fifteen years old. I went to Michigan State University in engineering and received a bachelor's degree in 1950. Later on, in 1960, I got a master's degree in business administration from the University of Detroit.

I went to work with GM in what was then called General Motors Product Study, which eventually became General Motors Engineering Staff after they built the Technical Center. Back in 1950, I was working on automatic transmissions GM wide. At that time, we were working on the Chevrolet PowerGlide, Buick DynaFlow and other more advanced transmissions. The automatic transmissions didn't become much in production until the early '50s, except for, perhaps, the Hydramatic which was the fluid drive type of transmission rather than the torque converter type.

I was a trainee, just out of school and ran dynamometers and took data. I was a general "gofor". The normal things a young engineer would do.

AG: How did the small block V-8 become a Chevrolet engine?
Dick: I joined Chevrolet Engineering in 1952. It was about the summer of '52 when Mr. Cole came to Chevrolet, before I got there. He pulled with him one of the Assistant Chief Engineers, Mr. Rosenberger, who I worked for back in the transmission days. I always enjoyed working with him, so I interviewed with Chevrolet and went over there. He was one of the people that Mr. Cole took with him when he transferred from Cadillac. He and Harry Barr had been involved in engine design at Cadillac.

When Mr. Cole came to Chevrolet, there was a new engine with overhead valves already designed within Chevrolet. That was the engine that Mr. Ed Kelley had designed. He was the

Chief Engineer at the time and Mr. Cole replaced him. Mr. Kelley then became Manufacturing Manager for Chevrolet Division.

Mr. Cole wanted to incorporate his own ideas in the engine, so in essence, we started over. Al Kolbe was a project engineer within the engine group at the time, and another young engineer was Donald McPherson. Mr. McPherson eventually became Vice President of all North American operations for General Motors. Eventually, I ended up working for Mr. McPherson. He was Staff Engineer for all engines, and I was Assistant Staff Engineer for V-8 engines from 1963 to 1967.

It was Mr. Cole's idea to start with a clean sheet of paper. He had the idea for short exhaust ports and the way inlet ports were designed. That was primarily his initial broad brush approach. Mr. Cole was, of course, the ultimate engineer. He never quit being an engineer, even when he became President of General Motors.

Harry Barr was also involved with that engine. Mr. Barr was the Assistant Chief of Design for passenger cars, and Mr. Rosenberger was the Assistant Chief in charge of experimental and development work. They both worked for Mr. Cole.

I found Mr. Barr to be a very open individual, a fine engineer and a fine person, always a gentleman. I never found him to be particularly one way or the other as far as V-8s or 6-cylinder engines were concerned.

Mr. Cole's engine went from the idea phase into production in approximately 1952 to '54. That was about the right length of time for a production engine. We had a full crew on it at the time, and we were designing a brand new car, the 1955 Chevrolet. The engine was designated to be THE engine for THE new car. The car, being a new model, was the first Chevrolet under the jurisdiction of Mr. Cole and his group. He was actually responsible for the entire car.

The design of the 1955 Chevrolet was started back in 1951, and of course, there were quite a few innovative things in that car, a new suspension, a new kind of drive, a wrap-around windshield, those sorts of things. The engine was designed to be an "up-grade" option for that particular vehicle. The 6-cylinder was still the basic engine for the car, but the V-8 became very popular. That was the beginning of Chevrolet as a high performance division of General Motors.

People started running cars with that engine up and down Woodward Avenue, north of Detroit, and in drag races all over the country. Kids loved to work on the engine, and it just took off. By 1956, it was already being established as THE power package for the young people who wanted to go out and have fun with cars. We had special transmissions to go with the engine, and we started to market many different options. In fact, I believe it was the first time we optioned dual exhaust systems. Up to that time, if someone wanted dual exhausts, he would have to go to a hot rod shop and have it installed. We ended up optioning 4-barrel carburetors. From there, we went to dual quads and three 2-barrels. In 1957, we increased displacement from 265 to 283 cubic inches.

During all those years, I was in the engine design group in the drafting room. I was an engine designer, and we designed whatever came along, manifolds and blocks, whatever. I was

involved in the 283. We came in with a new exhaust system with the "ram's horn" manifold. It was high performance and was a highly efficient manifold. Interestingly enough, we used it first on Corvettes, but we eventually ended up using it on everything.

You must remember that the exhaust ports were pointing toward the sky. They were not turned downward. It became a better design to let the exhaust manifold go up to extract the exhaust gases much more efficiently, then bring it down. The result was in the shape of a ram's horn.

During my years in drafting, I also worked on a V-6 with a balance shaft. The engineer on that was Johnny Burnell. I also worked on the Corvair engine, another of Mr. Cole's ideas. He took the best designers in Chevrolet, six of us, and sequestered us back in R&D in a room all by ourselves to design this engine from scratch. That was also under the tutelage of Al Kolbe. We started early in '57, and the car came out in '59.

During that same period, Zora Arkus-Duntov was working on improving V-8s for the Corvette. He was working on the fuel injection. I joined Zora in 1958. There were just three of us. I was the engine man and Harold Krueger was the chassis man. Before that, Zora did his own engine design as an engineer, but he always had drafting people doing work. I did some drafting work for him back in the middle '50s. So, we knew each other. About then, he was looking for an engineer, and he asked for me. I got promoted from designer on a drafting board to a project engineer.

The 283 was already in production, and one of the first things I did was bore out a 283 to make it a 302 cubic inch, short stroke, large bore. That was one of my projects. We didn't know whether manufacturing could make a package like that because of the 4-inch bore in what was then considered tight conditions for bore centers. Nowadays, you do it every day.

That was the engine that eventually became the Z-28, really, but it had an evolution in between, the 327. That was the 283 which was bored to the size of the 302 but with one quarter-inch longer stroke than the 283. So the 327, in some respects, came after the 302 yet the 302 in the Z-28 came after the 327.

The first 302 was an experimental version which we played with in the Corvette, Mr. Duntov and I. We also put the fuel injection on it and the Duntov cam. It was a going machine. Compared to the production 283 Corvette, it was way beyond that. The 302 was a real performance type engine, but it never went into production until the Z-28 Camaro. It was strictly a performance experiment to see how far we could go, and to prove to management that there was a hellofa potential in the small block with a larger bore. At the time, we were primarily doing development work.

Zora was a good person to work for. He always let me do my own thing. He was full of ideas, and I was full of ideas. We would sit after work and talk about what else we could do to get even more power out of the engine.

The 348 was the other project I worked on with Zora. The 348 and the 409 were the same family, called the "W" engines. I was very much involved in it when I was in the drafting room around 1955-57. I think we went into production with that engine in '57 as both a truck engine and a passenger car version. It was not a very high specific output engine so, Mr. Duntov was given the assignment, or maybe it was his suggestion, that I work on that one when I got into his group. It was a very important project, as I remember, to make the 348 a decent engine. We were developing manifolds, carburetors, different pistons, and above all else, new camshafts. I had many different valve configurations and did a lot of work with induction systems.

I was working for Mr. Duntov on the 348 when Jim Rathman was the driver doing development of that engine for stock car racing. It was for high performance for both the passenger car and the Corvette although we didn't put the 348 in the Corvette. Mr. Duntov had responsibility for what amounted to high performance engines regardless of where they were used whether in the Corvette or passenger car or stock car or boat. That was in 1958-'59. The major projects were camshaft work, induction work, getting power out of the 348, developing the small block into a high performance engine and general power development on almost anything. Junior Johnson won the Daytona 500 in 1960 with the 348. In 1963, Rex White was a driver with Lou Clemmons as his partner. Ray Fox was the builder of Junior's cars, and both he and Smokey Yunick built engines. Those were the three teams.

The 348 did not get a good image although it had good durability and a good beginning because it had the Chevrolet name on it, but it never responded to the normal hot rod activity that we expected. For one thing, its combustion chamber was too convoluted. It was a machined chamber partially in the block because it had a 16-degree angle normal to a flat top piston and the top of the block. The top of the block was not square with the top of the piston and not square with the center line of the bore. It was a wedge shaped chamber with a domed piston with a pent-roof on each side. To get the valve clearance, we had to notch the piston and the side of the cylinder bore in the block.

Also, the exhaust port was extracting exhaust gases from the furtherest point of the chamber. The exhaust valve was square with the deck of the cylinder head, as was the inlet valve, and actually opened into the block because the chamber was partially in the block. With respect with the world, both the inlet and exhaust valves were at 16-degree angles normal to the centerline of the bore.

The 409 was a better engine than the 348, but it also had a 16-degree slab angle at the top of the block. All the engines like that were designated the "W" engine family. The 409 had a larger bore, four and five-sixteenths (giving us more room for the valves opening into the bore), and that's one engine that we really spent a lot of time on as an "up option" for passenger cars. It was also what we finally ended up with as a NASCAR engine in 1962.

In 1959, when I was still working for Mr. Duntov, the other major project I worked on was the aluminum engine. During that time, I had responsibility for small block high performance development, the 348-409 power development and the aluminum engine development. We started working with an eutectic alloy for aluminum cylinder heads for the small-block that was scheduled for a Corvette package. We had other aluminum parts: aluminum intake, aluminum water pump, aluminum clutch housings along with aluminum cylinder heads, and we just happened to call it the aluminum program. Back then in 1957-'58 there wasn't anything like that in production except for some aluminum cylinder heads that Ford had made years before for the flathead.

The aluminum engine work that I did was intended for Corvettes because Corvette was the premier car for Chevrolet. I was assigned the task of making aluminum cylinder heads work with a high silicon alloy, a 17% silicon eutectic alloy. Silicon, as you know, is basically sand, and it proved very difficult to cast. The goal was to make an engine in which the valves would ride right on the aluminum without inserts and where the valve stems would ride in the guides without inserts. As you know, all aluminum cylinder heads today have inserts and guides. Our project was unsuccessful, but that project would have been a tremendous breakthrough if it had been. We ended up wearing out the valves very quickly because the silicon was abrasive.

When we thought that engine was close enough to be put into production, Chevrolet transferred the engine and myself away from Duntov and out into the production group where I went to work for Mr. McPherson. That was about 1960. After about six more months work, we just couldn't make the aluminuim head engine live. We also had special application casting machines manufactured in Germany which we brought over to do low pressure casting. About that time, we also built an aluminum foundry in Messena, New York because of the St. Lawrence Seaway and dams for making electricity.

It was really all tied together. There was a lot of planning and coordination around what we as a corporation could do, what the country could do for supplying electricity, what Alcoa and Reynolds could do with supplying cheap aluminum. It was the beginning of trying to come up with low cost, high volume aluminum alloy that we would then be able to make all these aluminum parts for our vehicles. The research was an effort to make as many parts out of aluminum as we possibly could in order to make a lighter car, a more fuel efficient car. The Corvair engine block and cylinder heads was made up there, but what made the Corvair engine live was that it had a cast iron cylinder. We went to cast iron cylinders because we couldn't get the aluminum to live in combination with aluminum pistons.

Compared to cast iron engines, the weight savings with aluminum was considerable. Not only was the engine lighter, but saving a couple of hundred pounds on the front end meant you could go with lighter suspension pieces and all the components such as the chassis could be lighter making the vehicle more efficient.

Later on, the completely aluminum small block engine with insert for the valves was raced with the Jim Hall Chaparral, but that was a completely different program much later in the '60s.

At that time, while I was in the production group and the aluminum cylinder head didn't work out, Mr. McPherson gave me a new assignment to design a new 4-cylinder and a new 6-cylinder which became the basis for the current modern 4-cylinder and 6-cylinder work. The Chevy II that came out in 1962 had a 4-cylinder (153 cubic inches) and a 6-cylinder. We actually designed three versions of the 6-cylinder, 194, 230 and a 292 cubic inches. Those were all designed by yours truly back about 1960 and '61, all production stuff. The 230 was designed for full sized Chevrolets. For 1960, '61 and part of '62, I was working on bread and butter stuff (non-high performance).

When I was in the production group, I also had the responsibility of the passenger car version of the 409. This was the basis for racing applications of the engine.

AG: Since the AMA ban against racing had been imposed in 1957, what was the politics of the time?

Dick: All of the high performance projects, especially Duntov's CERV-1 and CERV-2 were always on the fringe of racing. And during those times, we had a whole group of people who wanted to make Chevrolet into the high performance and racing division of General Motors. They were led, primarily, by people like Mr. Duntov and Mr. Rosenberger and Mr. Cole. It was always a difficult situation for Chevrolet, because the corporation had made a policy statement that said we, General Motors, are not involved in racing, and we had the only American production sports car, the Corvette. Duntov was always trying to make it faster and better, that was his job, and he did that. But in all the work that was going on, nothing prevented someone from putting a Corvette engine in a Chevrolet car or hot rod and going racing. So Chevrolet engines ended up in drag races and hot rods, in California and wherever, without Chevrolet involvement because the small-block was such a good package. We kept developing options people could buy, like compound carburetion and fuel injection and different camshafts, plus all the work that outside hot rod people made. We certainly didn't dissuade people from developing high performance parts, because it was such a good deal for us as a GM Division.

Somewhere in the middle of '62, Bunkie Knudsen "jumped the traces" and became General Manager of Chevrolet from Pontiac. He gave us the go-ahead to build a racing engine for stock cars to replace the 409 that was currently being raced in NASCAR. Harry Barr was the Chief Engineer at the time, I believe. I got the assignment in, I think, July of '62. I still remember writing an Engineering Work Order stating, "Please design an engine per instructions of R. L. Keinath."

You normally didn't do that. Normally you'd say design something with such-and-such specifications, this size valves, ports here, bore, stroke, deck height and so on. But that engine, the Mk II, was very secret. All there was for instructions was a one-liner to design an engine per my instructions, and there was a blank check. I could do anything. It was a tremendous program. We were free from bondage, a clean sheet.

I started with the 409 bore centers. That was the only thing I kept, although the bottom lip of the crankcase looked a lot like a 409 as far as the oil pan was concerned. From there on up, it was completely different. The top of the block was

square with the piston rather than at an angle, normal to the centerline of the piston. I knew, from an induction stand point, that we didn't want to make such a sharp valve angle as the 409. We wanted to make a larger angle. That's one of the reasons that when I designed the Mark II (later christened the "Mystery Engine"), I gave it 26-degrees. The Mk II was square with the world, a completely normal engine. The combustion chamber was in the cylinder head rather in the block, and of course, the cylinder head was designed with canted valves which became known as the "porcupine" head. I have the patent for that cylinder head design and the canted valve design.

Several years later, Ford adapted that design in their engines. All that is a story within itself about how NASCAR made us sell one of our engines to Ford if we were going to race the Mystery engine. During that time, which was really just weeks, we did many new things on that engine, some of which we were not able to pull into production because they were too unique and perhaps too exotic for production. During that time, I developed special ports which as recently as three or four years ago, people out in the field rediscovered. The Reher-Morrison group, for example, came up with what they called the "short port" which was really a development I made in 1962 in the Mk II, but because of production limitations, I had to go with a long port and a short port. I couldn't go with all short ports because it would have been too expensive to make at Tonawanda. We also had, at one time, a right hand and a left hand cylinder head. That also was discarded.

The uniqueness of that engine was from the pan rail up. It was all new. All castings were brand new. The block was a four and five-sixteenths inch bore and three and half inch stroke giving 409 cubic inches to start. That was the way it was in July of 1962. The big thing was the cylinder head, valve arrangement and valve train. All the calculations for the valve angles were done by hand, there were no computers. The lifters were at different angles because they had to be in line with the push rods which were not in line because the inlet valves were inclined at 26-degrees and the exhausts were at 16-degrees. Plus, they were canted outward, double angle, and I had an awful job with the machine shop getting these heads machined. Back then we didn't have computer aided equipment.

Duntov had given the racing 409 the designation of Mk I, so that's why this new engine was called the Mk II. The word "mark" comes from Europe and Duntov, being European, wanted to call everything "mark" something. We could have called the engines Phase 1 or Phase 2 or something like that.

About October or November, we stroked it and it became the Mk IIS, "S" meaning stroked. That took it from 409 cubic inches to 427 cubic inches. We had to scramble to make all-new crankshafts because we were negotiating "politically" with NASCAR on displacement, and they permitted us to go up to 427 cubic inches because that was what Chrysler was doing with their hemi head engine that they were coming out with, and what Pontiac was running.

One morning, I got a phone call that said, "We're going to

change displacement."

I said, "MY GOD! How am I going to change displacement. I've got all these parts coming in. We were making drawings, making designs, making castings, we're doing this, we're doing that, and you're going to change the engine on me."

"Yeah, you can do it."

We had to design a new crankshaft and stroke it, new rods, new pistons. We changed all that and started over again in these areas. The 409 version had a 409 crank, but when we stroked it, that killed the crank. So, the only thing left that was 409 was the pan rail holes and the main bearings. The 409 W-engine bearings were in the 409 Mk II and the 427 Mk IIS. Both the Mk II and Mk IIS were called the "Mystery Engine" by the public.

When we changed the stroke, we had to make new parts and still get it all designed, get patterns made, get core boxes made, and castings made and everything machined in time for the race in February. You just don't go out racing. You've got to run the engine, develop it, run the durability on it and see how everything does, change it to make everything live.

The exhaust manifolds I designed for the Mystery engine is a story in itself. They were really cast headers. They were single tubes made out of cast iron that culminated in a flange with four holes. They were about two feet long. That is one way you can tell a Mystery Engine instantly, by these exhaust manifolds. We made them out of cast tubes and joined them into the flange that mated with the exhaust pipe. The Mystery Engine was completely unique.

I supervised all the testing of the engine. We had a test engineer, Bill Howell, and one of the dynamometer operators that was very good was Tom Poole. The difference in output between the 409 W-engine, which was factory rated at 425 horsepower, and the Mk IIS was a lot more. The Mk IIS was good for about ten more miles per hour which was a lot of horsepower.

I still have the piston which was in the car that Junior ran when the engine dropped a valve and went right through the piston. That was the Daytona 500 in 1963. They plated the piston and presented it to me as a memento. Freddie Lorenzen won in a Ford, but Junior was leading off and away, along with Johnny Rutherford in Smokey's car. Both Junior and Rutherford won the qualifying races.

Two guys walking around Daytona Beach were Mr. McPherson and Mr. Keinath wearing dark glasses and slouchy hats. The project was all secret. It was all within Chevrolet, and the rest of the Corporation didn't know anything about it. What an embarrassment for the General Motors hierarchy. But the Chevrolet hierarchy knew exactly what we were doing, but no one would admit it.

We finally did get pressured into granting an interview. Ray Brock of *Hot Rod Magazine* interviewed us at Daytona in a motel room, and the stipulation was that we would grant him an interview only if he promised not to mention anybody's name. We had to take vacation time to get down there. We couldn't go on the Corporation's time. It was that secret.

I could tell you a lot about the secrecy surrounding that engine. At Daytona, we were running about ten miles per hour faster than the nearest competitor and the press was clamoring to find out who did the engine? What has Chevrolet got? What is General Motors doing? They are not permitted to race because of a "no racing" policy, yet how did this engine get into a Chevrolet? Everyone denied knowing anything about the engine from the brass on down.

It was in April of '63 when General Motors handed down the "no racing" edict again. There was so much embarrassment for General Motors when they made that public announcement, and here was Chevrolet running away with all the races. It was a direct edict; either you do it or you get fired. After that, the car owners such as Ray Fox and Smokey raced the cars on their own. We got rid of as many parts as we could to keep them going, somewhat clandestine, but we were not able to make any new parts. My records are not complete enough to determine how many Mystery Engines we made.

I don't remember exactly when the Mystery Engine project stopped, because after we were told in no uncertain terms, "Thou Shalt Not", the enthusiasm went away. We had an entire engineering department and the entire shop geared to machine cylinder heads, manifolds, exhaust manifolds, blocks and everything, and we had the pattern shops working, the foundry working, the different machine shops in the Detroit area making camshafts and the crankshafts. So, there were a lot of people involved very intensely.

It was a tremendous undertaking with a lot of esprit de corps. People would work nights, Saturdays and Sundays, anything just to get the job done. We went on three shifts. I would take calls at home at 3 o'clock in the morning because we would run the engines all night. Something would happen, and I'd jump in the car and go somewhere like 3 or 4 in the morning. We had "48" hour days. In the morning, I would park the car and make the rounds where the work was going on, and the people in the front office wouldn't see me until just before noon. I'd be all over the building because I'd go from the laboratory to the machine shops, the pattern shops, the motor room, to inspection, to all the different departments. I had to find out what happened the night before. What was working and what wasn't, and make plans for the day. That's how it went every day.

The Mystery Engine time was a tremendous time. I don't think you'll ever see it again, not in the auto industry.

AG: At that point, were there plans to go into production with that engine?

Dick: Oh, absolutely, but the plans were also that we've got to try and make it even better. So, we came up with what was called the Mk III. That engine had a different bore center, and during the summer of '63, we were working on the Mk III, and we decided to go back to the old bore centers, and that became the Mk IV. That was the engine that finally went into production.

There were some differences in the engine, mainly the induction system. We had about three different inlet manifolds. One was a tuned runner manifold. One was an H-type and one was a plenum type inlet manifold. These were all different versions that would fit on the same cylinder head pairs. We did not go with a right hand - left hand cylinder heads on the Mk II engine when we finally went racing with it. The heads were interchangeable. We never even made individual heads, and we did not go with individual ports like we wanted to. We had to compromise. The Mk. II was really not as much as we could have done if we had had more time. We just ran out of time.

In the cylinder head, I had to put a long port and short port. The short port was the one that entered the chamber on the side of the cylinder so that it gave a swirling effect to the induction charge. The other port came straight down and did not give a swirling effect. Because of production, I had to go with two of one and two of the other for every cylinder head. It was not until about twenty years later that people on the outside discovered that the short port was better.

That development goes back to '62 when we took over a portion of the carburetor flow room and used it for the induction room for evaluating ports. I had some people working in the pattern shop making patterns out of wood for different ports nearly every day. We were trying to come up with better flowing ports. We had some pattern makers that were so good that they could make furniture better than furniture because they could make it exact, beautiful work. A lot of this is just unknown to anyone else.

I was looking for how to make more horsepower versus more torque, but I was also looking for manifolds that would give us more torque coming off corners at the race track, rather than just pure horsepower.

AG: How did the Z-11 drag racing engine fit into the Mystery Engine picture?

Dick: I don't recall just how the Z-11 came about, precisely, but I think the Corvette Group was looking at the engine for the Corvette. I had control of the Mk II parts, so nobody else had any parts. I may have given them some engines when we quit shipping them out. We never made the 409 after the initial Mk II. It sort of went away after that. If Mr. Duntov's group was developing the Z-11 for the Corvette, they may have used some experimental parts which were Mystery Engine parts.

After we got the politics straightened out and we were denied racing, we continued to develop the Mk II as a production engine that finally became the Mk IV. My involvement from 1963 on was the production version Mk IV. We had it in a 427 passenger, a 396 passenger which was made for the Chevelle, a 366 cubic inch truck and a 427 cubic inch truck. The trucks had a higher block, a four-ring piston, much higher durability than the passenger, and of course, higher weight. The passenger engine was modified. We played with the valve angle a little more than the Mystery Engine had.

In some aspects, I think we were hurting ourselves rather than helping ourselves. We reduced the bore size from four and five-sixteenths down to four and a quarter because the production people in Tonawanda were giving us fits. They didn't like the big bore. They were telling us they were having bad castings. So, we had to increase the stroke a little bit, which we didn't want to do. It went from 3.65 to 3.75-inches.

The changes made it a little more difficult for the free-flowing valve system I had designed originally. The chamber ended up being a little higher than I really wanted. By higher, I mean the roof of the chamber was higher and that gave more volume than I wanted to see. We ended up narrowing up a little bit because of smaller bore.

We went into production with the 396 in the 1965 model. The 427 came around because of NASCAR. Pontiac was running a 428 in 1963, and that's why we chose 427 for the Mk II. The 396 might have come about either because NASCAR limited displacement to 6.5-liters around then, or someone in the corporation might have said we couldn't go beyond 400 cubic inches. My goal was to get as much power out of the 396 as we got out of the 427. We did that. The 396 was a higher winding engine because of the way we cammed it. The 396 Chevelle became known as the "ultimate muscle car" for that era. It would really run.

The Mk II was strictly experimental. When we started with the Mk IV, we started with almost a clean sheet of paper. I wrote the SAE paper on the Mk IV as I did on all the engines I designed. The only thing that was the same as the Mk II were the bore centers. There wasn't anything used on the Mk II that could be used on the Mk IV without a lot of changing. Head port locations of the Mk IV were different, bolt locations were different, and you couldn't make Mk IV heads work on the Mk II without a lot of welding and machining.

When the edict came down of no more racing, we started to work on the production version which ended up as the Mk IV. Again, that was my design. I was by then a supervisor so I had a couple of engineers working for me helping me on that engine. The little things that were put together and improvements that were made by so many engineers and so many people became the Mk IV. We all had a hand in it. Mr. Duntov had ideas, and Mr. Barr had ideas that improved the durability of the engine. Myself and the people who were working for me; we just kept plugging at it and plugging at it. We changed the material by adding tin to the cast iron to improve durability and strength. Many different things were involved in materials and processing selection. Finally, it came to the point where it is today.

At that time, in the middle '60s, Vince Piggins was involved in product promotion, which was the ability to capitalize on exposure at race tracks. To do so, many times we would come up with what we thought was a good idea to sell to management. That's how we came out with the Z-28, for example. I believe that one was hatched in my office one day.

The Z-28 was an outgrowth of the idea of coming in with a product that the public would identify as high performance. I think the Trans-Am regulations for 5-liter engines was the reason for the 302 cubic inch configuration. The limit was 305 cubic inches, and we had a 302 that we had been playing with earlier. The Z-28 seemed like a normal outgrowth, and that's what we did. The Z-28 was primarily, in my opinion, a chassis dominated vehicle. That concept influenced how the car was designed, handled and developed. The race concept had to be understood, as part of the vehicle, as it was being designed. I can't comment from an insider viewpoint because, at that time, I didn't have much to do with the chassis. I was asked to make sure we had a good engine for the car.

I remember when the Camaro first came out. We had widened the front track for improved handling, and there was quite a discussion about that.

Another idea that was very much a goal at that time was the Central Office Production Order cars, because COPOs were about the only way you could come in with a limited production option that would permit you to put in special products for customers interested in that sort of thing and who would be interested in paying top dollar to get it because those things were not cheap.

AG: How did the public know about COPOs since they were not advertised?

Dick: It's fantastic how the public finds out things when you don't advertise. Even today, there are special packages available that the normal public never finds out about. But the people who need to know, they know.

The Product Promotion group are the people that handle those sorts of things.

During the latter years of the '60s, I was transferred to GM Europe and came back to Chevrolet in Detroit as Chief of Research & Development in 1970. Later I became Chief Engine Engineer for Chevrolet with the overall responsibility of engine programs.

Since my retirement, I have continued my association with Chevrolet as a consultant for race car engines with Herb Fishel's group in the Chevrolet Race Shop. I worked a lot with Junior Johnson before he went to Ford.

I'm still doing development work on race engines, especially heads where several aspects of the port designs I did with the Mk II engine are proving beneficial. We didn't have computers back then, but now, we're able to do a lot more a lot quicker, and that has improved NASCAR engines.

Fred Frincke

**Chevrolet Engineering
Reviews his years with engines**

My work as a draftsman and project engineer for Zora Duntov was from 1959 to 1971. I worked with Zora on the Corvette fuel injection from the beginning and on the SS

Corvette, then on the Chevrolet Engineering Research Vehicles (CERV-1 and CERV-2) that were put together here. Then there were the light weight Corvettes that were built here that did go into some races. The SS Corvette was raced earlier.

I worked for Duntov as, lets say, a component designer. I designed a number of cylinder heads for him. I designed manifolds, high performance fuel injection intake manifolds, and special connecting rods for durability. I was in drafting, and he was really the engineer who called all the shots as to what was to be designed, and I designed it.

Later on as I became an engineer, I also worked for Duntov. I would design something and go out back and get it made and put it on a dynamometer and try it. It was just a constant design, build, test; design, build, test; trying to get all the performance we could out of our engines. We were doing that not only as a means to get high performance engines into full production but also to learn as much as we could about getting power out of our engines so that we could advise any outsider that wanted to race Chevrolets.

It was with that in mind that we did a lot of this work, a supportive effort to advise racers and racing programs and to, in some cases, make material available over the counter. We wanted to have a good street machine in production but we also wanted our customers to win some races. It was a little difficult to do both. We would carry equipment so far and make a good driving street vehicle out of it, then we would go on with the design and try to provide enough material that the racing enthusiast could buy over the counter from Chevrolet dealers.

Vince Piggins used to get involved in a lot of this "hand out" kind of work. We would do special parts and some parts would go to people like Smokey who knew what to do with them. In the early days, Smokey was the central figure.

Some of the engines we did were the "Mark" engines. Before the Mk II, or the mystery engine, there was the Mk 1, the W engine 409. We increased the displacement of the 409 engine to 427. Something like two dozen drag packages were built. They were called the Z-11. That was the Mk 1. The Mk II was the "mystery engine", with same bore and stroke, but all new block and heads, etc.

I think that was what magazine writers called it. We didn't give it that name. It was really a prototype engine of the "Mark" series, a big block V-8 engine which was designed primarily with high performance in mind. I guess it was called the mystery engine because it disappeared at races and it was something that nobody could get. At that time, it wasn't a production engine.

That would have been Vince Piggins working in the background, getting parts out to the people who knew how to race and try it out for us and see how it would go. The Mk II engine had larger bores and a shorter stroke that any Mk engine does today. The Mk III, I understand, was just a paper study of some other engine which, I guess, just passed through in a couple of weeks time. It was nothing serious.

The Mk IV was really the mystery engine, the Mk II, with a longer stroke and smaller bore size. There were some head bolts that were eliminated. You might say it was designed around the induction system, around the intake ports and the exhaust ports and combustion chamber, and there were two places on each cylinder head where intake ports existed where you would have wanted to put a head bolt. They were left out, and we put bolts as close as they could go.

There are two places on each cylinder head where, if you look you would say there are a couple of bolts missing. The tendency today is to look at them and say we have two too many, the other two ought to be eliminated. Then we could really do a job on the intake port. We have actually spent time running tests with the other two eliminated and they have been successful, but we would have to do an awful lot of testing before we could approve taking those off.

I would say the Mk II was designed with NASCAR and the 500 mile race in the back of some engineers minds. Another way of looking at all of this is kind of paradoxical. The 348 engine was designed with trucks in mind. It was designed and put on paper as a big truck engine, but it ended up in passenger cars and became a 409 racing engine. So, after getting enthused about racing, we wanted to design a new engine so we started with the Mk II engine to design a high performance engine. Now it is our truck engine.

The lineage of the Z designation of the Z-11, ZL-1 and Z-28 was, the Z represents a vehicle oriented designation. In other words, if you had a Z engine, it was really an engine that went with a vehicle package. Like a Z-28 is more than an engine, it is a vehicle. Z-11 was a whole vehicle. It was a drag racing vehicle with a big block 409/427. I actually worked on that engine, the increase of displacement of the 409 to 427 with special cylinder heads and intake manifolds with separate valley cover. There was another group that was designing the mystery engine, the Mk II. I think both engines used the same crankshaft and rocker arm stud but everything else was different.

The ZL-1 actually went into production in 1969 or 1970.

There were a few made. You take an L-88, convert it to aluminum and it more or less became a ZL-1. The ZL-1 was 427 cubic inches, with aluminum block and aluminum heads. I worked on that engine and did the block and heads. I was the project engineer. I was the ZL-1 man, as far a doing the block and doing the heads and intake manifold and pistons and things like that. When it came to putting it all on the dynamometer stand and tuning it up to get it to run for fuel and carburetion and spark, that was somebody else.

I was the hardware person, not the controls, not the fuel or spark control person. I designed the hardware. There were three people in the engine group that worked for Duntov full time, Denny Davis, Cal Wade, and myself.

The ZL-1 came after the Corvette Engine Group disbanded. We were working for Duntov on Corvette racing projects. Then they decided to put the engine group back together again. So, they took us, the three engineers that were working for Duntov, and we were put on other jobs. I went to the main engine group and the other two guys went to other places. So, when I worked on the ZL-1, I wasn't working for Duntov, although he was still around promoting the Corvette with the ZL-1. The direction for the design was over with the main engine group at that time. I was made assistant staff engineer about that time, then I supervised the design work on that engine.

The LS-6 gets you into the 454 cubic inch engines. Let's say, if you take what used to have been an L-72 (an L-72 was mechanically like a 427 with an equivalent carburetor on it), the LS-6 was about the same thing except it had 454 cubic inches. It also included cylinder heads that were made of iron which were nearly a dead ringer copy of the aluminum ZL-1 heads. That iron head is still around today and is still being used in boat racing. The LS-7 was like a 454 cubic inch L-88. Then we had a 454 cubic inch ZL-1 that was called the LT-2. LS-7 and LT-2 never came out. The ZL-1 had an aluminum block and aluminum heads.

We worked with Bruce McLaren on basic engine components for the Can-Am, but at the time we were working on it, it was big bore, short stroke with 430 cubic inches. We made the bores as big as we could go and then de-stroked it. So, we had a big bore, short stroke engine for Can-Ams. I worked on that project, too. I did some of the blocks and cranks for that engine and the pistons.

Now you take that kind of an engine with such a big bore in it, put the biggest stroke in it you can get in, and that is when you start getting 490 cubic inches. However, all of that kind of stuff was done on the outside. We had the ingredients here. We had the big stroke crankshafts, something like four and a quarter inch stroke - similar to the one used in the 454, and we had big bore block castings.

Back in 1969, I became manager of high performance engine design, and Herb Fishel was one of the first engineers to work for me. Piggins was not exactly in charge of design at that time, but brought back inputs from the outside. Polkinghorne was the design group leader during that period.

At about the time, in the early 70s, when the Monte Carlo came out and Chevrolets were NASCAR racing, I kind of lost touch with all that. About then, high performance was turned over to the product performance group as it exists today. That was Vince Piggins' group. From 1972-1973 on, I've worked on production engines. I finished up with the last of the Corvette "Mark" engines in 1974. That was the last year for the big block in the Corvette.

On the small blocks, I worked on the LT-1. It was a 350 cubic inch Z-28. The Z-28 in the beginning was a 302. It had a mechanical lifter camshaft, big holley four barrel, and short stroke crankshaft. When they made it 350 cubic inches, it was the LT-1. Then we also worked on the big aluminum cross ram intake manifold with two four barrel carburetors that appeared in Trans-Am series 302 engines. In time, we designed every kind of manifold you could think of for Duntov. We also designed every kind of cylinder head you could think of, too.

The first thing that I designed for Duntov was the three valve, overhead cam cylinder head and intake. Then we worked on a hemi, a hemi head with push rods; then a hemi head overhead cam; then we had a double overhead cam shaft gear driven hemi head. The last thing we designed was a four valve 454, a cylinder head with four valves per cylinder, and dual overhead camshafts.

That's the kind of stuff you hear of today, four valves per cylinder. That would have been the ultimate, I guess, but we didn't really finish it. We got to the point where we said it is time to quit, (1970-71).

We designed performance engines such as hemi-head or overhead cam or push rod engines, and we put it on the dynamometer stand and take a few shots at horsepower. We would do design and development up to a point, and then put it away. I guess this gave us the opportunity to flex out engineering muscles. It was a good design exercise, and it kept us in shape. I was primarily a hardware designer. I designed the hardware and Denny Davis, Cal Wade and others tuned it.

I think there was never any intention, when we did an engine, to put it into production. But we wanted to be ready. If we ever got to put something like that into production, we would have had the expertise to do it and do it right.

Bill Howell

Chevrolet Test Engineer
Recalls more than twenty years with Chevrolet

I was hired directly into the Chevrolet test laboratory in July, 1961, just out of college, and I worked in the test lab on engine development from 1961 through 1967. Then, in the fall of 1967, I went to work for Vince Piggins in what has been known by different names but was then called product performance engineering.

The test lab was under Max Rensch. Zora Duntov had a group of his own that tested in the lab. They designed the Corvette engines, but they were a separate entity from the V-8 engine group. The inline 6 engine group was a separate group also, but they were all in power train development. Vinces's group used anything that was developed by any group for Chevy's racing interests.

The Corvette was rather unique in that they had Zora, the unique personality. But also, whoever was in charge of the organization chart gave them their own branch where they could coordinate the chassis as well as the engine. They had a continuous engine development program, but it was basically an offshoot of the basic V-8 group who also had a continuous development program at the same time. So, there were always two parallel groups going on any engine that the Corvette group was interested in and obviously the Corvette group was not interested in everything that Chevrolet had going. They were, in effect, in charge of the high performance development of both small and big block V-8 engines.

When I went to work, the big block was the 409. It went by the name of the W-engine. The Z-11 was one of the options of the 409. The Z-11 was a 427. The Corvette group had the responsibility for high performance development of that and the 327. The basic V-8 group had all the other development for those engines, the truck application and the passenger car application. There was some overlap of design responsibility. In other words, Zora couldn't design a whole new cylinder head without having it coordinated with the basic V-8 group, because you had to utilize it in more places than just the Corvette. So, it had to have a wide application in the Chevrolet Division.

When I joined Chevrolet in 1961, they were finishing the initial design of the Mk II. In late 1961, the parts for the engine started to appear. That is when they started calling the W-engine the Mk I to distinguish it from the Mk II. There became, inside the corporation, a competition between the V-8 engine design group who had the responsibility for the Mk II and Zora's group who still had the responsibility for the Mk I. There was an actual competition between internal groups to see if the Mk II engine was a better engine than the Mk I, and in fairly short order, the Mk II won out.

The Mk II was a completely different engine except for the crankshaft and the rods which, I think, were common. But those were about the only parts in it that were common. For some reason, whoever was in charge over all V-8 engine design decided not to let Zora's group design and develop the Mk II. It was designed as a racing engine right from scratch with the idea that you could de-tune it for street use easier that you could take a truck engine, like the W-engine, and make a race engine out of it. Management decided that was their mistake because the W-engine was such a flop as a race engine. They took a truck engine and tried to make a race engine. The new philosophy was to build a race engine, then de-tune it for passenger cars.

The Z-11 package didn't come along until well into 1962 or 1963. Zora's group had it on the drawing board at the same time that the Mark II engine was well underway and running on a dynamometer. The Z-11 was still a flop compared to the Mark II. However, the Mark II got set back in its introduction until 1965 through internal corporate decree, but some of the Z-11s did get out. There were actually some of them sold, but none of the Mark IIs. Some of them got out, but they were never put in a vehicle and sold like the Z-11s were.

Smokey, Junior Johnson and Rex White all had Mark II engines in late 1962 and early '63. The plan was to go to Daytona with that engine in 1963, and go into production with it as a racing engine, probably by making some token offering of it in vehicles so that it could qualify as a production car. All was going along full steam until February, 1963 when we were actually at Daytona. The corporation pulled the rug out from under us and said, "you are doing what you are not supposed to be doing".

So they, in effect, cancelled the Mk II, but nobody cancelled the Z-11, or the Mark I, engine. Chevrolet was allowed to go ahead with the development on the Mark I engine, and the Z-11 kind of came along in 1962 or 1963. The only reason that it got a reputation was it was the only thing we had. As far as ability, it was overshadowed by the Mark II, but the Mark II never got out. A few slipped out in 1963 when they went to Daytona. Out the back door, we fed some pieces to try and keep them alive through 1963. Rex White, the 1961 NASCAR Champion, had to drop out of that program by the middle of 1963 because he couldn't get hardware. Ray Fox was the man who owned the cars that Junior Johnson was running, and Smokey chose not to run very often. So, Vince kind of funneled the hardware over to Ray Fox to keep Junior running. I think he ran the whole season on it.

At this time, Ray Fox and Junior Johnson actually had a direct tie-in with the factory that was set up before Smokey. In fact, we ran vehicle tests at Mesa, Arizona in November of 1962 and Smokey wasn't even a part of the program. We tested with Rex White. Rex built two new cars specifically for this test in November. They were brand new 1963 automobiles, and Junior Johnson and Ray Fox were invited out there for the tests. Smokey was not yet a participant.

Smokey had been running Pontiacs with Bunkie Knudsen in 1962, and when our tests were done in November and Smokey heard how fast our cars were, he jumped on the band wagon. Since he had the influence through Bunkie, he was able to get the hardware before Daytona. He may not have even built the car he raced at Daytona. It may have been a Rex White built car. Johnny Rutherford drove at Daytona.

Rutherford was pretty much a rookie then. As a matter of fact, he looped it out of turn two and lost a lap or more. He wasn't able to be a factor in the race, but I think he was the only one running by the end (the only Mk II running at the end).

Smokey was not captain of the ship on the Mk II until after Daytona, but there are not very many people around that can deny it anymore.

Ray Fox, Rex White and Smokey were the three people that received the Mk IIs. However, we sold one other one to Ford and one to a guy who drove the car it went into, named Bubba Farr. If you can find any of the entries from the 1963 Daytona, you will find there was a fifth car. There was Rex who had one, Ray and Junior had two, Smokey had one and the fifth one was Bubba Farr. G. C. Spencer drove the second car for Ray. Every Chevrolet in that race led the race at one time except for Bubba Farr.

It was a real hassle trying to get enough good parts to go racing as fast as that engine design came along. It was probably the middle of 1962 before we found out that it was significantly better than the 409. We were making major strides in development by the fall of 1962, but there just weren't many parts. So, to try and push these developments into production in time for the race in 1963 was almost more than we could do.

The 409 had so many problems that never got developed out of it that it was a basket case to try and race in stock cars.

I don't know the politics that allowed Pontiac to do what they did up until that point, or allowed Chevrolet to race out the back door with Rex White in the early 60s, but somebody on the 14th floor got their back up, probably because out stuff was suddenly so fast by Daytona time, that Ford and Chrysler, through their presidents and vice presidents got back to the president of General Motors saying, "Hey, you guys are cheating" and our vice presidents probably didn't know it.

After Daytona, I can remember Vince telling me the story about getting the phone call from his boss and having to call Daytona and tell them that the deal was off and to fold up their tents and tell the people that we were not going to support them for the year. That was a big deal, but I wasn't in Vince's group at the time, so I got it all second hand. I was at Daytona for the race, but I was on my own nickel in 1963.

The Mk IIs were like engines that were built on the production line. It was similar to engines that went down the line as a high performance passenger car engines, no head work, no polishing, none of that stuff. In those days, the racers did their own engine building, their own assembly, their own blue printing. Both Ford and Chrysler tried to keep the racers out of it. They didn't want someone "improving" their stuff, so they made them run it the way it was, and they didn't sell their parts, either.

Chevrolet actually sold engines. We always have. That's why every Saturday night racer in the country ends up running Chevrolet instead of Ford or Chrysler.

In 1963 and 1964 locally here at Mount Clemens, and I am sure in a lot of other parts of the country, there were some very fast running Ford stock cars. I think they were 427s, and they dominated racing around here. No one ran Chevrolets. So as late as that, they were a viable option for Saturday night racers. By 1969 or before, you couldn't find a Ford anywhere or a Chrysler, either.

The vast majority of racers in this country are semi-pro racers; Saturday night racing at the local track for money. I guess that is what makes them semi-professional, they get paid for it. That market was dominated by Chevrolet because we kept the good parts in the catalog and sold them for a fair price.

During my days in the test lab, we did a variety of interesting engines under Zora's direction that never saw the light of day as far as production goes. The sequence that happens after you design something and get it ready to run, you then turn it over to someone else to run it. The designer does not run it, so the man who directs the testing of it is usually the development engineer.

You are never happy with the first results, so the design engineer and the development engineer get together and try to make it better. Well, what if you try a different camshaft? So you make four or five different kinds of camshafts. The designer does that, then the development engineer plugs them into the engine and schedules the tests. Little by little, you develop a viable engine out of this design.

In spite of what the Europeans will tell you, nothing comes off the drawing board perfect. The success of racing engines in the real world is a product of design and development. We have had a recent example in the form of the Chevrolet-Ilmor Indy engine, where the program was sold because it would come off the drawing board perfect. There isn't a part on the Ilmor that hasn't been redesigned several times since the first design came off the drawing board.

You can be fairly creative. A development engineer does have a lot of input into the finished product because it is up to him to find the mistakes of the design engineer. It is also up to him to find them in a way that they can be improved upon and not junked. The Mk IV is an example.

In 1962, we had 427 Mk IIs up to about 510 to 520 horsepower. When I went to work for Chevrolet in 1961, the Mk I would put out 425 horsepower at about 6000-6200 rpms, and that was all it would do. By the time we put the 396 on the market in 1965, the street engine would put out 440 horsepower.

After 1963, we kept running the Mk IIs for another year or two as developoment engines for the Mk IV because the design concept stayed the same. The "porcupine" head with staggered valves, all that stuff stayed the same. They changed a lot of the basic design of the Mk IV based on the weaknesses that the Mk II showed. For instance, they put four bolt main caps and larger mains on it.

The main caps would walk around as a result of just two bolts, and Smokey did contribute to that. He pointed out early in the engines that he ran that the main caps were not staying where they belonged, and he came up with a support that went over the two bolt cap with two extra bolts on the outside, which in effect, kind of gave it a four bolt pattern. That was one of his modifications.

Even though they were both 427s, the Mk II had an expensive cylinder head and push rod guide arrangement. So they got some economy into the design by changing that in the Mk IV, but they retained all the performance values of the Mk II. It had a different and stronger connecting rod, bigger bolts, everything just by evolution. By the time it was the Mk IV, it was quite a bit different.

We almost always ran into high rpm valve train problems.

Even on the dyno, their true potential never was illustrated because the power curve would still be going straight up at the time the engines would run into valve train problems. Other than an engine or two that Zora had, there was not much in the way of exotic engines. Fred Frincke designed single and double overhead cam heads, and when he finally got one for the small block, it was really an impressive engine. But as long as they were push rod engines, we never really got anything that I was to impressed with, even though the power was good.

Although Penske raced a Mk IV at Daytona and Sebring early in 1966, that engine actually didn't make it to market until later, as the production version of the L-88. There were always 427 versions around, from the very beginning, both 396 and 427 Mk IV engines, and I ran both of them as test engines from 1962 to '67. I was the sole test engineer on high performance Mk IV engines.

The 396 generation came about as an accident. In 1963, NASCAR said that they were going to quit running 427s and back up to 396. So that was when we started looking at the Mk II as a 396 instead of as a 427. The 396 had the same bore as the 427 but with a shorter stroke. The Mk II 396 was a humdinger of an engine.

We tested that engine in NASCAR trim the fall of 1963. We had Smokey do a Chevelle, the first Chevelle bodied stock car. We tested it down in Fort Stockton, Texas, again with an eye toward running the Daytona 500 in 1964 as an under-the-table deal. Anyway, the 396 came about only as a result of this NASCAR edict that they were not going to run 427s anymore.

From then on, we stayed with the 396 until they decided that there was no reason to stay with it, and Chevrolet offered the 427 as a product in 1966.

All the RPOs had an L designation. There were three versions of the 396, a mild hydraulic cam version called the L-35; a hotter hydraulic lifter version called the L-34, and the L-76 - a mechanical lifter 396. The 427 came along in 1966 as an L-72 with the mechanical lifter version and the L-36 as a 427 hydraulic lifter street engine. There was only one street version of the 427 and one high performance version with cast iron heads. Then we had the aluminum 427, the L-68, I think, was the three-carburetor Corvette engine. Then we had the L-88 which was a very limited Corvette production engine with aluminum heads and a race cam and a single four barrel. The L-89, I think, was a single four barrel, aluminum head street high performance engine.

There were several other versions with aluminum heads with hydraulic lifter cams and mechanical lifter cams. There was a very limited run that was put in the Chevelle 396 in 1965. It was a very unique engine. It was only available in 1965. It was a hydraulic lifter cam engine, but it had big valve heads on it, so it was a real odd ball. We had a lot of stuff that we could mix and match. There were lots of RPO numbers. You almost need the AMA specs for that period.

There was a rivalry, a jealously within the Chevrolet Division. The Corvette people always wanted to do their own thing compared to Vince's group. Vince had the "responsibility" for all racing program liaison with Chevrolet, but the

Corvette group always resented that, and because Zora was a strong enough personality, he didn't have to live by that edict. So, he was able to do his own thing, with people like John Greenwood. His small group had their own feelers out into the world and the people that they worked with, but any other type of racing got referred to Vince. When I went to work for him, Vince was reporting to Public Relations. Then, they changed that and put him under Research and Development about 1969 or 1970. Then they later changed that name to Advanced Design.

When we did the ZL-1 in 1968, we were trying to take what was developed as a Chaparral big block engine and turn it into a production racing engine. Originally, the 1965-66 Chaparral was a small block, an aluminum small block. Then Penske, with a Traco engine, blew their doors off. The early Can-Am series was dominated by the small block. When Bruce Mclaren started running in 1967, he won with a small block, then we got acquainted with him in 1968. By '68 the Chaparral had been converted to a big block aluminum engine. It was a pretty exotic conversion. It had a built-in dry sump pump in the front of the engine, a cast alloy oil pan with dry sump pick ups in it. It was a factory designed dry sump engine. This was an R&D designed Mk IV racing engine, all aluminum with all this exotic stuff. That was the Chaparral.

In 1968, Vince decided to sell that engine to Can-Am customers. It became evident if people like Penske and Mclaren could come around and beat the Chaparral that we better have somebody else out there besides Chaparral running Chevrolet products, so we had deals with Penske on the Camaro to run the Camaro at Daytona and Sebring and in the Trans-Am from then on.

His 1965-66 Corvette big block was a deal through the Corvette group. Vince wasn't involved in that, but by 1967 we had a deal through Vince's group for Penske to run Camaros in the Trans-Am, and Penske was doing his own thing with the rear engine Lola in the Can-Am and USRRC series.

Then McLaren came along and blew everybody's doors off in 1967 and 1968. During the latter part of 1967, it was rumored that Mclaren was going with Ford, so Vince put out some feelers and we got Bruce McLaren in and met with him and convinced him that he would be much wiser to stay with Chevrolet. He had a proven winner and we had this coming along and this and this. For one year we made the Chaparral aluminum block and dry sump parts and everything available to the Can-Am racers, the 427.

In 1969, the ZL-1 was actually a legitimate option. We sold the ZL-1 blocks in quantity. It was a 427 only. The ZL-1 was always an aluminum block. In 1968, we didn't have it in production enough for the Can-Am yet, so we sold them the Chaparral version. The Chaparral version had the built in dry sump pump and it had some different oil passages drilled and cast into the block. It was actually a different block. It was off of unique pattern equipment. It was a physically different casting. Even though the bore centers were all the same and bore sizes were all the same, it was unique. The ZL-1 was a production version of that casting. We did that for one year. Then by 1970, we were offering a large bore aluminum block with iron liners to the Can-Am racers.

For one year, we offered the steel liner 4.440-inch bore aluminum block to the Can-Am racers. This was the second evolution of the ZL-1 block. And then the following year, we offered the A-390 alloy all aluminum block in which we ran the pistons right on the aluminum bores.

A-390 is a high silicone alloy. It is the same alloy that we used in the Vega engine. In the Vega, we found out we could run on aluminum bores, and we wanted to demonstrate that capability in racing. In a sense, Vince never did anything that wasn't in some way going to benefit the other groups in Chevrolet, either from a publicity stand point or product development. The Can-Am 390 alloy V-8 was to demonstrate that you could use this alloy in a different environment, other than a bread and butter grocery getter like the Vega.

The Can-Am pistons were special, too. They had to be iron coated by electrolysis just like you would tin plate something by electrolysis. They had a process for iron plating on an aluminum piston, a very thin coating like a few ten-thousandths of an inch thick. That was to prevent galling of the aluminum on aluminum. The rings were a chrome plated. There was a compatibility problem if you ran aluminum on aluminum.

We offered that engine for two years, the A-390 alloy block, then we got out of it when the Can-Am died with the advent of the turbo Porsche. McLaren lost their sponsor, but in the period from 1969 on, all of our Can-Am development was done by McLaren under contract.

McLaren did their own engines. Gary Knutson, who did their engines, was a "graduate" of the Traco school. Gary worked for McLaren in 1967, then he hired in and worked for Jim Hall at Chaparral in 1968. Then McLaren hired George Boltoff who was a Traco employee. George ran the McLaren program for two years, one year in England and one year in the U.S. Then they hired Gary Knutson back from Chaparral in 1970, and Gary ran it for a number of years.

They did contract development for us starting in 1969, and in 1970 they pitched all the high performance development out of the laboratory at Chevrolet because the emission requirements were so great on our facility. We had to go 100% outside of Chevrolet to do our high performance development.

We did most of our development work with McLaren's dyno shop in Livonia, and worked with them starting in 1969 through 1978. We didn't work with anybody else, but by then there were active NASCAR programs, and the NASCAR guys pretty much did their own development.

It was 1971 or 1972, when the Monte Carlo started to become a force in NASCAR. Those were big block race cars, 427s. We had a lean period after 1970 and 1971 when we didn't have any money to spend. But again, Vince was persuaded that we could be competitive if we had the right man running the stuff. Vince convinced Junior Johnson to try Chevrolet, and the real essence of what we were able to do then is something that has never been disclosed or expounded on.

From 1963 on, we had no money to spend, so anybody that

we got to run Chevrolet stuff was mostly an arm waving job, a few trick parts deals, but no money was involved. That took a little bit of a break in 1967 when they decided that they had to make the Camaro famous, and they hired Penske to run the Camaro. They paid him some (never enough, according to him). Then, the Chaparral era; I don't believe that Jim Hall was ever on the payroll. I think that it was just research that he was being supported by. The McLaren program involved some money at first to keep them from going to Ford, but the money disappeared, and we had them on a development contract, parts and stuff like that. We kept the racing scene alive at Chevrolet, really, on just talk and a few parts, and we built loyalties over the years. That was very difficult to do, but sometimes they are better loyalties than you can buy with money anyway.

Vince had a philosophy that it was a good deal if both sides came out a winner, the racer and Chevrolet, so you can strike a lot of good deals that way, and it doesn't take a lot of help to get things going. The empire, if that is what it could be called, was built between 1963 and the 1980's when Herb Fishel came in, and performance again had a good name.

There was a change in management philosophy about racing. They finally saw that you could sell cars with high performance. The whole 1970's decade, we were struggling to meet the emission requirements and spending every dime we had on that. Vince's group was barely able to stay alive on a minimum budget because we always operated on engineering funds. Chrysler and Ford always operated off of their sales department, their merchandising budget. They've always had more money to spend than engineering does. That always seemed to be a handicap for Chevrolet, but in a sense, maybe it wasn't a handicap because it kept the program small and kept the quality high.

I retired from Chevrolet in September of 1987. At the time, our group was involved in the return of Chevrolet in racing on a major scale.

Now for a little bit of philosophy. In the middle and late 1960's when Chrysler and Ford were battling in NASCAR, we just stood back and watched because we didn't have any money to buy in, and those guys were spending a lot of money trying to out do one another. That is why you didn't find any competitive Chevrolets, from 1963 on, in NASCAR. Then when Ford and Chrysler got tired of hitting each other over the head with their money and they backed out, NASCAR was willing to put in rules that made Chevrolet competitive.

They outlawed the hemi, and I think they outlawed the BOSS 429. All of a sudden the best show in town was the Chevrolet big block. So, we were back competitive again. Vince's philosophy was that we didn't want to buy into NASCAR, that they were just another race group like the guys at Indy. Anyway, we didn't have the money to buy in.

I believe that Ford's philosophy was "win on Sunday and sell on Monday". The people at Chevrolet that controlled the purse strings didn't agree with that. In the 1980's, they finally could see that racing sold cars. It came about because of the Monte Carlo. You almost could not give them away in 1982 and '83.

Everybody running GM cars in NASCAR were running Buicks or something other than the Chevrolet, because the Monte Carlo was such a brick. So, in 1983, they did the aero nose for the Monte Carlo. I sat in on the meeting where they decided that they were going to do six thousand cars, and they were afraid that they were going to have to eat five thousand of them because they were so ugly, at least they were ugly to the guy that originally designed the Monte Carlo. They were so concerned that they only put one interior option with them and only wanted to go with two colors. All this stuff because we knew we were not going to sell these cars. "Nobody is going to buy them", but history will tell you how good a seller it has been. If nothing else proves that racing sells cars, it kept the Monte Carlo alive when it was a dead duck. The Monte Carlo rear glass was just self defense. We had to do that to keep up with the Thunderbird. I think that the Thunderbird ate our lunch in 1985 when it came out. NASCAR let Pontiac and Chevrolet do a fast back, and I am not sure why they ever bought it, but they did. The Monte Carlo couldn't get any rear down force with the notch back car. The cars were going fast enough, but they were flying. They couldn't keep them going straight. So, I think maybe NASCAR let us have that sloped back window for safety reasons.

AG: What do you think of the latest development, the engine in the ZR-1?

Bill: I saw it out at Riverside last fall, and I was very impressed with it. I don't know if they are struggling to get it on the market or not. As a high performance street engine, it has all the bells and whistles. I don't know where we are going with high performance street engines. I am a little nervous about 180 mile per hour cars.

The people who are spending the money to do that stuff are still spending money, so the designers are going to do it. It has always been that way. If the money was available, you could do new stuff. If the money wasn't available, you had to get along with the old stuff.

The Japanese are able to bring these exotic engines into the main stream at a reasonable price. I have no idea how they can do it and make any money on them. Maybe they aren't, but they are upping the ante. They are putting the pressure on the Germans and everybody else to make exotic stuff to keep up with them. When you look at that SHO Taurus, for instance, with that 24 valve Yamaha engine in it, that is pretty zoomy, but I don't think that is the bread and butter part of the industry. And I don't think that it is the bread and butter part of racing.

If you look at the serious areas of racing, they are all going along a path which they are trying to direct as the right path. NASCAR is really trying to figure out some way to use less horsepower and be less exotic because there is only so much money available for racing, and you can sure spend it in a hurry when you get exotic. And Indy cars, they wish that they hadn't done some of the things they have. They don't know how to get back to an economical engine. Formula one is now going back to the naturally aspirated engine from the turbos hoping that is going to save them something.

AG: Do you think that the Ford Cosworth and the Chevy

Ilmor will go head-to-head in Formula-1?

Bill: I hear rumors about that, but if they are ever going to do anything, it all depends on whether someone wants to spend the money. If the corporation decides that they have the extra money and somebody appropriates some of it to do Ilmor, then it will happen, but I don't know if it will be a winner. I am still a push rod engine man myself from all the years that I spent on them. From all the development that hasn't been done yet, there are lots of areas yet, even though we have made break-throughs over the years.

When I went to work for Chevy in 1961, we were getting 425 horsepower out of a 409. When we started racing the Camaro in 1967, we were getting 425 horsepower out of a 302. It still had one four barrel on it. That was 100-plus inches away with the same power. We essentially stopped developing big blocks in 1967 or 1968, and any big block development since then was done by the drag racers. Herb Fishel's group kind of fell back on it out of self protection and has done some cylinder head stuff, but too many people are cashing in on our reputation by building cylinder heads to put on our blocks

and call them Oldsmobiles and Pontiacs and Buicks.

The small block development has gone along pretty steady. I have seen 335 inch small blocks pull 650 horsepower, and you can get about an equivalent power per inch out of a V-6, or even a little better that that. The V-6 is a hell of an engine as far as I am concerned.

We have valve train development that is up to the 9000 rpm range now. Again, development is the key word. The development engineer, and I am saying this with a bias, is the unsung hero. The designers get all the credit, but it is the development engineer that makes the design work.

A lot of things have happened over the years from 1957 on that Vince orchestrated, and he is the man who should really get a lot of credit. He has never gotten it over the years because he had to operate behind the scenes and with a low profile. There wasn't a racer out there that didn't know Vince Piggins. Vince really kept the Chevrolet program alive, even when everybody else cancelled all of their programs.

A good percentage of the reason that Chevrolet is where it is today is because of Vince Piggins.

Drag racer Wally Booth, left, chats with Paul Prior and Vince Piggins, right. Photo courtesy Paul Prior.

Paul Prior

**Relates his years with Vince Piggins'
Product Promotion Group**

I hired in during 1950 out at the proving grounds, and then I went to work at Chevrolet for Walt Mackenzie in 1951. In

1955 when Chevrolet introduced the V-8, 265 cubic inches, it was originally available in two versions, 2-barrel and 4-barrel, 162 horsepower and 180 horsepower. These very quickly became popular with people in competitive activities, primarily round track racing.

At the very beginning, Cole, who was the Chief Engineer in those days, told our big boss Mackenzie to coordinate racing activities. Mackenzie was a staff engineer and reported to Cole. He had a number of activities under him, though none of them included racing until Cole asked him to do something about this. Under Mackenzie, Mauri Rose was the first head of this activity. Rose had one fellow working for him, Bill Konopacke. I think he is still working out at the proving grounds.

That was a fairly short lived arrangement, and it got kind of chaotic. At about the same time, Hudson and Nash formed American Motors, and one of the guys that had worked for Hudson was Vince Piggins. With this merger, I guess he became available and must have approached someone at Chevrolet and Mackenzie hired him. So Vince headed the group and Mauri was part of the group for a while.

Ralph Miller was also one of the group. He later went to the sales department and became a district manager out in the middle of Kansas. There was one other fellow who left the group and went to the sales department and started the *Corvette News* magazine. This was in 1957 after the AMA agreement, after Vince's group had split up.

GM embraced the AMA resolution hook, line and sinker, and Vince went into production engineering. He became a field rep for service problems mainly on trucks, and the various fellows that had worked for him went to other places. The whole activity was abolished, and that held for some time. But people on the outside continued their competitive activities. By one way or the other, they would try to get information or help or whatever they could get from various people in engineering.

It turned out that there were a number of people as individuals helping various outsiders with varying degrees of effect. Cole, by this time in 1960, was general manager, so he decided that even though we were adhering to the AMA resolution, there had to be an activity, or at least it should be centralized to eliminate all of these little groups that were working individually (and not accountable). Vince was pulled out of the production engineering job and put back under Mackenzie. At that time in 1960, I went to work for Vince.

When Cole decided that there had to be some form of activity, again under Mackenzie, Vince and I were the group. At that time, there was very little we could do. We had a very small budget, but one thing we were able to do was set up a channel to merchandise parts. Ironically, many dealers at that time didn't like to mess with performance parts, so we set up an arrangement with Jim Rathman who was then a marine dealer in Miami and not associated with Chevrolet in any way.

Jim knew the racing business, and he also knew Cole pretty well. Geographically, he was about right for the NASCAR group, so he was set up as a place to sell parts. It wasn't long after that arrangement started that Rathman became a Chevrolet-Cadillac dealer in Melbourne, Fla. That is a little story in itself.

Melbourne was a sleepy little town, and the dealer there was about to retire. Rathman took over, I think Cole probably had something to do with it, and Rathman hadn't been there but 2 or 3 weeks when the government announced that Cape Canaveral was going to be the headquarters for everything in space. All of a sudden, Rathman was setting on this gold mine, but he still functioned as a dealer to the NASCAR crowd.

We were also able to maintain small developmental programs like Rex White who was Grand National champion in 1960. We were able to help him somewhat by using him to do certain developmental work for us. Rex and his chief mechanic Louie Clemmens were a lot of help. I think Clemmens is retired now from the GM Desert Proving Grounds.

I was not in the group that Vince originally formed in 1955. Physically, they were close to us and we all worked for the same big boss, Mackenzie. I am sure you have heard this story before, but from 1955-1957, until June of '57, racing was a wide open thing. They had the "seed company", Southern Engineering Development Company, in Atlanta. Virtually everyone ran out of that place. It was under Mackenzie but Vince handled the details of it.

Let's digress a little bit. When Zora came to Chevrolet in 1953, I believe it was May of '53, back in those days we were down in the GM building on Grand Boulevard, Detroit. On the GM building, there is a Chevrolet annex on the back side of it, but Chevrolet had out-grown this annex, particularly the engineering part of Chevrolet. I was a technical writer in those days, and we were in what had been the auditorium of the GM building. On the stage, what had been the stage was now this little group that Maurice Olley had, which was later to become R&D.

Mauri Rose was part of that group, and he had a lot to do with development of the chassis and drive line on the original Corvette. Zora came into that group when he hired in. The Corvette was already an accomplished thing by then. In fact, I went with the original Corvette to the Motorama in Miami, Washington, DC and Chicago that year. Zora, if I recall, took some kind of leave that year, maybe the summer of '53, and went over and drove in Le Mans for Porsche. Then, I didn't hear a whole lot about Zora for awhile. Later, he flipped a car and broke his back at the Proving Grounds. Again, I don't know what year that was. It must have been some time in 1955. During the period that the "seed company" existed, Corvette racing was handled out of SEDCO in Atlanta.

I think a guy named Red Byron was the head of Corvette activities at the "seed company". Rathman's involvement as a parts dealer did not start until 1960 when Cole, through Mackenzie, had a group reestablished. During that period, things went along very smoothly. We had a few development programs with Rex, with the 348 and 409, and he won the 1960 championship with the 348. Of course, the 409 never did quite as well as a lot of people thought it should in NASCAR racing. It was fine in drag racing but not in NASCAR. The 409 years were kind of nothing spectacular, although Ned Jarrett won the national championship in 1961 with a 409, but not by winning many firsts. Rex White was second.

That led up to what is often referred to as the "mystery engine", the Mk II. It had the same bore centers as the W-engine. The W-engine was our terminology for the 348 - 409 family of engines. I think there was a fair amount of politics involved in the mystery engine.

It was Dick Keinath's development, and right off the bat, it showed real promise on the dyno. We had a couple of cars built. Rex and Louie built them. They were essentially Grand National cars. I bet you can't believe how much they were built for! $5,000 each.

By this time, Knudsen was the General Manager. Knudsen had a reputation for being pretty racy, and Smokey was fairly privy to what was going on with the Mk II development. Smokey and Knudsen were very close.

Well, Knudsen became enthused about the Mk II. Of course, everyone else was also. The cars that Rex and Louie built were out at Mesa (Proving Grounds) for development. We sent a couple of the Mk II experimental engines out there, and they ran great. The Mk II made its debut at Daytona for the 500 in 1963.

It seemed like, in those, that everybody expected a lot out of the 409s, but Pontiacs with the 389s were going faster, and someone got to asking some questons and wondered if the road load requirement was less on the Pontiac. Nobody really knew the answer. The road load requirement is the horsepower requirement for any given speed. NASCAR set the weights. So, we bought (Rathman bought a 1961 Pontiac from Ray Fox) that I think David Pearson had run during some of the 1961 season. We fixed it so that we could put a Chevy engine in it. We also got one of Ray Fox's good Pontiac engines. We also took Rex White's car at the same time, a Chevy with a 409 engine. This was about September, 1962. We were still trying to make headway with the 409, trying to find out why it wasn't performing as well as it should.

It turned out that the Pontiac did not require as much power as the Chevy, Rex White's Chevy. We eventually found out why. I don't know why, but Rex preferred to have the front end a little high, and Ray Fox ran with the nose down. The "Cd" factor is a lot better going over the top of the car versus going underneath the car. So that is really about all it was. Although we didn't discover that until they were running them out of Mesa, we knew that Rex White's car was nose up and Ray Fox's car was nose down, but we really didn't stumble on to it until that time.

At that test series at Daytona, we did discover plenum air was a good source of cooler air, from the ventilation plenum at the base of the windshield - cowl induction. What we did was, we instrumented those cars very thoroughly under the hood. We took temperatures at about ten different places under the hood, and carburetor air going in the throat of the carburetor, and air coming off the back of the radiator and air in front of the radiator, about ten different places, and we could see that under the regular NASCAR set up, which was just one big dry element air cleaner in those days, the carburetor air was pretty hot.

Just to see what the effects were, we made some runs with just a simple scoop on top of the hood directly over the carburetor. There was something like a 60 degree drop in air temperature. Naturally, it went faster.

Then we tried air from the back edge of the hood, that is, air from the ventilation system's plenum. Louie Clemmens and I made up the first cowl induction air cleaner hookup. What we did was, we took a stock air cleaner and fashioned some sheet metal that went backwards from it. We made a hole in the dash panel into the plenum and instrumented that. It gave all the air you wanted! Ambient temperature air ran about 4 inches of water slightly pressurized.

I would say that we ran the first cowl induction down there, and the Mystery engine set up ran cowl induction, too, although they got it from a slightly different location than we did, but the principal was the same.

As I understand the politics of the thing, Knudsen went to Bill France, and between the two of them, it was decreed that Chevrolet could run the Mystery engine at Daytona even though in all the world there were not more than 18 of them at that time. They were running real strong, and as race day drew near, Ford was getting more and more upset. They wanted to buy some of these engines. They would call us, and we didn't know anything about them.

They must have gone to Bill France. He called up and said,

"If you guys are going to run that engine, you have to sell two of them to Ford, Holman and Moody." So, we sold two of them to Holman and Moody.

Also with that program, Chevrolet set up some fairly elaborate deals with Ray Fox and Rex White (Junior Johnson was driving for Ray Fox). As I recall, I think Junior did not drive for Ray Fox until the Mystery engine thing. Anyway, Fox built two cars for Johnson, one for short tracks and one for long tracks.

Well, as everybody knows, the cars went fast and that aroused the interest of the press to no end. A few weeks after Daytona, I think it was Donner and Gordon (Chairman of the Board and President of GM) were holding a press conference about something else all together, because for one thing we weren't into racing in those days. I guess Donner and Gordon went through what they wanted to go through, and then the press jumped on them about this so called Mystery engine, and they didn't know anything about it.

That is part of the reason it was called the Mystery engine. Another part is, we were told that we were not to acknowledge the existence of it. But after Holman and Moody bought these two engines and sent them up to Dearborn, they ran them on a dyno there, then they took the heads off for some reason and then realized that they had no new head gaskets. They called us to see about them.

In those days, we knew our counterparts at Ford and they knew us, so they called us and asked us if we would sell them some head gaskets. We played dumb and wouldn't acknowledge anything about it. It was a very awkward situation. It wound up that Henry the second had to call Knudsen to arrange for head gaskets for these engines. That's how dumb it got, but because of the embarrassment that it caused, Donner and Gordon (I don't know how these things happen on the 14th floor), caused Knudsen so much trouble that he eliminated our activity. Vince went back to the service department, and I went into R&D where they were building up a group to work on the Corvairs.

I was in R&D about 6 months when Knudsen was promoted to group vice president, and then Pete Estes became General Manager of Chevrolet. He pretty quickly decided, if only for negative reasons, we still needed an activity like that because in the absence of an activity, people don't know who to go to. So, they go to everybody, and it gets chaotic.

So, Vince and I were back in business, and it stayed that way until I retired in 1980.

AG: In the early 1960s, Dan Gurney raced a car that, I think, was built by Bill Thomas and had a 409 in it. Do you know about that?

Paul: Bill Thomas used to do some development work for us. Bill built a stock car (a '61 Impala) that Gurney drove out at Riverside, maybe in a USAC race. He only drove it twice, I think. It was very light and very fast. That was prior to the Mk II. When Knudsen eliminated us, he also had to wrap up those programs with Smokey, Rex White and Ray Fox. I think Knudsen pretty much did that on his own, although I think that Vince might have been involved in it at some point.

We had to saw off any relationship we had with them. The

144

deal was, they could run as long as the parts lasted, which wasn't very long. Then everybody went to other things. I think that Rex White went to work as a service manager for a Chrysler Dealership in Atlanta. As far as I know, he is still there.

Louie Clemmens floundered around for awhile and then Doug Roe got him a job out at Mesa, the Desert Proving Grounds. I think Louie is retired now.

Going back to the 409, it was always more successful as a drag engine; Hayden Proffitt, Don Nicholson, Dave Strickler. Bill Jenkins built Strickler's cars. Fred Sanderson of Phoenix also ran a 409 successfully. Don Nicholson and Hayden Proffitt were probably the best known drivers. Originally, Nicholson was from California and later moved to Atlanta. He preceded Proffitt, and both of them worked more or less for Bill Thomas on their drag engines. We were a little bit of assistance, but development wise, it didn't amount to very much.

There were several versions of the 409. There was the original 409 that had 360 hp and then the 380 hp. The 409, per se, did well by itself. Don Nicholson won the Winternationals in 1961 and '62. The engine was virtually brand new, just out of the crate. NHRA didn't have too many National events in those days.

AG: Was it the 409 that the drag racers ran or was it the 427 inch Z-11?

Paul: In 1961 and '62, it was the 409, and the Z-11 came along in 1963. The Z-11 427 had a raised deck manifold. It was the only V-8 that Chevrolet had built that had a separate manifold valley cover. That version was originally built for NASCAR. A few of them ran a single 4-barrel version. The Z-11 was a dual 4-barrel and therefore not allowed in NASCAR. The 409 single 4-bbl was the NASCAR engine. The raised port heads, intake and seperate valley cover were also made in a single 4-bbl version 409, and that would have been the NASCAR set-up were it not for the Mystery engine.

I guess one of the reasons we were running that road load business down in Daytona in late '62 was in anticipation of running this high manifold on the 409, the raised heads and high manifold from the Z-11.

NHRA was always changing their rules. In those days you had to have so many in order to call it Super Stock. I think 50 was the number you had to have. Actually there was more than that built, 55 or so.

AG: There were 55 Z-11 cars built?

Paul: Yes. That arrangement with the high manifold on the 409 looked pretty good, though as soon as the Mk II started showing promise, everybody forgot that. The Z-11 should have been recognized as a Super Stock. It was not.

Even though the so called Mystery engine kind of died, it was in a sense reborn as the Mk IV, or the 396. I think it was 1965 when it went into production. It was not like the Mk II. The Mk II had the smaller bearings and a 3.48-inch stroke where the Mk IV had the 3.76 stroke and smaller bore. It was a good performer but not as good as the Mk II. In 1966 when we had the 427 version, I think that it started performing somewhat better.

AG: When the Camaro came out, were you involved in its comptitive activities?

Paul: I was somewhat involved in that project. Penske was probably the first guy that came along that really had his act together. He was well known to us. He was a dealer in Philadelphia, and he also had the ears of a number of people on the 14th floor. There were a number of things that were occurring in the early Camaro Trans-Am racing that needed some developing, like axle shaft failures and spindle failures.

AG: From the Camaro design, when I read these things, I think it looks like the designers and engineers were designing a race car. Have I analyzed that correctly?

Paul: I think you might be. I think the principal thing was that we needed something to compete against the Mustang. I won't say that they just threw something together, either. Of course, programs down the road were to include that same stub frame and suspension. The first application of the stub frame for Chevrolet was in the Camaro, but the same part number for that whole assembly was used in the Chevy II as well as Camaros.

I think it's true of all racing series that when they first start out, you don't have to be too sophisticated. But then as the perception of it becomes more valuable to people, you have to become more sophisticated. When the Trans-Am first started out, it was a nice SCCA fun thing to do. Then Ford got in it with Peter Revson and Parnelli, then Roger and the Camaros and it started escalating and taking the fun out of it.

AG: Were you involved in the big block Camaros, say the ZL-1?

Paul: The ZL-1 was on the Camaro. Those were COPO (Central Office Production Order). After the COPO program was established. The COPO L-72, for instance, anybody could order it, any dealer could order it as the COPO L-72 Camaro or COPO L-72 Chevelle. But some COPOs were limited, like police cars were limied to legitamate police use. The ZL-1 COPO was limited because of the availability of the aluminum block. The L-72 was the 425 horse 427 iron engine. The ZL-1 was the aluminum block L-88. I think there were 57 COPO Camaros built as ZL-1s.

What the COPO amounted to was virtually just a production L-78 Camaro, which was a 375 horse 396, with deleting the 396 and substituting the ZL-1. Although one of the other changes was the axle ratio, I believe that all the ZL-1 Camaros came with the 4:88, and the close ratio four speed. That was the coarser geared M-22, or "rock crusher". That was the aluminum case Muncie. The aluminum case was common to all Muncie 4-speeds. Other than that, the parts list didn't have to be very long for the COPO. Only a few items were deleted and superseded.

AG: What was the horsepower rating of the ZL-1 from the factory? The Yenko, for instance, was rated at 450 on the sticker, but those were iron block engines, not ZL-1s. Would the ZL-1 also been rated at 450?

Paul: I think 450 is about right, but I would need to look it up.

AG: At this time, were you still in Piggins' group?

Paul: Yes. It was a small group, about 5 people. My responsibility was primarily drag racing.

AG: Did drag racing sort of "go away" like other forms of racing such as Can-Am and Trans-Am in the mid-70s?

Paul: No, I can't say that it ever really decreased in popularity. Of course, the drag rules have always been a very flexible thing. I think we would have preferred it if stock meant stock. The more you could relate stock to a car you bought off the show room floor, the more it meant to us. Pro Stock was an exception to the rule because the guys that did well in Super Stock also were the guys that did well in Pro Stock. So, right away, there wasn't a whole lot to talk about Super Stock, as compared to Pro Stock, and Pro Stock was much closer related to stock back then. Pro Stock today is almost like the funny cars that ran back in the '60s.

In all those years, we were not really involved in racing. Whatever we did we had to justify as a development program.

We weren't really racing. Everything I know of that was done had to have some kind of development program behind it. Maybe that got kind of thin at times, but nonetheless, I think some of us at Chevrolet felt like the corporate bean counters were watching us more closely than they were other divisions.

We did a lot of other things other than racing, maybe not as exciting, though. We did things like the Pure Oil trials that became the Union Pure Oil trials and later the Union 76 Performance Trials. We did all of that. Mobile runs, things like that. Our purpose was to show the product to its best advantage. We always sort of felt we could do it better than anyone else could.

"We" were Vince Piggins, Doug Roe, Bill Howell, John Pierce, Jim Kuhn, Bill Horton, Herb Fishel and Louie Clemmens.

Gib Hufstader

Chevrolet Engineer for Transmissions, Clutches and Chassis Recalls his Racing Days

AG: Gib, how did your get started in racing?

Gib: Well, it starts before I even started school. I worked with some friends in Tacoma Park, Maryland, Joel and Preston Welsh. They started racing stock cars in West Lantam, Maryland, a 1939 Ford standard coupe with a small flathead Ford.

From there, I went on to GMI (General Motors Institute) and was active in the motorsports club up there. I had been building and modifying my own cars for drag racing, mostly just street type cars, and continued on to finish school. Then, I worked in Chevrolet Research and Development with Maurice Olley.

I was drafted, and after the army, I came back to Chevrolet Research and Development. That was in the late 1950s. I worked as a shock absorber engineer, then riding and handling, then in the early '60s, I did the clutches for the Chevrolet manual cars including Corvette and Corvair, and also developed the high speed clutch that was used on the first Mk II engines at Daytona when they were first introduced.

We had a "high burst" driven disc, aluminum backed and nodular pressure plates and flywheels for the car. That design has basically been there ever since. They were small, lightweight flywheels, low inertia, and have been used continually in high performance service ever since; everywhere, small block and big block.

Also, in the early 1960s, I went with Zora Duntov and the Corvette Group to do chassis, transmission, clutch, drive train and axle work on the Corvettes. It was a small group of about four or five engineers. From there, we would help solve known concerns about durability in the production cars as far as being used on the race track, especially when the L-88 came along with higher torques, higher speeds, and higher horsepower. We had to develop a good drive train, and I was involved with that. The racing evolved from that, too.

When the public started using these cars, we would monitor their activities at the track to be sure that the car wasn't abused, and to see if there was any production component that warranted any update or reinforcement. We would provide that in the regular production or service area. There are quite a few examples of that from the drive shafts and spindle bearings, axle bearings, gear cuts, axle lubes, brake pads, brake structure and on and on. There was just a whole host of things that evolved from that activity.

That was the hardware to support racing. Of course, we were not officially involved in racing, and this was all done to protect the users and to see that the car was adequate to get the job done, the job of racing. We had no problem doing that. We didn't do it openly, and I continued on with my first involvement with Penske and Daytona.

I was involved in the Grand Sport program only at the end of the project. They were finishing up about the time I started working for Zora in the Corvette area. So, my real focus was on all the production cars, but we learned a lot of things that we could provide for the future racers of Grand Sports. When Wintersteen began racing them, and other people, we had learned how to make axles quite successful. We could run 24 hours behind a 600-700 horsepower engine without any major problems. We had worked out proper attitudes and proper clearance and braking, etc, and had no problems with cooling. All that was developed in our areas here at Chevrolet.

We had a new transmission, the Muncie option, the M-21 and for high capacity, the M-22 which was often called the "rock crusher" because it was a noisy box. It obviously wasn't designed for noise reduction, and that became the standard for any racing Corvette. They were built at Chevrolet, in the Chevrolet plant, nothing special, just had a different cut on the gears.

AG: As specified by high performance?

Gib: Well, we knew at the time what loads we had to make it for and it worked quite well. We used some higher alloy gears but primarily it was the low helix angle that gave it the much greater capacity. It was primarily for the L-88. That's where it really had to be developed. We carried it on into the ZL-1 and to the 454s, and it was raced successfully. But we did add coolers. Many of the racers wanted coolers and it was a good idea.

AG: When did you get involved with racing with Corvette and Roger Penske?

Gib: It was Daytona. When Sunoco was the direct sponsor of Roger, and Roger was getting Dick Guldstrand to build the car and run it with George Wintersteen and Ben Moore as co-drivers. That started Roger and he went to Sebring. Later, Roger got into the Lolas with Mark Donahue and eventually got a deal to run the Trans-Am Camaros.

AG: Were you involved in racing in the Camaro and Corvette era of the Corning cars?

Gib: The Owens-Corning cars were run by Jerry Thompson, one of the partners in that operation, and most of his crew all worked here. So, they were development engineers at Chevrolet, and they were very close to the product, as close as you could get. But it was not a Chevrolet sponsored car, and, of course, Penske at that time was a different operation. He had many bigger sponsors, but they still had to have, or be advised of all the important information that we had developed. It was certainly to our benefit to have them as well versed as anyone. My driving the Owens-Corning car at Sebring was strictly on the side. That was my opportunity to drive a car.

AG: In the design of the Camaro, I have seen some semi-technical papers showing what appears to be some thought toward application to racing. Were you a part of that?

Gib: I don't know how true that really was. I know a few things that were done that we implemented quickly. One thing was, we changed the upper control arm to provide more camber change. That was a pattern you could lay against the upper control arm mounting pad and relocate holes. We gave them drawings for bushings that would stiffen up the front suspension and the front of the body. Anything that had been learned could be passed on, and it was also available to other Trans-Am racers. Again, they used the "rock crusher" transmissions.

I was involved in designing the four wheel discs for the Camaro. Adding disc brakes to the rear; we just picked up on the Corvette. This was to provide a production release. It was packaged so that it could be homologated in FIA as a production arrangement. It was set up for the racers to overcome the problem of continuing difficulty of balancing disc front - drum rears and overcoming the wear of a rear pad. Prior to the disc brake rear, we had developed a forward adjusting drum brake, but the disc was the best solution. In fact, Jim Patterson who was the SCCA czar at the time even bought one such car as proof that it was in production.

AG: Tell me about your drive with the Corning team.

Gib: It was quite interesting. The cars were pretty good, well set up. A lot of work had been done on them. The one I drove was the first one of that team to finish a long distance race. They had run at Daytona and not finished. I think they had run twice at Daytona and not finished. That was important; to try to get a finishing car.

The problem is driving them to keep them durable. It is tough driving down there. It's a rough course, and it's at night and very crowded. I think we might have lost our class to Don Yenko in another car at the time. It was nice to just see the car finish. That was Sebring in 1969. I never drove Daytona.

AG: The big engines, the L-88, the ZL-1, the Can-Am 494, were they all Chevrolet engineering efforts?

Gib: Yes, the ZL-1, we designed and built it here. In fact, the plant manager in St. Louis during the ZL-1 time had a company car, a ZL-1, and drove it as his assigned car for awhile.

AG: How would you compare the engines, the Mk II mystery engine that became the Mk IV L-88 with some changed in head bolts, bore and stroke and some other things?

Gib: Dick Keinath and Fred Frincke are both experts on the Mk engines, and another one who was an engineer here, Tom Langdon, was development engineer on the LS-6 and LS-7. Ray Shrex in the next office was the production engineer at Tonowanda on the 454s and the LS-7 stuff.

AG: Which was the hot version, the LS-6 or the LS-7?

Gib: The 7 was the full race, high rise engine. The LS-6 was the low rise production version but with big ports, hydraulic cam; really a terrific package. I think that was the real sleeper, and we kick ourselves over it. We had the opportunity to buy them out of our own fleet but passed them by.

There is really a lot more to say. This really just scratches the surface.

You see, we had to run discretely on this during that critical time. There were "minimum involvement" directions from central office. We felt totally honest in observing and updating the components and hardware for the purpose of safety and to improve the quality of the cars so the customers would have a more raceable purchased vehicle. There would be less that you would have to do to it.

AG: In all fairness, Chevrolet was not racing?

Gib: Right, but we obviously had a lot of enthusiasm.

The L-88 version of the Mk IV big block. Chevrolet photo.

The ZL-1 version of the Mk IV big block. Chevrolet photo.

Mk IV Big Blocks

The legacy of the Mk IV series of big block engines has become a lasting tribute to the Chevrolet engineers and production people who made it happen. After more than 20 years since the Mk IV was first introduced, collectors, restorers and Chevy buffs have become increasingly interested in how many of the engines were actually built. There are all sorts of semi-authoritative stories about production numbers, but in order to arrive at accurate information, Chevrolet records are the untimate source.

While talking with Fred Frincke, Chevrolet's engineer on the evolution of the Mk IV, the new generation of Mk V truck engine, I inquired about production figures. Fred contacted Don Rust at Chevrolet's Tonawanda, New York big block engine plant, and Don, along with Ken Kayser, researched the production figures.

Don relayed the history of the Tonawanda plant as having first produced engines in 1938. Since then, the plant has provided many American market 6-cylinders, small blocks and big blocks. The aluminum Corvair and Vega engines were produced at this site, and Tonawanda is now the assembly plant for today's modern 60- and 90-degree V-6 engines. The Flint plant, which is the high volume Covette engine plant, and the St. Catherines, Ontario plants have produced small block engines, while Tonawanda ended small block production in 1981 after having started in 1955.

For the big block fan, the primary significance of Tonawanda is that it is the home of the big block. All production big blocks including the W-series 348 and 409 were built at this site. The facility is the machining and assembly location for these engines.

Ken Kayser researched the plant's records and arrived at the following production numbers:

```
1958-65: (348 and 409) - 570,000
         Mk II and Mk IIS - 60
1965:    396 - 61,126
1966:    427 - 226,459
1967:    427 - 173,972
         L-88 - 20
1968:    191,993
1969:    254,760
1970:    163,399
         LS-7 - not released
         7 shipped to St. Louis plant, 5 returned
1971:    158,108
1972:    196,648
1973:    241,764
1974:    217,441
1975:    132,461
1976 - 1986

total: 3,204,554
```

6

We Don't Race

Pontiacs were the favored cars in the Daytona 500 of 1960, but Junior Johnson won the race with this '59 model 348 Chevy by drafting, a technique he discovered during qualifying. Johnson averaged 124.740 mph to win. Daytona Speedway photo.

Stockers Go Big Time

Chevrolet's 348 inch W-engine was released for production in the 1958 models. Rumor had it that Ford was going to release its FE series big block, the 390, which was in fact on schedule until the AMA ban killed everything in 1957. The 390 was held back a few years but the 352 was released. Thus, Ford still had the distinction of the largest displacement engine and Dearborn also claimed victory in the horsepower war. The top 352 with a single 4-bbl carburetor was rated at 300 hp @ 4600 rpm while Chevy's 348 produced 250 at 4400. That was a big difference for the growing number conscious public. If Ford could build engines with 300 hp, whether or not that rating was actually real, why couldn't Chevrolet?

To help solve that problem, Duntov and his engine group went to work developing a three 2-bbl carburetor manifold for the 348. With that done, the engine was now rated at 280 hp @ 4800 rpm. The difference was clear, though. Ford only offered three V-8s, all in standard form with no multiple carbs, no supercharging or other power boosting equipment. That was purposely done in accord with the terms of the AMA ban. Ford's Robert McNamara saw to it that his com-

pany was towing the line.

Although the corporate edict had been handed down, deep in the heart of Chevrolet, high performance parts were still being developed and marketed through optional equipment for assembly line cars or across the counter parts. The small block was fast becoming the dominant engine among racers and hot rodders, and there were the Duntov cams, dual-quad manifolds, fuel injection, 4-speed transmissions, heavy duty clutches, heavy duty driveline and chassis components, none of which Ford had.

1958 was an all-new year for Chevrolet. While Ford did a facelift on its '57s, Chevrolet released a totally redesigned and unique car. Gone were the vertical fins and crisp lines of the mid-50s. This was a new era, and it was beautifully expressed in the '58 Chevys. Swoopy and curvaceous, these cars were a magnificent blend of contours accented by chrome, and lots of it. Also new for '58 was the Impala marque. While the earlier 1955-'57 cars remained very popular, the '58s were so different that the public either loved them or hated them.

Chevrolet Division designers, stylists and engineers had produced their own car. Nothing was shared with other divisions. It was to be the last time that Chevrolet would do that. The '59s and later years went to shared body shells with other divisions. Styling disguises appeared to make the cars distinctly different. Thus, the 1958 Chevys were a unique car in the Chevrolet lineage.

The shared body shell concept was to follow through to

Dramatic new styling and a new all-coil spring suspension were the features of the '58 Chevys. They were the last year of a Chevrolet-only product. Chevrolet photo.

modern times. Olds, Buick and Pontiac builds very similar cars today that are only thinly disguised as different makes. And with the introduction of Chevrolet's Lumina in mid-1989, the fleet of cars from GM's four groups are now very similar visually and differ only in details.

Not so during 1958. The Chevrolet Impala received unique styling, a four coil spring suspension replacing the earlier leaf spring rear suspension design and the largest engine Chevrolet had yet offered. Meanwhile, an economic downturn spread across the nation. Chevrolet production dropped over 266,000, a healthy 17.5%. Across town in Dearborn, Ford was hurting. While Ford sales had almost matched Chevrolet's in '57, 1958 production dropped off nearly 484,000 units, 31.8%. Clearly, Chevrolet was doing the right things in the marketplace and buyers rewarded themselves with more Chevys than Fords.

On the race track, it was a different story. Stock car racers found the radical change in suspension so different that they had difficulty adapting it to oval track racing. Racers stuck with their tried and true '57s, and Glenn "Fireball" Roberts came through at Darlington with a victory in the Southern 500. Although a year old car, his #22 Chevrolet set a new race record by averaging 102.59 mph. Later, the Rebel 300, Curtis Turner turned Darlington's highbanks in a '58 Ford and set a 300 mile record of 109.62 mph average speed.

Thus, 1958 was a mixed bag as usual. With the economic influence brought by reduced sales, Ford was having a tough go of it, and McNamara no doubt thought that a "no racing" policy was justified in reducing expenses. Chevrolet's NASCAR Grand National wins exceeded Ford's '58 total 22 to 16, and Lee Petty was Grand National champion with 9 Oldsmobile victories. Ford was done for.

And so it was in NASCAR's Convertible Division: Chevrolet 13, Ford 6. Bob Welborn once again brought his Chevy in as the reigning champion with 10 wins, all in Chevrolets. Short Track Division? It was Lee Petty again, and again in

Oldsmobiles. Chevys won 7 races, Ford 12, but the season end point total favored Olds.

In truth, Ford had pulled out of racing. And so had Chevrolet, but there was so much knowledge and ability already in the hands of the racers that competitive racing went on in spite of corporate decrees. The three successive '57 Chevy wins in the Southern 500 with progressively higher average speeds indicate just what the racers could do.

The market for high performance cars was growing steadily and Ford would have to get back into racing if for no other reason than rebuilding its tarnished image besmutted by Chevrolet domination of racing. Public awareness of wins translated directly into sales, and Ford was losing that battle in a big way. Meanwhile, Chevrolet maintained its hands off policy, too, but it was administered in a different way.

The AMA ban had specified no factory racing, no high performance parts in catalogs and McNamara interpreted its meaning as total non-involvement in racing. GM? Maybe they weren't directly involved in racing, but advertising displays of products at races sure was a good way of putting before the racing conscious public that GM had high performance cars and equipment to offer. At Daytona for the opening of the giant speedway in 1959, there was Ed Cole and Chevrolet staffers everywhere. Their cars were paraded before the stands, and fans could check out the new cars at will. Where was Ford? Nowhere. Only Jacque Passino represented Ford, and Cole offered him a seat in the Chevrolet booth along with a box lunch.

During '58, Passino had helped John Holman and Ralph Moody team up in Charlotte and arranged for them to get Ford's racing parts inventory for a nominal investment. Smokey Yunick had been paid off for his two-year contract, and most of Ford racing was by diehards. On GM's side was the knowledge that Holman & Moody had all that inventory, and it was hard to believe that two old racers had the finances to mount such an extensive racing program without factory support. It was easy for GM racers to conclude that Ford was cheating by putting out all that racing stuff right in the middle of racing country at Charlotte.

What had actually happened was that Holman had been able to purchase a lot of reject parts at junk prices, particularly for Thunderbirds, that they were running. His crew could build them into racers, and no one would be the wiser. That was the primary source of contention between Ford and Chevrolet. Were these really homebuilt stockers or factory cars out the back door in defiance of the ban?

The 350 hp Lincoln 430 cid engine was offered as an option in the 'Bird in 1959, and although the Lincoln engine was large, it certainly wasn't a high performance mill. But every racer knew that cubic inches translates into torque, and 430 inches has a lot of it (490 lb-ft at 2800 rpm compared to the 335 horse tri-power 348 at 362 lb-ft at 3600 rpm). A little tuning can take that many cubes into the league of stock car racing wins. While the 348 had the edge in power at a higher rpm range, which was clearly much more suited for racing, events were to unfold that created heated controversy.

Semon "Bunkie" Knudsen, whose father had left Ford thirty years earlier and built Chevrolet into the industry leader, was building Pontiac into a force. Olds was building, too, and rumors of infractions on both sides flew like mad. Nobody was sure just what was going on, and interpretation of events gave rise to all sorts of differences of opinion. Lee Iacocca, Ford Division marketing whiz, saw that GM still had performance parts offered in catalogs and suggested that Ford do likewise. McNamara reiterated his no-racing directive, and a letter was sent to GM in February 1958 reporting the infraction. A reply came back after Daytona that promised to remedy the problem, but a year later they were still there and everybody at Ford "knew" why. GM was racing, or so it seemed. All Holman & Moody could do was race their 'Birds on a shoestring budget in hopes that Passino was right; Ford would have to return to racing soon to compete with Chevrolet.

"Red" Curtice may not have thought out the entire plot, but his coup over Ford was complete, at least for a time. Ford's view was simple; GM was cheating. Complete cars built especially for racing by GM, and lots of high performance parts and financing was suspected to be in the garages of several GM racers. In fact, like the Ford racers, the Chevy racers were diehards, too, and were also hit by the ban. All except Jim Rathman.

The Rathman Connection

What happened with the Rathman connection was in association with Zora Arkus-Duntov; Harry Barr and Ed Cole saw a spin-off application of Chevrolet engines in marine applications. Under the guise of developing both the small block and 348 engines for marine applications, Rathman was selected as an outside source to turn the 348 into an engine for stock car racers. The marine application part was acknowledged, but the racing aspect was not.

On the Chevrolet Engineering Department Build Order dated 8-14-57, Duntov assigned to:

Advertising the high perfomrnace angle of the all-new '58 Chevy with daredevil stunts like this championed Chevy's 4-coil spring suspension. Chevrolet photo.

J. R. Rathman, President
Advanced Marine Industries, Inc.
Miami, Florida.

"To cover the design and development of a marine adaptation of Chevrolet V-8 engine in accordance with the attached description of work to be done...

"Material to be forwarded for conversion;

"6 complete 283 cubic inch high performance V-8 engines including all engine accessories

"4 complete 348 cubic inch high performance W engines including all engine accessories

"These engines are designated to be shipped as soon as available from production tools 'that is, not to be built up experimentally'.

"The development and test to be conducted:

"Laboratory performance and physical tests and tests under working conditions in various types of water craft such as cruisers, runabouts and hydroplanes, checking performance and durability as directed by Z. Arkus-Duntov."

Contained in a second letter from the Experimental Shop dated 11-28-58 was an outline for further development work, and a purchase order was requested:

"to cover the development and test of marine adaptations of Chevrolet V-8 engines...This invoice, the amount of which to be arrived at between Mr. Rathman and Mr. Arkus-Duntov is not to exceed $15,000."

On 6-8-59, Chevrolet Chief engineer Harry Barr sent a memo to Duntov saying,

"We should avoid further overruns this budget year." H.B.

A memo dated 7-29-59 outlined charges accrued by Rathman of $27,472 and noted that, "the project is now overrun by $160."

Another document tabulated annual expenditures paid to Rathman which were:

By 1960, it had been a long time since Oldsmobiles and beach racing at Daytona for Junior. This was his first Grand National car. Junior Johnson photo.

Junior Johnson and the Harley Earl Trophy for winning the Daytona 500 of 1960. Darlington speedway photo.

1958 budget year: $165.52
1959 budget year: $21,072.00
1960 budget year: $21,924.41

and tabulated all charges including labor, parts and payments to Jim Rathman paid out under this project as:

1958 budget year: $31,658.00
1959 budget year: $34,449.00
1960 budget year: $36,404.00 (through March of 1960)

Given these figures and according to Duntov's recollection of the Rathman liaison, Chevrolet engineering was deep into performance development of the 348. In the Duntov interview, he relates that the Marine engine project was "a subterfuge" to divert funding to develop the 348 for the racers.

The 1958 round of the Rebel 300 at Darlington looked to be in serious doubt for Ford when both the Turner and Weatherly Holman & Moody prepared cars were heavily battered in a minor race that Turner won prior to the 300. Somehow, a miracle was achieved when the mechanics managed to get the cars together for Darlington. Then, they put on an all-Ford show to win 1-2 and they were followed across the line by two more Fords. Nobody in the GM camp believed Ford was out of racing after that.

In at 5th was one of racing's favorites, Fireball Roberts in a Chevrolet. Ford didn't have a seat for him, and soon the loss was a big gain for Chevrolet when he won the Southern 500 in record time.

Ford was in a vicious circle; no money to promote racing to increase sales to get the money to produce high performance parts for racing. The AMA ban worked to GM's great advantage. Sales were up while Ford's were down. How to get buyers back into Ford showrooms was helped considerably in 1959 in one of Chevrolet's rare styling blunders. The winged batmobiles were not popular cars and Ford production rebounded past Chevrolet's calendar year '59 to reach 1,427,835 units compared to Chevy's 1,349,562. For the first time since the first Chevy V-8s in 1955, Ford surpassed Chevrolet in sales.

Stock car racing was changing a little as it became clearer

The 1961 Chevrolets came with fins, chrome and a 3-deuce 348 as the highest performer.

Interiors thirty years ago featured the fashionable jet age look.

to everyone that GM was hanging on to its high performance parts. The opening of the new Daytona International Speedway and the fanfare GM gave the inaugural running of the Daytona 500 was all it took for Ford to let go of some financing to develop high performance parts.

To most observers at Daytona, Ford was behind the six Holman & Moody Thunderbirds that started. Corporate Ford actually had nothing to do with the cars other than manufacturing the parts that were sold to John Holman for junk, the same deal offered anyone else. Although the 430 inch Lincolns were not strictly legal under NASCAR regulations, Bill France allowed them to race to add some spice to the 500. To the delight of Ford fans, and equally convincing that Ford was playing hard ball, four of the 'Birds finished, and unknown driver, Johnny Beauchamp of Harlan, Iowa drove one to a photo finish with Lee Petty's Olds. The excitement of the race and suspense following it went a long way toward rebuilding Ford's performance image. The fans saw the strong running Thunderbirds run with the best in the 500.

Unlike Chevrolet that had Duntov and his men turning out more and better high performance parts, only a fledgling crew of three men was allowed to operate within a framework of "limited re-entry" at Ford. With little funding and no priority, what they did was produce a 4-bbl intake for oval tracks and a tri-power induction system for drag racing. Both were for the FE series engine, and the 390 was back on line. Hotter cams brought the engine up to 360 hp, the highest in the industry. And once again, Ford and Chevy were fighting a new round of cubic inches and horsepower.

Along with Daytona, Darlington was joined in 1960 by two more super-speedways: Charlotte and Atlanta. Now there were four top showcases for stock car racing. With eight major races each season followed by millions of fans and growing radio and television audience, along with widespread newspaper coverage, stock car racing had by now evolved into a media blitz offering immense sales potential. Bill France had achieved what he had wanted to do when he brought together Ed Cole, Smokey Yunick and others on that hill over-looking North Wilkesboro. There were all the major

Joe Lee Johnson drove a '60 Chevy to victory in the first World 600 at Charlotte. Darlington speedway photo.

American brands racing on NASCAR tracks all over the southeast, not to mention Buck Baker's win in a '57 Chevy on the road course at Watkins Glen in 1957. The sport that was once the domain of boot-leggers was now a high dollar showcase with its own stars.

Winning stock car races was becoming a higher priority with the manufacturers as the sport grew to professional status. The result of the Jim Rathman/348 engine development effort still left Chevrolets well down in power compared to the much larger Pontiac engine, but the Chevys were effective just the same. During the first of the qualifying 100-mile races preceding the 1959 Daytona 500, Bob Welborn brought his Chevrolet across the line ahead of three Thunderbirds. The single

Ned Jarrett and Rex White (#4) were the tough guys driving the USA-1 brand in 1961. Jarrett was NASCAR champion that year, the second of two consectuive W-engine championships, 348 in 1960 and 409 in '61. Darlington Speedway photo.

lap record had been set by Everett "Cotton" Owens in a Pontiac, yet here was Welborn matching that record in the race, 148.198 mph. Chevrolets were not supposed to do things like that. In the second race, four '58 Fords crossed the finish line first. Lloyd "Shorty" Rollins posted an average speed of 129.50 mph. With the 348 now a force, many racers were convinced that Chevrolet was definitely behind the engines.

The day of the Daytona 500 opened with more Chevrolets on the starting grid than any other make. At the green, Welborn pushed his Chevy out front and battled Tom Pistone's T-Bird. For the next 147 laps, one Chevy or another lead the race at times. First Pistone, then Joe Weatherly battled the 'Birds. Jack Smith got in the fray and led for 54 laps in separate intervals. Although more than half the race was a Chevrolet versus Thunderbird battle, in the closing laps, it was Lee Petty who moved up to battle Johnny Beauchamp's T-Bird to the finish. At the end, it was a photo finish! NASCAR officials spent 60 hours debating the outcome while the racing press and fans waited anxiously to find out who won the Daytona 500. By then, it didn't matter that Petty was declared the winner because Ford had reaped enormous attention.

There were 16 Fords, 6 Thunderbirds, 2 Mercurys and 1 Edsel in the race. Opposing them were 25 Chevrolets, just about equal in numbers. Oldsmobile and Pontiac were clearly out-numbered by a sizable margin. Out of the top 20 finishers, half were Chevrolets. Four Thunderbirds and 3 Fords rounded out the Ford Motor Co. contingent, and everyone could see that stock car racing was now Chevrolet versus Ford.

Fireball hammered his Chevy to victory in the Rebel 300 at Darlington to set a record with the highest race average speed (115.380 mph) in the speedway's first four years. The 348 could get the job done. His record stood until 1961 when Fred

Chevy man Rex White, NASCAR's 1960 champion. Darlington Speedway photo.

Lorenzen's Ford pushed the average up more than 4 mph.

There were a few other major victories for Chevrolet on the top tracks, but Jim Reed winning the Southern 500 in a '57 model wasn't quite what Chevrolet marketing could use to sell new cars. That didn't affect the fans, though. They saw Reed set by far the fastest race in Darlington history. At 111.840 mph for 500 miles, that proved that old Chevys could still beat the best. Reed's record stood until 1961 when Nelson Stacy's Ford set a new mark at 117.787 mph.

Then came another round in 1960. The 500 mile races at Daytona and Darlington were widely covered by the press and were of deep, and growing, interest to the manufacturers. The 100 mile qualifiers were dominated by Knudsen's Indians. "Fireball" Roberts put his Pontiac so far out in front in the first race that he posted a new record over 8 mph faster

Johnny Rutherford with Smokey Yunick's "Mystery engine" Chevrolet of 1963. Junior Johnson called his similar factory backed "Mystery engine" Chevy, "The most superior car the sport has ever seen." Daytona Speedway photo.

than the previous year. His 151.556 mph average speed was well ahead of Junior Johnson's 348 powered Chevy that finished that qualifier in 5th position. The second 100-miler was dominated by Jack Smith in another Pontiac, and in 3rd, 4th and 5th positions were Jim Reed, Rex White and Bob Welborn in Chevys. The 348s were still in the hunt.

One of the largest crowds that had ever attended a race was at Daytona for the 500 of that year. On the starting grid were 23 Fords, 4 Thunderbirds and 19 Chevrolets. As expected, Fireball lead away in his record setting Pontiac, and for 19 laps, he was untouchable. Then his indian broke, and seven Fords were out by the time Fireball's Pontiac was pushed behind the wall. Five Fords were out of the race before the first Chevrolet dropped out.

Junior Johnson drove a masterful race and led for a total of 61 laps including the final 8 to take the victory. Although the 348 engine had been well developed, the question of how a Chevrolet could win that race was due mainly to Johnson's driving strategy. He invented "drafting" that year at Daytona, and the announcers, not knowing what he was doing, kept everyone in suspense with what looked like a succession of rear end collisions. Junior was just setting up each car in front of him to pass in a sling-shot move as he relates in his interview following this section. He freely admits that the 348 powered '59 Chevy he drove into history was not nearly the fastest car, but it was the biggest win of the year anyway.

The total number of Daytona 500 finishers in 1960 that were Chevrolets was once again half of the top twenty. Only Johnson's car was a '59 model, and he beat Bobby Johns' Pontiac. Johns was followed by Richard Petty and Lee Petty

in Plymouths. Johnny Allen's Chevy was 5th. The 5-9-10-12-13-14-15-16-18 positioned cars at the end were all 1960 Chevys.

The 348 was making history elsewhere, too. Joe Lee Johnson of Chattanooga, Tennessee, took his Chevrolet to victory at Charlotte in the inaugural World 600 while posting a 107.735 mph average in NASCAR's longest race. That was Chevrolet's only World 600 victory until the coming of the Monte Carlo and Darrell Waltrip in 1978. Of the top four races in 1960, Daytona, Charlotte, Atlanta and Darlington, Chevys won two. Pontiac took the other two, Atlanta (Johns) and Darlington (Baker). In other shorter races, Rex White won the Old Dominion 500 at Martinsville in his '60 Chevy, then won again at North Wilkesboro.

Lee Petty was once again Grand National Champion in Oldsmobiles, and Chevrolet's 13 GN wins in 1959 surpassed Ford's 9 (although Thunderbird won 6 more for a total of 15 Ford Motor Co. wins). Joe Lee Johnson was Convertible Division champion with four victories and several high finishes in Chevys.

Speedy Thompson took the other Charlotte feature of 1960, the National 400 but this time in a Ford. Atlanta opened its gates that year to a packed house who saw Pontiacs dominate both the Dixie 300 and the Atlanta 400 in its first two years. Atlanta was tough on Chevys, and the first Dixie 300 claimed was at the hand of Bobby Allison in 1972. In the first race of the year at Atlanta, Chevrolets can only count five wins in 27 years. The second feature of the year, the 500 miler, Rex White and Junior Johnson claimed victories in 1962 (White) and 1963 (Johnson). However the 1963 win was with a new

Johnson and Rutherford won the 100-mile qualifiers for the '63 Daytona 500, and Rutherford was the fastest qualifier with a sensational new Daytona record of 165.183 mph. He finished the 500 in 9th place. Daytona Speedway photo.

Louie Clemmens and Rex White after winning at North Wilkesboro. Darlington Speedway photo.

engine from Chevrolet, Dick Keinath's Mk IIS "Mystery" engine.

Stock car racing by then had reached a fever pitch. Chevrolet and Ford were going at it hot and heavy. New and better equipment showed up, and suddenly Chevrolet was way out in front. People began asking questions.

Although Pontiac dominated the 100-mile qualifiers at Daytona in 1961 and '62, it was Chevrolet that cleaned house in 1963. Junior Johnson set a blazing pace during the 1st

round of qualifying and raised the record by over 7 mph. Johnny Rutherford won the 2nd round in Smokey Yunick's mystery engine Chevy by posting another victory, this time 17.57 mph faster than the year before, and just 1.1 mph off Johnson's pace.

In qualifying for the 500, Rutherford was the fastest qualifier and set an astounding new record of 165.183 mph. That was over 6 mph faster than Fireball's Pontiac record of the previous year. The first Chevrolet to leave the race was Bubba Farr's '63 mystery motor car. Johnson was next after leading through the 23rd lap. Only two of the new 427 cubic inch Mk II Chevys finished. Rutherford was four laps behind the five Fords that led across the finish line to victory, a stunning blow to Chevrolet. The Daytona 500 was an all-Ford show during the final 84 laps.

When the dust settled, the fact that Ford had won so overwhelmingly did not overshadow the curiosity raised by the fast Chevys. Where did the new Chevrolet engine come from if General Motors was, in fact, adhering to the AMA ban against factory racing?

During a news conference in Detroit during March, that question was posed to General Motors Chairman Frederic Donner and President John Gordon. They didn't know, and being put on the spot indicated that either GM's top management were not aware of what was going on within their own corporation, or they were secretly racing. Either way, it did not look like GM adhered to its own policy.

How that simple question changed the course of Chevrolet's racing involvement is staggering. If it had not been raised, many great things might have come from Chevrolet and the other divisions of GM. However, it didn't take long for the Chevrolet Division boss to answer for what was going on, and the result was the restatement of the AMA ban on factory racing in all forms. Suddenly and completely, the people inside Chevrolet that were doing what gave the make great prestige were threatened with the loss of their jobs.

The shutdown was so thorough that not a single Chevrolet placed in the top ten at Daytona for years, and the next

Daytona 500 win for Chevrolet didn't happen until 1975 (Benny Parsons). Nowhere could a competitive Chevy be seen after the make's 8 wins in '63. In '64, Wendel Scott scored his only win (Jacksonville, Fla.), and it was Chevy's only win for two years. No super-speedways wins were by Chevrolets for 9 years. Bobby Allison broke the drought when he put his '71 Chevy into the winner's circle at Darlington and Charlotte in '72. That was a long dry spell for Chevrolet in stock car racing, and the fans wondered where the fast Chevys went.

This is Smokey's Chevelle that caused NASCAR officials so much heartburn. Daytona Speedway photo.

After this, it didn't matter. Smokey Yunick photo.

Junior Johnson

Stock Car Racing Legend
Recalls His Chevrolet Days

The basics of where I really started gettin' into the sport strong was in 1954 and 1955, along in there. Of course, that was when the bootleggin' business was pretty strong around in the area here where I live. So, I got in trouble with bootleggin', got sent off to prison, and when I came back in late 1957, in early 1958, that's when I got pretty devoted to the sport of racin' and gave up the whiskey business, you might say, and devoted my full time to it. It just kept multiplyin' itself to a bigger sport, a better sport, and a way to make money out of it. I continued to get deeper and deeper involved in it, and year by year, I chose to go with various kinds of cars and drive for people that owned dealerships and stayed with the sport up to now.

Back in 1954 and 1955, it was very tough to go racing. You basically got out of it what you put in it. The person that put the most money in it, they got the most out of it. The proof of that was when Carl Kiekhaefer came in here and he dumped tremendous amounts of money in it, and he was very successful. He didn't come in and steal off a bunch of racers that was already here. He brought in raw, unaware people of what the sport was about, but he did bring a lot of technology and smarts into the sport. What he did, he really classed the sport into another demand saying, you can't keep up unless you have the money and the sponsorship to do so. It has went from that to where it is today. Not saying that he caused what has happened, but what he did, he showed them a better way, and they picked up on it and built on it, and I think he is one of the big reasons that the sport is a class sport such as it is today.

In 1955 and 1956, I ran a car out of N.Y. for some boys, a Chevrolet, a 1955 Chevrolet at Darlington. Then, in 1956, was about the time I got sent to the pen for bootleggin', but in 1957, I came back and I ran against them a lot in the latter part of 1957 and 1958 in a 1957 Ford. Chevrolet had fuel injected cars and Ford had supercharged cars. When I came back, they was down to one carburetor. I never run any of the supercharged cars or the fuel injected cars that Chevrolet had. The racin' ban while I was gone took care of that.

I basically worked with people in the motor business, not manufacturers but people that had motor companies that sold cars, dealers and such, so it didn't affect me as much as I think it did a lot of other people. I wasn't used to the factory backed stuff. I didn't really know the benefits of having it, so I basically survived without it and with the help of friends and people that wanted to be involved with racin', like Holly Farms. I used more of a sponsorship approach than everybody else did.

I could do without racin' or I could race. It wasn't an obsession with me. When I didn't have a good car or good support, I didn't go to the races. I just simply stayed home. That is one reason that I dabbled in it. I was in and out of it because I didn't want to go unprepared or unprofessional even though a lot of them did do that; just go and ride around. They weren't really racin', they was just appearin' and bein' involved, and I never did get to that point. When I went racin', I went to win and nothin' else.

I ran Fords in 1957. I drove a little bit for a man named Paul Spaulding out of Syracuse, N.Y. the later part of 1957 and 1958 and part of 1959. I drove for him and the factory people, but the Ford factory got out in 1957. I was drivin' a 1958 Ford, and then I switched to a Dodge and drove a Dodge for a part of 1959, a 1959 Dodge. Then, in 1960, the Pontiac seemed to be the dominate car, but I went to Daytona with a 1959 Chevrolet and won the Daytona 500.

At Daytona in 1960, I think that Pontiac was the dominant force in racin'. No way could you outrun them with a Chevrolet. That is where the drafting came from. The Pontiacs blew up, the motors blew up in several of them, and some of them had other problems, but what basically won the race for

us was drafting. I picked that up in practice on the race track. I realized the closer I could run to the fast cars, the easier it was for me to run fast. I kept playing around with it, and I figured out that if I could stay close to one of those fast cars, no matter how fast he ran, I could run that fast, too. Then, it wasn't long that I figured out that it was a drafting situation, and it didn't have to be a fast car. It could be any car that I ran up on. I would run right up to it and pull out and pass it and pick out another one up in front of me and just keep step-stoning along. I could just keep on going if the cars was strung out all the way around the race track. I could keep that up all the way around the race track. I didn't have to have a fast car in front of me.

The way I'd pass, well, you got a running start and you would run up to them, you had the momentum goin', and you just ran on out around them and kept on goin'. Most of the time, you tried to set up another car in front of you so when you got around him, you could pick the other car up and keep right on goin'. It was a pretty well cut and dried plan that you had to do to work it to your advantage. You didn't run out into the wind by yourself and get caught setting out there. You always made sure there was a guy ahead of you. When a fast car came along, you just hooked up with it and went with it.

We had a good car and it ran good, but if you were to win Daytona with a car like that, it would be a miracle. To take a car with the disadvantage that car had and win it was a miracle.

This was done with Ray Fox and through the effort of the dog track in Daytona Beach. They called me and wanted to know if I wanted to drive. They didn't have a driver, so I agreed to go down and drive the car for Fox and the Daytona Kennel Club. I did a few favors for Fox during the 1955-1956 season when he was runnin' Herb Thomas in a Chevrolet. He was basically runnin' against Carl Kiekhaefer in the Chrysler cars for the championship. At that time, he raced all out in California and up north. They ran about sixty races a year. Fox had called me to drive and let Herb Thomas start the car and I would finish the race for him. So, that is basically how me and Fox hooked up with driving a Chevrolet for Herb Thomas.

Then I got a Chevrolet. This was a car that Ray Fox built his self. Ray was sort of a fabricator and car owner, sort of like Smokey was. So, the people that I was involved with with the Chevrolets was Fred Lovette, Rex Lovette, Dwayne Church and Bruce Church, and Fred Gaddy of Gaddy Chevrolet of North Wilkesboro.

We had bought a car, me and Holly Farms and some friends of mine, off of Cotton Owens, which was a Pontiac. They was the hottest cars on the circuit at that time. I ran in all the races up to the Charlotte race. At that time, they had a dirt track called the Fair Grounds of Charlotte, N. C.

We ran the Chevrolet up to a point, and then Holly Farms, which Fred and Rex Lovette was basically operating at that time, they wanted to get a Pontiac. So at that point in time, we bought a Pontiac, and we raced a Pontiac for the rest of 1960, which was about half of 1960, and 1961 and part of 1962. By then, Chevrolet was coming into racing factory backed in a big way, so me and Ray decided to switch from Pontiac to Chevrolet. That is when we ran the 1963 Chevrolet, which was the dominant car in NASCAR that particular year.

The mystery motor was very famous because it was a sort of an unheard of motor, an unavailable motor type of thing. It came through Paul Prior and Vince Piggins. We re-did them. Smokey Yunick got one of their cars and Rex White got one of them and we got one of them. That was basically all they had was the three teams. Now, we did borrow a motor from Smokey because Smokey wasn't runnin' a full circuit and we was having a lot of trouble with the motors. We ran pretty much out of motors about two-thirds of the way through the season.

We sat on the pole several times, and we won seven super speedway races that year and pretty much dominated the sport 'til we had problems of some sort. Well, NASCAR pretty much outlawed or banned the 1963 Chevrolet motor, which was the mystery motor, and at that point in time, I signed a contract to drive for Ford Motor Company.

In 1963 when NASCAR announced that they were not going to let the mystery engine run in the Chevrolets, there wasn't any use in me pursuing that any farther because without motor support, you couldn't beat the Fords and the Pontiacs. And Chrysler was getting into it very strong, too. The Chryslers had the hemi engines which was a doll of an engine in its time. Ford was getting into it with factory help against no help at all. There was no contest to the way you had to go, you either had to go Chrysler or Ford one, because Chevrolet had chosen to honor the AMA specifications that were set down.

So, I just figured that Ford would be my best way to go. I had never had any luck with Chrysler. Although, in 1964 I had a contract with Chrysler before I switched to Ford, they didn't live up to the contract, so I switched and I drove for Banjo Matthews in 1964 and was sponsored by Holly Farms. I drove for Holly Farms in 1960, '61, '62, '63, '64, '65, and then I retired in 1965. I only raced full time about from 1960 through 1965. I won 50 Winston Cup races, or at that time, it was Grand Nationals, probably more in a Ford than I did in a Chevrolet, but I also won in a Pontiac, and I won a race or two in a Dodge.

I have driven a lot of cars for different motor companies. I was always sort of a shopper type person. If you had a fast car and wanted me to drive it, I would drive it. If it wasn't a fast car and you wanted me to drive it, I just wouldn't mess with it. I didn't want to be involved with something I couldn't win in.

I drove for Ford in 1964 and 1965, then I retired from racin', drivin' wise, but I stayed on in racin', and I hired drivers to drive my cars such as Bobby Isaac, Darel Dieringer, Lee Roy Yarbrough, Cale Yarborough, Darrell Waltrip, Bobby Allison, and these types of drivers. I stayed with Ford on through 1970, and then I chose to get out of racing again.

In 1970, I stayed out of racing the rest of the year. I just quit. In 1971, I built a car, a Chevrolet to run the World 600 in Charlotte. Me and Richard Howard got together, Richard Howard the promoter of Charlotte Motor Speedway. Charlie Glotzback, we brought him in to drive that particular race.

He sat on the pole, and he was leading the race three hundred miles into the race and dominatin' the thing. Then, him and Speedy Thompson got together and he wrecked and tore the car up. But, we ran the car on the rest of that year and won some races, then pretty much dominated the sport in 1971. We won with an unheard of and non-factory backed car.

That car was a 1971 Monte Carlo. We ran a 427 engine. That was the biggest engine that you was allowed to run. That was like a L-88, but we had to do a lot of work on the engines. It wasn't a full-fledged racin' engine. It took a lot of knowledge of past racin' experience to make the Monte Carlo into a race car and the motor into a racin' motor. The engine block, it was cast iron and the heads were aluminum.

In 1972, we hired Bobby Allison, and with Bobby came Coca Cola sponsorship. We won 12 or 13 races that year and dominated the sport with Chevrolet. We should have won the championship but down at Talladega, we had a problem and for some reason of which we don't know, Bobby chose not to drive the car anymore that day and that cost him the championship. From that point on, in 1973, he decided he would run his own car and we hired Cale Yarborough. Well, Cale didn't do a whole lot in 1973, but in 1974 he started to come on. All the way into 1979 and 1980, Cale was drivin' for us in the Monte Carlo.

We raced the Monte Carlo and a Leguna that we ran on the super speedways. We ran the Monte Carlo mostly in the mile and mile and a half races, and we run the Leguna at Daytona and Talladega and that type races where you needed the aerodynamics mostly. We went on into the 1980s, and Cale chose to cut back his activities and we brought Darrell Waltrip in. Then, he dominated the sport basically up through 1983 with the Chevrolets, and we won two championships those years.

From that time on, a lot of mechanics choose to go to a lot of other racin' teams takin' a lot of information away from our team and we scattered a lot of good help out among the other racin' teams. It wasn't long until about everyone knew how to run a Chevrolet and work on the motors and stuff, and it advanced on to where it is today. They still probably win more races today than any of the other make of cars, but the competition is greater now, and that could change. It could be scattered out among all the cars; you know, Ford, Pontiac, Olds, Buick and Chevrolet. I look for them all to win four or five races each per year. I don't look for one car to go out and win twenty races like the Chevrolet has done in the past. It is just too competitive for that now.

We built our own chassis along in the 70s, like '71, '72, '73 and along in there, but then because the chassis are pretty much designed the same and there is not a whole lot of difference you can make in them, we chose to buy the chassis from Banjo Matthews and then finish them ourselves. We've been doin' that mostly ever since. I don't see any real advantage in buildin' the chassis or we would be doing it ourselves.

The Monte Carlo we raced had a lot of work done to it. It has been there since 1983 and that thing has had so much work and technology put into it over the last six or seven years that it is a good car aerodynamically. You slow them down to restricted situations, they are as good as anything on the race track. The reason that Ford did not dominate Daytona (1989) was NASCAR's rules; the restrictor plate and some things that went on in the manifolds in the Chevrolets that they were not allowed to do with Fords. That made Chevrolet a dominant force at Daytona.

They have rules that they go by, and if somebody comes along and says, "Can I do this?" and they say, "Yes, I don't see anything wrong with it," and that shows up on the race track and it is a dominant idea that beats the other car, well nobody knew what it was going to do except the people that was runnin' it. They had an unfair advantage at Daytona. Chevrolet did, yes sir. It was not any disadvantage imposed on the Fords; just that the Fords, without doing some of the things that helped the restrictor, weren't competitive.

It's a total deal where the people that have been working on the Chevrolet motors and stuff since in the early 70s, so a lot of the problems are already worked out in the Chevrolet motor, and a lot of the problems still are not worked out in the Ford motor because they haven't had anyone except Bill Elliott running the Fords much for the past 5 or 6 years. But now in 1985, he hurt the sport as far as being able to take one car and go out and dominate the sport, but that is NASCAR's fault again. They let a small dimensional car run against the big dimensional cars, the Thunderbird versus the Monte Carlo. That is basically what happened at Daytona this year in February. The Monte Carlo has an unfair advantage with their manifold the way they had fixed their manifold, that should not have been OK. It allowed the Chevrolet to have about 40 more horse power then the Fords, even with the restrictor plates.

Don't get me wrong. I am not knocking the Chevrolet, but I am not praising them either because if you have an advantage in your favor, you should win. They had the advantage and the Fords was at a disadvantage. Car for car under the same basic rules, they should have run about the same but they weren't. They weren't the same, and they weren't competitive. There was two or three cars there that were Chevrolets that was untouchable by a Ford.

The reason I switched to Ford is, well, there is several basic reasons. I just don't like the way that Chevrolet is doing business right now. I think that Ford is in racing to stay, and my relationship with Ford in the past was a good one, and I don't think that my relationship with Chevrolet at this point is in good shape. And I don't want to be involved with somebody that I don't feel good about, or they are headed in one direction and I am headed in another. Whether it is right or wrong, I just have my beliefs, and I don't want to be involved with Chevrolet right now. I'm not saying somewhere down the road I might not want to go back and run a Chevrolet, I don't know, but I don't plan on it. You know, when I have had enough, I've had enough, and I have had enough.

Well, you know it is basically a politics sport. It has not bothered me in the past, but this time it did bother me. I really think that Ford has the best race car right now. I think it will finally prove itself, although up to this point Chevrolet and Pontiacs and stuff has pretty well dominated the sport, but you know, that is the funny thing about our sport. What happens in two or three months don't mean it is going to keep on happening. It can turn around. I think it is going to turn around. It is getting closer and closer to turning around.

We have raced Fords before, and we understand them and know their basic car about as good as General Motors cars, and we pretty much had a lot to do with both motor companies over a period of years, you know, helping them from where they were to where they are now. We were involved in that stuff all the way up through the line. We feel like, not so much this year, but in the next three or four years, Ford is going to be the best car.

We built one of the first Luminas here, and we also went to the wind tunnel with it and worked on it quite a bit before I switched to Ford. There is nothing there that is shocking to me. If NASCAR makes them stick to the rules with their bodies, they are going to have a hard time. If they don't let them mis-form the body on that car and change a lot of configuration on it, it is not going to be any better than anything that any one else has got. It is certainly not going to be as good as Ford.

Ford has the edge on all of them in aerodynamics. They have put more effort and more work and more time in building their cars for aerodynamics. Now, if NASCAR chooses to say, "now that Ford has the best aerodynamic car, we are going to let General Motors chop their's up and cut them down in size and make them get competitive, then that is a different story. They will get competitive. But if they stick to the rule like they are supposed to stick to it and make those cars stay to the template that they are supposed to stay to, Ford is going to have the best car.

I think the approach that they are taking right now is a stand off position. I think they are being mis-guided by two or three people that doesn't have their best interest in stock cars. They have it some where else; Indy cars, sports cars and stuff of that nature. I think that stock cars are secondary to them.

Stock car racing is primary to Ford. Ford should, with no more companies than they have to look at, they should do a better job. They are only running one model car where General Motors is running four brands of automobiles. How long they can stand to run four brands of automobiles, no body knows. I don't think it is to their best interest to get beat by a Pontiac, to beat a Chevrolet. I could be wrong. I don't think it is to their best interest to get beat by a Buick. I think it is just basically pretty stupid myself.

I think stock car racing is both a drivers sport and a make loyal thing with the fans. I think it is two thirds driver and the team and a third for the brand of automobile. I know when I first started running the Chevrolets again, the sport did not jam the grand stand with people. But it wasn't long after I started running the Chevrolet that they started having sell outs and tremendous crowds. That had to be General Motors fans coming back out to watch Chevrolet. There was some of that in the 60s but more noticeable in the 70s.

160

Jack Chrisman's dual Chevy AA/Dragster was NHRA drag racing World Champion in 1961. It's been a long time since top fuel dragsters were just breaking into the 8 second range at 170 mph. Bob D'Olivo photo courtesy Petersen Publishing Co.

It's a Drag, Man!

The greatest single boost to drag racing was the birth of the Super Stocks. Up until 1961, there had been long lines of drivers in stock class from A to Z. The fans cheered on drivers of their favorite make, but the big drawing cars were the loud and fast "slingshot" rail dragsters. They came in all sorts of single, dual and quad engine construction. Most were rear wheel drive, but a few were four wheel drive.

The second most popular class was composed of the "gassers" and "altereds". Like the rails, the Gas and Altered cars were homebuilts using production car bodies and frames but with modern power equipment. They also came in all sorts of varieties, and provided thrilling drag racing.

When the rails, gassers and altereds were through running, the hordes of stock class cars rolled to the line. Two-by-two they faced off against each other. At NHRA National events such as the Winternationals or the US Nationals, the stockers usually were running into the wee hours of the morning. When they got to run, it was usually after the excitement of the fast cars was over. Fans packed in by the droves to watch the fast, noisy and quick "real" drag racers, but went for a hot dog or to make a pit stop when the stock classes ran.

Then came the heavies from Detroit, the Super Stocks with over 400 cubic inch engines. They roared into the imagina-

The glory days of the 409 are still alive in vintage drag racing. The cars are once again favorites.

tions of millions of drag racing fans every weekend at hundreds of drag strips all across America. These were the cars that anyone could go see at their nearest dealers, and auto magazines inflamed the spirit of America's youth with a continual barrage of action-packed automotive material. There were "how-to" features and lots of action. Chevrolet's entry into the bucket seat, four on the floor, high performance era was the 409 of 1961.

Chevrolet's top engine of 1960 was the 335 hp 348, a not so inspiring powerplant. But with the debut of the 409 and big inchers from Ford and Chrysler, drag racing fans had more excitement than ever before. Factory built cars along with

The Gardner-Waldman team brought their 409 all the way to the final A/Stock round of the US Nationals of 1963 only to lose to 16-year old Don Gay's 421 Pontiac. Gold Dust Classics photo.

homebuilt rails and gassers produced ardent make affiliation and intense rivalries grew among Super Stock fans. These were the cars that everyone identified with, but where they came from was not due to drag racing, although that sport was a huge benefactor.

The Super Stock engines that seemed to suddenly appear in 1961 were due largely to professional stock car racing. Larger and more powerful engines were the quickest way of upholding the factory's name. The car that won at Daytona, Darlington or Charlotte affected new car sales. "Win on Sunday, Sell on Monday" had become a very real aspect of automobile showroom traffic. Buyers wanted to be seen in and drive the cars of the speedway superstars. What that meant was that the factories produced their high performance engines and super cars to benefit sales through advertising and not for general public consumption. Thus, the cars were rather rare, and although an owner may never exceed the legal speed limit in his 409 Chevy, 406 Ford, 413 Plymouth or Super Duty 389 Pontiac, big inch engines were bragging rights. They were engines for the kids, and their emblems became cult symbols.

In truth, the manufacturers had offered heavy duty, high performance cars and equipment for years, but that sort of hardware was usually associated with police cars and stock car racers and not available in public showrooms. But by 1961, hot rod kids could be driving a fully engineered, completely developed, brand new, high performer for no more than a down payment and monthly payments. These were factory built hot rods. It was a new and exciting era of cars,

and the kids gave some of that legacy to the future when they immortalized the cars in rock 'n' roll songs. "Hey little Cobra" and "She's real fine, my 409" were songs by the teenagers for teenagers simply for the fun of it and certainly not today's 40-year old singers doing teenage music for the money in it.

What the 409 Chevy and all other super stock showroom models were to most people was far more hype than reality. The full size sedans that received the engines remained as heavy as ever and even with 360 hp as in the 409's case, street performance was mostly on the starting end where the cars could spin their narrow tires into clouds of smoke. That wasn't fast, but it was awesome.

Even though the 340 hp single 4-bbl (the tri-power was rated at 350 hp) 348 of '61 was within about 6% of the output of the 409 and torque was within 12.4%, there just wasn't the magnetism for that engine that the 409 generated. Both were virtually the same engine except for bore and stroke. The dual valve spring, big valve 348 with solid tappet cam and 11.25:1 compression ratio was really a 409 of lower displacement.

The 409 was not a bored 348 but a re-cored block designed for larger bores that retained the same cylinder wall strength. The block's main bearing webs were machined to clear the 409's thicker crankshaft counterweights because of its 3.5-inch stroke, 1/4-inch longer than the 348. The 348 and 409 cranks differed in more than stroke, though. The larger piece was fitted with an additional counterweight at the flywheel end. Another small difference in the 409 was the use of improved steel backed shell type main bearings. Both used

The 409 W-engine was tough to beat in A/Stock drag racing during 1962, but Chevrolet's engineers were never happy with it and invented the Mk II "Mystery" engine. Chevrolet photo.

The 409 hp dual quad 409 became a legend in its own time, but what it did on drag strips was not matched in NASCAR.

Drag racers with factory connections knew about the 427 hp dual quad Z-11, but most people thought it was another 409.

two-bolt main bearing caps.

Cylinder head castings became either 348 or 409 depending on machining and were identical except for spot facing around valve guides that the 409 had and the 348 didn't. The spot facing was there to accommodate the 409's larger diameter single valve spring rather the 348's dual setup. Valve stems were also larger in diameter in the 409, 3/8 versus 5/16-inch.

Pistons were also similar except wrist pin location on the 409. Chevrolet called the pistons "impact extruded" but in hot

rodding parlance, they were forged. Each one received a machined relief of 16-degrees at the top to clear valve heads.

Both engines received the same cast aluminum intake manifold although the runner inlets of the 409 were larger because of using a larger carburetor.

Although Chevrolet won this round of the cubic inch war with Ford, Dearborn produced its own tri-power intake for the 375 horsepower high performance 390 and claimed 401 horses, the highest offered in 1961. Whatever one manufacturer did, the others had to do also, and all of them feared

Probably the runningest street version of the Mk IV big block was the 396. This was the engine that made Chevrolet known on the street in 1965. Chevrolet photo.

After the Mk II was killed, the Mk III paper study led to the Mk IV big block. Here, a factory technician runs an L-88 on a dyno. Chevrolet photo.

being left behind in the marketplace. But Chevrolet seemed to get more of it right. When the dust had settled, Ford was having to scramble to catch up.

The unusual feature of both the 348 and 409 was the combustion chamber in the block rather than the head. Valves were in the normal, inline position similar to the small block design, but the deck of the block was inclined 16-degrees. The mating head surface was flat except for valve recesses. Although the engine ran well in drag racing applications, it did not prove as effective in stock car races. According to Chevrolet engineers Zora Arkus-Duntov, Dick Keinath and Fred Frincke, the combustion chamber was the fatal flaw in the design and the reason that Keinath was assigned the job of designing the 409 cubic inch Mk II that became the fabled "Mystery" engine when it was expanded into a 427 and called the Mk IIS.

The 409s launched themselves into history among the thundering cheer of enthusiastic spectators, but in 1961 "Mr. 409" wasn't Hayden Proffitt. That year Proffitt was pushing Mickey Thompson's Optional/Super Stock Pontiac during NHRA's US Nationals at the newly completed quarter-mile facility known as Indianapolis Raceway Park. "Mr. 409" was "Dyno Don" Nicholson of Atlanta who would soon become a legend in Mercury Cyclones and Cougars. Proffitt had clocked a qualifying best of 13.07 seconds at 112.21 mph while Nicholson's 409 was classed one notch under Optional/Super Stock and turned in a best of 13.25/110.29 mph in Super Stock.

When the eliminations came around, none of the estimated 30,000 in attendance left their seats. In those days, the cars were flagged away by a flagman who stood out front between the cars and gave them the "go" signal. "Christmas trees" and foul lights were off in the future. When the full-bodied cars blasted through the lights, Proffitt had nailed Optional/Super Stock at IRP with an awesome 110.29 mph run in 12.55 seconds. For a stock class car to run in the 12-second range was history making. The next year, similar cars were known as A/Factory Experimental. Then Nicholson faced off against Arnie "The Farmer" Beswick's S/S Pontiac and had a tough time beating the haulin' Indian. Later he was disqualified and Beswick claimed victor in Super Stock.

What was most unusual about the US Nationals that year was the domination of Chevrolet power. Of 39 classes including four eliminator titles and top speed and low elapsed time setters, Chevy power took 24. Ford powered cars won only 2 and Mercury took 1. Top speed, 177.87 mph, was posted by Atlanta's Pete Robinson in his "Pete's Engineering Co. Special" AA/Dragster. Low ET was grabbed by Dode Martin of Carlsbad, California in his twin engine "Two-Thing" AA/Dragster blasting an 8.68 second pass.

What this showed was that from coast to coast, Chevy power had become pervasive. Anyone from anywhere could build upon the factory parts and put together a winning, record setting drag racer.

When looking through the list of NHRA's 1961 class record holders nationwide, of 53 classes recognized, 27 were nailed down by Chevrolet powered cars. Mercury held 2 and Ford tallied just 4. Although the sensational '60s had just begun, Chevrolet was already in the driver's seat, and Ford was history as the hot rodder's make. All those high performance parts that Ford had not developed during the post-AMA ban of 1957 and Chevrolet had were paying off handsomely in the bowtie brigade.

What looked like a run-away Chevrolet decade when the '60s began was to reach spectacular proportions with the 427 cubic inch "Mystery" engine in 1963. Then came those embarrassingly fast NAS-CAR Grand National Chevy's that closed the door on super speedway wins for a decade when GM management restated, "we don't race". After GM got out of stock car and sports car racing, the drag racers and hot rodders kept Chevrolet in the thick of exciting racing because the Chevy stuff was that good.

The bowtie brand was here to stay. Ed Cole, Harry Barr, Zora Duntov and all the supporting Chevrolet engineers, technicians, designers and draftsman could afford a satisfying grin for having overwhelmingly disposed of Ford as the hot rodder's make.

Each year of the decade brought more Chevy powered drag racers. There were many top stars of drag racing, but Jack Chrisman was probably the favorite nationwide. He set drag strip crowds ablaze with excitement. Chrisman toured the country in his quest to win drag racing's World Championship. His machine was the Howard Cam Special sponsored by Howard Johanssen's speed shop. He and Howard's son, Jerry, built and raced the dragster using twin small block engines. Each engine was supercharged and fuel injected, and 19-year old Jerry was the tuner that traveled with Chrisman while on tour. He won Top Eliminator at the 1961 Winternationals with a fabulous 170.13 mph blast at a phenomenal 8.99 seconds. With that winning round, Chrisman received a brand new hardtop Thunderbird as grand prize. The 'Bird was presented by George Hurst and showed to what extent Ford Motor Co. regarded drag racing. Ford wanted drag racing's World Champion to drive a Thunderbird!

The most powerful Mk IV big block was the 500+ hp ZL-1. Road racers got over 700 hp with fuel injection and dominated the Can-Am. Chevrolet photo.

The ultimate Mk IV. All the goodies that made the ZL-1 production aluminum alloy engine. Chevrolet photo.

Chevrolet powered cars took four out of five eliminator titles available at the Winternationals that year. Dick Manz won Little Eliminator in his Devin-Chevy running in B/Modified Sports Production (12.09 @ 114.21 mph). The Street Eliminator title was taken by Johnny Loper in his B/Gas Willys-Chevy that clocked a 12.77 second pass at 108.95 mph. Then there was "Dyno Don" taking Super/Stock Eliminator with a 13.59 @ 105.88 mph.

The World Finals at Indianapolis was nearly an all-Chevy show. Four Eliminator trophies were available, and Chevy powered cars took three. Some 40,000 fans packed the stands as Jack Chrisman aimed for Top Eliminator, but "Sneaky" Pete Robinson blasted an 8.52 run that had everyone shaking their heads. In the eliminations, Chrisman and Robinson faced off against each other. Chrisman left the line with the front wheels off the ground and stretched his lead by mid-

The first of the 55 Z-11 Chevys built was delivered to Ammon R. Smith Auto Co. just before Christmas, 1962. As an RPO, its list of options included aluminum bumpers, special sheet metal, a 427 cid W-engine with special cowl induction, vented metallic brakes, 4-speed transmission, positraction, tach and deleted sound proofing and insulation. According to Bill Jenkins who prepared the car, Dave Strickler won about 90% of some 200 races that year. Gold Dust Classics photo.

way. But at the lights, it was Robinson that stopped the clock first, and Chrisman was out.

The final round and Top Eliminator was accompanied by more noise from the crowd than the dragsters produced. Tom "Mongoose" McEwen had cracked a water jacket and was running his blown Olds with no water. This was the run for all the marbles. He faced off against Robinson's single engine, blown Chevy small block. Anticipation grew; the flagman waved them away and everyone held their breaths. It was Robinson laying down a quick 8.86 @ 170.77 mph to take the win.

That was drag racing at its best in 1961, but it wasn't over yet for Chevrolet. Willie Ragsdale rolled his fuel injected B/Street Roadster to the line against Tennessean Milton Potter's blown A/Street Roadster. It was a close won, but the Texan took Little Eliminator with a 11.55 seconds @ 122.44 mph.

Junior Garrison's B/Gas Chevy nailed down Street Eliminator (12.44 @ 111.66), and in the final round of World Stock Points Championship that year, two fuel injected B/Stock '57 Chevys pulled up to the line. Bruce Morgan in the left lane had already accumulated enough points to claim the championship, but was beaten by Richard Hilt in the right lane. With that victory, Hilt received a new '61 Pontiac as grand prize, but later, he was disqualified for having non-stock valve springs.

After all the running was done at Indianapolis, Chevrolet powered cars had taken four of the five Eliminator titles. Officially, though, Chevys had nailed down three of the four Eliminator titles awarded when Hilt was disqualified in Stock Eliminator.

By 1962, an entire cadre of drag racers running Chevys in all sorts of configurations had overwhelmed the sport. Chevys were everywhere. In the Dragster classes, a new generation of very light weight rail dragsters were making big waves in the sport. These small machines could be built in any garage and were knocking off some big iron. With no more than full-tilt fuel injected small blocks, these B/Dragster and C/Dragster class machines quickly became favorites of the crowd. It was a case of David and Goliath. For instance, a 302 cubic inch small block B/D was capable of 10 seconds flat, and when given four car-lengths against a AA/Dragster that were running in the low 9 second range, the "giant killers" were tough to beat.

At Indianapolis for the US Nationals, three of the Chevy dragsters won their class, A/D, B/D and C/D. Jack Chrisman had gone to a Pontiac engine and won the AA/D title.

When all the smoke had cleared and World Points Champions were crowned, it was Chevrolet powered machines at the top of both categories. The Competition World Champion was Jess Van Deventer of California topping the points total with his B/Modified Roadster. Stock World Champion was Tom Sturm, also of California, who piloted his 1962 409 C/Factory Experimental Chevy to the title. The next four runners-up were two Pontiacs and two more Chevrolets. Ford wasn't to be seen. General Motors owned drag racing, and Chevrolet was way out front.

Things looked like more of the same in 1963. A special production version of the 409 was now up to 426.5 cubic inches, but Chevrolet wasn't the only manufacturer to have an engine with that much displacement. Ford was there with its crossbolt main 427 developed from the high performance 406. This engine with its inline twin 4-bbl carb intake was under-rated at 425 hp. Chrysler's new 426 II "Super Stock"

166

The "young-at-heart" convertibles for 1965 were a major marketing theme for Chevrolet. Floyd Joliet of Chevorlet's photography team chose settings for marketing brochure photos that brought customers in by the droves. Sales that year reached 2,587,509 for the first time over 2.5-million, the largest sales year on record. Chevrolet photo.

engine with cross-flow dual 4-bbls was also rated at 425 hp, less than it produced. Pontiac's aged 389 was bumped to 421 for the 1963 racing season and was rated at 410 hp.

Chevrolet was in the thick of things with the the Z-11 version of the W-series 409, and outwardly, it looked very similar to the old 409 hp, 409 inch engine. The 409 had been a real charger and had its way about everywhere it was drag raced, and the Z-11 was to prove equally competitive. On the high-banks, another 427 cubic inch engine was needed. More about that later.

The Z-11 used the same block as the 409 with the same 4.3125-inch bore but with a 3.650-inch stroke, .150-inch longer than the 409. This longer stroke crankshaft (part number 3838396) required new rods (3837686) and new pistons (4 each 3837682 and 3837683). New "high port" cylinder heads (3837730) and a new matching intake manifold (3830623) were the main components that made the Z-11. With dual 4-bbl carbs and a hot .511-inch lift cam (3837735), the Z-11 was rated at 425 horsepower. A new cast iron exhaust header was part of the Z-11 package. The idea of the "high port" heads was to raise the intake manifold so an aluminum cylinder block valve lifter chamber could be used underneath. That separated the intake manifold from contact with engine block heat and kept it cooler.

Both the 409 and Z-11 used the same size valves, 2.023-inch intakes and 1.734-inch exhausts, and valve actuation hardware was also the same. The purpose for updating the 409 to become the the Z-11 was to make Chevys more competitive. As confirmed by Dick Keinath, Chevrolet's en-

gineers were never satisfied with design problems of the 409, and although the Z-11 proved an even better engine, it didn't have the potential of becoming a winning stock car racing engine. And that was, after all, THE reason that the factory went to the Mk II engine.

The primary differences in that engine was in the heads. Outwardly, the valve covers were very different. The double convoluted covers of the 409 and Z-11 were simply rectangular covers on the Mk II. This design became standard with the later Mk IV big blocks. Larger intake valves of the Mk II, 2.19-inches, could accommodate the healthy increase in breathing of the engine. Everyone knew that horsepower is made with improved air-fuel flow in and out of combustion chambers, and that was the limitation of the W-series engines. The combustion chamber in the block and piston-to-head mismatch of 16-degrees insured that little could be done to improve breathing.

The Mk II was a significant improvement. Rather than cant the combustion chamber, the valves were canted. That put the combustion chamber in the head in semi-hemi fashion. By using the rocker arm, stud and ball pivot concept of the small block, designer Keinath could cant the valves where he thought they should go. Once on the dyno, the Mk II showed great advances in power over the W-series engines, and development on them was stopped. Much of the Mk II design carried over to the later Mk IV 396, 427 and 454 big block engines, but there were enough differences that the Mk II should be considered a completely different engine. It was, however, the granddaddy of all of Chevrolet's big blocks.

167

Hayden Proffitt

Remembers his "Mr. 409" days

The press put the name "Mr. 409" on me. I feel honored to be called that, but there was a lot of people involved in it. Don Nicholson, Jenkins, Strickler, there was many of us that helped make the 409 Chevy's famous car.

My very first racing was during World War II. I drove the circle tracks, believe it or not, in a 6 cylinder Chevrolet with a Wayne head on it, and I used to shut those flat head Fords down pretty good. If it stayed together, then I could beat them. Then I quit that and got into drag racing in 1954, in a 1954 Buick, and won one trophy the first year. With the 1955 Chevrolet, I won 12 trophies. In the 1956 Chevrolet, I was almost unbeatable; had track records in old Santa Ana, San Gabriel, Long Beach. In 1957, I got a Corvette from the factory and did very well.

AG: How was the Corvette set up?

Hayden: It was stock. Everything back then had to be stock. You couldn't even use headers. Even the seven-inch tire was not in rule at that time. You had to use whatever came on that car; couldn't use anything any wider.

AG: How about fuel injection and four speed?

Hayden: It had a four speed but not fuel injection. It had two fours at that time. Class was B/Sports Car. Anything blown was A/Sports Car, and it was just those two classes. The only thing we ever run was just the T-Birds and the Corvettes, and the Corvettes just absolutely hid from them. It was a run-away.

Then I went into a 1937 Chevrolet blown B/Gas. Broke Doug Cook's record one day, and it held one hour. He came back and broke it again. So I gave that up and went into dragsters, C/Dragster first with a Chevy engine.

AG: What size Chevy was that?

Hayden: It was bored and stroked out to 292 because you had to run under 300 cubic inches. That was injected. When we put a blower on it, that shifted us to B/Dragster, and we had a national record in that. It was set at Long Beach, CA. That was my home track. My first track was old Santa Ana; the very first legalized drag strip in America, Santa Ana, California. It was owned and operated by "Pappy" C. J. Hart, who is one of my dear friends.

From the B/Dragsters, I went to the A/Dragsters with a big Chevrolet. I drove two Chevys in-line, supercharged. They were 350 inches at that time. To get that many inches, you had to stroke the engine a half-inch. We had a national record with that car, top end. The car would not ET, it was too heavy, but we would turn top end everywhere.

At the 1960-1961 Winternationals, I was inducted into Pontiac at that time. Pontiac took me over for 1960 and 1961. One of my height of glories; we took 5 Pontiacs to the Winternationals, plus that dual engine dragster. We set top time of the meet and we won all five classes. They were all stock classes including the, no I am getting ahead of myself because the next year was when I built the very first A/FX car, A/Factory Experimental Tempest, and we won that plus three more classes that year. That was in 1961.

Then in 1962, Chevrolet; well, General motors didn't want to drop me, but they were going to drop Pontiac, so they put me in the seat of a 409 Chevrolet, which actually I think I got more ink - more publicity. If you want to call it fame, we will. Absolutely, the phone rang 24 hours a day, congratulations and all that stuff.

The 1962 409 was factory-backed Chevrolets. We had over a hundred cars at Indy that year, and they were all factory backed. There were 33 factory-backed Mopars, and man, I had to go through them. I kicked the hell out of all their asses and sent them home licking their wounds, and remembering that makes me feel good.

MoPars, Fords anything that pulled up there. The last two to run was a RamCharger, Jim Thornton, and myself with the 409 red Chevrolet. Everything had to click to win these kinds of things. I don't think I can stress this enough; the factories were trying to get the jump on the other one, the drivers were good, and the tuners had to be good.

I moved first, and his was automatic coming up beside of me. I went to second, and I pulled him about a half of a car. Then I went to third, and I pulled him about another half. I knew then if I got it in fourth gear, I had a couple o' miles-per-hour on top end. As soon as it went in fourth gear, everything was straightened out, and I turned around and I gave him the bone. That was the first time I'd ever done that, and I never will do it again.

I tell you it was really something. Back in those days, you go to those Southern "run what you brung" races, it was a lot rougher than people thought. It was two-by-fours and the boys fought then, just like they do now in the stock cars at the oval tracks. They'd get to fist-a-cuffs sometimes.

When we got there, it wasn't to love them. Man, it was to beat them. Really, the fun quit for me when I had to call the factories on Monday morning. They didn't know what it meant for me to say, "Well, I lost." I mean, they gave you the best of everything, how come you can't win. But I got to report that I had won more than I had lost.

Then the funny thing about it, Chevrolet quit racing. I already had my 1963 Chevrolet, and I had won my first two match races.

AG: Tell me how the cars were set up. Did they come from the factory built?

Hayden: No sir, absolutely not. You had to be stock, it was only little tiny things that you could do.

AG: You mean, start out with a car off the show room floor?

Hayden: Absolutely. Everyone started the same, but the Plymouths, as far as buying them off the show room floor, they were as hot a car as you could buy.

AG: That was the 413 cross ram?

Hayden: Yes, at that time. Then in 1963, it would have been the 426. A Chevy could beat them, but you had to know what you were doing. People thought that going in a straight line, you set the chassis up just like it came from the factory, but that is dead wrong. You have to get the shock towers higher, which was legal. You could put any Chevy part on them, so I would take Chevy station wagon coil springs, and I would put them in the front and a different spring in the back to let the car go down. I set my cars up a lot different than the others. The chassis on my cars worked. The RamChargers kind of set theirs up solid. I had 10/90 shocks on the front and 90/10s on the rear. The front would jump up, transfer the weight, and then as you were going down the track, it would gradually level out again so you wouldn't have the wind turbulence. It would take a good month to take a stocker and get it ready to drag race. You could bore .060 over, and if you didn't bore it sixty over and put good pistons in it, you were not a winner.

AG: Have you ever totaled up how many wins you had with the 409?

Hayden: No, I haven't. The only thing that I have kept track of is, I have won 365 trophies, but see, a lot of the tracks didn't give trophies. They gave you a $25.00 bond or something like that, a little kiss from a pretty girl or something. In 1962 the very most money that was ever paid at that time to a drag racer was a guy at Atlanta, Georgia paid me $3600.00 to come from Garden Grove, CA. to Atlanta to run Phil Bonner. Well, Nicholson and I had two Chevrolets so we were going to run Phil Bonner and Dick Brannan in Fords, and we beat them three straight. It was really no contest.

That is still the worst year that I ever had. Thinking about it, though, I am still the only man that has ever driven for all four manufacturers, and was paid to do so. I drove American Motors the last three years, as far as in the Funny Cars. From a zero end, we took it to a 70% win in the second year and also the third year, in 1970. That was the last year that I drove the Funny Cars.

I drove for Chrysler right after I got out of the Chevy in 1963. Remember, I said I had my 1963 Chevrolet all ready to go, and Chevrolet called and said they had to quit racing. So, they quit racing, and I sold my 1962 and 1963. I loafed around for a couple of months, then called the boys in Detroit at Chrysler

and they said come on up and talk with us. In two days I left there with five cars, two dual cab pick-ups and a check for $188,000.00 for a year. Then we duplicated that in 1964.

Here again, that was one of my heights of glories. Factory racing was heads-up again in the AHRA in 1964. I had one car stationed in New Jersey and one in Seattle, Washington, and I had one in Houston, Texas, and I had two in Garden Grove, California. I would fly in to race the others, but the two in Garden Grove were the hottest cars because we got to work on them all the time.

Then there was another all factory-backed car thing again, 90 or something, Fords, Chevrolets, Plymouths, everything. Then, on Saturday for class, my two cars raced each other. I had another guy by the name of Roger Caster driving for me, and it was my two cars against each other. And we repeated that same thing on Sunday.

In 1965, Plymouth was gradually getting out of it. That's when Mercury came in hot with their Cammers. Louie Unser, the brother of the famous Unser brothers, he bought five of those Mercury Cammer cars. Nicholson got one. Arnold Burchett got one. I got the very first one because I was there at home. I forget where the other two went, I think a guy by the name of Delorian got one.

Anyway, the engine would do good on a dyno, but on the drag strip it just would not stay together. Everytime I let out on the clutch, I would either break an axle or a clutch. The engine would blow. I had the worst year I ever had. I knew I could get another deal with Chevy any time I wanted, so I called them and told them I wanted to build a Corvair, put the big motor in it (427). Cleaned up! My smartest one was a 430. That one was injected and no nitro. Then I built a 450 incher, and after that I built a 488. I never did use the 488 but one time, that was in Denver, because it had too much power. It would break the tires loose. I had 60 match races that year with the Corvair, and I won 56 of them.

AG: What class was that?

Hayden: Funny Car/Fuel, (engine in front, fiber glass body). This time we had over a hundred cars at the very first East versus West race. They were all there at Long Beach, California. "Pappy" Hart pulled this off, and by golly, I sent them all home talking to themselves. That was the Corvair. That was another highlight in my life.

We built the USA-1 rocket car. My oldest son wanted to go racing, so we did, and we held 18 state records. He still holds the fastest quarter-mile record, 349.77 miles per hour in a quarter-mile at 4:35 ET. Now that was a rocket car, a rocket powered by Hydrogen Peroxide. Then I got the idea that I would like to go back racing. A gentleman that had worked for me named Les Shockley had started on a jet car, so I bought the jet from him and got back under the wheel. It was named the Hot Streak, and we set a lot of records again and kicked a lot of ass again.

Building one of those things is like painting a house. You work on it for a year, but when it's done, it's done. All you do is put fuel in them, diesel, and pop the chute, and you're racing. I really had a ball for four years, but I have been out of racing now four years (1988). We just had a lot of fun.

The 375 hp SS 396 Chevelle Malibu of 1965 was Chevrolet's first muscle car. It's styling was very appealing. Chevelle was second to Chevrolet in sales volume that year with 370,188 units. Just 200 were the RPO Z-16 like this one. Chevrolet photo.

Baldwin Motion's 427 powered Biscayne "Street Racer's Special" was a going machine. Squire Gabbard photo.

Street Racer's Special

The first publicly available muscle car from Chevrolet was the 396 Chevelle of 1965. By that time, there were all sorts of big inch pure stock cars, and Chevy's Mk IV 396 could hold its own pretty well against the toughest. Although the street hemi Plymounths and Dodges were both faster and quicker, there were far fewer of them, and those lightweight 427 Fords were even more scarce. That left rivalries on the local level to brew between production cars. Each weekend, it was open war at drag races, and every town had its "strip" where Satur-day night cruisin' often turned into street racing between stop lights.

Drag strips everywhere were host to one grudge match after another. The cars faced off where the numbers don't lie. In the stock classes from top to bottom, big block Chevys were always a threat, and occasionally some very plain cars made big waves.

Performance minded Chevrolet dealers offered their own versions of hot street machines by matching up low bucks cars with high performance engines. One was Baldwin Motion and their "Street Racer's Special" that came in any 1967 Chevrolet product a buyer might want.

If anything looked like a granny's grocery getter, it was a bottom dollar Biscayne. But if one had 427 emblems on the front fenders, it was probably a Baldwin Street Racer's Special. "Plain Jane" Bicaynes had no sex appeal at all and certainly didn't bring the "wows" like the immensely popular 396 Chevelle. But they had thrills of their own and cost a lot less. Although inexpensive, another reason for their popularity was the rise of the "sleeper", a car that was fast but didn't look like it would be.

As the number of muscle cars grew, they became increasingly commonplace, and the idea began to grow among young buyers that the manufacturers intended for their showroom model muscle cars to be compromises. Not so with Baldwin Motion, and their advertising was explicit.

"If you've had it with Detroit compromise performance and styling...you can outfit any car purchased from us with any of the SS-427 Special Performance Options..."

The Baldwin Motion Street Racer's Special was such a car. Built on the 2-door Biscayne sedan body, buyers could order any of three 427 cubic inch engines:

the L-88 with aluminum 12:1 heads;

the L-89 with 11:1;

the all-aluminum ZL-1 full-spec racing engine.

Prices were $750, $500 and $3,000 respectively. Thirty-three other pure performance options were available from Baldwin for their Street Racer's Special. The base price? A bargain basement $2,998! The 425 hp Turbo-Jet big block option cost $447.65 from the factory.

Special ignitions, racing cams, heavy duty clutches, racing flywheels and NHRA-approved scatter shields were on the list. The legendary Muncie M-22 "Rockcrusher" close-ratio 4-speed with Hurst competition shifters and a modified 3-speed TurboHydramatic autoshifter was there, too. Headers, traction bars, a choice of racing tires, cast alloy wheels, special gage package, and special suspension set-ups could also be purchased, and all the above wasn't as expensive as might be imagined.

Except for the engines, most options ranged from $29.95 for a special gear drive injector kit for the Holley 3- or 4-bbl carb to Corvette-type side pipes at $275. Things really have changed.

One of the cleanest and most appealing styling jobs was the Nova Super Sport Coupe of 1967. Chevrolet photo.

The 350 hp Turbo-Jet 396 was the top factory engine for the Chevelle in 1967 and was available only on the SS 396 model. Chevrolet photo.

The Ribicoff Effect

Although 1965 had been a great year for automotive sales in this country, the vast number of cars on the nation's highways and the growing number of high performance cars also produced the highest number of highway accidents in this country's history. Newspaper headlines relayed the "fantastic carnage" that automobile accidents had caused. Public opinion was mounting that said the auto manufacturers were not concerned with occupant safety in the design of their cars. Public outcry reached a fever pitch for what was called the auto industry's failure to act responsibly where the public was concerned. The division of opinion between the kids, who were fascinated with more powerful and faster cars, and the adult segment of the population, who were convinced that the auto industry was irresponsible, reached Washington and Senator Abraham Ribicoff. He was chairman of the Senate Subcommittee on Executive Reorganization. One of his staffers was Robert F. Kennedy, US Attorney General during his brother's Presidency. Another was attorney Ralph Nader. Soon, "Nader's Raders" were branding car after car as "unsafe at any speed".

General Motors chairman Frederic Donner, President James Roche and Chief Engineer Harry Barr were grilled in Ribocoff's hearings. Perhaps it was GM's $1.7 billion dollar profit and enormously successful sales campaign that gave Donner and his men an air of over-confidence. But whatever it was, they were ill-prepared, and they looked miserably inept when answering questions concerning safety of GM cars.

There were all sorts of studies showing GM cars were less safe than competitors. Vehicle safety and crash-worthness were the themes of the hearings, not high performance cars. For instance, statistics showed that doors on GM cars were almost 10 times more likely to pop open during a crash than a Ford car. How much money did GM spend on Safety? About $1.25 million, answered Roche.

That revelation changed the automotive industry forever. It was open season on the Detroit manufacturers, and the public demanded that they "clean up their act". Government mandates began placing requirements on the manufacturers because it appeared that they were not capable of regulating themselves. New car costs and insurance premiums went up even higher. Crash testing began, and engineering of saftey features became top priority. It took time, but steady improvements were made. By the early '70s and the near decade-long economic slump that followed, the auto industry was hurting. With the return of high performance cars in the '80s, enthusiasm and sales are up, but growing concern from the public, insurance companies and law inforcement authorities over the increasing numbers of 150 mph cars may cause history to repeat itself.

Baldwin and other performance dealers had a lot to build on. Chevrolet offered a fleet of super sport cars in '67. The new Camaro led the way followed by the Chevelle, the full size Chevy, the Chevy II and the Corvette. The standard 427 was the L-36, but Baldwin and other dealers in the know could get literally anything you wanted with a Central Office Production Order (COPO).

The top Camaro from Chevrolet was the SS 350 with the L-48, but the Baldwin Motion or Yenko Camaro or Nickey Camaro put the driver behind an L-88 or a ZL-1 when it became available. The 350 hp L-34 Chevelle 396 was a bigger car for '67 and didn't have the zip of the '65 model, but Baldwin could take care of that. The top Chevy II Nova SS came with the L-30 275 hp 327, but for a few dollars more,

Harrisburg PA's Bruce Larson took his patriotic red, white and blue USA-1 match race Chevelle around the drag racing circuit in the mid-to-late '60s. This fuel injected 427 with 4-inch stroke measured 454 cid and was capable of 8-second passes at 170+ mph. Larson was just one of the multitudes of match racers and super stockers that toured the country during the time that has become known as the "Olympics of Drag Racing", the sensational '60s. Gold Dust Classics photo.

the 365 horse small block or later LT-1 350 could have been a COPO. The Yenko Deuce is an example of this special edition car.

The 427 Corvette was already the hottest running car on the street, except for the rarely seen 427 Cobra, and Corvette buyers got the top factory car in the mechanical cam, 435 hp L-71. The tri-power 427 also came in the hydraulic cam L-68 with 400 hp, and the single 4-bbl L-36 rated at 390 hp. Special orders through the dealers were the L-88 and ZL-1.

For 1968, the Turbo-Jet 427 engine came in six versions. All were 4.251 x 3.76 inch bore and stroke, but output varied as follows:

Output	Comp Ratio	Induction
385 hp @ 5,200 rpm	10.25:1	1 4-bbl
390 hp @ 5,400 rpm	10.25:1	1 4-bbl
400 hp @ 5,400 rpm	10.25:1	3 2-bbl
425 hp @ 5,600 rpm	11.00:1	1 4-bbl
430 hp @ 5,200 rpm	12.50:1	1 4-bbl
435 hp @ 5,800 rpm	11.00:1	3 2-bbl

Estimates of the number of Baldwin Street Racer's Special sold runs as high as 1,600. With 4.88:1 positraction gears and a wheelbase of 119 inches, the full size Biscayne weighed around 3,650 pounds in production form. And like any of these special big block cars, they could turn quick quarter-miles, but narrow tires limited getting the power to the ground. They were, however, good for under 14-seconds right

out of the box. In a Super Stock magazine test, a '68 427 powered Biscayne with 4.56 gears laid down an impressive 13.65 at 105 mph.

For 1969, Baldwin advertised the same Street Racer's Special with the L-89 427 engine turning up 450 horsepower. This was the same 427 engine with a different label. The factory still said 430 with a single 4-bbl. Since the L-88 was the same for both years, it is probable that all the high performance big blocks exceeded sticker horsepower ratings by significant margins, insurance regulations and all that. Insurance companies tended to believe factory figures, and that saved buyers a lot of dollars in insurance costs.

Chevrolet horsepower ratings were one thing. What a buyer could do with his engine was another. The factory offered a multitude of high performance equipment to go well beyond ratings. In the factory's Chevy Power manual, they offered the know-how and specified the equipment. This manual was produced in association with Chevrolet's engineers and outside racing and high performance parts development firms. It has been published in several editions for years.

One item of interests to road racers was fuel injection. Since last offered in 1964 on the small block, the factory had not offered FI engines in any form although development went on. Chevrolet engineer Jim Kinsler was involved in big block fuel injection and went on to establish his own company making equipment that pulled over 700 hp out of ZL-1 engines.

The reason that the Rochester FI system was dropped was

that it was a temperamental and costly option. When the big block engines came along, they were both cheaper and less troublesome.

Whether it was drag racing, street racing or road racing, Chevrolet had the parts and knowhow. Adding to factory efforts were people like Baldwin and Yenko who brought Chevy's fastest hardware to the people. The Baldwin Street Racer's Special was one and Yenko's COPO Camaro was another.

Driving the Yenko Super Camaro

Don Yenko's Chevrolet dealership in Canonsburg, PA offered 427 powered super Camaros. Squire Gabbard photo.

After driving three of the '69 Yenko Camaros in Cliff Ernst's magnificent collection of muscle cars, my preference among the Yenkos I drove was the 4-speed car. Having once owned a daily driver '67 RS 327 Camaro for nine years and run a built version of an LT-1 with even more power, I can fairly compare the small block and big block cars. My Camaro was also a 4-speed car, and that probably explains my preference for the manual. Shifting the Yenko through the gears brought back many pleasant memories. Its feel was no different, except for having more power. Bringing the big block up to power seemed less crisp than the small block, but the 427's enormous torque simply hurled the car in a way the small block could only wish it could do.

The car has a light driving feel and is very responsive. It is easy to drive and gives no sensation of being unbalanced. With immense power from the L-72 big block, the Yenko Camaro must be rated as among the ultimate muscle cars.

Overall, the Yenkos were clearly very well thought out. As a COPO item, factory engineers made sure of that. Zeroing in on the 4-speed car I drove, I concluded that the 427 engine is not too much for this car at all. It was docile in traffic, easy to handle at low speed and a solid road car at highway speeds. As usual, the character of the Hurst shifter is very smooth and light. No question: it is a very solid performance shifter. While driving along in fourth gear at a modest speed, interior noise for a car this big (this one has headers on it but is otherwise stock), was not at all noisy. Being a premium fuel big block, though, meant frequent visits to the gas station with the highest octane gasoline. These days, 10 or so mpg is an expensive way to go.

While driving through the Tennessee countryside with other Yenkos and drivers, it was fascinating to see several of the cars in one line. That was probably the first time in the history of the world that all of the colors of the Yenko Camaros for 1969 were on the road at one time.

I was pleasantly surprised that this car was quiet and so easy to drive. But one thing that I did wonder about was that it had no tach. For the kind of power this car made, and for its overall driving appeal, it certainly should have had full instrumentation. However, that was a function of the options selected in originally ordering the car. It did have a 140 mph speedometer giving some indication of its potential.

This Yenko showed 49,796 original miles and was in pristine condition. Its distinctive styling features added to the already aggressive profile of the 1969 Camaro included bold stripes and interior upholstery unique to the Yenko line.

Taking curves at about road speed was easy enough for women drivers. Although superbly mannered, its very solid suspension transmitted the feel of the road back to the driver. At posted speeds, the car handled all turns with a comfortable margin. It was very capable of perhaps twice the posted speed limit on any turn. The Yenko Super Camaro was also referred to as the Yenko Sports Car, and the suspension under this car illustrated that the latter description was apt.

Later, some power runs on a private section with another 4-speed Yenko fitted with a tach and slightly modified engine fully illustrated the awesome performance of the Yenko marque. After driving around to acquaint myself with the car, it too proved just as easy and docile to handle as the unmodified version.

This car was easy to drive, and came to life as a thoroughbred muscle car of the highest caliber. The suspension tightened up under the load of massive torque, and the car leapt through the gears. Having done that many times before with my own Camaro, a quick winding small block, I was surprised just how quickly the big block turned up.

Then - BOOM - the car came alive like it was meant to be! First gear to redline and the Yenko was still pulling hard with no sign of letting up. A quick shift to second and the car was really pulling. The rear tires broke loose momentarily, then caught hold and slingshot the car in a neck snapping launch toward 3rd. Snatching the third cog broke the rear tires loose again, and while the tach needle arched toward 6,000 rpm, my thoughts raced to the conclusion; "This thing will fly!"

Topped in 3rd was about all the road that was available and just as I backed off, I noted that we were in triple digits. And there was more to come? Some muscle car indeed! This car could simply get it done in a hurry, the legacy of the muscle car era.

Don Yenko's entry into the specialty muscle car market began in 1967. By the '69 model year, the Yenko Camaros were well proven performers. No more than 201 Yenkos were built that year. This is Cliff Ernst's Super Stock magazine test car.

The line-up; 450 hp of Chevrolet muscle, the heart of Yenko Camaros. Cliff Ernst collection.

tested the car and titled his article "Yenkamaro Z/427/28/SS".

He told readers that, "What all that means is that Yenko Sports Cars has taken the best of the Z/28, added 427 power, their own trim, and created an 11-second street bomb that works!"

Aside from Yenko's COPO on the car, all that was changed was addition of Doug Thorley headers, drag tires and 5-spoke mag wheels. Then test driver Ed Hedrick nailed down a best of 11.94 seconds at 114.50 mph at York, Pennsylvania's US30 Dragway. At the time, Hedrick was campaigning a similar Yenko in Super Stock, and both of the cars were there during the tests

The Yenko Camaro was indeed a top drawer muscle car. Don Yenko built a lasting and respected legacy, first as a racing driver and later as a Chevrolet dealer offering the best

One of the Yenkos in Cliff's collection is the feature car of the July, 1969, issue of *Super Stock* magazine. Ro McGonegal of Chevrolet's special products. Unfortunately, he was killed in a private plane crash on March 5, 1987.

Bill "Grumpy" Jenkins went full-time professional drag racer in 1969. He prepared and drove this 427 Camaro to the first 9-second pass in the new "heads-up" Super Stock class that became Pro Stock. He swept the Super Stock Nationals that year and clocked the only 9-second runs during the entire event. Gold Dust Classics photo.

"Grumpy's Toys"

There were lots of Chevy drag racers in the late '60s, and several come to mind. Malcolm Durham and his "Strip Blazer" Chevelle; Tom Sturm's "Just 4 Chevy Lovers" Chevelle; "Jungle Jim" Liberman and his Novas; Terry Hedricks "Super Shaker"; and Dave Strickler's "The Old Reliable" match race 'Vette are among many memorable bowtie drag racers. There were many more, but because of Bill "Grumpy" Jenkins's long commitment to Chevrolets, he alone deserves the title of "Mr. Chevrolet".

The Malvern, Pennsylvania Chevy man had prepared the cars that Dave Strickler drove to win the 1962 Winternationals Super Stock/S class. The next year, Strickler took Street Eliminator at Pomona, and followed that the next year with an A/FX victory in the US Nationals at Indianapolis.

Bill decided to do the driving in 1965 and slid behind the wheel of a 426 Plymouth and won Stock Eliminator at Pomona on his first outing when he posted the win in 11.39 seconds at 126.05 mph. He returned to Chevrolets for good

in 1966 and began running his now famous "Grumpy's Toy I" Chevy II with a full house 327. With that car out-running the hemi cars, fans came to respect and admire his ability. His concentration left little time to chat with fans who affectionately dubbed him "Grumpy".

After retiring the Chevy II in 1967 in favor of a 396 Camaro, Bill won SS/C at the US Nationals, then took Super Stock Eliminator with an impressive 11.55 @ 115.97 mph. Except for a red light in the semi-final round, he came close to repeating in the World Finals at Tulsa. (In Street Eliminator, Gordon Matney won with his fuel injected A/Modified Sport Production Corvette turning 9.57 @ 144.68 mph.) By then, it was not uncommon for Jenkins to set 20 or more national records in a single season.

Bill recognized that thorough attention to every detail and getting each one right added up to a more competitive machine. It was the attention to detail that gave him his competitive edge. In all the national events he entered in 1968, Jenkins was undefeated. It was a tough year, and to gain that kind of record would have been regarded as impossible in the beginning of the season.

For the World Finals, he qualified four cars, and three of them made it to the final rounds. For the Super Stock title, Jenkins faced off against Dave Strickler in his own A/MP Z-28 Camaro and lost by a narrow margin.

For the 1969 season, Jenkins went full-time professional

175

This is the all-conquering small block powered Vega Pro Stocker that Bill Jenkins won ten 1972 National events with and set records everywhere he raced.

drag racer with a 427 Camaro. He was the first to run 9-seconds and swept the Super Stock Nationals with the only 9-second runs. He and the Camaro were tough to beat.

Jenkins was the central figure in drag racing's return to what it once was when he and Don Nicholson and Ronnie Sox formed what became Pro Stock. With all the handicaps and indexes in Super Stock at the time, there was a bewildering system in place. Jenkins, Nicholson and Sox proposed a simple formula based on engine size versus car weight with only production-based equipment allowed. The proposed regulations was for heads-up racing like days of old. The quickest car wins, and in Pro Stock, there was no sand-bagging at the end of the strip. Indexes meant that drivers braked hard just before the lights to get their elapsed times up and hoped they didn't break out of their index. The new Pro Stock rules did away with indexes. It was "no break-out" drag racing, and it quickly became the most popular class for full bodied drag racing. Jenkins wanted the class to be called Super Stock, but NHRA formed a new class for the professional drivers and called it Pro Stock.

During the '70 season, Jenkins jumped out to a huge lead when he won the NHRA Winternationals, Orange Country Raceway's US Pro Stock Championships and NHRA's Gatornationals in a span of just 15 days. He earned $30,000 for his efforts.

The big block "Rat" engines had powered his cars for five years when Jenkins went back to the small block "Mouse" mills in the fall of 1971. He introduced a new Pro Stock Vega. The reason for the Vega was three-fold: small cars had become a major Detroit priority; gasoline prices had climbed to 60-cents a gallon (soon to sky-rocket to over $1.00 a

gallon); and highway speed limits were dropped to 55.

A showroom stock Vega was hard pressed to cover the quarter-mile in under 20 seconds and might achieve 70 mph. In the early '70s, high performance was dead in Detroit, but Jenkins chose to build a dual 4-bbl Pro-Stock Vega with a 330-inch small block. By then, he was the all-time Pro Stock win leader with ten victories to his credit, but he had gone 22 months without a win at the hands of the hemi Plymouths and Dodges. With his new short wheelbase Vega running 8.5-seconds at 159 mph, he was to win lots more.

In 1972, Jenkins stunned the ChryCo crowd by shutting them out. He added 11 more Pro Stock wins to his list and earned more than $250,000. He set both ends of the NHRA Pro Stock record; 9.42 second ET, 146.81 mph top speed and left nothing for the Chryslers in national event competition. He later went 9.36 at the end of the season.

For his excellence in drag racing, he was voted to the American Auto Racing Writers and Broadcaster Association All-American Team and received at least 16 *Car Craft* magazine All-Star Team awards along with Pro Stock Driver of the Year accolades in four out of five seasons preceding 1973. Engine builder and Jenkins associate since 1965, Joe Tryson, also was general manager of Jenkins Competition research and development and received Pro Stock Engine Builder of the Year awards.

During the '72 season, Jenkins earned drag racing's first "Grand Slam" title by having won on each of NHRA's National tracks. He was the first driver to win all 8 Nationals on NHRA's calendar. He went on to four more 1/4-Million dollar seasons in 1973, '74 and '75. Jenkins Competition also built the engine that won the pole position for the Daytona

500, the work of Tryson.

For the 1974 season, Larry Lombardo became Jenkins' first protege driver and put the Jenkins Vega on the Pro Stock winner's deck at Englishtown, NJ turning 9.11 @ 150 flat. In '76, Lombardo drove Grumpy's new Monza to victory in the NHRA Winter Classic at Phoenix, and posted four major victories to finish the season by winning the NHRA World Championship.

Jenkins' second driver, Ken Dondero, came on board and won the AHRA Pro Stock World Championship with 6 victories in 9 scheduled AHRA Grand American events in 1974. Ronnie Thacker, George Areford and Richard Wright were other members of Jenkins' "Super Crew".

During that season, Jenkins scored an impressive series of wins in the UHRA Springnationals at New Yorks' International Speedway. Primary competition came

Back with the big block in 494 inch form for match races in 1976, da "Grump" introduced the Monza and a new driver, Larry Lombardo, who won the NHRA Winter Classic at Phoenix. Bill Jenkins photo.

from "Fast Eddie" Schartman's new BOSS 429 powered match race Mustang II. Jenkins shut down the Ford in six straight runs and notched a low ET of 8.54. His consistent wins were some of the quickest and fastest recorded by any Pro Stock type car in the entire 1974 season.

And after a 3-year lay-off from active driving in national events, Jenkins returned to the driver's seat in 1980 in a Camaro. But that was the first year of the famed Lee Shepherd Camaro versus Bob Glidden's Fords. From then on, its been Chevy against Ford like the old days.

Into the '80s with a new Pro Stock Camaro, Bill "Grumpy" Jenkins and his "Super Crew" found the going tough against Lee Shepherd and Bob Glidden in NHRA national competition. Bill Jenkins photo.

Bill "Grumpy" Jenkins

Recalls More Than 20 Years of Racing Chevys

I started getting interested in cars in the 1948 and '49 time frame when I was in high school. I went to college in engineering in '49 but didn't get a degree although I was in college off and on through '55. In between, during the "off" times, I worked in a dealership that handled Cadillac and Oldsmobile. I also did some work on six-cylinder Chevys.

The nineteen fifty-five Chevrolet V-8 really started it all and provided me an excellent opportunity to learn more through tuning. I moon-lighted with my own business, Competition Tune-up Service, through 1958. That was mostly with street cars for drag racing and SCCA sports cars and hill climbers; mostly local cars. A fair portion of my work was with Chevys, and it slowly drifted into building engines. I got involved with Dave Strickler in '59. We ran the "Old Reliable" cars from 1961 through '63.

I changed the name of my business to Jenkins Competition in that year, and its been the same ever since. We owned the cars and had no factory support. We were independents. "Old Reliable" numbers 1, 2 and 3 were 409s. In '63, "Old Reliable" number four was a Z-11. We built the engine for that car from pieces we could buy. It wasn't provided by Chevrolet. In '63 at Indianapolis, we won Little Eliminator. That was our first NHRA championship.

From '62 to '64, drag racing was a high percentage of my work, maybe eighty to ninety percent. Super Stock was really big back then, and we did a lot of match racing. It was a good bit of business for me in '61 and became very heavy by '63

when we were running A/Factory Experimental. In '64, Dave and I ran a series of Dodges with 426 hemi engines for the factory. During the '64 and '65 time frame, I did a lot of stock car engines in addition to drag racing. At one time, my products had won around thirty-five national records in different classes, and we won Junior Stock Eliminator at Bristol in the Summernationals in a customer car, a '55 Chevy called "Monster Mash".

The first two "Grumpy's Toys" were my '66 Chevy II, with an L-79 small block. I did a lot of drag racing and match racing in that car. The next year, I ran a Camaro with an L-78. I thought the Camaro had more "product appeal" for the sort of thing I was doing. That was "Grumpy's Toy" III.

A lot of people don't know it, but not all the L-88s in '67 came with aluminum heads. The L-89 was the aluminum head option on the L-88. You could build one with non-production pieces as far back as '65, and by '67, they became a Corvette option. The variations depended on the carburetion, mostly, three two-barrels or the 850 four-barrel. I ran my Camaro in class races and match races both with iron head engines. In match races, I ran the car with an L-88. That classified the car A/Modified Production. I raced that configuration a lot in match races.

At the US Nationals in '67, my class win in Super Stock/C was a slow run, didn't have to run hard, but the L-78 ran strong in taking Super Stock Eliminator. That car was very successful. I won numerous class wins and quite a few match races with the L-88 in that Camaro. That was a very busy season. I raced full time.

In '68, I had three "Grumpy's Toy" cars. One was a '68 Camaro in Super Stock/C or Super Stock/D depending on the engine. I was working with Strickler again, and we had four cars at the World Finals at Tulsa. Ed Hedrick, who had won the world championship in a Cobra a few years earlier, drove the '67 Camaro A/Modified Production to runner-up in Modified Eliminator. I drove the '68 Camaro Super Stock/C but got eliminated in the second round. Dave and I changed to a SS/D class and were in the final round. His car was another "Old Reliable", a Z-28 Camaro in Super Stock/E, and I raced my Super Stock/D Chevy II L-78. He won Super Stock Eliminator. I was runner-up.

After the NHRA season, the AHRA season had some races left, and I raced AHRA a lot. Overall, I won about three out of five races. By the end of that year, I was becoming disenchanted with Super Stock and invented Pro Stock in '69. The indexes were all screwed up and it wasn't real drag racing. Pro Stock was "heads up" Super Stock, the way drag racing should be. It hadn't been since '65.

Drag racing went index because of a lot of things. The manufacturers weren't building high performance engines for racing any more, they were into production muscle cars, and none of them were really competitive with each other. Indexing attempted to equal things out, but the whole thing turned out to be a mess.

Ford and Chrysler built cars for certain classifications, mostly for the lightest class the car would fit into like the 426 hemi 'Cuda, around 3400 pounds or less. The 428 Mustang was another one. There wasn't much of that from Chevrolet. Whatever class their cars fit into was what happened.

Going into '69, Super Stock had a lot of problems. The Super Stock Drivers Association, which was started by Strickler, campaigned for a "heads up" Super Stock class. It was composed of around fifty drivers. Strickler, Buddy Martin, me and Nicholson, and to a lesser extend Dick Landy, wanted to have a Super Stock class without indexes.

NHRA called it Pro Stock. I always thought that was a lousy name. They should have left it Super Stock and made everything else stock. Up through '71, the cars were really reinforced stock bodies and should have been Super Stock, not Pro Stock. It was a satisfying class, though. Its growth and popularity was good.

I started the '70 season with three major wins. I raced the '68 Camaro Pro Stock, "Grumpy's Toy" IV and won the Winternationals. After that, the Gatornationals and the Pro Stock Invitational at Orange Co. Quite a few cars had been at the Winternationals, and I'd guess around twenty-five showed up a week or so later at the Invitational. Pro Stock was a new class, and to have some of the east coast cars there, too, was good for the class.

During most of '70, I ran what would be a Pro Stock Camaro, and from about May, a '70 Camaro. The '69 was more successful. In 1970, I qualified #1 at Indy, but had bad luck for the remainder of 1970 and early '71. I did win AHRA and Super Stock national events. I was the first Pro Stock driver under 10-seconds, a 9.96 the first time out in '70.

The '71 season was so-so. Late in the season, I built the first "Mountain Motor" for my '70 Camaro. That was a Can-Am 494 aluminum engine that came from Chevrolet. Late in '69, I got quite a few engines that could be made 430 or 465 or 494 cubic inches depending on the crank. They all had poor ring

wear and required an awful lot of rebuild time. The 494 was good for around 750 horsepower and gave 9.60s at around 140. I won three or four races at the end of the season.

In September, NHRA changed the rules and allowed the Vega. That was the most successful of my Pro Stock cars. I was defeated only once, at the Gatornationals, and that was in the second or third round when I had lost a head gasket. At the Winternationals, I qualified the car 17th out of a thirty-two car field and won Pro Stock Eliminator. That was with a small block. That was my best year, over $200,000 in 1972 dollars. I was well sponsored, at least $100,000 was on the car. I won the NHRA Pro Stock World Championship at Tulsa.

The next year was pretty successful, but not as many wins as '72. I red-lighted in the Winternationals, and later won the Summernationals, AHRA World Championship, and was runner-up in the World Finals. That year, I was the first Pro Stock driver under 9 seconds, an 8.98 at the Super Stock Nationals at York, Pa.

The reason I went with the Vega was that cars were getting smaller and smaller, and there was a pending fuel crises. I thought the car was more in line with the promotional interests of Chevrolet. I raced the Vega through '74 and won the NHRA Winternationals again.

From 1975 to the present, I always stayed with production type cars. They always looked like the best kind of market to be in. Funny Car didn't look like it would become marketable and it didn't fit my ideals. Most of my involvement with Chevrolet, as far back as the '67 Camaro, was never more than parts and pieces. I did some development work from time to time, but there was not any type of real racing money. Now, I'm doing a lot of development work for Chevrolet, but I don't race anymore.

By 1967, Ford Motor Co. involvement in Trans-Am racing was a dual-pronged attack; Dan Gurney and Parnelli Jones in factory-backed Cougars and Jerry Titus in factory-backed Mustangs. Mark Donohue in the Penske-Sunoco Camaro was independent and gave them fits. Ford Motor Co. photo.

Trans-Am Racing

The Early Days

At Sebring in March of 1967, a young racer the press had dubbed "Mr. Nice Guy", wheeled the 12th Z-28 Camaro built onto Sebring's grid to start the Sport Car Club of America's first Trans-Am race. He was Mark Donohue, and that was the first showing of a Camaro in road racing competition.

The 12-Hours of Sebring was one of America's premier international races at the time, and Sebring's 1967 Trans-Am was the second year the famed airport track was host to sedan racing. The previous year was the beginning of the Trans-American Sedan Championship. The event was the 4-Hour Governor's Cup race held March 25, 1966.

SCCA officials were not enthusiastic about racing production sedans. The cars were a bit too close to stock car racing to be attractive to sports car racers. Although sedan racing had long been a major segment of the sport in Europe, it was not considered a viable series in America. Alex Ulmann, promoter for the Sebring track, saw the advantage of having another race at his facility. He was the man behind that first sedan race. The Trans-Am turned out to be an immensely exciting form of racing just waiting to happen in this country.

The early- to mid-sixties was a time when American auto manufacturers were turning up the heat with high performance cars. The new, smaller cars with hot V-8 engines such

as the Dodge Dart, Plymouth Barracuda and Ford Mustang became instant marketing successes. Young buyers liked smaller cars with power, and they liked racing. With a sedan racing series, manufacturers could capitalize on that interest, and the ponycar revolution was born. It was just a small step to go racing and see which make was a better racing car. The Trans-Am became another facet of the heated Ford versus Chevrolet battleground that drew spectators by the droves.

The cars were the stars, but so were the drivers. The factories were quick to get involved in the Trans-Am. With growing corporate money behind the teams, this new racing series attracted famous professional drivers who drove their machines in some of the most exciting road racing in this country. Dr. Dick Thompson was in a Mustang at that first Sebring Trans-Am, and in another of Ford's newest sensations was A. J. Foyt. They brought the fans, and manufacturers increasingly saw the Trans-Am as a marketing tool to increase sales, but Chevrolet fans could only watch. They had no suitable entry.

The old adage of, "race on Sunday, sell on Monday" was working better than ever, although the early Trans-Am races were confined to Friday events preceding main features. In time, that would change to feature events of their own. The first year of the Trans-Am (1966) went by with Mustang winning the Manufacturer's Championship.

Insiders at Chevrolet realized that they were missing an important segment of the market without a car of the ponycar type. The Camaro was in the works, primarily as a marketing response to the Mustang, and secondarily as a car to race. First offered in 1967, the factory announced that a full range of equipment was available including a special car for the

George Wintersteen in one of the Penske-Sunoco Camaros at Daytona, 1967, being passed by a Porsche 906. Wintersteen raced 1737.4 miles only to be classified as Did Not Finish. Daytona Speedway photo.

road racing enthusiast, the RPO-Z28. The equipment for 1967 was not as fully developed as it would become, but it was a healthy start.

In the Dick Keinath interview in Chapter 5, he relates that the idea for a high performance 5-liter car was fleshed out in his office one day. Behind closed doors, with coffee nearby and without telephone interruptions, he and Vince Piggins saw such a car as the natural development of the existing 302 cid engine. That engine had been fully developed some years before according to Zora Duntov, and fitting it to a specially prepared Camaro offered a new market niche for Chevrolet.

Consistent with Chevrolet's thorough engineering program, the design of the Camaro was fully analyzed by computer simulations to predict handling characteristics, directional control and overall vehicle dynamics. Roll angle and roll center were specified to provide stability at high lateral accelerations. This effort was meant to produce the best handling vehicle possible. Keinath relates that the track was widened from the orignial specificaions to further improve handling. In other words, the designers and engineers at Chevrolet were thinking "race car" when they created the Camaro, even it was not admitted. Confirmation of that conclusion has come from several sources although the general theme has been that the Camaro was first meant to be a good handling car, and secondarily, it could be effectively raced.

The result was the closest thing to a Corvette that Chevrolet has yet produced, but in four-seat form. The Camaro was so impressive that the new car was selected as the official pace

The new Camaro SS 350 was the Indy 500 pace car in 1967. Chevrolet photo.

car of the Indy 500 in its first year. Both coupes and convertibles were built, but only coupes were raced in the Trans-Am series. It all contributed to 202,917 Camaros sold that year. Among them were 602 Z-28 special performance Camaros. The Z-28 was offered only on the Sport Coupe. This option cost $400.25 and included a 327 cylinder block with a special 283 crankshaft to produce 302.4 cubic inches. That was off-the-shelf hardware that just happened to fit within the 305 cid limit imposed by SCCA. For the Trans-Am series, SCCA had adopted international regulations set down in FIA Groups 1 and 2 specifications.

At a production curb weight of 3355 pounds, the Z-28 was not a lightweight, but they were able to post top speeds over

181

130 mph at 7100 rpm in stock form. That made their price of $4435 a lot of car for the money. However, the Z-28 did not officially meet SCCA's homologation requirements of 1,000 units built during the production year, but to increase corporate involvement in the Trans-Am, officials bent their own rules slightly and legalized the cars by homologating the Camaro 350 with the Z-28 option.

Building quickly on the racing potential of the Camaro, Roger Penske and driver-engineer Mark Donohue selected the car shown here as their first Camaro. They were, however, going up against seasoned racing teams with well developed cars. Carroll Shelby's factory backed team of Terlingua Mustangs with lead driver Jerry Titus was a formidable foe. Add to that Bud Moore's factory backed Mercury Cougars driven by top stars Dan Gurney and Parnelli Jones in one car and Ed Leslie and Peter Revson in another, and the Trans-Am opposition was fierce.

Donohue at Marlboro, Maryland, August 16, 1967. He was still trying to make a race car of the Camaro. Ford Motor Co. photo.

Donohue was thirty years old during 1967. It was also his first full season as a professional driver. He capped off the season by wrapping up the United States Road Racing Championship in Penske's Chevrolet powered Lola T-70 known as the Sunoco-Special seen elsewhere in these pages. Donohue had been associated with Roger Penske since the late fifties when he raced and wrecked his new 1957 Corvette. Penske advised Donohue to buy a real race car rather than race a converted production car, and the result was an Elva Courier. Donohue acquired such a car and raced it first at Lime Rock in 1960. He then went on to win the 1961 Sports Car Club of America E/Production National Championship in the car, entirely as an independent.

With his boyish good looks, Donohue had received the moniker of "Captain Nice". He looked like a teenager, but he was becoming a seasoned amateur and was certainly an aggressive competitor. He followed his first national title with two more in the seats of a Lotus 23B and a Shelby G.T.350 Mustang. He received SCCA's highest award in 1965, the Kimberly Cup for outstanding driving and was also named "Amateur Driver of the Year" by the New York Times.

But for 1966, Donohue was on the sidelines. He had received a degree in mechanical engineering from Brown University in 1959 and was an engineer by profession, but his income could not cover his interests to race at the level he wanted. Fortunately, he had been noticed by veteran driver Walt Hansgen who offered him a seat in a Ferrari as co-driver at Sebring where they finished 11th after averaging 79.3 mph for 951.6 miles in the 12-Hour enduro. It was Donohue's first professional drive. He soon became known as "Hansgen's protege".

All Camaro Trans-Am entries were by independents such as Jim Rathman whose entry ran the Daytona 24-Hour of 1969.

Hansgen was a team driver for Ford Motor Co. and chose Donohue to co-drive with him in the Daytona Continental of '66. Had he ever driven a car like the 427-powered, 500 horsepower Mk II Ford GT-40? No. Had he ever driven over 200 mph? No. Had he ever been on a high banked track like Daytona? No. But Hansgen wanted him anyway, and John Holman of Holman-Moody fame in Charlotte, NC was in a pinch. Ford had planned to enter five cars in the Daytona Continental, but entered six because Hansgen HAD to have Donohue. The result? Hansgen and Donohue finished 3rd among the Fords that swept every major race that year with a 1-2-3 finish. There pace was 106.20 mph for 2548.89 miles during the 24-hour contest.

Clearly, Donohue was a talented driver with the ability to handle the fastest and most sophisticated racing cars in the world. This was also his introduction to the engineering side

182

The Penske-Sunoco Camaro was very popular with the fans.

Donohue was always at ease as a driver. Marlboro, Md. '67.

By Bridgehampton in '68, the Camaro was finally a race car.

The Trans-Am was a tough and exciting series. Quebec '68.

of racing. The Fords were Ford Motor Co. cars and engineers were everywhere.

It would be a few years before he could exercise his own desire to thoroughly "engineer" a racing car. When that opportunity arose, it was the Camaro. He was strongly motivated to know why something worked or didn't work, and that took a rigorous effort. When Penske chose a Camaro for the Trans-Am, it was Donohue's job to make it do what was needed to win. It was his job to discover the unfair advantage.

After Daytona, he accepted the chief engineer position at Griffith Cars on Long Island, NY, and moved his family from New Jersey to Stony Brook, a small town on the northern shore of the island. Unfortunately, Griffith Cars was soon out of business, and Donohue had no job. In June, 1966 his occupation officially became "professional race driver" for Roger Penske Racing when he signed on to drive a new Lola in the USRRC and the Canadian-American Challenge Cup series, the Can-Am. He won at Kent, Mosport and Nassau, and finished 2nd in the Can-Am driver standings ahead of a lot of world class drivers.

Like all drivers, Donohue wanted to become known as the best driver in the world. Although he had never been much

of an athlete, there was something about driving that brought out the best in him. He wasn't the fastest driver, but he was consistently quick. He followed Penske's philosophy to the letter; always finish. It always paid off. His blond hair, chubby cheeks and smile gave him an all-American boyishness frequently seen in the winner's circle. Although it has been said that nice guys finish last, Donohue proved that nice guys can finish first. His "Mr. Nice Guy" image was little consolation to competitors that he soundly trounced even though he was known to apologize for winning by wide margins.

Donohue tended to race against himself by making changes in the car's preparation or his own driving style, and then go out to beat his own lap times. That made him tremendously competitive. Race car development and driving was his full time job, and few people could compete with that dedication.

For 1967, Donohue had three major goals; Trans-Am racing, Can-Am racing and driving one of Ford's Mk IV prototypes. He and Bruce McLaren finished 4th overall at Le Mans in a Mk IV. By then, Donohue was a world class driver. Can-Am racing was dominated by Bruce McLaren's Chevrolet powered McLarens, and Trans-Am racing with the new Penske-Sunoco Camaro was tough.

183

The Daytona 24-Hours was the longest bout for the 5-liter American sedans. Here Don Yenko fights off the pack in the early stages in 1969.

In January 1967, George Wintersteen, a Penske associate, picked up the 12th Z-28 built from the factory and drove it back to Penske's shops in Reading, Pennsylvania. They had just three weeks to prepare it for the Daytona-300 Trans-Am (Feb. 3, drivers Donohue and George Wintersteen) and the Daytona Continental 24-Hour (Feb. 4-5, drivers Wintersteen and Joe Welch). This car, #36, raced under the dual banner of Roger Penske Chevrolet and Wintersteen Racing, Inc.

With little experience with such cars, no one was sure how to set it up. Mechanic "Murph" Mayberry and Donohue "guessed" what it would take to produce a sedan that could handle the infield road course and high banks at Daytona. Their selection of 1200 lb/inch front springs and 400 lb/inch rears made for rock-solid, if not atrocious handling.

The proof of their selection was during the Daytona-300. Two of the factory Cougars driven by Parnelli Jones and Dan Gurney had qualified fastest and were on the front row. But at the flag, Donohue's Camaro was clearly faster than either the Cougars or the Mustangs. From his 4th place grid spot, he passed all the cars in front and went by Jones into turn-1. That was the beginning of a heated contest between them, not only in this race but during the next three years.

Donohue's intuition about springing for Daytona was pretty close. But after only a few laps, he was out with a clogged fuel filter. When the checkered flag shown after 79 laps, neither the Cougars nor the Mustangs were there to win. It was Bob Tullius in his #44 Dodge Dart. That turned out to be the last victory for the Dart and Chrysler products in the Trans-Am. One of the Z-28s entered was driven by Canadian Craig

Fisher (also a Penske entry) who finished 2nd overall.

In the grueling Daytona Continental 24-Hour, three Camaros were on the starting grid. Fisher and George Eaton were entered among 9 Grand Touring Over 2-liter class entries. Joie Chitwood of his famed "Thrill Show", along with Jack McClure, handled their Florida based Camaro team. Wintersteen and Joe Welch in the Penske-Wintersteen Camaro pounded out 456 laps around the 3.81-mile Daytona circuit only to be classified as DNF.

Not one of the three Camaros on the starting grid finished. The Fisher/Eaton Camaro dropped out after 258 laps and the Chitwood/McClure car was already out after 186. It was an embarrassing showing of the new Camaro, especially since Paul Richards and Ray Cuomo brought their Mustang in 11th overall to lead the American sedan finishers and win the Grand Touring Over 2-liter class. A lowly Ford Falcon was 12th overall followed by the Tullius Dodge Dart in at 15th. Another Mustang was 16th and still another Mustang finished 20th.

Over in the GT-40 Ford pits, Donohue watched the Mustangs beat the Camaros and no doubt wondered if he made the right choice to drive for Ford. His Holman-Moody Mk II Prototype dropped out 230 laps before Wintersteen's Camaro, and 12 laps before the Craig Fisher car he could have been driving.

Of the three Camaros, the Wintersteen team set a qualifying record over the 3.81-mile course (2:10.60 minutes at 105.022 mph). That was 9.5 seconds a lap behind the record setting Ford GT-40 in the Sports Car class, 15.5 seconds behind the

Prototype record set by the Gurney/Foyt MK II Ford.

The next Trans-Am on the schedule was the Sebring 4-Hour where Jerry Titus ruled with his Shelby sponsored Terlingua Racing Team Mustang. Among thirty-one entries, sixteen were Camaros! Donohue's Camaro was still ill-prepared, and he crashed it during practice. But the Penske team, now combined with Terry Godsall into Penske-Godsall Racing, measured up to the task and had the car ready for the race. Donohue was the only driver to stay in striking distance of Titus and finished a distant second.

At Green Valley, Texas, for the third T-A race, a 300 miler, Donohue was still sorting out the car and managed a 4th behind a Team Cougar 1-2 finish (Gurney and Jones) followed by Dr. Dick Thompson's Grady Davis sponsored Mustang.

The Trans-Am attracted a lot of competitors who wanted to race but didn't have major sponsors. The Z-28 Camaro was an ideal package to begin with as did Warren Fairbanks who raced this car in the series. Today it is a vintage racer.

After a 2nd place finish in the 4th round, The Green Valley 300 in Texas, Donohue was off to Le Mans as a Ford team driver. He and Bruce McLaren drove to a 4th overall in one of two Shelby American sponsored Mk IV Ford Prototypes. As a consequence, he missed the 5th Trans-Am race held at Mid-Ohio, and George Follmer, star to be, was hired to drive the Sunoco-Camaro. Follmer gave it a 3rd place finish behind Titus' winning Mustang and NASCAR driving ace David Pearson's 2nd place Cougar.

At this point, it was clear that the Camaro's brakes were not up to the rigors of Trans-Am racing. Donohue went to Chevrolet for help. Gib Hufstader at Chevrolet Engineering had been working on improving competition Corvette brakes and lent his help to the Camaro, but all the attempts Donohue tried only proved to be of little benefit in the beginning. After the car was fully instrumented in tests at Bridgehampton, some useful information began to accumulate.

Perhaps the most useful bit of data was that the Camaros weren't doing well in racing, and that was obvious. For their newest market entry to look bad against Mustangs and Cougars was all it took for someone within the Chevrolet management to decide to do something, even if higher management prohibited such actions.

Although the "we don't race" edict was still in force, Chevrolet engineers did some clandestine brake testing with the car. This was the first time the factory was involved. Donohue was invited to take the car to GM's testing grounds at Milford, Michigan. When he showed up at the sea of asphalt, there were Chevrolet engineers ready to help sort out the car; Dick Rider, Al Rasegan, Don Gates and Paul van Valkenburgh. After the tests, the engineers had no solid recommendations on how to better prepare the car, and Donohue was not impressed with their lack of knowledge. He decided it was up to him to sort things out to improve the car's handling and braking.

It simply took time. Both sides were learning. Not only were the engineers lacking in answers, all of GM's engineers had been handcuffed for years by the corporation's no racing policy. There were no answers because they had been kept from learning what made a car go better or handle better than stock.

Racing durability was an unknown quantity and involved a great deal of development. Donohue was demanding a lot from basically stock equipment, and the warning provided by Paul Prior that axles would not hold up under racing stresses proved to be accurate.

Someone pulled some strings and got Camaro body panels stamped out of lighter gauge metal. With that new equipment, Donohue showed up at Bryar, New Hampshire for a rain-soaked Trans-Am. He promptly crashed the car when an axle broke and all those expensive body panels on the front were junk. Prior and Piggins had been working on stronger axles, and by the next race, Donohue's Camaro had one less problem when he received the new equipment.

Chevrolet's R&D engineers had several sets of springs made, and Jim Musser delivered them to Donohue while he was testing in preparation for the next round at Marlboro. This was, of course, not happening officially, so Donohue installed a Pennsylvania license plate on the Chevrolet tool truck to get it into the pits. With those springs, trial and error homed in on what the proper spring settings should be; 550 pounds in the front and 180 in the rear. After Musser drove the car, he suggested that a rear anti-roll bar would eliminate some of the remaining handling problems.

After reading through the Trans-Am regulations, Donohue

concluded that he could strengthen the chassis of the car with the addition of a NASCAR-type roll cage. While the car was stripped following the Bryar crash, he had a welder build in an enormously strong structural cage that tied everything together. Now the car was rigid, if not heavier than needed. He later went to a thinner wall tubular steel roll cage construction.

Donohue and Roy Gane worked around the clock to completely rebuild the car in preparation for Marlboro. By now, Donohue was certain that he had a car equal to the best Trans-Am cars. When he qualified on the pole, the Camaro was now the front-runner he had been searching for.

The Marlboro Double-300 was run in two segments of five hours each. The races divided the under- and over-2-liter cars into their own separate race. In the big bore round, the Donohue/Craig Fisher Camaro crossed the finish line two full laps ahead of the nearest Mustang, and neither of the Cougars finished. This was the first win for both Donohue and Camaro. The date was August 13, 1967, a time when the '68 model Camaros were about to appear in showrooms.

The testing had paid off, and what was learned contributed to the growing competitive edge that Donohue was developing with the Camaro. Now, he and the car were a force to be reckoned with, but Trans-Am points were still in favor of Ford Motor Co. Mustangs and Cougars had won all but one race through mid-season. However, the points were divided between the two teams and the Penske-Camaro team had a shot at winning the Trans-Am championship in the latter races of the season.

By now, it had been learned that the other teams were building lightweight cars with acid-dipped bodies rather than using expensive panels stamped from thinner metal. Flush with new success from Marlboro and prospects of a winning season, Penske decided to build a new, lighter Camaro, and

Z-28 #12 was given to Craig Fisher and Bob Johnson to drive as a back-up car in the following Trans-Am races. But while the new car was under construction, Donohue was able to drive the older car to a best of 8th overall in the Continental Divide Trans-Am held in Colorado, and Camaro was well out of any chance to win the Trans-Am championship. Titus won another one in that 7th round in his Terlingua Mustang, and was followed by Ed Leslie's Cougar.

On the way further west for the Crow's Landing Trans-Am in California, Fisher fell a sleep at the wheel of the transporter and rolled the truck and everything down a cliff and demolished everything. The new roll cage saved the car, though. The chassis was still straight, even if the car looked a wreck. With the help of two Chevrolet dealerships in Oakland, Donohue and his crew managed to rebuild the car.

Meanwhile, the super-light car had been flown out to California at the last minute. It was completed and painted the night before the race and just made the starting grid. Although a full 1,000 pounds lighter than a production Camaro, the car was fitted with wrong gearing and Donohue could place no higher than 3rd behind Titus in the Shelby Team Mustang. Pete Revson was 2nd in the highest finishing Cougar.

That was the 8th round of the Trans-Am season, and it was now a Cougar versus Mustang shootout. Stock car driver David Pearson led Leslie in a 1-2 Cougar finish at Riverside in the Mission Bell 250. Bob Johnson posted a third in a Camaro while Tony Settember was the alternate driver for Donohue who was in a Can-Am race at Bridgehampton where he did not finish. Karl Kainhofer maintained the Sunoco-Special Lola T-70, but Donohue blew the engine during the race.

The 11th Trans-Am of '67 was the Stardust 350 at Las Vegas where Donohue and the Parnelli Jones Cougar were on the

During the 1968 model year, not enough Z-28 Camaros were built to conform to SCCA regulations for Trans-Am racing. To keep Chevrolet in the series, SCCA bent their own rules and homologated the SS 350 with the Z-28 option. Chevrolet photo.

Trans-Am Racing

The Early Days

At Sebring in March of 1967, a young racer the press had dubbed "Mr. Nice Guy", wheeled the 12th Z-28 Camaro built onto Sebring's grid to start the Sport Car Club of America's first Trans-Am race. He was Mark Donohue, and that was the first showing of a Camaro in road racing competition.

The 12-Hours of Sebring was one of America's premier international races at the time, and Sebring's 1967 Trans-Am was the second year the famed airport track was host to sedan racing. The previous year was the beginning of the Trans-American Sedan Championship. The event was the 4-Hour Governor's Cup race held March 25, 1966.

SCCA officials were not enthusiastic about racing production sedans. The cars were a bit too close to stock car racing to be attractive to sports car racers. Although sedan racing had long been a major segment of the sport in Europe, it was not considered a viable series in America. Alex Ulmann, promoter for the Sebring track, saw the advantage of having another race at his facility. He was the man behind that first sedan race. The Trans-Am turned out to be an immensely exciting form of racing just waiting to happen in this country.

The early- to mid-sixties was a time when American auto manufacturers were turning up the heat with high performance cars. The new, smaller cars with hot V-8 engines such

as the Dodge Dart, Plymouth Barracuda and Ford Mustang became instant marketing successes. Young buyers liked smaller cars with power, and they liked racing. With a sedan racing series, manufacturers could capitalize on that interest, and the ponycar revolution was born. It was just a small step to go racing and see which make was a better racing car. The Trans-Am became another facet of the heated Ford versus Chevrolet battleground that drew spectators by the droves.

The cars were the stars, but so were the drivers. The factories were quick to get involved in the Trans-Am. With growing corporate money behind the teams, this new racing series attracted famous professional drivers who drove their machines in some of the most exciting road racing in this country. Dr. Dick Thompson was in a Mustang at that first Sebring Trans-Am, and in another of Ford's newest sensations was A. J. Foyt. They brought the fans, and manufacturers increasingly saw the Trans-Am as a marketing tool to increase sales, but Chevrolet fans could only watch. They had no suitable entry.

The old adage of, "race on Sunday, sell on Monday" was working better than ever, although the early Trans-Am races were confined to Friday events preceding main features. In time, that would change to feature events of their own. The first year of the Trans-Am (1966) went by with Mustang winning the Manufacturer's Championship.

Insiders at Chevrolet realized that they were missing an important segment of the market without a car of the ponycar type. The Camaro was in the works, primarily as a marketing response to the Mustang, and secondarily as a car to race. First offered in 1967, the factory announced that a full range of equipment was available including a special car for the

Donohue the was fastest Trans-Am qualifier for the Daytona 24-Hour of 1968. He and Craig Fisher finished 12th overall and 2nd the T-A class.

One piece of equipment that went through the testing was a Fred Frincke designed cross-flow, staggered dual 4-bbl setup that Chevrolet development engineer Bill Howell had tweaked to perfection. It ran extremely well, and Donohue had been given what he called another "unfair advantage".

About half way through the test, Smokey rolled in with his beautiful gold and black Camaro. The factory engineers happened along about then, and Smokey didn't have a driver. So he talked Donohue and Fisher into taking his car out. The Sunoco car compared more favorably in handling while Smokey's car was faster, but that was after a half-day of high speed laps on Donohue's car. Donohue qualified fastest among the Trans-Am entries and was gridded two spots in front of Titus in the Mustang. Smokey's Camaro qualified second. After completely rebuilding the new car for the 24-Hours, Donohue and Fisher were hampered with another cracked head. It cracked in the same place, across the valve seat. Over the years, for engines fully stressed in racing applications, that has come to be recognized as one weakness in the small block design. Changing the head dropped the Sunoco team well down at the finish. Lengthy stops to change brake pads, compared to the Mustangs, also forced the car to finish a respectable 12th overall after 2152.65 miles, but a distant 2nd in class to Titus and Ronnie Bucknum who finished 4th overall in the Mustang.

Smokey's car also didn't finish, and as usual, he had difficulty getting through tech inspection. Lloyd Ruby and Al Unser drove the car to equal Donohue's Trans-Am pole position, but the car failed to finish either Daytona or Sebring.

To solve the problem of lengthy brake pad changes, Howell invented a quick method for changing brake pads that became another "unfair advantage" and was kept secret. By rigging a vacuum line from the brake vacuum booster to the master cylinder, with an inline valve for the driver to actuate, when the car came to a full stop in the pits, by the time the crew got the car jacked up and a wheel off, the brake pistons were retracted for quick pad changes.

During the March 23rd Sebring 12-Hour, the method worked so well that it caught the attention of the Ford guys. Even when they saw it happen, they couldn't figure out how

the Camaro's brake pads could be changed so quickly. In the Penske-Sunoco pits, stops for fuel, a change of tires and new brake pads were accomplished in less than 2 minutes. And while the Mustang team was still putting their car's brakes back together, Donohue and Fisher in one Camaro and Bob Johnson and Joe Welsh in the other were in-and-out and gaining a lap at each 3-hour stop.

The Johnson/Welsh #6 car had been "inspected" and accepted at Sebring by a slight-of-hand. It was the old acid-dipped car that SCCA had warned Penske about. It was not legal and would not be allowed to race. Donohue rigged the number circles on the cars so that they could be interchanged, and took the new #15 car to inspection first. Once it was approved, the car was taken back to the garage where the numbers were switched on the cars. Then the same Camaro with #6 on it went back through inspection again. Both Sunoco Camaros were now in the race!

Sebring was a huge success. After 12-hours, the Penske-Sunoco cars rolled in 3rd and 4th overall (car #15 followed by #6). They were 1st and 2nd in class, and both cars finished about 4 laps ahead of the Mustangs.

Afterwards, Chevrolet was even more interested in Donohue's Camaro. He was invited to Detroit for some engine tests on a dyno. After blowing up one of two engines brought along, the second was cranked up and showed about 420 hp (out of 302 cid). Then the factory engineers showed him another trick. The heads were yanked off, and another set of high compression heads were installed. Instantly, there was a more than 20 hp gain. The trick was to "season" a newly-built engine by running it several hours. That allows all the parts to become worn-in, then change to a fresh set of heads.

Howell and Chevrolet's test engineers had lots of stronger parts in development, and Donohue gained some new knowledge although his engine builders were Traco, Jim Travers and Frank Coon, rather than the factory.

With the two long distance races of the year evenly split, 1 - Mustang and 1 - Camaro, the season's shorter length Trans-Am races unfolded as another tough contest. Penske's Sunoco Camaro was entered in only 9 of the 13 races, and Donohue won decisively at War Bonnet Park in Oklahoma. In front of the Ford brass at Mid-Ohio, he won again after being gridded last. He wasn't able to qualify because of running in an Indy car race and accepted the last position while making the casual comment that he expected to be running up front after about 12 laps. He was leading after 10 laps, and thoroughly embarrassed the Mustangs.

At Bridgehampton, Donohue and back-up driver Pete Revson were on the front row in Penske Camaros. Donohue set the fastest lap and finished well ahead of all the competition for another victory. With all the "unfair advantages" he had learned and with his thorough preparation, the Camaros he raced were now the front running cars in the Trans-Am in spite of no factory support. When the Ford teams ran the 289 cid engines that were successful in 1967, they were down on power compared to the 302 Z-28. When they tried their new "tunnel port" 302, it didn't survive, and Donohue cleaned house.

The 1969s were a handsome styling improvement for the third year of the Camaro. 19,014 Z-28s were built that year.

Donohue went on to win at Meadowdale and then made it seven wins in the 3-hour Trans-Am at Mt. Tremblant in Canada. Then he won at Bryar, then Titus broke Donohue's 8-race win streak at Watkins Glen. He won again in the Continental Divide 250, but was unable to fend off the Mustangs at Riverside. He did, however, win at Kent to make it 10 wins to Mustang's 3.

The '69 season opened with all new cars. Ford was hot on the Trans-Am trail with new BOSS 302 Mustangs. Although bigger than the previous Mustangs, they were the response to Chevrolet's Z-28, a special performance package from engine to suspension. The BOSS 302 engine was developed when the 302 "tunnel port" heads failed in 1968. Ford was preparing a new engine series for their '70s cars. This was the 351 Cleveland, and their bolt pattern and water passages were rather closely matched to the four-bolt main "tunnel port" 302. By adapting those heads to that block, the BOSS 302 was born. Its main features were canted valves that were strikingly similar in design to Dick Keinath's Mk II Mystery engine of 1963. (Remember those two engines that Bill France forced Chevrolet to sell to Ford in order to run the Daytona 500 that year.) Although the Ford engines were not called "Porcupines" like the big block Chevys, their similar valve train, huge ports and large valves made a high winding performer capable of 480 hp in Trans-Am form. Suddenly, the Z-28 had a new adversary.

The 1969 T-A season was another Chevy versus Ford

shootout, but they were not part of the endurance races at Daytona and Sebring. Finishing 4th and 3rd overall the previous two years had made the high-buck sports car crowd nervous. If an American sedan was to actually beat a Ferrari or Porsche, their image would be tarnished to no end. However, under international regulations, Trans-Am type cars could run the endurance races, and no less than 9 Z-28 Camaros were entered at Daytona. Another Z-28 powered car was the 3rd place finisher, a Firebird! Four more of the engines were in Lolas counting Donohue's car. Two of the Lolas were movie actor James Garner's American International Racing team cars.

After racing twice around the clock, it was Donohue and Chuck Parsons winning the Daytona 24-Hour, this time driving the Chevy powered Sunoco Special Lola coupe. The car ran a Traco 302 Z-28 engine fitted with fuel injection and ran in the FIA Sports Car class. All the Ferraris and Porsches failed, and Donohue rolled into the winner's circle more than 100 miles ahead of the nearest competitor. In a sense, the Camaro had won after all.

SCCA opened its 11-race Trans-am season on May 11 at the Michigan International Speedway. Although there were tough competitors such as the American Motors Javelins and Pontiac Firebirds, the Camaro-Mustang battle raged anew. Donohue and Parnelli Jones fought it out throughout the year. The races drew more fans than ever before and swelled the cheering numbers in the Camaro and Mustang camps.

The striking '69 Z-28 remains one of the most beautiful Camaros ever built. This is the car that "starred" in the movie, At Close Range, with Sean Penn.

Rated at 290 hp, the Z-28's horses were thoroughbreds!

Unexpectedly for the bowtie brand, the BOSS 302 Mustangs won 4 of the first 6 races and had a huge lead on Camaro. Donohue teamed with Ronnie Bucknum to score Camaro's only win, at Mid-Ohio on June 8th. Then, in the 7th round, three of four of the team Mustangs crashed at St. Jovite, and Donohue took over from there. By Laguna Seca on August 4, Camaro had won three straight, and Mustangs lead had evaporated and Camaro was leading, 67 to 56.

Bucknum won at Seattle and Donohue scored again over Jones in the Sears Point 200. In the final race of the '69 season, Donohue and Bucknum made it a 1-2 grand slam at Riverside for the Mission Bell 200 on October 5, and Camaro won the

Trans-Am title for the second straight year. The score: 78 to 64. The Penske-Camaro team had done it in the last half of the season.

The following year was to prove just as decisive, but this year it was spelled Mustang. Penske was lured over to American Motors, and the Bud Moore Engineering BOSS 302 Mustangs made the Trans-Am an all-Ford show in '70. The Mustangs won 6 of 11 races. With Penske's defection to A-M, Jim Hall was brought on to handle the new generation Camaro. There were out-spoken ties with Chevrolet and the Chaparral Camaros, but the cars were not as much a threat as had been expected. Dan Gurney's All American Racers ran factory-backed Barracuda, along with Sam Posey in the factory connected Dodge, did not materialize as a force, either. Such big names in the driver's seat of sedan racers indicates the drawing power of the Trans-Am. And 1970 is considered the best year on record until the return of factory racing in the late 1980s. Perhaps history repeats itself each twenty years.

Owens-Corning, the fiberglass people who sponsored the Corvettes of Tony DeLorenzo (son of a reportedly embarrassed GM vice president) and Chevrolet project engineer Jerry Thompson, entered the Trans-Am with Owens-Corning Camaros. With two major Camaro teams, Chaparral and Owens-Corning, bowtie fans looked for a great season but were disappointed. Two-time Trans-Am champion Jerry Titus handled a strong running Firebird, but, sadly, was killed in the car. He was a great sportsman and was among Trans-Am's most popular drivers.

The competition in 1970 was very tough, and Ford fans savored "their" 3rd Trans-Am championship while Camaro

Jim Hall put his Chaparral logo on the sides of two Trans-Am Camaros in 1970. Here at Kent, Washington, on Sept. 20, 1970, this car was one of 17 Camaros entered.

fans wondered what happened. Jones, followed by George Follmer, won the title, and the two of them piled up 72 points for Mustang. The Penske Sunoco Javelins were 2nd with 59 points, and Camaro finished the season with 2 victories and just 40 points. Plymouth and Dodge were also-rans with 15 and 8 points, respectively.

Then the Trans-Am collapsed. After an illustrious decade of racing with great victories in about everything there was to win, Ford announced in late 1970 that factory racing was being disbanded. Chrysler withdrew support; Jim Hall backed out of the Camaro; and the Trans-Am no longer had the big names or the drawing power to attract the fans. For the next 15 years, the excitement was gone.

Another important aspect that affected the Trans-Am was the industry-wide down-turn in automotive sales. Total sales of Ford cars steadily declined from 1968, and Mustang dropped off 40% from 1969 to '70. General Motors experienced a strike that lasted over two months, and that reflected in sagging sales. Total Chevrolet sales dropped 494,695 from the volume of calendar year 1969 to '70, and Camaro sales dropped nearly 10%. Overall, GM was down 32.6% and lost almost 3-Billion dollars in sales during 1970 as compared to 1969 when sales were down less than 4%.

The signs of the time were a drastically changing worldwide

Ed Leslie was the driver of the 2nd Chaparral at Kent and finished 6th overall.

economy and the first public effects were such huge losses. Rapidly escalating gasoline prices three years later killed the public's willingness to pay for performance, and both muscle cars and ponycars were a thing of the past. The decade of econo-boxes had dawned.

Z-28 Camaro: Always even tempered. Always mean!

Trans-Am ad slogan.

Bill Preston

Sunoco PR Man
Recalls the Sunoco Era

Roger Penske raced a wide variety of cars very successfully during his driving career. I watched him in the period when he drove the Porsche RSK and RS60 with Bob Holbert. He ran production Corvettes in SCCA racing, and drove a Maserati Birdcage Type 61.

Back in those years he bought a Formula-1 Cooper which had been crashed at Watkins Glen and built it into the "Zerex Special" sponsored by DuPont. It retained its central driving position but had all-enveloping bodywork to make it into a super light and quick sports car. The required passenger seat was offset to one side. The car was allowed to run for one year, I believe, before a rule could be added to the rulebook that said something about seats for two people positioned on either side of the center of the car.

During this time Bill Scott of Newtown Square, PA worked for Roger as a mechanic and was also an expert machinist who worked for Sun at the Applied Physics Lab in Newtown Square. He went racing with Roger by taking his vacation in days.

Roger's career high point has to have been at Nassau in December of 1964 when he did a hat trick by winning all three of the major races, two in one of Hall's Chaparrals and the Grand Touring race in a Corvette Grand Sport.

After that, Roger retired as a driver. He had gotten to know George McKean, owner of a large Philadelphia Chevy dealership, when they both raced Corvettes in SCCA. George's son had died as a teenager, and thereafter he more-or-less adopted Roger as a son. As George was thinking of retirement, he permitted Roger to buy a share in his dealership in 1965. I imagine that Chevrolet was delighted to have the dealership move on to Roger. George's game plan was that Roger would be able to buy the dealership from his share of the profits over, say, two years. But Roger was running on a different timetable, and I believe that he probably took it over in 6 months. George retired a little ahead of schedule.

In late 1965, Roger sold a 1966 Corvette with a 427 inch street engine and four-speed to Elmer Bradley, vice president of Marketing for Sun. The car was dark blue. It was from this association that Roger got Elmer interested in having Sun sponsor a race car. As far as I know, neither Roger nor any of his relatives owned any interest in Sun.

Roger set up a meeting with Sun in late 1965 to which I was invited. He described the new L-88 engine that Chevrolet was building with aluminum heads and how he intended to win the Grand Touring class at Daytona with it. At that time Sun was marketing Sunoco 260, which was honestly the highest octane commercial fuel available anywhere. I recall the Research octane number (RON) as being 103.6.

I was working in Product Development in our Applied Research Division in Marcus Hook, and had a background in both fuels and lubricants. I was one of two engineers selected to provide technical support to Penske. Jack Ziegler was the other engineer. Briefly, our assignment was to make sure that our products (gasoline, engine oil, gear oil, and grease) were available at the track in sufficient quantities and that none of them failed. During the years we supported Roger, we had failures that led to the development of some excellent new products, but that is another story.

The Corvette we raced was a 1966 model and was originally red. It was built at Chevrolet's St. Louis plant and had an L-88 engine in it as produced. It also had an "L-88 hood" which was newly-designed and had its air inlet in the high-pressure area at the bottom of the windshield at the rear of the hood. A heater was a "delete option" for an L-88 Corvette. This was Chevrolet's way of trying to say that the car was for racing and not for road use. I believe that the engine was built in Warren, Michigan and shipped down to St. Louis for installation in the car. The car also had the Muncie M-22 "rock crusher" gearbox.

Dick Guldstrand, whom Penske had selected as one of the three drivers (I understand on Zora's recommendation), flew from California to St. Louis, picked up the car, and drove it to Newtown Square in the dead of winter with no heat!

George Wintersteen had a small shop right in the center of Newtown Square, and Dick and George's mechanic Bill Mayberry (known as "Murph") prepared the car for competition. Bill Scott built all of the special bits and pieces needed, like the aluminum spacers used to replace the normal rubber spacers in the suspension. I remember that George Wintersteen wanted to make sure that the car had plenty of lights and had added a pair of huge Lucas (Flamethrowers?) driving lights on the front. As it turned out, they were relatively ineffectual and didn't really contribute anything to night driving.

At that time the #6 1966 Chevrolet Stingray L-88 was painted red. Roger had always favored red cars and had this one painted red at the factory in St. Louis. This was the first race Sun sponsored the car. The three drivers were George Wintersteen, Dick Guldstrand and Ben Moore.

In the pits with Scotty were myself, Sam Wooters, also from Sun's Automotive Lab in Marcus Hook, PA (as was I) and Gib Hufstader, supposedly on vacation and just watching the proceedings as a "tourist". The "tourist" wore a stopwatch around his neck. They were analog then, and still made out of steel. Maybe he was timing something.

When it was time for the car to depart for Daytona, the eastern U.S. was caught by a really deep snowstorm. Route 3, which goes through Newtown Square, was blocked and so was the driveway to the shop. When the crew couldn't get the race car out of the shop and on the road, Roger called Elmer who called the manager of Sun's refinery in Marcus Hook and asked (ordered) him to send heavy snow removal equipment including a bulldozer to free the car.

The car was transported to Daytona on Wintersteen's pick-up truck/trailer combination. I arranged to ship thirty or so 55-gallon drums of Sunoco 260 to the track in a commercial truck. It was transferred in Florida to a local Sunoco van. When that truck tried to enter the Daytona track to deliver the drums, it was stopped by a Pure Oil representative. Pure (later Union 76) had invested a lot of money in Bill France and NASCAR, and wasn't about to have publicity going to a competing oil company. They made the Sunoco truck unload its drums outside the track, and we had to rent a pickup truck (which I recall was pink) and bring the drums in a few at a time.

Practice was run with the "production L-88" engine the car had in it when delivered. I think the engine was Chevrolet engine red. The night before qualifying this engine was pulled and replaced with a gray TRACO L-88 that had been flown in from L.A., which then did both qualifying and the race with no other service other than valve adjustment.

Along with tools, etc. I had packed a couple of big, four-cell black plastic flashlights. During the night Dick Guldstrand hit the wall. As I recall the incident, Dick had been sleeping and was awakened to go out after a pit stop. Some people thought he wasn't fully awake. I think he was just getting back up to speed after a nap, and found the car and the track a little different. I think it was where you come up from the infield course back onto the tri-oval. The front end pushed too much, and he went nose-first into the outer wall. The whole grille and front was torn from the car (including those Lucas Lights) and something punctured the radiator. When Dick called in at the pits, we used "racer tape" to fasten the two black flashlights onto the remainder of the fenders, put radiator stop-leak in the cooling system, and sent him back out to circulate while the team located a replacement radiator. The radiator came from someone's Corvette that was parked nearby in spectator parking. After the race the radiator was returned to that car.

Dick had to resort to following other cars and using their headlights until dawn came. The car soldiered on to finish first in GT and maybe 12th overall.

This race was the first time I met Gib Hufstader who was on vacation from Chevrolet; he worked long and hard to help the car win. The car was then returned to Pennsylvania, painted blue (I worked to get the proper DuPont and Ditzler paint formulas to produce Sunoco blue paint in a lacquer) and readied for Sebring. Roger didn't want the enamel we used to paint our tank trucks, but wanted the same color blue in lacquer. A Corvette Grand Sport roadster was also prepared for Sebring. Ben and George shared the Stingray, and Dick Guldstrand and Dick Thompson drove the Grand Sport. The Stingray won GT again.

The Grand Sport had plenty of power but was relatively unaerodynamic against the Ford GT-40 Mark II's which also had 427 inch engines. The Grand Sport could out-accelerate them, but on the faster parts of the course, the Fords simply drove by. Thompson finally touched a Morgan and went

down through some back yards, bending the frame which was comprised of large diameter tubes. This was during the period when some homes were right alongside the course!

After the race we walked over to where Dick left the course and could see the tracks where he went through the yards. The part that hurt the car was that the driveways for each home were sunk down about 12" or so and the car had crossed about three of them.

The Sunoco Cars

Compiled by Bill Preston
Listed in sequential order
and by year raced

1966
1. 1966 Corvette Sting Ray L-88 Coupe - won GT at Daytona, Sebring
2. 1963 Corvette Grand Sport Roadster s/n GS001 - Sebring
3. 1965 Lola T-70 Mk II (ex-John Mecom) - St. Jovite (427 cid engine), Mosport (427), Watkins Glen (333) destroyed
4. 1966 Lola T-70 Mk II - Kent (333), tub destroyed at Riverside (337)
5. 1966 Lola T-70 Mk II - Riverside (377 - 333), Laguna Seca (333), Las Vegas (333)

1967
6. 1967 Camaro Z-28 - (Follmer, Donohue) Daytona, Sebring; (Donohue) Trans-Am at Green Valley, Lime Rock, (Follmer) Mid-Ohio, (Donohue) Bryar, Marlboro, (Fisher) Las Vegas, Kent
7. 1967 Camaro Z-28 - lightweight Trans-Am (Donohue) Las Vegas, Kent
8. 1967 Lola T-70 Mk IIIB - (Donohue) - Won the Can-Am
(5.) 1966 Lola T-70 Mk II - (Donohue) - Won the USRRC, Riverside, Laguna Seca, Mid-Ohio, Road America, etc. (Follmer) in the Can-Am

1968
9. 1968 Camaro Z-28 - (Donohue) - Won the Trans-Am
(7.) 1967 Camaro Z-28 (Lightweight '67 rebodied to '68)
10. 1968 Gurney Eagle USAC car with 320 cid Chevrolet
11. 1967 McLaren M-6B with 427 cid Chevrolet

1969
12. 1969 Camaro Z-28 - (Donohue) - Won the Trans-Am
13. 1969 Camaro Z-28 - (Leslie)
14. 1969 Lola T-70 Mk IIIGT - Daytona
15. 1969 Lola T-152 Sunoco-Simonize Special Indy Car - (Donohue) Rookie of the Year, 7th (turbo-Offy and 4-wheel drive)

16. 1969 Lola T-163 Can-Am car with 430 cid Chevrolet

17. 1969 Lola T-150 Chevrolet USAC car (both 2- and 4-wheel drive

18. 1969 Lola T-190 Formula A (302 Chevrolet), Sebring in December

1970

19. 1970 AMC Javelin (development car)

20. 1970 AMC Javelin (Donohue)

21. 1970 AMC Javelin (Revson)

(17.) 1969 Lola T-150 Chevrolet USAC (2-wheel drive)

(15.) 1969 Lola T-152 Ford Indy car - (Donohue) 2nd

22. 1971 Lola T-192 Formula A (302 Chevrolet) - Mosport, Mid-Ohio, Sebring

1971

23. 1970 Ferrari 512M s/n 1040 - (Donohue & Hobbs) Daytona, Sebring, Le Mans, Watkins Glen

(15.) 1969 Lola T-152 Ford Indy car - (Hobbs) destroyed at Indy

(17.) 1969 Lola T-150 Chevrolet Indy car 24. 1971 AMC Javelin - (Donohue) - Won Trans-Am championship

(20.) 1971 AMC Javelin with '71 sheet metal as a development car

26. 1971 Lola T-192 Formula A (302 Chevrolet) - Questor GP @ Ontario

1972

27. 1972 AMC Matador NASCAR Grand National Stock Car - (Donohue), crashed at Ontario

28. 1972 AMC Matador NASCAR Grand National Stock Car - (Marcus)

29. 1972 McLaren M-16B Indy Car - (Donohue) - Won Indy 500

30. 1972 McLaren M-16B Indy Car - (Bettenhausen)

31. 1972 Porsche 917-10K Can-Am car - (Donohue) - destroyed at Atlanta

32. 1972 Porsche 917-10K Can-Am car - (Donohue)

33. 1972 Porsche 917-10K Can-Am car - (Follmer)

34. 1972 McLaren M-19 Ford Formula-1 - (Donohue) - Mosport, Watkings Glen

1973

35. 1973 Gurney Eagle Indy Car - (Donohue) - Qualified 3rd, DNF

36. 1973 McLaren Indy Car - (Bettenhausen), 5th

37. 1973 McLaren Indy Car - (Allison), DNF

38. 1973 Porsche 917-30K Can-Am car - (Donohue) - won Can-Am championship

39. 1973 Porsche 917-30K Can-Am car - (backup)

(28.) 1972 AMC Matador NASCAR Grand National Stock Car - (Donohue)

40. 1973 Lola T-330 AMC Formula A - (Donohue) burned at Riverside

41. 1973 Lola T-330 AMC Formula A - (Donohue)

42. 1973 Porsche 911 Carrera 2.7 - (Donohue & Follmer) - Daytona

43. 1973 Porsche 911 Carrera 3.0 - (Donohue & Follmer) - Watkins Glen

End of the Sunoco Era - After 1973, the cars were CAM2.

Roger Penske looks over his Sunoco sponsored Corvette at Daytona, 1966. This was the first race for Chevrolet's new L-88 427 engine. After 24-hours of racing, it was the winner in the GT class. Daytona Speedway photo.

"If I can make it through the night" Guldstrand smacked a wall and Bill Preston taped flash lights to the fenders, the Sting Ray went on to finish 12th overall; 575 laps and 2190.75 miles at over 90 mph. Daytona Speedway photo.

Jerry Thompson and Tony DeLorenzo on their way to a hard-fought finish at Daytona, 1968. Daytona Speedway photo.

More Corvettes

For the Daytona 24-Hours of 1967, six Corvettes were entered but none were to finish. The 63-car starting field drew the best cars and teams in world, and 24 of them were Trans-Am cars. When the Titus/Bucknum Mustang finished 4th overall amongst the prototypes, it didn't make the Grant/Morgan Corvette that finished 10th overall, and won GT class, look so good. The excessive weight of Corvettes has always hindered their performance when compared to other sports cars.

The following year, 1968, seven Corvettes were entered at Daytona for the season opening 24-Hours. The grind of such a long race was tough on all the cars, but the torque of the big block Chevy 443 cubic inch, 585 hp stump pullers was tough on every component of the cars. The #30 'Vette of Jerry Thompson and Tony DeLorenzo broke its transmission, broke two spindles and two discs and had eight flats, and still finished 27th.

DX Sunray Oil Co. entered a team of three cars that year, two '68 Sting Ray roadsters (Don Yenko/DeLorenzo and

Gerald Thompson/Jerry Grant) and a '67 coupe for Dave Morgan and John Ryan. However, when the race ended, it was Corvette #31, the '67 coupe, finishing highest and winning GT class (10th overall) with Grant and Morgan driving. Pete Revson and Yenko brought Sting Ray #29 in 25th overall, and 434.3 miles behind the '67 'Vette was #30.

Dave Morgan paired with Hap Sharp at Sebring where the pair nailed down another 1st in GT. Their Corvette finished a much more respectable 6th overall, but there were both Penske Camaros and a Shelby Terlingua Racing Team Mustang (Titus) in front. Donohue brought his Camaro in 3rd overall behind the high buck Porsche 907 Prototypes.

For the 1969 enduro at Daytona, Actor James Garner fielded a pair of American International Racing Corvettes, and Owens-Corning was there with a pair of L-88 big blocks. Since Thompson was a Chevrolet engineer and DeLorenzo's father was a GM V-P and Gib Hufstader was driving the cars, the Owens-Corning cars were for sure considered a factory team. The cars showed that O-C was into more than just sponsoring. The cars were fitted with fiberglass molded shell seats, and the drivers were wearing safety fire suits made from Owens-Corning's new Fiberglass Beta cloth that had been developed for the Apollo Space program. The Corvettes, though, experienced the worst luck again.

DeLorenzo had qualified 13th overall and was easily leading GT class when the first flat was encountered by running

The DX Corvette team finished the Daytona 24-Hours intact. The Grant/Morgan #31 Corvette won GT and finished 10th overall in 1968. Daytona Speedway photo.

over debris on the track. The right rear tire blew and severed the fuel line. He limped into the pits when the trailing fuel ignited. The fire was doused quickly, but the car was done for. During the night, he took over as relief driver. When another tire blew and he hit the wall, both 'Vettes were trailered out. The #66 and #67 'Vettes were out.

At Sebring in '69, the Owens-Corning team of Corvettes made a good showing but still couldn't get the best of the Trans-Am cars. While Don Yenko and Bob Grossman rolled their Camaro in 10th overll (1086.8 miles) for GT class honors, Lang and Hufstader were drivers in the leading Corvette and completed the 12-hours finishing 14th overall.

Their O-C 'Vette completed 1019.2 miles at an average of 85 mph around the rough airport circuit.

Later in the 1969 season, Thompson put together a winning year by capturing the SCCA A/Production crown and broke the string of Cobra championships that dated back to 1963. It was the first of four winning seasons for Corvette. John Greenwood took two successive A/P national championships in 1970 and 71, then Jerry Hansen added the fourth in 1972.

For four straight years, B/Production was dominated by Alan Barker's '63 Sting Ray, and throughout the '70s decade, only Bob Tullius' Jaguar would break the Corvette hold on B/P, and that happened only in 1975.

Jerry Thompson in the Owens-Corning Corvettes won the SCCA A/P title in 1969. Note the side pipes; Corvette "Kustom Header" side pipes were invented by Dick Simpson in association with Junior Johnson in the early '60s. Daytona Speedway photo.

John Greenwood built this 427 Corvette and won the SCCA A/P National Championship in 1970. John Greenwood photo.

This is the Corvette that the Greenwood team raced to victory in the Elkhart 500 km Trans-Am and the Edmonton Trans-Am of 1973. John Greenwood photo.

Allan Barker won back-to-back SCCA B/P National Championships in this 1963 Sting Ray in 1969 and '70. He set lap records at 9 tracks and won 14 consecutive B/P races with 22 total wins. Vintage raced today by John Baldwin.

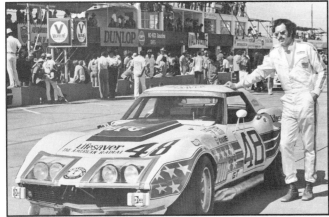

Greenwood and his B.F. Goodrich car at Sebring '71. He and Dick Smothers won GT class and made the Sebring race magazine cover of 1972. John Greenwood photo.

Greenwood and Smothers finished 7th overall at Sebring and beat a lot of imports. For 218 laps and 1133.6 miles, they averaged 94.47 mph. John Greenwood photo.

John Greenwood

Recalls his racing days

My first car was a 1955 Pontiac, that was in 1960. Basically, I was a street racer from Detroit's Woodward Ave. I got hold of a McKeller NASCAR 421 Pontiac, and I put it in the car. It was a hot engine. It was a legal NASCAR engine at the time. Then I converted the car over from an automatic to a four speed.

McKeller was the name of the man that was doing the heads and camshafts, probably an engine builder. I really don't know, they just called it the McKeller equipped engine.

So, I had this four door Pontiac with this big engine in it. That was when I started learning about older cars. So the first thing that happened was the brakes went out. I would be down shifting going down Woodward Avenue, going through lights, missing cars and everything. I got all kinds of experiences out of that car. Then I started running Impalas.

I started boring and stroking them. I had a 452 cubic inch engine in 1963 out of a 409. I had the NASCAR Z-11 heads and all that kind of stuff on it. I never had a real Z-11. I just bored and stroked a 409 and put the Z-11 heads on it.

I used to race on Woodward Avenue every night, 7 days a week, and I probably ran the car 150 miles a night. I put the gas in $2.00 at a time, and I did that for years. We got to know everybody.

Woodward Avenue was just an amazing place back then

because the stretch that we would use was probably 20 miles long, and there was probably 30-40-50 drive-ins along the way. And every 10 miles there would be a whole different group of people. It was like you were in a whole different world. We got to know everybody from one end to the other because our car was fast. We would go out and run the hot cars from every different area.

When we stopped racing in about 1968, it had got to where we would get like 200 cars and go out on the expressway and pair off two at a time down through the center and keep going two after two after two. When the police did come, everybody would just go in different directions. All the fast cars would get away anyway.

So I was racing the big Impalas, and I could beat anybody up to 100 mph. Then I started running into Jaguars with hemis in them and 1957 Corvettes with big blocks. All of a sudden at about 100 mph, these guys would come by me. At the same time while I was doing all of this, I was working on other people's cars in my garage at the house, doing clutches and engine work on late Corvettes and Chevrolets. I used to build engines in the basement and carry the short blocks out, or build them in the den, in my mother's den, and carry the short blocks out.

I know I drove my parents absolutely crazy. I'd buy a new car and have it towed home the first night, and I would have the engine out the second day. That is what they went through with me.

Anyway, I switched over in 1964 to Corvettes because of the weight differential. I could clearly see what was happening with the 1957 Corvettes and the Jaguars, so I switched to Corvettes to get the weight down. I bought a 1964 coupe. It was a 327, and I immediately pulled the engine out and put a 427 big block in it.

AG: If you got one of the 427 engines in 1964 you must have gotten one of the "inside" engines?

John: Well, living in that area, I just had a lot of friends at General Motors, and there was always somebody that knew where I could buy something. In that area there was always good sources of high performance parts. Most of the stuff I did, like the 421 Pontiacs, were before they came out. A lot of the drag racers had stuff a year or two before, like that Pontiac engine I bought from one of the drag racers. So there was always good stuff that was a year or two ahead of when it went on the street.

I would take the engines and blue print them. Like my 1964 Corvette, I had 14 different engines in that car. Every time I turned around I would come up with something new, a new combination of something and stick it in the car. I would, absolutely, every night after work come home and pull the valve covers off the car, re-lash the valves and tweak the engine, and then I would go out.

AG: How old were you in 1964?

John: I was about 18.

AG: Where did you get the money to do all of this?

John: I quit school and worked construction doing engineering type of work. My dad was in contracting, so he got me good jobs. Back then money for construction work was good. I also got the right price on the cars and everything, I paid $4000 for the Corvette. I paid $2300 for the loaded big block Impala. I mean, it was a whole different ball game back then. I was making good money and cars didn't cost what they cost now. The cost of a car now has gone way beyond a person's salary. Our salaries didn't go up when everything else went up.

I changed engines. I changed suspensions, brake work and all kinds of stuff. My whole deal was to come up with combinations that would hook up and be very usable. I could feel whether or not it was getting the job done, and I learned how to drive the car, too. It all depended on who I was racing and where we were and all the conditions.

I got real good with carburetors. I would epoxy runners in my intake manifold and change the distribution of air in the runners and go into the carburetors and drill out idle circuitry. Again, I would cut air horns off or add air horns to learn how to get the power curves that I wanted. Then I started feeling the flywheel weights versus the cam shafts. Fortunately that kind of thing came very easy for me, because I didn't spend a lot of time going backwards. I think one of the reasons was because I was very motivated and very dedicated and very single focused. When I would come home and lash the valves every night, seven days a week, that was pretty dedicated. But I could feel what changing a gap of 1 thousandth or 2 thousandth on an exhaust would do.

My engines worked so well that when I started racing, I was way ahead of everybody. Porting and the power curves and everything. I mean, I just didn't have any trouble with anybody.

All that led up to road racing. I went to a road race and I thought, "Look how slow they are going. I can do this!" I was convinced right up front that I could, so I decided to try out and joined the club to go to drivers school.

So I bring this Corvette with the big engine in it out to drivers school. At the time, I had big Mickey Thompson tires on it. I liked the big diameter for acceleration. The instructor walked the whole group around the track and talked us through the turns. Then he'd have somebody drive through the turns, then he would drive through right ways and wrong ways to show us the difference.

He wanted to drive my car. He saw something with a lot of horsepower. So he goes and gets the car and goes through a couple of turns with it. Then he takes it back and asks, "Whose car is that?" When I said it is mine, and he says, "Boy, you have your work cut out for you. Those tires, man, that thing isn't going to stick".

My instructor was a blond haired guy called Dennis the Menace. He drove a 1963 split window coupe, and he was one of the fastest people in the club, especially in big cars. He took me for a ride in my car. By the time he had finished with the first lap, I was trying to con him into letting me out because I could see better from the side. But he took me for two more laps. I went for three laps in a car with a crazy man. The car didn't stick anyway, and with a lot of horsepower, that was about enough for me. I didn't like it.

My interpretation of what racing was had totally changed right there on the spot. All of a sudden I realized that these guys were driving on the limit. It is not 40 mph; it is 40 mph on the limit everywhere you are. There is no breather. It just looks easy from the side.

Anyway, I went through that school. For that first year of racing, I went ahead and got some other tires on the car, but I had a terrible time for the first three events. That winter, I really thought about quitting. I really wasn't having any fun. I was getting passed by women in Fiats! You get on a course where people know what they are doing with race cars with race tires, well, it took me awhile.

Then I went through the whole phase. What you do is, you go talk to people and buy all their parts. I bought $10,000 worth of parts that didn't work. Just buy what everyone is recommending, right?

So that went on, and I didn't have any satisfaction. The car didn't work. I didn't know if it was the parts or if it was me or what. That winter I thought about whether I wanted to go out there and do it again or not. I started to do some work on my car, and I went out to the first race the next year and started setting records.

By now I was in a 1968 Corvette. I really just visualized it and thought about what the car was and wasn't doing on the track. I started concentrating on it and basically started doing what I had done on my street stuff, coming up with combinations to make the car feel and do what I felt it should do. I got lucky again. The car came in fast, so all of a sudden, I had something that would handle, too. I had some Chevrolet engineering people that helped me out some. They were giving me some pretty good advice.

Gib Hufstader gave me a lot of help. The stuff he was recommending was working. He had tried to help me the year before, but I was so far off; I had a lot of horsepower and no way of putting it down. I was un-helpable. But then I started coming around. I joined SCCA and started doing good. By the end of the 1969 season I had my national license and was racing national races. I was winning national races.

AG: *How many races did you run in 1969?*

John: I ran 10 to 12 races. I ran about 4 regionals to get my national license and then started running nationals. We had some problems that year, but I had the car working real good. I was going to come up against Owens-Corning for the first time. One of the guys from the club at Waterford Hills was a real good driver in his car, he was a winner in one of those Lotus 7s, and he wanted to drive my car on the track. I had just been out testing that day and got my car working real good. He pestered me and wanted to drive it so I told him, "Don't put a wheel off the track and drive it easy." Three laps later he absolutely totalled the car, just wiped it out.

AG: *This was at Waterford Hills?*

John: No, this was at Gratten, Mich. So that was another big set back. I had just lost my car and that guy ended up walking away from it. He was going to take care of it, but naturally nothing ever happened. He never offered to do anything or help fix it or do anything. I left there pretty upset. I got home on a Saturday morning after getting drunk on Friday night, and by Sunday I was over at the shop taking the car apart, stripping it down. My mechanic that was working close with me, Art Jerome, was good. He came over that Sunday and we just started building a new car. We finished the car in a month and started running the long distance races, Daytona and Sebring and stuff. We had pretty good luck again.

AG: That was in 1970? Did you actually get an FIA license?
John: Yes '70. In '69, we ran some long distance races like Sebring, so I must have gotten some kind of license to do that.

I was racing in A/Production at the time. That was really the toughest class, like Owens-Corning had won 22 straight times with two cars every race, I mean one-two finishes, and there wasn't anybody out there that could beat them. There were obviously easier classes to be in.

My engines at the end of 12 hour and 24 hour races would actually be stronger that at the beginning. Everybody else would just crawl around at the end. The tolerances I chose and the way I set the cars up, the way I broke the engine in, well, they just got better as they went. We were so focused, so dialed in to it that we had real good reliability. In 1970 we got into nationals and won the Central Division which was, again, the toughest division for A/Production. We won the national championship that year in the run-offs where all the divisions come together. I won that, at Road Atlanta. That was the first time they had run at Road Atlanta.

One month earlier was the first test at Road Atlanta and I was there. That was the first time that I had met Peter Gregg. He was in a Lola, and I out-qualified him. He came up to me before the race and said, "If you beat me, I am going to protest you because I know you are illegal". I tried. I mean, I really tried to beat him. I hung on to him for a couple of laps but he finally got away from me. I really did want to beat him, bad.

Anyway, I liked that kind of track. I had the car really working and set up good. It seemed like the best people that I had going to races with me were volunteers. I had a crew and a group of volunteers that were excellent. They could really get the job done.

AG: Back then, it looked like you went racing with a group of guys that just wanted to race. You were up against the pro teams, and you probably had less equipment but more heart.

John: Yes, that's right. We didn't have the big semis and didn't have all the stuff that they had. But, I got pretty dedicated, and I was pretty confident about what the outcome would be at the races because the car was performing so well.

Just to give you an example of the things that I did that were so different from what everybody else was doing, I guess, my biggest advantage was not ever looking anybody else's car over. I just did what I thought I needed to do to make my car work. So I didn't make all of their mistakes. Even today when I go look at their cars I see mistakes that the pros are making. They are all doing it. And all of a sudden, they are all going in one direction thinking that is what they need, and they lose contact with the sport. I see it happen all the time. There is so much money in it nowadays, there are so many people involved in it, you can't get the level of communication you need. Car-to-race track-to-design, everything.

What I had was that I built the engines. I put them together. I put together all the moving parts in the car. So when I got

in the car and drove it, I could feel everything, and I knew what everything was. I could feel exactly what the engine was doing and exactly what I needed to make an adjustment to make it do something a little different. To give you an example of what I was doing and how different it was, I was gearing my car for 8000 rpm in high gear with a big block and Owens-Corning and everybody else was running 7000 rpm. If they ran over 7000, they bent valves and had all kinds of problems. I didn't over-torque the car. I could put full power on coming off the turns in second gear. At Road Atlanta, I could put full power on at every turn on the race track. I could drift with full power on because my car hooked up.

I had a good combination of power curve. The power came on right, and it wasn't over-powered torquewise on the bottom end. I could come out of a turn and hook up a sling shot. I could beat people by about six car lengths coming off the turns. The other advantage was the gearing. By being able to run the gearing that could run an 8000 rpm straightaway speed, I had the right gear on about every turn. So, what would happen was, we would go out there and the other guys would try to follow me around for qualifying. I would put a third of the straightaway on them. I mean, they would come in just shaking their heads. They were beaten before they ever started the race at Road Atlanta. I overheard them, "He has too much power." "I can't race with him." That kind of deal.

It wasn't that at all. It was that I came on to the straightaway a lot faster than they did. I took it up to 8000 rpms in every gear, and I was gone. But in the race, I might do that for one or two laps, then I'd drop it to 7000 rpms. That is where I would leave it from then on. I only used what I needed, but it gave me a big advantage. It gave me big power curves and all that kind of stuff. Nobody out there was really into the combinations.

My key thing has always been a development driver. I have a real good seat-of-the-pants feeling for what the thing does, especially if I am touching the parts that I'm riding in. If I am really involved in doing the alignment on it, I'm closely involved with the car.

I might not do a great job of driving somebody else's car. I'm a pretty good driver, but you could stick somebody else in there and he may be faster than me. I might be the fastest in my car because of the way I set it up and the way I know it needs to be driven.

Looking back, I got started driving by accident, my wife got me involved in it. That was 1968. I started by driving in regionals while I was maintaining a Camaro for the A/Sedan national championship which we won in 1969. I didn't really want to drive because I am too defensive. I didn't get totally comfortable driving for two and half years. I hired other drivers. I built the cars and the engines. The drivers were hard on both the cars and the engines.

The Camaro was a 1969. I had another driver drive it. My driver would go out and tear the oil pans off the engine and just keep going until the engine blew up or blow the fan belts off and run them out of water. Then the engine seizes.

It was getting aggravating, so one day I got in the car at Black Hawk and drove the A/Sedan in a test. I just drove around comfortably, and I was within one-tenth of a second of my driver's fastest time. All of a sudden I go, "wait a minute!". I took him to the national championship because I told him I would. I had three engines with me and put the weakest one in. He went down there and just blew everybody away. I didn't even bother to put the next two engines in the car.

I tuned that car, and I also tuned Alan Barker's B/Production Corvette that same weekend. Ike Nupp was beating him in the Javelin and Barker was like 5 or 6 seconds behind him. I'd just started, and here I am with these guys listening to me because they could see what I was doing with my car.

I pulled the distributor out of the Covette and took it over to the Champion people. I recurved the distributor and relashed the valves a different way, and I had them put a different gear in it. I started changing all kinds of stuff to get the car to turn more rpms with more gear. By changing around some of the things that they were doing, and they did everything I told them to do, he just kept going faster and faster. Finally, he was faster than the Javelin. Then I worked on Kirt Rienhold's Formula 5000 type car, and he lead three quarters of the race until he broke a rocker stud in the valve train.

It worked out pretty good for me. I was the only mechanic on my car and my car was so ready all the time, I had time to work on everybody else's cars. So, again, it was really doing a lot of thinking about what you are doing. I found that same thing when I started racing. You can do the whole thing on paper. You have to do your homework. I went to races when I knew I was going to win and I won. That's all there was to it. I went to races where I knew I was not prepared and I didn't win. I have never done anything since I have been in racing that wasn't black and white; you could write it all down on paper and add it, subtract it, multipy it, and it is going to do everything that is says it is going to to. I did a lot of winning my first 3 years.

The years following when I was doing a lot of winning, I wasn't doing my homework. I wasn't involved in my program anymore. I was traveling and I had seventeen people working on my cars. I wasn't there and that is where the racing program went. We were still developing stuff and I just wasn't there to be on top of it and make it all happen.

We could have won everything all the way along. We could have beat anybody. I mean, the cars that we had back in 1976 would have beat anything in IMSA all the way through 1985, that is how far those cars were ahead of everybody.

I really wasn't connnected with Chevrolet, but they would tell me who had the engines, brand spanking new ones. I would buy up everything that I could get my hands on. At one time, I had all the aluminum engines. I finally bought everything there was around and there weren't any more that anyone knew of. I bought everything that was out there, figuring that I was going to need them.

As I got into the BF Goodrich programs, I did need more and more engines. All I needed was to make sure that I had more of them because every time I would sell my old race cars, I would sell one or two engines. In 1970, I had two Corvettes. One was my '69 car, and I drove another car in

1970. No, I guess it was 1971 before I had two cars. So, the car I won the national championship in 1970 with is the one that went to Denny Long. Then I built a new car. I built two new cars, and in 1971 I started running them in the long distance races. During that season, I only had two cars.

Then, toward the end of that season, I started building a third one. So, I went into '72 and '73 with three cars. In 1973, I started building those upper A-arm, anti-dive, anti-squat rear suspension cars, the trick ones with the coil shocks in the front and all that stuff, and I just didn't get done until 1974. I still had the other cars at the same time, and I was building three of those new ones. So, I built three of the tricky cars. I was really going to use them for the BF Goodrich program. Again, I wasn't staying on top of the program and that is where the Goodrich deal went away.

We could have won the races on the Goodrich tires. We were fast enough to win the races. The things that got us was oil pan cracking and stuff like that. It wasn't for lack of speed or durability. It was real stupid stuff. I mean, I just got burned out after three years and never came back. That and other business pressures, driving the cars; it was all a real burden when you owned the team, ran the team, developed everything, brought the money in. I didn't like driving the car. To me, that was a real burden. It was dangerous.

I would say I am a natural driver only when the car is right. When the car is set up the way I want it, I will drive it. You will never get me in a position where I will push anything that doesn't feel right, ever. All I ever did with any of my cars was drive them the way they wanted to be driven. You see, my cars had personalities. Like, if I had three cars, I only drove one of them. You never got me into one of the other ones because I would get that one car so refined, so tweaked and everything, it ended up being like an animal. It had a personality, and I could make it do what I wanted. I just had a feeling for it to where I could actually visualize the changes that I could make on the car and then go make the changes and go out on the track and do exactly what I visualized.

At the time I figured that everyone else was doing the same thing, but they were not. I never ran with anybody that helped me with the whole relationship of what I was doing and what the whole thing was about, ever. I had to quit and get out of it for ten years to figure it out. That was 1977.

During that period of time, I had three of the tricky cars and four of the others. I had seven cars up to the tube cars which I did in 1976. I built two tube cars, so nine cars altogether. Then I started building a lot of customer cars, I built maybe a half dozen of them at a time in 1976-1977, but of my own personal cars that I would use, I had about nine of them.

The whole time that I was racing, I was looking for what niche I wanted to be in because I could understand the promotional value behind it, the engineering value, all the different things. So that is why I tried race track programs. I ran Riverside, Michigan National Speedway and Sebring. So then, all of a sudden, I was promoting the races while I was working with the sponsors on three car teams and driving everything. It got very burdensome. I was trying all of these things to understand the market place, and basically I was ten years ahead of the market. But I didn't have anybody to back me up as far as management. So, I couldn't do things or know what to do or what not to do because I was so focused on creating, innovating; I just prototyped myself to death. I designed one new body after another for street cars, and I was doing new fuel injection manifolds and new suspensions. I would do one suspension, and then I would make another one, and I would not use them for anything. I just got carried away because it was so interesting to me to develop new stuff that I just kind of lost track of things. I figured I could use it somewhere along the way.

Then I got involved with different partners, and a lot of those things didn't work out. I really didn't care because starting in 1972 I was just getting overloaded. From that point on, I was going backwards because I was totally over-stretched in what I could handle myself. It took me all the rest of this time to figure out where I had made my mistakes, and how to do them differently.

Now, (1989), this late into the program, in the past couple of years, I have done a lot of R&D work on the late model Corvettes. When I was racing, Zora Duntov and Gib Hufstader, the engineering group at Chevrolet, were always behind me. The product promotion people, the ones with the money, were always asking me to stop racing. I mean, it was just a real political deal.

When I beat Owens-Corning the first time, the guy that ran the *Corvette News* magazine who lived in the same town that I did asked me if I wanted to come over to his house to get the first issues of the new magazine. I go over to his house and he hands me the magazine and I am on the cover of it. He said, his words were, "I didn't want to put you on the cover but I had to." I just sat there. Now I know where I stand with this guy.

You see, I had just gone out and beat Owens-Corning. I won the race. I won the central division, I won the national championship and a lot of people at Chevrolet were saying that's it. The "stars and stripes" car, that's the car we want to go with. He was against that because he was tight with Owens-Corning. That is where it started, and it never got any better.

It was just politics; it is still politics. Chevrolet is still the worst politically motivated organization of them all, but the guys that are running product promotion now, they understand marketing and the promotional value of such things. Herb Fishel knows what he is doing, and as we get back into some good things, I hope to be working with someone like him because he is a good man. He is not playing the political game, but there are still too many people in that organization that are. For me to come up with new or good ideas was just absolutely a no-no. It was a situation of where I was taking some of their color away. They didn't like that and they still don't.

I tried to switch over to Ford so many times, but I just couldn't find the right way to make the move. Ford was new to me, and I was really into development of Chevrolet stuff.

Back then, most people thought I was factory backed, but I got zero from those people. I did it all. I made my own manifolds. I designed them. I did all that stuff. Back in the 1972 era when I was running the old swing arm cars, Zora Duntov would get me pallets of parts, suspension pieces and stuff like that. When I had the tube cars, I would get Zora to go out to the skid pad with me. Zora was always a good sport, but he was just not in the position to get the money to make the thing happen. Other than that, there wasn't any support. The product promotion people had asked me to stop racing, and every time I went in there with a good idea, they would say, "Well, I don't think it will work". They never supported me, even in ideas, let alone anything beyond that.

So, that is the way it was. They were just not there for me. Had they been and had I gotten a little support from different areas, we could have done a lot. That was another thing that just made me tired of racing. I just wasn't getting anywhere. It was costing me too much of my own money; it just wasn't rewarding. It was too much work for the reward. And then to have to drive the cars, with me being a very defensive person, I would go to all the races tired. My week was so hectic that going and getting in a race car was relaxation. It should be the other way around. You should have all of your mental and physical focus going into that race car, so having to go out there and drive when not in good physical condition told me that I wasn't right. I was still quick because my cars worked.

From 1976 on, it just wasn't worth doing anymore. I wanted to get a business operation going that would benefit by the visibility and credibility of winning races. But I will say one thing; what I was doing out there opened a lot of eyes. Maybe not here in the USA, but those European manufacturers, tire manufacturers for example, they are racing people. When they see a certain thing happen, they know what they are looking at.

There are people over here that are so into their own thing, their own egos, that they don't know the difference. Racing has changed so much, it is in a totally different state. I believe I could take one of their cars that they are out there racing right now and spend thirty days making minor adjustments to it and go out there and go two to five seconds faster. There are guys out there just playing with each other.

You see, when I started racing, I never went out on a race track and raced another driver. I raced myself. I made sure that I had my concentration on what I was doing and didn't make any mistakes. The whole time I was out there racing, I was fast and I didn't crash cars. And I didn't blow engines. I didn't get off the track at all, I never believed in it.

AG: A little earlier you made a comment about your drivers, Dicky Smothers for instance.

John: Dicky was about the most successful co-driver that I had. He was like me; he was defensive. He wasn't going to go out there and embarrass himself and do something stupid. He wasn't going to take the car and push it over the limit that he was comfortable with. He wasn't going to crash the car. He ran about 3 or 4 seconds behind my time, and he was satisfied with it, and he and I won a lot of races. He would use his head and run the speed that he could run at consistently and not get in trouble.

AG: How did you two get hooked up?

John: I called him to see if he wanted to drive a long distance race, because I knew he had gotten out of his Formula 5000 deal and that he was doing well in Formula 5000. He had his own team. He had two cars and he drove one of them.

I guess we teamed first in 1971. We won Sebring in 1971. He was careful. He was smart, and he did not go beyond what he could do. That is what made him my best co-driver. I ran with him later, too. I took him to Watkins Glen in 1977; we drove the tube car. We also went to Le Mans once or twice.

AG: Tell me about racing the Corvettes at Le Mans.

John: In 1972, 1973 and 1976. It was a good experience because, unlike Penske's and a lot of other's experiences, we were well taken care of over there.

AG: By whom?

John: The people of the race sanction body. I mean everybody. They liked us. They liked the way we did things. So we didn't have any problems at all.

AG: What were the problems?

John: Penske and all these other guys, their numbers were not the right color; they had to repaint the numbers on their cars; they couldn't go through tech, and they didn't run the first session. It just went on and on. It didn't matter. For little things, they didn't get to do the right things.

During practice sessions, if our car broke down on the race track, they took our mechanics and put a jack in their turbo Porsche pace cars and took them around the track and towed the race car back. I mean, they would just do anything for us. It was amazing. It had a lot to do with the Corvettes. The "stars and stripes", the whole nine yards. We got more publicity in 1976 than anybody in the history of the race. The people liked the "stars and stripes", and they liked the Corvettes and they liked what we were doing. So, it was just a real good experience every time we went over there.

AG: How did you do?

John: We always had engine problems. We had Moldex cranks and on the long straightaway, we would break a crank in half or something after about 8 hours. The same thing at the Daytona 24-Hours; we would have a lot of problems with that. The heavy parts in those big old truck motors didn't like long durations of high revs along straights sometimes four miles long.

Even on BF Goodrich street tires we qualified on the poll. I loved it. The European tracks are smooth, the turns have little banks in them. They really go for racing over there.

AG: Are you going to race your GTP team at Le Mans?

John: No. It will be awhile before we do anything like that.

AG: Are cars better now than in the past?

John: Yes, it is all better. All the technology is better, and if you are going to be competitive, you are going to use it. Like I said, most everyone lines up and uses the same information, and they all do everything the same way and they stick their driver in their cars and tell him to drive it.

But I like racing. Don't get me wrong. I wasn't out of racing for the last 10 years because I wanted to be, I just couldn't get out of it what I wanted to and able to put into it what I needed to.

When I go racing, I am going to be looking for some volunteers again to race with me because that was the best crew I ever had. Those guys believed in what I was doing and did everything I said and they did it the way I said. They didn't question it.

The people that work for you, that you are paying, it's a whole different ball game. You are continually, constantly having to be on top of them. They are always trying to find a way to do less. I will find some good volunteers again, but you always have to have some full time people.

AG: What about the car that you would race. Is that something you would build here at your shop?

John: No, I think I would go out and buy something that is out there right now. I'm looking at a GTO Corvette, but the more I have been thinking about it, the more I have been thinking GTP sounds interesting to me. They cost the same amount of money. You might have a $100,000 more in a GTP car that you build than in a GTO car, maybe because of carbon fiber technology, but other than that, the maintenance is all about the same. If I went GTP, I would probably go normally aspirated engine.

AG: If I could wrap this up in John Greenwood's philosophy on racing, it would be; the true racer is the guy that builds his car and puts his heart in it?

John: Yes, but there are some things missing. In racing right now, you have to run it like a business. It is a business, but racing goes beyond business into the emotional side. There is another level, another depth that is missing in it right now I call it a loss of communication. You could get that loss of communication in any business situation, any business where you have a bunch of different people. You need to build your systems around trying to find a way to check that as fast as you can so you don't loose any depth any longer than you have to.

Racing is the same way. As you go through your whole spectrum of what you have to do from the concept through being on the track and actually doing the job, you make a lot of mistakes. Most people think that because they are racers that they have all the answers.

It takes an artist. There is an art form to racing. That is what goes beyond where they are now.

I am real excited about what is beginning to happen in racing and what is happening in the automotive industry. It is absolutely exciting and obviously racing is coming to its own, even with some of the present short comings.

7

Return in the '80s

Dale Earnhardt drove the Wrangler Jeans Monte Carlos to his 4th Winston Cup Drivers Championship in 1988.

Monte Carlo

The New Beginning

When the Monte Carlo was introduced as Chevrolet's full-size luxury coupe in 1970, few people could imagine it would become the winningest marque in the history of stock car racing. Junior Johnson's Coca-Cola sponsored 427 Monte that Bobby Allison drove to 10 wins, including the Southern 500, and the NASCAR manufacturer's title in 1972 proved the Chevrolet had the right stuff. 1974, '76, '77, 79 and '80 were also championship years, but these were with small erngines. NASCAR had imposed a 366 cubic inch maximum, and while the big blocks could be built to that limit, stock car racing was now the domain of the small block.

Then, in 1981 and '82, Buick won 47 races while Chevrolets could muster only 4 wins. But the next year, the Montes were back with 15 victories and the title. Ford had only 4 wins, and Chevrolet has won every championship since.

The roll was on, and the following year, Terry LaBonte drove the Piedmont Airlines Chevrolet to the make's second NASCAR championship in back-to-back years. Chevys won 21 races and Ford still hung at 4.

Darrell Waltrip brought his Chevrolet in as champion in 1985, in spite of Bill Elliott's famous million-dollar year, and secured his third championship year (1981 and '82). Chevrolet had won three Manufacturer's titles in a row! Elliott led Ford's rise with ten more wins than the year before, and the Chevrolet-Ford rivalry reached a new high. Both were evenly split at 14 wins each.

For 1986, it was the Monte Carlo again. Dale Earnhardt captured the crown, and Chevrolet led Ford 18 to 5 in the win column. Earnhardt had won his first championship in 1980 and won again in 1987. His yellow and blue Wrangler Jeans #3 Monte Carlo was among the most recognized cars in America. The number three carried on his Monte Carlo was symbolic. He made it 3 championships in a row with the car.

Monte Carlos combined for 15 wins to Ford's 12 that year, and by that time, Chevrolet had taken five consecutive Manufacturer's Championships. Elliott broke the string by winning the championship in '88, but the combined might of Chevy's Monte Carlos tallied enough points to just get by Ford by 2 points. Earnhardt's Monte Carlo was now showing the black and silver colors as Chevrolet's own Mr.

Benny Parsons won the NASCAR title in 1973 by finishing 21 races in the top 10, 15 of 28 in the top 5. That proved the Monte Carlo was durable. Daytona Speedway photo.

The top running Winston Cup Monte Carlos have now become Luminas. Waltrip, Bodine and Earnhardt in action at Charlotte during the '88 Coca-Cola World 600.

Goodwrench entry. It was an unprecedented SIX Manufacturer's Championships in a row, and Chevrolet was deep into factory sponsored racing like never before. And so was Ford.

When the torch was passed to the new Lumina at Talladega for the Winston 500 on May 7, 1989, over 150,000 spectators and millions of racing fans watching on TV saw Ford's new Thunderbird score a decisive 1-2-3 sweep. Maybe the Monte Carlos had been retired too soon.

The change was made and the score board still lists the Monte Carlo as the winningest car in stock car racing history. In various configurations, the cars were in 183 races and won 95 between 1983 and May, 1989.

One of the teams that has contributed so much to the Monte Carlo legacy is the Rick Hendrick team of three cars. Each one has its own driver and crew. With three top teams with top drivers, Hendrick is NASCAR's top entrant, and all other teams face a fierce triple attack from the Hendrick stable.

Darrell Waltrip, shown here driving the Rick Hendrick Tide car, has won three Winston Cup championships.

Although modern stockers are far removed from as-manufactured cars, fan allegiance to the shape of the Monte Carlo had become enormous, and passed to the Lumina with just as much enthusiasm. Today's stock cars are no more than a silhouette of the production car they are made to look like. Nothing but the shape and the engine is similar. GM cars must run GM engines, and that means the small block in 358 cubic inch form or less, and Fords must run Ford engines. All cars are built with similar tubular frames on a wheelbase of 110 inches. And even though there are other GM makes in Winston Cup, they all run Chevy small blocks, perhaps with different heads, but small blocks just the same.

Although the shape of the cars changed to the GM-10, the engine remains the small block. It is an enormous tribute to Ed Cole's initiative that specified the engine and to small block project engineer Al Kolbe's design that, after 35 years, it is THE dominate engine throughout the world of racing, not just Winston Cup.

In the garage area with Junior Johnson's Monte Carlo. The great Chevy man of NASCAR defected to Ford in '89.

205

Geoff Bodine

He came south to race

The Geoff Bodine story? Well, it has been told a lot of times. I grew up around a race track. The year I was born, both my grandfather and father (both named Eli) built a race track. It was on a farm, just a small farm in New York state, Chemung, New York. It is farm country up there, and we lived on a dairy farm. We had a chicken farm and a dairy store, and the fellows in the area went up to my grandfather and said, "we want a race track." So, they took an old corn field kind of down in a little hole that had a slight hill where they could have seats and people could sit on the ground and watch, and he and my father went out there and plowed it up. They dug out a race track. That was in 1950. It was a quarter mile dirt track, and inside that quarter mile, they had a small track for kids to race on.

The kids raced in what were called micro midgets. They were just simple home made cars, go cart type cars with a little body on them and had about a two and a half horsepower Briggs & Stratton engine. I went to the races every Saturday night when I was just a little tyke. When I was five years old, my father decided, I don't know how he decided, he just decided I was old enough to start driving, so he went and built me a micro midget. He hand built it from the ground up, and I remember going down there and watching him build it but I never got involved in working on it. I remember the shop was real dark and real cramped, but he built that thing, and I started driving when I was five years old. I have been behind a steering wheel ever since.

I drove those things for about four years or so. Then I drove some go carts. We ran a home made job for a couple of years, then we bought a manufactured micro midget and kind of stepped up a little bit. I drove some go carts a little bit after that, but mostly, I stayed at my father's track and raced. We went to a few other places and raced but mainly stayed right there.

My father has never, never raced a car. As many years as he has been around racing, and he ended up promoting that track when my grandfather got older, he has never been in a race car, never had a ride in a race car. He left the driving to his sons, but I had uncles that drove. I had uncles that built cars and did the mechanical end of that stuff, and that is where I learned that side of racing. I had an uncle Earl that was a real good driver. He was the best out of the three that tried and so they put him in the driving chores and the two other uncles, Maynard and Jimmy, were the mechanics. When I got a little older, ten or eleven, I started hanging around with them in their shop, sweeping the floor, cleaning the parts, and slowly moved up, advanced up to where they let me work on the cars a little bit.

All through those years, I was also helping my father at the track. There is a lot of maintenance to a dirt track. You have to work it all week long. So, after school or during the summer, I would go up there with him, and I would drive the tractor or work the grader. Back then, it was a hand or manual grader. You had to turn the wheels to make the blade go up and down. I drove the tractor to smooth it out or picked up rocks or I drove the water truck. You name it, I have done it. I helped build the grand stands that were there.

After I got done there, I went to my uncle's shop and hung around there and learned that side of racing. So, really, racing has been my life since I was a year old. I have always been around it and always been involved in it one way or another. I think the involvement with my father on the promotion side has helped me through the years to understand the promoters a little bit better, the problems they have, and the things they go through.

Of course the experience that I had with my uncles has been invaluable. That has been a real key to my success. I used to build my engines. I used to build my cars from the ground up when I started running modifieds.

I ran two years at my father's track in modifieds. I couldn't start racing there until I was eighteen, that was a track rule. So, I built a car, a late model. It was a 1956 Plymouth with a six cylinder engine. That was my first car. I ran that my first year and won Rookie of the Year. I didn't win any races but I had a lot of seconds. I won the point championship but never won any races.

That was the Late Model Division at Chemung, Speedway. No big thing, but back then it was. The next year, I stepped up a division. We put a V-8 in that same chassis, a Plymouth V-8 and changed the body to a 1966 plymouth. I went out and won, I think, 12 out of 16 races. At the end of that second year, I had the opportunity to drive a modified car on asphalt for a friend. When my father's season closed down, I drove that car two or three times and did pretty good with it. The next year, I left my father's track and moved into the modifieds on asphalt. That was a tough time. That was a tough decision to make to stop racing at my father's track. I felt like I was abandoning them, deserting them and it didn't seem right, but they understood what my goals were.

When I was younger, during the winter we would go to Daytona. We had relatives down there, so we would go visit them, take a little vacation and see the Daytona 500. I was maybe 9, 10, 11 years old and I would say, "Hey, I am going to be out there some day." My hero was Richard Petty, and I said, "I am going to go out there some day and race with him." No one thought I could make it, and I didn't even know if I could make it. That was my goal; some day to get in these cars and go to Daytona and race against Richard Petty and all those other fellows. Of course they all laughed at me.

Back then, from New York to Daytona took you two days to drive. Now you can make it in an hour and a half by air. Back then, it was a long way away, physically, plus the thought of going there and racing; it was a long way away in many ways.

When I left racing at Chemung, my parents knew what I was after and what my goals were. They didn't hassle me about it. They wished me good luck, and of course I always watched what I was doing. If they could go to a race they would go, if they weren't racing Saturday nights. They have always been very interested in my career and very helpful.

During that same period when I got out of high school and started racing at my father's track I went to college, to Corning Community College, in Corning, N.Y. to study Mechanical Engineering, to learn more about how to build things, how to put things together, how to make things strong. For three years, I went there while I was racing.

In the mean time, I joined the national guard. It was a pretty busy time doing all this stuff; racing, school, and national guard, trying to keep all that together. But being in the national guard allowed me to race. I didn't get drafted and have to go away for three years and miss racing. That was really the main reason that I joined so I could continue racing and not miss that. The national guard worked real good with me. They allowed me some time off where I would make it up during the week. If we had a meeting on the week-end, they would let me miss that meeting and make it up during the week. I thanked them many times for doing that. It was six long years of a good relationship with them.

I got into modifieds and ran in New York State in that circuit up there for three years. During that time, I owned a car at one point with some other fellows and went broke being a car owner. I had to sell a lot of stuff to pay the bills, so I went looking for a ride again and found a ride out in New England with a modified owner named, Dick Armstrong.

We had always won races, but during my first year in modifieds, we didn't win any, didn't win any main events. The second year, I won about twelve. The third year, I won twenty, and the fourth year I won 25. I have always increased my number of wins. So my wife, Kathy and oldest son Matthew and I moved to New England just so we could race.

We had just bought a house in New York state with a garage so we could race and went broke. We didn't have any money.

We didn't have any sponsors, so we had to go somewhere else. We packed up and moved to New England. We lived in a twenty-four foot pull behind trailer for about three months. That was all we could afford. Finally we moved in with some friends for awhile and that was a successful year. We won races, and the next year I started building cars of our own design for Dick. That's when we really started winning. I would have to look up to see exactly how many races we won, but it was in the 20's. The next year it was in the 30's, and finally in 1978, which was my last year with Dick Armstrong, I won 55 out of 74 main events. That is just main events and does not include the preliminary heats or the other races that we ran during the night. Fifty-five main events; that is a record for modified racing and still stands today and is in the Guiness Book of world records.

That was my best year, but it was my last full year in modifieds. We were winning all these races but we were not getting anywhere, kind of like spinning our wheels. We raced all up and down the east coast. We raced at Daytona on the road course. We raced Martinsville. We even ran a race at Charlotte with a modified, but it just didn't seem to matter that we were winning all those races to the people that counted. They were the people that owned these Winston Cup cars, the crew chiefs of these Winston Cup cars. They all knew me and saw all the races I had won but it didn't mean anything because modifieds are so different than Winston Cup cars. So Kathy and I knew what we had to do; we had to move. We had to move again. We had to get down South. We had to get into a late model or a Winston Cup or whatever we could to get the experience, to get the exposure that would prove to these people that I could drive this type of car. We had the confidence. I knew I could do it, so we took the chance. We left racing modifieds the best year of our career, winning all those races and making good money. We put all that behind us and moved South. We spent all our money to move and bought a house. We moved to a little town of Pleasant Garden, near Greensboro, N.C. We knew some people there; they were the only reason we moved there. And Richard Petty was only ten miles from Pleasant Garden, so I said, "If that area is good enough for my hero, it is good enough for me".

That is where we settled. There was a fellow in New England named Jack Bebe that had a Winston Cup car and was looking for a driver. He kind of had the same problem. He was from the North trying to get into the sport and was new at it. He was having trouble getting a driver. He couldn't get a good driver, an experienced driver, because they didn't want to go with a rookie team and a guy from the North. He knew I was looking for a ride and we got together and struck a deal. I mean, it was a tremendous opportunity; I leave modifieds and I get a ride in a Winston Cup car right away! The only problem was the crew chief of that team. I didn't have any problem with him, but we used to race against each other in the modifieds. I beat him a lot. He really didn't like me. A lot of people said it wouldn't work, but I said I'm going to go for it anyway. I couldn't pass that opportunity up.

So I went there and we worked on the cars and we got them

ready and we went to Daytona. We led the race at Daytona, first time in the Daytona 500, 1979, in an Oldsmobile, but the engine blew up so we didn't have a good finish. We went to Atlanta, no we went to Rockingham next. First time ever there we weren't doing too bad, but the engine broke again. The camshaft broke. Went to Atlanta and was running pretty good in practice, and the crew chief decided he wanted to try some new things. He changed the car around and really messed it up; couldn't hardly drive the car. I went out in the race, and it was just terrible. After the race, we could see that it wasn't going to work and the car owner and I decided that we had better split, which we did. Unfortunately, I had already moved to North Carolina. I had already spent all of my money moving, and after the third race of the season, I didn't have a job. It was pretty tough times. I didn't know what to do there for a while. Kathy and I both didn't want to move back to the north, and we had had another son by then, Barry. He was just a little over a year old.

We had a lot of responsibilities, a lot of bills. So what do you do? I ended up going back North to work for a man that wanted some work done on his cars, some modifieds. He had two and I ended up driving one of the cars for him along with Satch Worley from Virginia. He raced part time, and I raced a limited schedule. They were big cars, they were fast, and I won a lot of races that year. We had a really good year, successful plus profitable, but I was living in New England in a little motor home and my family was in North Carolina. It wasn't a very good situation, but we had to survive. I had to earn the money to pay those bills.

That wasn't what I wanted, obviously, so I came back down to the South after that season. That was 1979. They were still racing late models down here, I went to one at South Boston and met a man by the name of Emanuel Sevacause from Richmond, VA. He ran late models. I talked to him about getting together with him, and we made a deal to run a few races the next season. One catch was I had to go to Richmond, Va. to build the cars, to work on the cars and maintain them so I could run them. Well, that was what I needed, that kind of exposure to that kind of racing. So, here I go again. I pack up this motor home and spent most of the winter up there building the cars getting them ready, family still in North Carolina. I would come home on week-ends.

The next summer, I raced one of the cars and had to stay there most of the week to work on it, maintain it, and get it ready for the races. I would see Kathy and the boys at the races on the week-end. I might go home on Monday after the race, and then I would pack up and go right back to Richmond, Va. to work on the cars.

We had a very successful year, we won quite a few races. The first time I drove the car, I think we finished second. The second race out, we won with that car, 1980, at South Boston. I won at Langley Field.

By running that division, it gave me the opportunity to run places like Charlotte, Rockingham and Darlington because the Busch Grand Nationals ran those tracks. That is really why I wanted to get in that division, it would give me the experience at these tracks where the Winston cup cars drove.

I ran a few of those races and had the same deal with the same man for the next season, and had to do the same thing; work during the winter to get the cars ready. We built a super speedway car for the Busch Grand National Series, and later on that year, we even built a Winston Cup car. My fan club collected some money and my friends donated some money. Sevacause had his shop and he sold race parts, so we built the car right there. He put a lot of money into that Winston Cup car. That was a Buick.

We ran Oldsmobiles in the Busch Grand National Series, and back then, Buicks were pretty good Winston Cup cars. We ran Charlotte, Atlanta and Martinsville with the car. It ran good, but we kept having engine problems. We built this car, put all this money into it, friends and fans, and we ran it only three times that year. Unfortunately, that was the last year that I drove for him, but still it was a good experience. It gave me some experience and some exposure that I was looking for.

We ran the Busch Grand National car at Charlotte, Rockingham and Daytona, but we didn't have a lot of success with it. We had engine problems with that car, too. But on the short tracks, we finished second in the points championship that year and won a lot of races. We didn't really chase the points, we raced where the big races were, but we still ended up second.

We had a very successful year. We turned some heads and got some attention. People down here began to know who I was, and they actually cheered for me. Here is a different face out here running against the guys they have seen for years and years and years and beating them and putting a good show on. It was good racing back then, and people appreciated that. They got behind me, and I had a lot of support. Of course, that made Kathy and me both feel good.

But living away from home and spending all that time away from home was getting pretty old, it was really testing Kathy's and my relationship. It wasn't fair to them, my two boys, so we decided, or I decided I just wasn't going to do it. I wasn't going to live in Virginia with my family in North Carolina. I was getting sick of that motor home, too. So, after that successful year, the car owner and I decided we were going to part ways under friendly terms, no problems. So, again, in 1981 I didn't really have a ride. I started that season without a steady ride.

I was driving for this guy and that guy and didn't have any problem having a ride. People knew I could drive the Busch Grand National cars, so I didn't have a problem there. I had a fellow in Maryland, Frank Plessinger, who had a Busch Grand National super speedway car that we ran Daytona with. It was a Pontiac. He owns Hagerstown Speedway in Maryland. Rex Cagle was the crew chief, an old race car driver and super guy; still is a crew chief. I did have that ride at the few select super speedway Busch Grand National races that year, but nothing steady on the short tracks or nothing else. I was just plugging away and of course I had gone through a bunch of Winston Cup shops that winter trying to promote myself.

"Hey, I'm available. I'm looking for a ride". I had gone to

the shop of Cliff Stewart right in High Point, which is real close to where I live. He owned the #50 car. Joe Milligan was driving it then and they were having some problems. Cliff said, "Well, we are going to let Joe try maybe ten races this season, and if things don't work out, maybe we will give you a call".

In the mean time, I'm driving these Busch Grand National cars and plugging along. I had a Winston Cup ride at Daytona with some people out of Maine, Dick and Bob Bahre. They owned Oxfordplain Speedway in Maine. They had an old Pontiac. They were just messing around in the Winston Cup and wanted a car. They always liked racing, so they had that car and were letting me drive it. That was a good opportunity. It wasn't a first class car but, it was still a car we could get out there and do some racing with.

We raced at Daytona with that car, the Daytona 500, and raced in the 300 with Frank Plessinger's car. That was what I was going to do that season until something else broke or an opportunity came along. That was a pretty tough time. We didn't really know what was going to happen. We raced Daytona and we raced some other races and we went to Darlington. I had the ride in Frank Plessinger's car on Saturday, the Trans South 200, and we won the race, 1982. That is when I won Rookie of the Year.

I beat the likes of Harry Gant. David Pearson was in it, and Allison. Back then, a lot of Winston Cup drivers drove in those races on Saturday. I won the race and impressed a lot of people. I didn't even stay there. I went home after the Saturday race. Kathy and I just packed up and went home. I must have impressed Cliff Stewart. After only the third or fourth race of the year, they were still having trouble with their driver. He wasn't running good, but they ran Darlington.

Monday evening I got a phone call from Cliff Stewart asking me if I wanted to come over to his shop and talk to him and his crew chief about driving their car.

Back then, Cliff Stewart had Performance Connection as his sponsor, and the good thing was his shop was only about 15 minutes from my house. So I jumped in the car that evening and flew over to his shop and talked to him and his crew chief, then came home and told Kathy we had a ride. I mean, that is how quick it happened, and pretty unexpected, too, because they had said they were going to let him drive ten races and see how it went. But it only went four and they made a change. A great opportunity for me. That's when everything started. I drove that car the rest of the season and went out and won the Champion Spark Plug Rookie of the Year.

I didn't win any races but we won Rookie of the Year and ran consistent. I drove for him the following year, still in a Pontiac. We should have won some races with that team but mechanical problems prevented that. We ran real good some times, but just had some problems.

Toward the end of that year, 1983, is when Rick Hendrick was putting a team together and they were looking for a driver. I had met Rick once at Charlotte. A friend who knew him introduced us. Of course, I knew Harry Hyde, who was going to be Rick's crew chief, and of course Harry knew me. Actually, a couple of years before, Harry and I had tried to get together when Donnie Allison had gotten hurt. Harry was crew chief for his car. We almost did get together, but the man who owned the car just quit racing when Donnie got hurt.

When Rick was looking for a driver, it was rumored that Dale Earnhardt was going to drive for him, then Richard Petty, then Tim Richmond, then none of this was happening. It was getting time when they needed a driver, so Harry suggested me to Rick. He called me, and we had a meeting.

I decided that everything sounded good. I liked Rick and his ideas. He was running a Chevrolet. He was a Chevrolet dealer in Charlotte, owned City Chevrolet, and I liked Harry Hyde. I knew from those first two years in Winston Cup racing, to be successful you had to be with the right people. You had to have the right team behind you or you weren't going to win any of these races, didn't matter who you were or how good you were. Harry Hyde had a winning record as a crew chief, a tremendous record in Winston Cup racing. That probably was the key that made me decide to go with Rick and Harry. It was Harry Hyde's experience. That was when I got involved with Chevrolet.

So, I made a deal with them for 1984 and went back and told Cliff Stewart that I was leaving him the next year. He got a little upset, and he wouldn't let me drive the last two races of the year, Atlanta and Riverside.

OK; 1984, Rick Henrick Team, Harry Hyde and Chevrolet. That was my first experience with Chevrolet, and it has been a great one. With that team, it took us eight races and I had my first win, in Martinsville, Va. A brand new team and go out and win a race in eight races - that is pretty good. That was my first Winston Cup win. We won three races that year on the Winston Cup series, Martinsville, Riverside and Nashville. That was the last race at Nashville, the last race ever for a Winston Cup car. 1984 was a fantastic year for a brand new team and my first year with Chevrolet. We were very happy with that.

Rick had just one team that year. I was his first driver. In 1985, he also only had one team. I went back in 1986 and drove for Rick, and Harry Hyde was my crew chief again, but unfortunately, we didn't win any races. We had a good year, finished good in the points and had a lot of good finishes and should have won some races, but we had a lot of mechanical problems with the engines.

Toward the end of the 1985 season, Rick came up with another team. He chose Tim Richmond as a driver and he put Harry Hyde as Tim's crew chief for 1986 and hired Gary Nelson as my crew chief. So, basically, I started over again with a new team and a new shop and we had to build cars. It was kind of a tough year, a transition year. We still had Levi Garrett as our sponsor and Exxon Motor Oil, and still had #5. I went out in 1986, first race out, at Daytona and won. We won the Daytona 500! What a way to start a year. Winning Daytona was one of the goals that I had set a long time ago. One goal was to just go there and race, and another was to go there and win. In 1986, I achieved both goals.

The thing that had been driving me through the years was to go to Daytona and drive and win. I am really proud of that. If you look at the list of winners of Daytona, it is not a very long list, and it is a pretty impressive list of names. This year, we have added another name, Darrell Waltrip. That race had eluded him for years. He has raced a lot longer than I have, and he finally won it in 1989.

It was a fantastic way to start the year in 1986, and Gary and I went on to win the first race that year at Dover, Delaware. After that, we developed some problems, a lot of engine problems and mechanical problems and we didn't win any more races that year. But, we finished well in the points, and we had eight polls (Busch Polls) that year.

I have had a poll every year that I have been in racing. I am proud of that fact. I hope that streak continues. I have been in the Busch Clash every year that I have been eligible.

I went into 1987 with Gary Nelson, again with Chevrolet and with Rick, and didn't do nearly as well. Again, we had a lot of engine problems, mechanical problems. We ran real good, had polls and all that, but just couldn't win a race.

In 1987, Rick formed another team with Darrell Waltrip and Tide as the sponsor. Waddell Wilson was Darrell's crew chief that year, and everyone thought that was going to be a great combination. But, it didn't work out very well. They had a lot of problems, so at the end of the 1987 season, they were looking for a different combination of people, a change.

With the bad year that Gary Nelson and I had, we were looking for a different combination, so Rick decided to switch things around a little bit. He put Waddell Wilson with me and put Gary Nelson on Research and Development and Darrell Waltrip got another crew chief. So, in 1988 I starting over again. I have been with Rick Hendrick for a long time, but I have had three different teams.

The #5 came from Harry Hyde. The numbering system in Winston Cup racing is a little complicated. It doesn't go by points or anything. It goes by car owners. The car owner gets a number and he can keep it for life if he wants to. Eventually, all the numbers are getting used up. Even if the car owners are not active, they can keep their number. Harry had run the number 5 as a crew chief a few years before that, I think with Neil Bonnet, and no one was using that number at the time. So, Rick went to NASCAR and said we would like to have #5, and that is how we came up with that.

In 1987, I got invited to race IROC, and I won my very first IROC race, at Daytona. I went on and won Watkins Glen, and won the IROC championship.

The IROC Camaro and the NASCAR Monte Carlo are, of course, completely different types cars. There is no comparison at all. The Camaros that they run in IROC are set up on an equal basis. The winning is up to the individual driver. That is the whole concept; get 12 of the best drivers in the world together and see who is the best in equally prepared cars. I am very proud that I won that championship. I was invited back in 1988 to run IROC, but we didn't win the championship. We did win a race, we won the Michigan race, and we went into the last race at Watkins Glen in the point lead again. Unfortunately, we had a problem at Watkins Glen and didn't win the championship. We didn't get invited back to run in 1989 because of some political reasons, but hopefully I can earn my way back into that series because I really enjoy

running the IROC. Racing against the best drivers in the world, that is the only place you can get that opportunity.

I like running Camaros. I drive one on the highway, an IROC Z. I love driving a Camaro and to go out and race them is an equal thrill. They are a real neat car and a lot of fun to drive.

After things were switched around with Waddell Wilson as a crew chief in 1988, it has been a super relationship. We won Pocono which ended a dry streak for me since the Dover race in 1986. It was a successful year, and I think we finished sixth in the points. We won polls last year, and now we are in 1989. We have already won a poll, and we are running real consistent with the Monte Carlo. We haven't won a race yet this year, but it is still early in the year. We are third in the points, which is only 37 points out of first, going into the Bristol race. Our consistent runs have done that for us. The car has been performing well.

Of course, now we are anxiously awaiting the arrival of the Lumina. The new Chevrolet. With the Thunderbird getting smaller and more aerodynamic, we thought we were going to be at a disadvantage until the Lumina came out. But, surprise, surprise, we have been very competitive and consistent, but we still believe that the Lumina is going to be a better car than the Monte Carlo.

You know, the Monte Carlo has made history in Winston Cup racing. It has been around, I don't know how many years, and there have been some changes made to it, the front nose and then the sloped back glass and all that stuff that have helped the car win more championships and more races than any other car in history of Winston Cup racing. I am a part of that because I won some of those races. I have won some of those polls and have added some of the points to the Manufacturer's Championship, so I am a part of the Monte Carlo history, and I am glad I am. I am glad that I got with Rick Henrick and Chevrolet.

It will be kind of sad to see the Monte Carlo go. It has been so good for us. I mean, we have just run the thing to death and it just keeps going. We already have some Lumina's built, but we will take the Monte Carlos and just change the body. We will have to shorten the frames a little bit because the Lumina is shorter but everything else fits right on.

With wind tunnel testing that has been done up 'til now, the Monte Carlo is a better car as far a drag numbers compared to the Lumina. It is a faster car in the wind tunnel, but we feel certain, with a little time and a little testing, we can get the Lumina as good as the Monte Carlo has been as far as the drag numbers. The advantage of the Lumina is the down force that it can generate. The Monte Carlo has the lowest drag numbers but it is very hard to generate any down force. To balance the car out aerodynamically with front down force and rear down force, with the Lumina we can turn that spoiler up a little bit and we can generate some down force in the back of the car. The front of the car already has down force. So, aerodynamic down force is what helps the car stick when you go through the corners. That is more important on some tracks than on others.

That is where the Lumina is going to help us do the things

to generate down force aerodynamically to help the car stick in the corners when we need it. The Lumina is shorter and more compact, and when you put the same amount of weight in a compact space, it is easier to control. You don't hang it over the back wheels as far or over the front wheels as far. You put it more towards the middle and that helps the handling of the car. Physical size and aerodynamically, there is going to be a gain for us so we are pretty confident that the car is going to be better.

There's a rumor that NASCAR is likely to go to the V-6 in 1990 or 1991 instead of the V-8. I don't think NASCAR will do that. At one time, that was the plan. That was why the Busch Grand National Series went to the V-6. It was to be a stepping stone, a testing area for Winston Cup to eventually go to V-6. But as long as the manufacturers keep building V-8s, I believe Winston Cup will keep running them. They have found that the V-6 is not a very economical engine to use. It costs a lot of money to build and a lot of money to maintain. They have raised the reliability of the V-6 up, at first it wasn't very good, but still the expense of running that engine is pretty high.

We ran a V-6 in the Busch Grand National car. The majority of the Grand National teams run a Buick V-6. It is a very fast engine, probably easier than a Chevrolet to build to make go fast, but we used a Chevrolet V-6. A shop in Winston-Salem built the engines for my car, and the Chevys are as good as, and sometimes better, than those Buicks. So, we are confident that if NASCAR were to switch Winston Cup over to V-6, we are in good shape, but I don't see that for a long, long time.

Geoff Bodine on pit selection:

In Winston Cup racing, your pit selection goes first by the previous year's point champion who gets to pick first. No matter where he qualifies, he gets first choice of all the pits. Then they go by qualifying and a point order. The top 10 in the points, if they qualify in the first round in the top 10, get to pick in that order. Pit selection is important at most race tracks, some not as important as others, but at short tracks like Bristol, it is very important. The pit rows are very narrow, the track is very small, and the prime pit sections are the first pit, the first pit area going into turn one. Toward the corner is the best pit area. When you come into the pits there is no one in front of you to block you in and you are the closest to get back out on the race track, and you don't have any traffic to drive through as you are exiting the pits.

Bill Tower

Corvette Man
And NASCAR engine builder

By the time I was 12 or 14, I was racin' motorcycles and hill climbin' on weekends. I went into stock cars in 1960-64. That was a 1933 Chevy 3-window coupe with a GMC 6-cylinder, 302 cubic inch. I was high point champion in my junior and senior years in high school. The sprint car I drove was very well known, called the Bardall Special. I run around Florida and went out in the mid-west in car #2. Then I went into top fuel drag racin' for years. The car's name was Rat Trap. It was the test car for Goodyear. I tested all the new rubber compounds for the Indy cars. Also, the car was the Motorama car in 1969 and won Best Engineered Car in 1970. The car was also a highly successful top fuel dragster, and I got out in 1977.

I worked in a dealership in Tampa, Florida, Dempsey Chevrolet, when I was goin' to high school. I was workin' for the dealership race team. They ran stock cars. The owner of the dealership liked my work, and he put me in to go to the General Motors Institute of Technology. I graduated from GMI, but I didn't pursue it until I sold the top fuel car. I was sponsored by Chrysler Corporation at the time. I did try a couple of the ZL-1 experimental aluminum blocks in my car, but it wasn't a durable engine for my application. The nitro that you burn in those cars really produces a lot of horsepower, and the aluminum block just would not stand the pressure. But after I sold the top fuel car in 1977, I got into different aspects of racin'.

When I was out in Pomona and Bakersfield, I won out there and got an opportunity to meet Mickey Thompson. He sponsored my car, Rat Trap AA/Fuel Dragster. They're called Top Fuel Dragster now, and when I won the race, I got myself into a movie with Steve McQueen. (The Islands Wonderer - 1968). Steve McQueen did all the motorcycle drivin'. He actually jumped the fences and did all the tricks himself. There were no stunt men. I drove all the segments of the drag racing part of it.

The movie prople presented me with a trophy 4-feet tall. It's inscribed:

For your participation in the great movie "The Islands Wonderer" and winner of the championship race at Bakersfield, California. Bill Tower.

Life Magazine was doing an article on racing at the time when I was runnin' my top fuel dragster in NHRA. I was out in California and I was doin' real well. Matter of fact, I set the speed record at Bakerfield. I won a lot that year. One of the Life Magazine people came and interviewed me for one of the awards. I won the "Outstanding Sportsman of the Year" award for the drag racing segment of sports. I went to the banquet and was very lucky to be with Richard Petty and A. J. Foyt and lots of the top name drivers that I admired over the years.

The trophy has incribed on it:

Bill Tower for contributing to completion of safety film
Life Magazine, Hollywood, CA.
Outstanding Sportsman Award, 1969-1970

By then, I was Top Fuel Dragster 4-time national record holder with the car I built, and that year it seemed like the car ran so good. Back in 1966, I was one of the first drivers to go over 200 miles per hour. At that time, I went 213 to 218 mph, then I backed it up in Bakersfield and set a new ET record way down in the 6's, around 6.23 I think. Also, I was one of the first drivers to go to 5-seconds and over 250 mph. That was with a front engine car, too. It was real excitin' that I could contribute to being in the records. I guess that is what brought the fame to receive the "Sportsman of the Year". That award is one of the cherished things I will ever have, to be with all the best.

My first love over the years has been Corvettes. One year I especially like is 1957. '56 was the year the fuel injection came out makin' 1 horsepower per cubic inch. The engines were 283, they developed 283 hp. All the races the Corvette was in set records. Chevrolet's new 4-speed was released then, too.

When I went through GMI and worked with Research and Development at Chevrolet, I happened to meet the R&D team, which at that time, was headed up by Vince Piggins. He is now deceased. He became a very good friend of mine. I was kind of a test pick for them at the time. Remember, Chevrolet was not into racin'. Basically, we did a lot of testing engine configurations and also worked on the Indy program for Buick, in the V-6 program. That year the two cars sat on the pole and outside pole at Indy.

Now I'm building NASCAR engines, but also I build sprint car engines and some All-Pro engines and top fuel engines. I don't know where it is goin' to take me, but I've been buildin' engines for several years now for the #25 Chevrolet (Rick Hendrick Motor Sports owns the car) when Tim Richmond drove it and now Kenny Schrader of Missouri. It's the Folgers car. Benny Parsons drove it after Tim Richmond. Harry Hyde is the crew chief of the car, and we work together somewhat, testin', tryin' to get the car goin' fast.

The key to the whole project is what you start with. You start with a nickel alloy block, special made, that comes from Chevrolet, out of Research and Development, a "bowtie" series or the high performance series. It is a small block engine in the same bore and stroke configuration as the 350. When I get an engine, I X-ray it. I make sure that everything is straight in it. By "straight" I mean if the line bore in the engine is correct and where the pistons go in the cylinders in direct relationship to the crankshaft. There is a lot to do, but the key is the block assembly. Then I go on to the crankshaft and camshaft. Everything I do to the engine is X-rayed and heat treated if possible.

I even heat treat the camshaft. I X-ray it first, then I put temper in it. I check the structural rigidity of the crankshaft and the camshaft, and see if I need to nitride them. That is a hardening agent. The critical thing is boring the block and getting the cylinders straight.

Next, you go into the head work. You have to flow the heads on a flow bench and use the proper way to flow them. In the last couple of years, we have come upon a real big snag that has dropped power from 650 horsepower to 425 to 450. That's called a restrictor plate. With 4 one-inch holes, it just kills the power of an engine. But we are managin' to get faster every day and technology is gettin' back there.

Some of the parts we use to build an engine are Chevrolet, some are not. The crank we use is an aftermarket, not Chevrolet. The rods are also different, non-Chevrolet. The crank is forged steel. When we talk of NASCAR engines, we don't talk of anything other than forged materials. We try to use hard materials so that breakage is a very minimal.

The pistons are racing varieties of aluminum that I have special built to my specifications, one of my secrets. I was the first to run a two ring gland piston. I learned that in my drag racer, but a NASCAR motor, they said "no way". But it worked and made 30-40 more horsepower. Pistons are the key on the whole thing, the flow factor and how they burn, how true they burn the fuel off, and the "squelch" area of the head versus the piston surface. The job is to get that geometry correct so the fuel gets totally burned instead of running out the exhaust. Sometimes in road racing when the drivers lets off coming into a corner, fire comes out the exhaust. That's what we call "fat", the engine is drawing in a lot of fuel and can't burn it off. It goes through the engine and burns out the exhaust. That's a waste. We have to look at every drop of fuel as critical in a 500 mile race.

We have to look at gas economy as well as performance. We try to get 4 to 5 miles to the gallon. That is also according to the track and depends on how hard we turn the engine. That's the key on gas consumption. We have really done well on that, to still produce the horsepower.

We are limited. The fuel cell has to meet the approval of NASCAR. They check it at every race, Daytona or Talladega or anywhere, and they put a seal on it. They make sure you get the proper amount of fuel that they recommend for that application.

It's very critical, too, that you have a very good carburetor man. The carburetor is like a computer telling the engine that it is going to produce that horsepower. It is really an art to get everything to work in harmony.

The carburetor is more secrets. Here again we stress gas economy. You have to flow the carburetor and make sure that it is flowing the amount of fuel that the engine takes. What we use is an aircraft air meter. A Holley is not a supply and demand carburetor. It will supply more than the engine can take, or it will lean the engine out so it will burn the pistons. The amount of air that the engine will consume mixes with the amount of fuel, the carburetor does it automatically, but a Holley will not do it that way. You have to jet the carburetor to what mixture you want. You have four jets. Stagger jetting is what a lot of people do. You have to get that carburetor down to where it really flows good, then you will be able to do a lot better with the jetting.

Everyone I've seen runs a Holley. To run the Daytona 500, I think it is probably a 390, but here again you can't flow that carburetor into one inch holes. Your flow is too much for one inch holes, so you have to watch how big you go with the carburetor versus not too small so you can atomize the fuel. It really takes an engineer to figure it all out.

There is a lot more to it than people just walking up to the car and saying it is running nice. There are hours and hours in assembly and a lot of time on the track; you have to test. A dyno only does so much; that track tells the tail. I have taken an engine off a dyno and put it in a car that wouldn't get out of its own tracks. I have also taken an engine that was un-dynoed, and it went unbelievably. So you see, a dyno tells you just a certain amount, but that experience on the track and knowing how to get it going is the key.

The aluminum heads are also non-Chevrolet. This has been a real touchy situation for the past few years.

GM makes a Pontiac head, a Buick head and a Chevrolet head. They are all competing as to which is the best. There is no preference really. We have run the Pontiac heads a lot and the new Chevrolet heads that are not even released yet. The ones I have tested are going to produce a lot more horsepower, too.

You have to consider the restrictor plate on the super speedway motors. On the shorter tracks, we run without the restrictor, so then you change and go with a different configuration on the heads. You can flow more air. The engine that Kenny Schrader won the Talladega 500 last year ran Chevrolet heads. I think the stage 5 or 6 heads had just come out. I believe those were the heads.

I try to stay around a 64cc chambers. You can get them with 58cc chambers, but I think the engine runs the best at around

64cc. The compression ratio is chosen according to what engine application, usually around 12-1/2. We've gone to 13 and found that the exhaust temperatures are different. A happy medium is around 12 to 12-1/2 to 1. Some people run a little more.

Each team runs different types of intakes. They are also aftermarket. What we are doing on the heads is making the runners taller. What I mean by "taller" is that the intake ports going into the head are taller. This lets air go into the head in more of a direct approach. Consequently, you have to go with a taller intake to get that what we call "reach area" in the heads in more of a direct form to get higher velocity air flow and a little more ramming.

Smokey Yunick really came up with that ram effect in the head area years back. Now we are seeing that it has actually proven out to make horsepower. For a while, the engineers thought that the direct approach into the head was not the way to go, but in the years since then, we have proven that Smokey was right. To make the real horsepower, the faster engines are running higher intake ports and so on. The technical term is "high riser" but I call it a "raised runner" intake. We consider it a new product.

See, the intake can fit only the raised runner heads. You cannot put it on a regular 350 engine. It won't work. So the intake is matched to the head. The intake is cast of an aircraft aluminum. It has some strengthening properties in it that they use at the foundry when they pour it so the warpage isn't bad.

I try to stick to 355 cubic inches. NASCAR rules let you run 358. I think some of the Fords will go 358. We use 2.05-inch diameter intake valves, larger than production LT-1 valves of 2.02 inches, and 1.65-inch exhaust valves. I grind them all, so when I put them in the head, they are probably a little less than that.

The restrictor plate affects valves, too. If you go too large in valve, the squelch area changes. The flow factor of the engine limits the valve size. Sometimes smaller valves make more horsepower. Sometimes we will grind the valve down even though we started out with the 2.05, we will come on down maybe to 1.95. We also try to "cc" the head as we grind the valves. The 650 horsepower engines need the larger diameter valves, but not with a restrictor plate. Another factor is blue-printing the motor.

I use triple springs for valve actuation. Triple springs are a must because at the end of a 500, a lot of strength has been taken out of them. In conjunction with the strength that we need, they work well at high RPM's (7200 rpm). I use roller rockers with a stud girdle that fits down the studs of the head and keeps the geometry all in play. If you don't run the stud girdle, at high rpm and constant running for several hours, your geometry goes away and your studs actually move. A long girdle keeps it all stable.

At Daytona, for instance, we try to run between 7200 to 7400 rpms. Sometimes we will run 8200. It is according to the driver and how much he wants to brutalize the equipment. That is just totally up to him. We try to run 7200 and kind of keep it until the end, and then we will go for it. I mean, anything goes at the end. If you are going to try to win, you have to be competitive. If the engine will turn 8200, you try to get to the front. If you are up front, you try to pull away from the train and be by yourself instead of fightin' with ten or fifteen cars.

It makes a big difference if you can pull away. The relationship from 7200 to 8200 might be 50 horsepower. You have to consider whether or not you are drafting. Lets suppose you are out single, not drafting. That takes horsepower away. When you pull out and go by yourself from 7200 to 8200 you are gaining very minimal. If you can pull away, that takes brute torque and horsepower. If you can pull away and maintain it, you know the other cars can't pull down and come to the front. If they try, they go backwards. So, if you are the dominating car and you are in the front. You can actually pull away like Elliott did three years ago. He just absolutely pulled down. If you noticed, he didn't blow the field back but he slowly did it. He had true 40 to 50 horsepower over the other cars.

Another key factor is when you are in the draft at Talladega and Daytona, if you don't study who is with you, you can pull down and nobody will pull with you. What happens? You go clear to the back of the line, and they won't let you back in. So you really have to use your head. At the end, you can make a mistake and it can cost you several thousand dollars. I call it "brain fade".I have been in the situation where I know exactly how they feel. It is a split second when you make that decision to pull down, but it could be fatal for you.

If you don't have much time to get back to the front, pit stops become real important. If you have a good bunch of guys that can get you out quick, that is a very contributing factor. If you don't, you are going to be back to 10th or 15th in a heart beat.

You might have a motor that can run 650 horsepower without a restrictor plate and be out there running roughly 200 mph at maybe 8000 rpm, but everybody else is, too. The crew chief has a lot to do with that. He determines how to set up the car, including the rear end ratio. On the Folgers car, that's Harry Hyde.

In addition to building racing engines for a lot of racers, Bill Tower is also a Corvette owner/restorer with a collection of several famous Corvettes. Among them are the Bill Mitchell SR-2, the Betty Skelton Daytona Beach record car, the Jim Hall/Roger Penske Grand Sport (# 5) and one of John Greenwood's SCCA Corvettes.

"The fame of the number 5 Grand Sport," confirms Bill, "is that it won Nassau every time it was there, 1963, '64 and '65. All the years it run, even when Penske had it, the car was a 'back door' Chevrolet race car. Chevy gave Penske parts, and it went back to Chevrolet for an aluminum motor. The last year it raced, Penske ran a Traco engine in it."

This is the car that beat Porsche and started the revolution in IMSA GTPrototype racing. Brian Redman conceived the idea for a Chevrolet powered, ground effect Lola coupe that became this T-600. Although missing the first four races of the 1981 season, Redman went on to dominate GTP and won the IMSA GTP Championship. Daytona Speedway photo.

The New Road Racers

And the GTP Corvette

The beginning of the new era of Chevrolet in top category road racing was in 1981 when the Lola T-600 ground effect coupe showed up for its first race at Laguna Seca on May 3, 1981. The car was so radical in styling that it caught everyone's attention. The typical sports-racer of the time was the aged Porsche 935 in its many derivatives, but here was a car dramatically new. With its rear fender skirts and - of all things - a fuel injected Chevrolet small block, The Cooke-Woods GTP Lola generated a few guffaws. An iron block Chevrolet going up against the big boys?

In qualifying, the Porsche turbos were quicker, four of them in the hands of top drivers. Brian Redman, driver of the new Lola, was uncharacteristicly nervous. He was a well seasoned driver having won on every major road racing track thoroughout the world, except Le Mans which has continued to elude his every effort. Having been on the works teams of five successive world champions including Porsche and Ferrari, why should he be nervous about another race in a new car? Everything was on the line. The Lola T-600 had taken so much of designer/builder Eric Broadley's resources that if it didn't win at Laguna Seca, Broadley would be broke.

Brian positioned the car a conservative 5th on the starting grid, then eased passed the Porsche's to take the car's debut victory. It was a historic moment. Suddenly, Porsches were no longer competitive. As the season progressed and Redman dialed in the car further, it became the fastest, best handling car in IMSA and won the championship that year by a huge margin. After missing the first four races of the season, Redman drove the car to a fantastic record of 5 wins and 5 seconds to take the IMSA title by almost double the 2nd place finisher, John Paul, Jr. who also drove a T-600, the second car built.

The brilliant yellow Cooke-Woods Lola was a radical GTP coupe, chassis number HU-1. It was also the first coupe Broadley had built since the T-70 Mk IIIB of the '60s. And just as suddenly as Porsche was eclipsed, Chevrolet was the new force in GTPrototype racing, America's top series.

The car was so influential that it spawned sufficient interest within Chevrolet's revived interest in racing that a new project was begun. A new Lola T-710 was to be the test bed for Chevrolet engineering analysis of the new generation

Not only did the T-600 revolutionize GTP racing, its radical styling introduced so many new aerodynamic features, that all subsequent GTPrototype winners can trace their styling to this car. Daytona Speedway photo.

turbocharged V-6. In time, the GTP Chevy also raced the small block as well and became another force to reckon with.

It is today's most advanced "Corvette". As a road racing machine, its life span could be counted on to be not much more than a year, competitive forces being what they always are. This was a car designed for racing in America's best series, and perhaps the Le Mans 24-Hour, the world's premier race.

Hurtling past the pits at Le Mans, then taking the fast right hander, followed by the esses and onto the long Mulsanne Straight was what the car would have done in that French classic. Up through the gears to flat out on Mulsanne, 250 mph, and the driver anticipates the sharp, 45 mph right hand kink at the end. Then brake hard and down shift 5-4-3-2-1. Up through the gears, and roar out of the turn followed by two dozen of the fastest cars in the hands of the most capable drivers in the world. Streak through left and right turns named Indianapolis and Arnage at the fastest speed possible, then back through the pit straight. Imagine that, lap after lap for 24-hours, day and night, rain or shine, for some 7,000 shifts over the 8.36-mile Le Mans circuit. It takes real men to survive that and tough cars to last the enduro.

The goal of the GTP Corvette was to enhance Chevrolet's international, high performance reputation by racing the 24-Hours of Le Mans and other Group C events on the European calendar. Along with America's own International Motor Sport Association (IMSA) GTPrototype series, the new Lola-Chevy had quite a task ahead of it.

Another facet of the project was to further develop Chevrolet's 90-degree V-6 engine technology. The possibility of that engine becoming a racing threat was very real, expecially with turbocharging and new generation electronics.

The T-600 was so superior to the competition, mainly Porsche, that not once did the car finish worse than 2nd. Daytona Speedway photo.

The Corvette GTP grew out of Redman's Chevy V-8 powered Lola T-600 as an evolution of the Lola chassis. The chassis was designated the T-710 and was designed and fabricated in the shops of Eric Broadley's famed Lola Cars, Ltd. in Huntington, England. Herb Fishel, manager of Chevrolet's High Performance Operations, put it this way,

"Our intent is to turn the knowledge gained through on-track experience into viable applications for our production cars and trucks. Thus, the rationale for the GTP Corvette. It's a rolling testbed for grooming our V-6 to carry on the winning tradition of our small-block."

The major difference between the V-8 T-600 and V-6 T-710 was turbocharging. Unlike the well developed and normally aspirated 8-cylinder, the turbo-6 offered new ground for

Inspired by the T-600, Chevrolet undertook a new generation Lola as a racing testbed for the turbo V-6. Chevrolet photo.

Many other Chevrolet powered GT Prototype cars came on the scene in the mid-80s making GTP the toughest series in this country. This is the Leon Brothers March-Chevy.

A number of Chevy engine builders rose to the occasion of GTP racing. Ryan Falconer and VDS proved to be excellent builders of GTP Chevy small blocks.

engineering. The V-6 is both smaller and lighter than the V-8 and produces more power in turbo form. Among many other advantages, the car's lower overall weight offered the dual benefits of reduced stress, thus lighter parts, and faster speeds through turns, thus reduced lap times. Top speed of both cars was similar, but acceleration of the turbocharged Corvette GTP proved to be considerably quicker.

The basic construction of the T-710 followed the styling lines of the 1985 Corvette to maintain product identification although the wheelbase of the GTP was almost 10 inches longer, 106.5 inches compared to 96.2. The GTP was also about a foot longer, primarily because of its extended and more aerodynamic nose that just cleared the ground by 2.5-inches.

The chassis of the car was a monocoque main section utilizing aircraft technology riveted aluminum panels sandwiching lightweight honeycomb aluminum. From monocoque pivot points, the front suspension was A-arms with coil-over shock absorbers. One interesting feature of the suspension's advanced push-rod and rocker arm design is its driver operated capability. In the cockpit, a lever could be used to alter the angular position of the suspension rocker blades, thus the car's anti-roll capacity could be changed during a race. The rear suspension was a similar mechanism, again with driver control. With 16-inch diameter tires, 23.5-inches wide on the front and 27.0 on the rear, the GTP

Rick Hendricks Motorsports campaigned the highly competitive Goodwrench GTP Corvette through 1988. Chevrolet photo.

Inside the GTP Corvette is pure function. Riveted sheet aluminum construction and full instrumentation became the norm after the Cooke-Woods Lola.

Tucked into its cramped engine bay, the highly reliable V-6 with turbocharging produced 775 hp in racing tune and 900+ in qualifying tune.

Corvette could exceed 2 G lateral acceleration, more than twice the production Corvette.

Unlike production Corvettes, aerodynamics of racing cars is a give and take situation. Because they are considerably heavier and usually driven at modest speeds, street cars need to be the best wind cheaters they can be, and the production line Corvette's drag coefficient of 0.341 indicates it is certainly a very slick design.

However, the GTP Corvette has the dual task of needing minimum air resistance and maximum down force. Without down force, tire spin limits power to the ground. The design of the GTP takes these requirements into account. Its flat underbody met Group C prototype regulations, and it incorporated ventures rising from the underbody and exiting between the rear wheel well extensions to create a low pressure area. Acting as an inverted aerofoil, the GTP shape and large wing kept the car glued to the ground.

The GTP body was made of high strength Kevlar fabric bonded with epoxy resin and incorporated a number of NACA type ducts for entry of cooling air or venting of high pressure areas. The left side inlet fed air to the turbocharger intercooler and to the engine oil cooler. The right side inlet fed the single large engine radiator and transaxle oil cooler.

Overall, the GTP Corvette was the showcase for Chevrolet Power. The car's heavy duty cast iron V-6 block was an adaptation of the 90-degree engine in a variety of production GM cars although displacement was reduced to 209 cubic inches from the standard 229. Stroke was reduced from

3.48-inches to 2.75 and bore was increased to 4.0-inches from 3.74 to produce a more favorable over-square form. The block, internals and cast aluminum heads were over-the-counter, but special parts were from Chevrolet's heavy-duty parts catalog. The heads were closed chamber with 64-cc volume that deliver a modest compression ratio of 7.5:1.

Using a compact Warner-Ishi Model RX9-L turbocharger provided maximum boost of 20 psi to produce 775 horsepower as first raced. Later, output was increased to around 900 hp. With a Hewland VG 5-speed transaxle, the 1950 pound GTP Corvette proved to be a formidable machine.

The car was fast when it debuted in 1985 and went through development to become the black and silver Goodwrench bullets sponsored by Rick Hendrick the next year.

While setting the fastest qualifying lap in record time, "Doc" Bundy and Sarel van der Merwe won the pole position for the Daytona 24-Hours of '86. They did the same the following year at Daytona, and set many GTP enthusiasts to wondering if another championship Lola-Chevy year was in the making. When the team took the power laden GTP Corvette's first win at Road Atlanta (Apr. 6, 1986) in convincing style, fans and competitors alike were looking more closely at the fastest Corvette.

The turbo-missile won the pole position, set a new track record while qualifying (124.998 mph) and went on to win the 313 mile race at Road Atlanta by establishing a new race average record of 120.951 mph. This victory broke a string of 16 Porsche wins and put an American make in the winner's circle for the first time in years.

Then came the Grand Prix of Palm Beach and another Corvette GTP win. Both Road Atlanta and Palm Beach were in the string of seven pole position performances (all by Merwe) that established a new IMSA record. The following year, 1987, looked to be a good one for the Hendrick Motorsport GTP Corvettes. They were quick, as usual, setting four poles and three race fastest laps, but the car rarely went the distance with no wins and scored a distance 2nd to Porsche in the manufacturer's point race. Durability problems continually palgued the car.

For 1988, the cars were improved about 3 seconds a lap with updated V-8 power, but so were competitors. The year was dismal, finishing 4th in the IMSA manufacturer's points race and no wins. At that point, the life expectancy of the GTP Corvette was about ended, and the project was retired. Crew chief Ken Howes thought the GTP Corvette could still be competitive. It just needed development.

Brian Redman

Formula-5000 and IMSA Lola T-600 driver

Recalls his many championships

I guess the first Chevy powered sports car that I drove was the Lola T-70, but it was a Can-Am car, in 1966 in England, a Group 7 car. After that it would be in a Lola T-70 Mk IIIB, the coupes that were so attractive. They had either engines that were 302 cubic inches for world championship races, which was the limit, or for non-championship races, we used 350 cubic inches. It was a very good car.

If the Chevrolet engine, at that time, had been able to produce the power that the Porsche 917 produced, then the T-70 would have won races, but it didn't win many international races because it didn't have the power of the Porsche. The Porsche at that time in its first form was a 4.5 liter. In effect, it was one and a half 908 engines, and it gave about 570 horsepower. Then it went 5-liter and by the middle of 1970 and was giving like 620 horsepower. The Chevy, I think, at that time was some where down in the 500 area, so it had substantially less power. That was the reason the T-70s were not able to beat the Porsches.

AG: From your experiences in the T-70s and many other teams during your European racing, how did the T-70s compare with the GT-40 Fords that also ran American 5-liter V-8 engines?

Brian: The T-70 Chevrolet engine was not as highly developed as the Ford at that time, because Ford had had a massive attack on Le Mans and various other sporting ventures, and the benefits had come down from that to the private owners in terms of very good, reliable engines. The Chevy at that time did not have that background.

AG: By the time that you came to the United States and did Formula 5000, what kinds of differences in the development in the engine could you see?

Brian: Well, there was quite a bit of work done in England on the engine. Allen Smith, an engine builder from Darby in England had developed his own inlet fuel injection manifold, and it was kind of a cross flow manifold. It was quite low down and it crossed over. The intake on the right side fed the cylinders on the left hand side.

The 5000 was also fuel injected, but before that the 5000 was on Weber down draft 48 IDAs, and the reason that the fuel injection was developed for them was not the power so much, but the throttle response. The carburetors suffered from fuel starvation. The Formula 5000s produced very high cornering power and because of that, the Webers either went rich or weak. They suffered from fuel problems coming out of a tight corner in second gear, like the corner onto the straight at Mid-Ohio for instance, the carbureted engine would just give a couple of coughs, bup, bup-bup, and that was enough for a fuel injection car to pass it. So eventually, fuel injection was on American engines. It was Lucas fuel injection on a McKay manifold that became the popular standard wear for Formula 5000. Then, of course, development on the engines went ahead slowly, as it always has done. You know you gain a little bit here and there. The engine builders would work on the engines and would get a bit more bottom end power, a bit more top end power, a bit more revs. You know, just a usual.

The engines were eventually 8000 rpm engines and very strong. We had tremendous reliability from our Chaparral engines built by Franz Weis, he used to be Jim Hall's engine builder and chief mechanic and chief car tester. He was a very good driver and wonderful engine builder. Today he builds the engines for Mario Andretti, and I think for Bobby Rahal as well. He is one of the best engine builders in the country. We had immense reliability at the time when Chevy's really weren't so reliable. We ran four years with Formula 5000 and we had one engine failure in that time. The T-70s with the Chevrolet engine were cast iron, and the 5000s were also.

AG: Given the changes from say 1966 to 1973, seven years of development, what kind of differences could you as a driver distinguish between the Chevy engines in those various types of cars?

Brian: None really, because in the different cars you have big differences in weight, 500 pounds difference between the Lola T-70 and a Formula 5000 car. So that in itself makes everything different. I didn't really take so much notice as to what was actually being done to the engines, and they certainly didn't tell me very much. Engine building is a bit of a magic art and the builders don't share the secrets, do they?

It was in 1971 Formula 5000 racing when I came to the States, but it was 1973 before I ran regularly in North America. I came to the States in 1972 with my own car to do some Formula 5000 events, and we finished second in the championship that year, to Jody Scheckter who became World Champion. But we missed three races because I was driving for Ferrari in Europe in the endurance events, and we only missed the championship by a few points. I think we won five out of the eight races, so we won most of the races that we ran in, just didn't do enough races. The total points weren't

high enough.

AG: Then in 1974 you were champion? And 1975 and 1976?
Brian: Yes, 1974, '75, '76.

AG: Were you ever in a Formula-1 car in 1972 so you could compare the difference between that type car and a 5000?

Brian: In 1972, I was driving Formula 5000 in Europe and three races in America, but I was driving also in the McLaren team in a M19 McLaren standing in when Peter Revson was busy doing American races. When he was doing Indianapolis and some of the other big Indy car events, I drove instead of him in the McLaren Formula-1 teams. So I had almost a direct comparison on a week by week basis. The Formula-1 car was lighter, and its power band was narrower. You had to work with the gearbox much more than in the 5000. The Formula-1 car braked a bit better because it was lighter, and it was a bit better balanced, but it didn't have the power coming out of the corners. So the actual difference in lap times between the Formula-1 and the Formula 5000 was almost nothing. Sometimes the 5000s were actually faster than the Formula-1 cars. There wasn't much difference. Formula 5000 became the "national formula" all over the world, really. It was in South Africa, New Zealand, Australia, America and England. It was the main national formula.

It didn't replace Formula-1, it was in addition to Formula-1. Several races both in America and in Europe were combined events. Not the world championship races, the non-championship events, and in fact Formula 5000 cars did win some of those combined events. And Skip Barber had a Formula-1 March in the Formula 5000 series. They were allowed in. There were races where the 5000s raced against the Formula-1 cars.

The main reason for Formula 5000 was, it was a low cost, powerful racing car. The cost was pretty low, it seems crazy when you think about it now. The engines were much less expensive than the Cosworth engines and easier to maintain. Otherwise, the cars were quite similar. It was just a cheaper formula of a very powerful racing car.

AG: It was in May, 1977 that you crashed a full bodied Formula 5000. Why had SCCA changed the rules to get rid of the open wheel formula?

Brian: Only because the race track promoters felt that the crowds that they were getting weren't big enough. The racing was good, but they felt that they weren't getting the crowds, and so they decided that because Can-Am had been very successful, it would become Can-Am. At one point in its history, Can-Am got a good name and was known throughout the motorsports world. SCCA said that they wanted to call the Formula 5000 series the Can-Am, but they couldn't do that because Can-Am cars were full bodied cars. So, you had to put full bodies on your Formula 5000 cars, which is what everybody did.

AG: When you were testing at St. Jovite in a full-bodied Formula 5000 and crashed, what happened?

Brian: I know that Jim Hall and Franz Weis in testing the car before the season started had decided that it did have a problem at the front, that it was too light in the front, and they had changed the front of my car. It wasn't the standard one, and just a bit before I turned over at St. Jovite, Elliott Forbes-Robinson did the same thing in the same place, but he landed on his wheels. He did a complete loop. I only did a half a loop. I went about thirty feet in the air at 170 mph, came down upside down.

AG: During the period after the crash when you were recovering from your extensive injuries, you raced off-and-on as I recall, but when you returned to racing on a full schedule, was the T-600 Lola-Chevrolet the car that you returned with?

Brian: Yes, it was. Up to then, racing in those days wasn't like today. There wasn't much money. I was really helped by Jo Hoppen who is the competition manager for VW-Porsche-Audi. He helped me a lot by providing me with rides. He would find me a car and he would pay me. I would go and drive, but I was only doing five or six races a year, at that point still living in England and not having any business in England, so that was my sole income.

By 1979, it was pretty obvious that I had really got to do something. This was about two years after the accident, so I talked to Carl Haas, and having driven for four years for him, he was a friend of mine, and he said if you would like to come and sell racing cars, come on over. So in 1980, we moved to Lake Forest in Illinois, and I went to work as a racing car salesman.

At about that time we had received the IMSA rules for GTP cars, and also at that time, I think that Porsche had lost only one race in four years in IMSA. John Bishop, quite rightly, was very anxious to change that. He wanted competition. He wrote a set of rules which kind of favored the Chevrolet engine. I read the rules, and I said to Carl, "Lola could build a car that could probably win races under these rules". He agreed.

I had to go to England anyway on some business to see Eric Broadley on some other business things, and I took the rules to Eric and told him, "Eric, you could build a car that fit these rules". He said, "Yes, we could". So I went back to Carl and told him that Eric agrees. Can we order two cars? Carl said. "No. I am not buying them".

They were $80,000 each, without the engines and gear boxes, and Eric needed the money up front for those orders before he could build a car. That was in 1980. Carl told me that if I could find someone to buy the cars, then he would split the profit on sales of future models and on parts. He is the sole importer for Lola, so any car made by Lola must come through Carl. I was friendly with Roy Woods, who I had known from the Formula 5000 days when he was entrant of the Carling Black Label car. He was kind of an owner, but he was a driver as well. He was a good driver that had driven in the Trans-Am. He showed some signs of interest in it, and so did Ralph Cooke. He and Roy decided to form a partnership and buy the first two cars. The project started to go ahead in July or August of 1980.

Ralph and Roy were going to have a big team that would also have Trans-Am cars that they would drive and incorporate Can-Am cars that Carl Haas would enter and the Lola T-600 that I would have in the IMSA Camel GT series. So, on one of my trips to England, Carl said why don't you meet with this guy, John Bright, who sent a letter looking for employment. I met with John at Lolas. We got on together right away, he said, "I would like to move to America right away, and yes I would love to look after building this car". So, my instruction to him was to build it and have it in America by the end of March, 1981, come what may, whatever Eric said. "It has to be in America by the end of March!" He really spear-headed that, and built both of the cars and sent them out.

The engines was done by Chaparral, who at that time, had a new engine builder, Gerald Davis. He had taken over for Franz Weis because Weis had joined VDS Racing, and that is still what his shop is called today. VDS Racing, that was Count Van der Straten who was a great racing enthusiast and supported Formula 5000 and other cars for many years. He built a shop in Midland, Texas and Franz was a part owner of it.

Franz had worked for Jim for many years back in the old Chaparral days. When they came to Europe, he was one of the mechanics. He is from Stuttgart in Germany and is just a great mechanic. He left and so Gerald Davis, who had been a sprint car engine builder, joined Chaparral cars and he built our engines. And again, they were great engines, 350 cubic inch Chevrolets.

We weren't allowed to use aluminum heads at that time. Later on, we did use them when IMSA changed their minds. We had the time when we could use Brodix heads, then we couldn't use Brodix heads, it was a big confusion. But again we had great performance from these Gerald Davis Chaparral engines. We only had one engine for a long time. We would fly it back and forth. John Bright would take it out of the car on Monday after the race, fly it back to Midland, Texas and we would have it back on Thursday. It went to Midland for overhaul and back to us for the next race.

The first race for this new car in the IMSA series was very important. We tested it at Sears Point in April of 1981, and we knew it was good right away because we were close on the lap times of the records held by Danny Ongias in the Interscope 935. We took it to Riverside a week later. We ran it around Riverside and again the times were good. We had some problems with the cars but nothing real drastic. It was basically a good car.

The T-600 had no real relationship to the T-70. At one time, though, it had been seriously discussed that we would build a more modern version of the T-70, but Eric said, "No, it is not the right way to do it. We should build a ground effect car along current technology lines".

It was basically Eric who suggested ground effects. But, of course, ground effects were the big thing at that time. So when the opportunity arose and the rules didn't ban ground effects, it was the thing that you obviously had to do because ground effects were already proven in Formula-1. It was taking Formula-1 ground effects and modifying it to sports cars. Quite a lot of work was done in the wind tunnel by Lolas, and the car came with full ground effects.

It was the ace for the early days for ground effects in relation to sports cars. We knew how good it was when we had good road holding and good braking, but the car had a diving about under braking problem. It had something to do with the suspension layout, we think, and we never really found out what it was. But the car, otherwise, was very good right away. The balance was good and you could change it by altering the wing or the roll bars. We had a very well balanced car.

We could have run it first in the Riverside 6 hours, but we thought that was really the wrong place for a new car. We didn't know how long the engine would run. We didn't know what the life of the engine would be, so we decided to run it at the one hour Laguna Seca meeting in May of 1981. 'Course, everyone came for the race. Eric Broadley was there, Carl Haas, everybody.

Carl says I was an absolute nervous wreck. I was responsible not only for driving it, but I was organizing it as well, team manager and driver. The night before the race, Carl takes a big draw on his cigar, blows out a cloud of smoke and says to me, "You realize, if this car doesn't win, it could bankrupt Lola".

I was an absolute ruin. I hadn't slept for days. I didn't qualify

very well, I was about fifth. The race started, and I immediately dropped back to about eighth because the car felt very bad going into Turn 2. Turn 2 at Laguna Seca is one of the most difficult turns in all of North American road racing. It is just about flat out or was in those days, and when I came off the power for just an instant going into Turn 2, the car was moving around. There was something wrong with it. It hadn't been doing that in practice.

The first thing that you think of is a tire going bad or a loose wheel and every single lap I said to myself, "I have got to go in the pits". But I knew if I did there was no chance of success because in a one hour race, you can't make a pit stop. I kept going and on about the tenth lap it was OK, so I started moving up, and eventually I won the race. I moved to the front at, probably, three-quarters the way through. I had a big run with John Paul Jr. in his 935 Porsche, and Bobby Rahal was in our other team car. Bobby and I had just won the Daytona 24 hours together, in the Cooke-Woods 935 Porsche, prepared by Garrison Engineering.

The Lola T-600 was a very, very good car.

Ken Howes

GTP Corvette Team Manager

At this time (1988), I've been racing for 22 years. I'm from South Africa and raced there or worked in racing since I was

18 years old. Boy, it seems like, you name it, and I have done it somewhere. Mainly single seater cars, Formula-1, F-2 and Formula Atlantic. Through the 60s, and in fact right to the 70s, we ran up-to-date, current Formula-1 cars. We started with a Lotus 49, and a few years later bought a Lotus 72, and we ran those for several years in the early 70s.

The next year, 1974, we ran a Lotus 72 again in the Formula-1 championship with the same driver, Ian Scheckter, and finished second in the South African championship that year. Then in 1975 we ran a Tyrrell 007 and came in second again. We won the championship in 1976, '77, '78 and '79, at which time we got a little tired of it. I was team manager, and I mean, literally, we were building cars, building engines, and racing all the time. The most people that I ever employed at one time was four. It is always a lot of hard work, no matter how many people you have, and we are still busting a gut somehow.

In 1980, we went into a GTO type of racing in South Africa. The regulations are very similar, and technically, we won that championship. We won enough races to theoretically win the championship, but through the year we had an ongoing struggle with the regulations and legality of the car. In a sense, we got "conned" when they let us race, because they needed us, but we knew that they were ultimately going to do us in.

That was kind of a low point in my career, and we all got a little disillusioned with it. At that point, Ian retired and I kept the work shop going but we really didn't run a team. So, 1981 was a little bit of a nothing year; just finding ways to pay the rent. Then in 1982, the championship changed a little where the cars had progressed to where they were really Formula-2 chassis but we used Mazda rotary engines, and I ran a car for a guy. We ended third or fourth in the championship.

Then in 1983 we ran a two car team and enticed Ian Scheckter back out of retirement. We ran a March chassis with Mazda rotary. We then won that championship in 1983 and again in 1984 with Ian.

That is when my life went upside down, because early in 1984, Kreepy Krauly, who are a manufacturer of swimming pool cleaners, decided to set up their own team in America, GTP, and approached me and asked if I would run it for them. Well I had a contract to run this Formula 2 team and I was in a bind. I spoke to the people in South Africa, and thought about it, and went to our sponsors and explained what was going on. They said, well, "we think that you are in good enough shape. Why don't you do both?"

So in 1984 I ran two teams, one in South Africa and one in America. I commuted, literally. I would be in America for two weeks, and in South Africa for two weeks. That was tough, but we had a reasonably successful year with that GTP car. We won the Daytona 24-Hour race, and we won again at Lime Rock. That was with a March 84G that we bought from Al Holbert. He had used it in 1983.

My thoughts at the time were that we are having to start up a new team in a strange country, and I needed a car that had some kind of potential, one that the problems had been solved. I didn't need to start out with everything against me. We ran Andial Porsche engines, and to this day am very good friends with Alvin Springer.

In 1985, I decided that I could no longer commute back and forth. I was nearly dead. I decided to come to America full time, and run the Kreepy Krauly team. We planned to do the full season but after the 24-hour race at Daytona, politics got involved and effectively Kreepy Krauly withdrew. What happened was an anti-South African Lobby in Florida were looking for publicity for their cause, and we were using essentially South African money and had South African Drivers and a South African Team manager. They approached the Miami Organizers for permission to have an anti-South African demonstration at the Miami Grand Prix. That was the beginning of it, and there was a lot of bad stuff flying around. They then threatened to picket Kreepy Krauly's retail outlets. The company was not big enough to fight something like that, and we decided to withdraw from the Miami Grand Prix. At that point Kreepy Krauly looked at their involvement and decided to withdraw their support.

They were good with me personally. They tided me over and left me here with this shop here in Indianapolis. We were based in Atlanta in 1984, but due to fighting the traffic, we moved up here to Indianapolis and have been happy here. At that time in 1985 things were looking bleak. I managed to keep the doors open for a little while. Kreepy Krauly had agreed to sponsor a trip to Le Mans, so we converted one of our race cars to Group C regulations and did the race at Le Mans in 1985, but we didn't do very well. Fortunately, we were able to sell the car in Europe, and get some of the money back.

Then about that time, I heard about this project with Rick Hendrick and Chevrolet. In 1984, there had been a lot of talk around that Chevrolet had this car and were looking for a team to run it. In 1984, John Pierce of Chevrolet Special Products had come to various race tracks talking with people. Everybody knew that this project was out there somewhere, and of course a lot of people were chasing it. We had spoken to John Pierce, and he knew who we were. I never thought any more of it. When our problems became known, this was around March of 1985, I was thinking, I have Le Mans to do and after that I don't know what's going to happen. Out of the blue, John Pierce called me and said, "I hear that you have some problems. What is happening?" I told him, and he gave me the number of a guy named Rick Hendrick. I phoned him, and that was the beginning of this project.

Chevrolet had approached Rick Hendrick to get involved, he was very interested but his background was NASCAR. He really didn't know what IMSA was all about. It was almost a perfect match. Rick had the car and Chevrolet's support and here in Indianapolis was an IMSA team that didn't have anything to do. Rick paid us to do some testing initially, because no one knew if the car was going to be competitive because it had been lying under covers. The car was built by Lola in England, commissioned by Chevrolet.

Chevrolet had gone into this project where their stylists and aerodynamics people had an idea of what a Corvette GTP should look like. Initially, a body was built in Detroit based on a Lola T-600. Aerodynamic tests were done in the wind tunnel at that point, and Lola was commissioned to build a better car with that body style. That car was built, and the V-6 engine was developed and Ryan Falconer was involved in that. Nothing really came of it. One story I have heard was that there was a management change at Chevrolet, and the new person really wasn't interested. When I first saw the car, it was in Detroit under a cover and had been lying like that for about a year. It had been tested a few times, briefly, but nothing had come of it.

Rick Hendrick and Chevrolet got together. So, through September, we were paid by Rick Hendrick to test the car and solve some of the problems, but it was fairly obvious that the car was going to be competitive. At that point Hendrick decided to enter a few races. I was thankful for it, because it helped me keep the doors open.

Our first race was at Road America in 1985, and we qualified reasonably well, but had engine trouble. I think the next time we raced was at Daytona, and again the car was competitive, but the engine program really wasn't up to speed. At that point, things had gone well enough that Chevrolet got serious about it. At the beginning of 1986, I was able to put a good team together. We continued in 1985 with that first car, and in May of 1986 we received the first of our newer cars. Lola built another car for a V-8 engine, and that car, somewhere down the line, was sold.

The 710 had got tidied up some. Then in June or so of 1986, we got our second car. At Riverside in 1986, Doc Bundy crashed the original car very badly and effectively demolished it. We did resurrect it here one winter, and it is now a show car, but it is not really suitable to race.

The three cars we have now all just evolved from those two cars that we took over in 1986. We have kept replacing them and updating them. We continued through 1986 with fair success. We won two races, Road Atlanta and West Palm Beach. In 1987 we really had the bit between our teeth. We figured we were going to do well, but we ended up with a lot of engine problems. It was mainly problems with the electronic management systems.

Chevrolet, in the winter of 1986-87, had developed their first generation electronic management system, and it seems like that killed us. So 1987 was a pretty bleak year, we showed promise. We qualified well but never were reliable and just really came away with nothing to show for the year.

In 1988, by this time, Chevrolet had a new electronic management system that they called Generation 2 which has turned out to be very good and very reliable. But the IMSA regulations changed and they put a restrictor on turbocharged engines. That took away the one big advantage that the V-6 engine had, which was very, very good horsepower.

The good horsepower hid a lot of sins. It made the average chassis look very good because we could just out-power anybody, but reliability problems got us. The restrictor took away the one advantage we had, so what we had was a car that was getting old and now down on power.

The basic design was laid out in late 1983 or early 1984, so by 1988, it's starting to show. The V-6 engine was no longer a good combination, and IMSA regulations had encouraged normally aspirated V-8 engines by this time. We felt like it was time to investigate that, so over the winter of 1987 and 1988 we assembled one car with a V-8 engine. We continued with the V-6, but took both cars to every race track we went to and did an lot of testing. It was apparent that the V-8 car was just about as good. It didn't have the throttle lag, and it wasn't difficult to drive.

In 1985, we were probably qualifying with somewhere around 900 hosrepower, racing at well over 800 horsepower with the V-6. That continued through 1986 and '87, qualifying at around 850-900. What the restrictor did was take us down to just a little over 700 horsepower. That's a big jump, and I began thinking that if the normally aspirated V-8 could make 680, that seemed like a good trade off. Complexity was down; didn't have throttle lag; and had a good power band. The V-6 had a very narrow power band.

The V-8 seemed like it was going to be reliable, but we were still a small team, and trying to run two cars with two very different engine layouts was starting to show. We weren't doing anything well. We were just doing both jobs badly. Then we decided we would concentrate on the V-8, and it looked promising. We built up a third car with the V-8, so we then had two V-8 cars. We put the V6 aside, hoping that development would continue, but it never did.

Jack Baldwin's 'Thunder' Camaro won 5 races and set 6 poles in 1986 as racing's most sophisticated Camaro.

Buz McCall's Skoal Bandit has raced on a shoestring budget, but carried the banner for Chevrolet fans.

There are now two sanctioning bodies in this country for racing Camaros, Mustangs and other production-based cars, SCCA and IMSA, and the Chevrolet versus Ford battles have burst back into prominence during the '80s. It hasn't all been Chevy versus Ford, either. Many other marques compete on the nation's race tracks. In IMSA, for instance, the GTO dog fights between Ford and Chevy was a grueling 17 race series in 10 months of 1986 and again the following year. Spread from Florida to New York to California, that many races in a single season is enough to grind down even the healthiest teams and drivers. The 1988 schedule brought some relief when the schedule was dropped back to 12 races, but. as always, every one of them was an exciting battle that drew huge numbers of fans.

Ford's ace driver, Scott Pruett, came from karting to real cars after proving his aggressiveness with 13 national championships, 10 professional titles and the 1983 Pro Karting World Championship. Pruett's killer instinct was keenly felt throughout IMSA GTO when he earned a seat in Ford's factory team of Motorcraft Mustangs handled by ex-drag racer Jack Roush. Pruett's closest competitor turned out to be his own teammate, Olympic decathlon winner Bruce Jen-

Darin Brassfield in a Corvette brought a new Chevrolet challenger to the Trans-Am in 1987. He won at Mosport.

Wally Dallenbach, Jr. and John Jones drove their Protofab Corvette to victory at Sebring, 1988.

ner. Although the Bob Riley designed chassis of the Roush Mustangs were three years old at the time, the prodigious horsepower of the Roush 5- and 6-liter engines was sufficient to make the cars highly competitive. Both Pruett and Jenner raced to win and for points, and that took tough cars.

The Brooks Frybarger Camaro handled by Willy T. Ribbs proved to be a great handling car, and was also highly competitive but didn't make it to the races until the season was more than half over. Willy scored two wins, two seconds and a third in six races to finish the '86 season 5th overall.

The big gun for Chevrolet was Jack Baldwin's wailing Peerless Racing Camaro. There were actually two Peerless Camaros that year. One was a 5-liter small block while the other was a 4.5-liter V-6 with fuel injection. The 5-liter car was so impressive in its debut win at Miami that Baldwin dubbed the car "Thunder". During the season, "Lotz o' Lutz" appeared on the rear bumper. That apparently was in reference to the car's factory connection and to Jim Lutz of Chevrolet Special Products. Baldwin captured 5 wins and three 3rd place finishes to end the '86 in 3rd overall, but still behind Pruett and Jenner. Baldwin was on the pole in 6 races (to Pruett's 9) and set fastest laps in 4 races (to Pruett's 5). (Pruett - 196, Jenner - 175, Baldwin - 159)

This beautiful yellow and white Camaro GTO was racing's most sophisticated car at the time. Riley had left Roush and did his chassis and suspension magic with Protofab to produce the Camaro with a carbon fiber tub, March Engineering suspension pieces like GTP type cars, an experimental transmission from Doug Nash, an ultra-modern rear end and computer-controlled shocks were just a few of the car's features.

From across the horizon came Dan Gurney's All American Racers turbo Toyota, driven by Chris Cord and Dennis Aase. But the manufacturer's race was all American. Due to Pruett's win in the season finale at Daytona, and Baldwin's 4th, Ford nudged out Chevrolet in the point battle, 256 to 252.

The 1987 IMSA GTO season fell to Gurney's Toyotas, and Mustang brigade was relegated to a distant 3rd overall.

(Toyota - 256, Camaro 248, Mustang - 187) Baldwin's Peerless racing Camaro won 3 races (Toyota took 8) and captured 6 poles followed by 3 fastest laps. Tom Gloy still finished the season 2nd in drivers points to Cord, and Baldwin was 4th.

Baldwin's spectacular vaulting exit over an embankment at Summit Point during a mid-season race, and missing the next race for repairs, was sufficient to hold him back from earning more points.

The '87 season was tougher than ever, and a new and exciting competitor appeared late in the season. Bob Riley had designed another car, a Corvette with independent rear suspension (is that something new coming from Chevrolet?). The car debuted at Sears Point where the heat got to Greg Pickett and robbed him and the car of a debut victory. That was the sixth from the last race of the year, and although the 'Vette matched anything speed-for-speed from there on, durability gremlins kept the Mobil 1 team from becoming a threat.

At Sebring of '88, the Protofab Polyvoltac Corvette of Wally Dallenbach, Jr. and John Jones teamed to win the 12-Hour. Pruett was back in Roush turbocharged 4-cylinder Merkurs and had won at Daytona, although Jack Baldwin, Max Jones and Paul Dallenbach almost won in Buz McCall's Skoal Bandit Camaro (it was Baldwin's old carbon fiber car).

With each of the long distance races split, one for Ford and one for Chevrolet, the new season opened into springtime with an exciting slate of races. It was, however, the last victory for the Corvettes and the Daytona 2nd for the Bandit was the last victory of the season until Wally Dallenbach brought his Corvette in the winner's circle at Lime Rock. Mechanical failures plagued all the teams that year, Ford, Toyota and Chevrolet, in the final point tally, that's the way they finished.

Over in the SCCA Trans-Am, 1988 was the year that Audi took the championship, but the series was a Chevrolet victory in that approximately half the cars entered during the season were powered by Chevy engines. And then there was Darin Brassfield's Mobil-1 Corvette that scored at Mosport.

By 1988, there was an enormous amount of racing going on

The Corvette Challenge for America's premier sports car put racing's most capable drivers behind the wheels of 40 equally prepared cars. This show room stock series of 10 races was created by John Powell and Chevrolet and began in 1988.

In 1988, the Cars & Concepts IMSA Barettas won the first-ever GTU championship by an American car. Tom Kendall won 7 races; Max Jones 1; in 12 rounds.

The International Race of Champions (IROC) is a showcase of equally prepared IROC Camaros handled by top drivers from several leagues, NASCAR, IMSA, SCCA, Indy 500 and Formula-1. Chevrolet photos.

in this country, and it's still growing at this writing. But this very brief accounting of modern road racing wars can provide little more than the flavor of what is happening on race tracks throughout the country. Road racing is more popular now than at any time in the past, and the competition is as fierce as ever. With increasing factory involvement in many forms, spectator turn-outs have grown tremendously, but it's not just cars on race tracks. Trucks and off road racing are also more popular than ever. All forms of motor competition has created a great new age of American motorsports.

If racing two decades ago is known as the sensatitonal '60s, this decade will go down in history as the exciting '80s.

226

"Little" Al Unser won 4 CART "street" races of the '88 season in this March 88C-Chevy. IMS photo.

Displacing 2.65-liters (161.5 cid) the Indy-Chevy produces 720 hp at 10,750 rpm on alcohol. Cast aluminum alloy block and heads; twin overhead cams; 4-valves per cylinder; 11.0:1 compression ratio; 325 pounds.

Indy-Chevrolet

The new master

The pride of Chevrolet is the new V-8, double overhead cam, pure racing engine for the CART series (Championship Auto Racing Teams). It was back in 1920 when Gaston Chevrolet drove a Monroe to victory in the Indianapolis 500. He averaged 88.5 mph. (Rick Mears won the '88 Indy 500 at

On May 29, 1988, Rick Mears made it 3 Indy 500 wins. He raced this Penske PC-17 Chevrolet to victory and scored the fastest lap at 209.517 mph. IMS photo.

144.81 mph.) Since then, the Chevrolet brother's name has become a household name recognized worldwide. Swiss born, the brothers Chevrolet made a great impact on American racing during the 'teens and 'twenties, and the Chevrolet name at Indianapolis returned in force in '88.

When the small block V-8 went into production in 1954, a new age of Chevrolet performance began, and during the early '80s, that engine actually raced at Indy in "stock block" powered cars and actually lead the race for a number laps.

Then, in 1986, came the all-new 2.65-liter Chevrolet Indy V-8. This was the Ilmor Engineering designed engine, and five years after the blueprints were laid down, the new Chevrolet engine was the dominant powerplant in CART. In 1988, Roger Penske added his 8th CART national championship, as a team owner, with the engine powering his own chassis. The Penske PC-17 chassis took 6 wins and his driver, Danny Sullivan, was CART champion. Then, in 1989, Emerson Fittipaldi won the 500 in a new PC-18 Chevrolet. He was the fastest ever, 222.469 mph!

During '88, Lola-Chevys took 5 wins, and March-Chevys won 4. With the Penskes, that adds up to 14. The new Indy-Chevrolet engine fulfilled even the most ambitious dreams when it scored 14 wins in 15 races during that year. Ford's DFX Cosworth that dominated the Indy 500 in '87 was completely shut out with no CART wins at all in '88. And the '89 Indy 500 was another shut out.

Danny Carr races the winningest Camaro in the country. Here he's with his 12.90 class 454 Nova, #1 in the nation.

Larry and Rick Green's 400-inch small block Camaro. Blew the engine, then insalled the tow truck's engine and raced!

Bill Kuhlmann's sensational 200+ mph Baretta is a "283 cubic in x 2" machine; fastest "doorslammer" in the world.

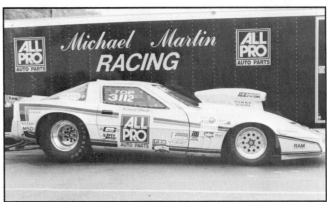

The quickest sportsman class, non-blown Corvette in the country, Michael Martin's 190 mph IHRA Top Sportsman.

Wally Stroupe's IHRA Top Sportsman Camaro is one of today's pro-built drag cars similar to Pro Stock cars.

Ken Koretsky's Superflow IHRA Pro Stock machine is a super Camaro capable of consistent 7.4 sec runs at 185 mph.

2-time IHRA Top Sportsman World Champion Terry Housley. Tom Swabe photo

Bill Kuhlmann

Fastest "door slammer" on earth

I got started in drag racing about 26 years ago as a junior in high school. There was a drag strip in my town. It woke me up on Sunday mornings, so I had to go out and see what was going on. Back then, a 1957 Ford was my first drag car. Then after that Ford, I went to a 1966 Mustang which, eventually, I put a small block Chevy in and ran it very successfully. That car was probably in a Modified Eliminator class. With the Chevy in it, it really picked up over the Ford motor, and back in the days of 1967 and '68, we were running in the 11.40 range with it, with a 331 Chevrolet in it. That was a built up 327.

We ran the Mustang to death. The Chevrolet motor had so much power for that unibodied car that it was pretty well beating the thing up. One day I came home and parked it in the garage and looked at it. The front wheels were so towed out from the unibody being beat up that I parked it. After that, I drove a Pro Stock Vega for a fellow in Wentzville, Mo. That was in 1976 and 1977.

After that, I have been all-Chevrolet ever since. The first car I built myself from the ground up was a Pro Stock Monza with a 331 cubic inch Chevy. That was in 1978 and '79. I went on my own and raced that Monza until about 1980.

For a low budget car, we did real well. We bracket raced and Pro Stock raced. We qualified at a few of the AHRA races, and they had people like Reher-Morrison and Roush. We ran fairly well, but nothing of real note. We got a couple of runner-ups in some outlaw events.

Then, I had Mike Spitzer in Indiana build a small block Chevy dragster for me. We basically bracket raced the car in a sand bag effort and just had tremendous success with it. It was in an 8.0 bracket, in that range.

We used a lot of Chevy motors. We tried everything from a 302 all the way up to a 400 inch small block. I even had an experiment once where we built a 380 inch small block, and we put fuel injection on it and nitrous oxide, and ADRA made it legal to run against the blown top alcohol cars. I didn't know anything about nitrous oxide at the time. When we went to the first race, I pulled up on the line against the world champion. By-the-way, we had a PowerGlide, a two speed PowerGlide and an injected small block against the blown big block. We put five cars lengths on him out of the gate, and I never got to shift into second because our nitrous melted the motor. We just coasted to about an 8.02 at 180 miles per hour.

I put that piece away and bracket raced the dragster for quite a few years. Then John Taylor, a local fellow in St. Louis, invited me to drive his Pro Stock 1981 Chevrolet. We did that off and on and qualified for most of the shows. Then he built a 1984 car. I got *Hot Rod* magazine's Rookie of the Year and UDRA Rookie Driver of the Year with that car finishing, I think, 6th in UDRA unlimited Pro Stock. Then I built the car that kind of got me a little attention, the Camaro with the big wing. That was a 1985 car.

The magazines were touting us as one of the possible cars that may go 200 miles per hour. The fastest we had ever been was 186, so we took that car to Darlington in the spring of 1987, and we were the only car over 200.

We ran over 200 fourteen times on different tracks that year, with a best at 204. We won the UDRA Pro Stock World Championship of unlimited Pro Stockers, and set 37 track records across the country. That really makes a person feel good when they've worked that hard. That successful season along with the awards that we received at the UDRA banquet, in a sense, landed the Summit deal with full-time sponsorship. I seriously don't know if I could have continued the next year with that kind of pace. The Summit situation is one where we race every weekend from February 'til October for sure and probably more than that.

Most people don't know that we have a schedule like that, and it may sound flamboyant and this and that to be a professional racer, but it can wear you down. We race two and three states away every single weekend, and we can't hop on a plane. We have to pull the whole rig, and pull it back home.

The new car a 1988 stretch Baretta. I wanted something aerodynamic, something Chevrolet, and stretched out for handling. It has 110 inch wheel base.

AG: Is the car built with your chassis?

Bill: Well, this is a High-Tech chassis. I have a chassis company, but racing full time doesn't afford me any time at all to build anything right now. I had a few guys that wanted cars built at the end of 1987 that waited for me to get done racing. So, I contracted Gary Heycheck out of St. Louis to build the bare chassis to my design, to actually do that while I did some customer jobs. That way the customers were satisfied, and I haven't taken on any new work since, because of the time. Then I completed the car.

I wanted something different with nitrous horsepower. The Sonny Leonard engines with Mike Thermos's NOS systems create so much power that the standard Camaro Pro Stock type chassis, I knew, could not handle that kind of power. It would have to be something with a double main frame more like a funny car. If you took a measurement of the bars in a single bar chassis, it would never be the same after a run.

The engines can produce as much as 1600 horsepower, honest horsepower measured on a dyno, 615 cubic inches, on gasoline, and the NOS nitrous oxide system that anybody can purchase. They try and gear what they sell to the individual customer's needs, but for all out racing, this was the system we got. I did very little to modify it.

AG: How much additional horsepower does that system give?

Bill: In spite of all the claims that all the nitrous companies make, in reality, pure honest horsepower - 400 on top of whatever you already have. What most people do not understand, and they wonder sometimes why those nitrous cars are so hard to get down the track, is that it is 400 instant horsepower. You push the button and you get hit by 400 more horsepower. It feels like another engine under the car. So it is something you have to learn how to drive.

Most of the guys that drive nitrous cars don't put on that little perfection type show that an NHRA type Pro Stocker puts on. Those guys don't have that kind of power. They don't have torque that is trying to rip the car in half. So, I compare it to the early funny car days when guys were just beginning to put in those big blown motors on what was the best chassis science at the time. We are in that "no mans" land right now where nobody knows exactly what to do because they have never had the combination of that much power with a standard configuration car. We like to think that we have a pretty good handle on it. We ran ahead of the pack so long, but right now there are some guys right there with us. There are even some cars that ran a tad quicker than we did. Our best (as of 8/88) has been a 7.11, but no one has beat the 207. I think Blake Wiggins ran a 206 in his Tran-Am, but you have to understand that when you attain speeds like that, one mile an hour is another light year. Currently, we're at 207.37, and we are working on the ET.

Drag Racing is fun. It is exciting, but it is also work like most people can't comprehend. We have calculated that it takes about 22 hours of work for every 7 second pass. It will take a sport that can be the love of your life and turn it into such work that sometimes you second guess yourself, but I have yet to burn out on it.

Wes Yocum, Jr.

At the Heartbeat of America
March 21, 1989

On Thursday, March 16, 1989, we had a big off-site meeting. At that meeting, we changed our Special Products group to what we now call the Chevrolet Engineering Race Shop. That is our new name. We have decided that, over the years, we are racing. Now, we are a race shop, and based on the chairman's letter of a couple of years ago, we are involved in racing now. We will be involved in racing to the point of development and testing, but we will not do sponsorship. We will run Camaros and Monte Carlos and Luminas in the racing game, and we will work with racing teams.

The teams in drag racing are Joe Lapone, Levi Garrett and Bruce Allen. In NASCAR, we are looking at Winston Cup and we have Rick Hendrick's with three teams. He has the Folgers team, the Tide team, and Levi Garrett also. We work with those three teams and we work with Richard Childress on the Goodwrench car. They are really the only four teams that we work with, development-wise. They test products for us, and we work back and forth to make sure we have the best performance parts out there.

We are still backing the Chevy Indy engine. We are doing development work with Ilmor. As you know, last year we just walked away with the CART series. We really feel we will do the same thing this year (1989). We have actually improved the engine from year to year.

We will continue to transfer technology from racing back into production. An example is what we have done with active suspensions. We put a car out last year with an active suspension on it, a GTP Corvette. That technology is being worked into, probably, production Corvettes in the next few years. But for this year, we have parked the GTPs. We are into an extensive design and testing development program for a new GTP car. You may not see that car on the road for maybe two years.

In GTU, we won the series last year. We brought in the Cars & Concepts people with Kendall and Jones. This year (1989) we decided to step up, so we are going into the Trans-Am series with basically those same Barettas modified to run Trans-Am. Jones and Kendall will be the drivers. It is a step up from GTU to Trans-Am.

I guarantee you, racing does improve production vehicles. There are a lot of things that racing can show us that we can move into production cars; safety items, brakes, steering. We even got into some seat belt tie downs that is now being looked at as far as production cars go.

Herb Fishel

Heartbeat of Today's Chevrolet

First of all, I am a car enthusiast. My first involvement with racing was in Winston-Salem, North Carolina, at Bowman Gray Stadium in the late '40s and early '50s. From there, it kind of became my first love; cars, racing, mechanics, engineering and that kind of thing. I followed it through high school, then got an engineering degree at North Carolina State University. I got my job with General Motors in 1963.

I came in at an incredible point in Chevrolet's history. In February of 1963, they debuted what they called the Mark IIS engine at Daytona Beach, Florida. Junior Johnson, Ray Fox and Smokey Yunick started as exciting an era as there has ever been in Chevrolet.

Go back and look at the speed increments from 1962 to 1963 and look at the qualifying speeds of those cars versus the competition, with that engine, we obviously had an unfair advantage. It caused NASCAR to dig pretty deep in their little book to find reasons to justify letting the cars run.

Chevrolet is really pretty basic as far as performance goes. It has a strong heritage and history of success. I think, fundamentally, because it has been important to Chevrolet. The Mark IISs and the ZR-1s, the Aerocoupes, Corvettes and Camaros; they don't happen without a purpose. They happened for a reason, and that is to be the products that create the idea of being performance minded. So, when those opportunities come up, they are products given to car lovers, to car enthusiasts. In the time that I have been here, we have never really varied very much from that.

For a company that is sprinkled with people like Duntov and Piggins, a phenomenal depth of engineering, and to take that product and put it in the hands of the racers, the results pretty well speak for themselves. We have continued to focus on the product, to make sure in our broad product line that the cars that have the image, the Monte Carlo, Camaro, Corvette and our trucks, that the potential is there for them to be very, very good racers. It is really a product focus in engineering and design. In 1963, it was fundamentally horsepower. In 1989, it is still horsepower but in a modern package. Racers are running forty miles per hour quicker with smaller engines and less horsepower today because of the engineering requirement of planning; the aerodynamics, the tires, the safety, just any number of reasons. So, 1963 was a horsepower battle and 1989 is still a horsepower battle, but it is a horsepower that encompasses every feature and every aspect of the car. It has been an effort to leave the racing to the racers and focus our efforts on developing products that have the ability, the quality and the performance capability in the hands of racers that they can go head-to-head with anybody anywhere in the world.

Our products can compete anywhere. They competed all over the world with Jim Hall. The Chaparral program competed in sports car type racing. I was here at the time, but I was not involved in racing. I was still a production engineer.

The small block V-8 is the most accepted engine in the world. In racing, it is used universally. It is raced in New Zealand, Australia, Europe, you name it. Chevrolet's success is directly attributable to the products. The fact that there were engineers here and visionaries like Duntov and Piggins that, through the political bureaucratic problems and federal regulations, continued to focus effort on designing products that made very capable race cars.

AG: When did you get involved in racing at Chevrolet?

Herb: In 1968. I spent from 1963 until 1968 in the basic engine design group. I was with the group that did most of the engine designs.

The evolution of the late '60s and early '70s was a very successful era for the Camaro and Trans-Am racing. A lot of work went into the small block V-8, the cross ram manifold and that type of thing. I think you will find it a very successful era for Bill Jenkins. That was the era for the Can-Am series. There was a lot of activity during that time, primarily focused on engines, designing and developing and continuing to work on the engine parts business.

I guess Chevrolet's modern return to NASCAR racing was with the Monte Carlo in 1983. When they introduced the new mid-sized cars in 1978, it turned out that Buick had the best one aerodynamically. Both were introduced in 1978, and NASCAR was reluctant to change. They really didn't allow the new mid-sized cars to race until 1981. That was mostly Buicks at the time. They were the bulk of the cars at Daytona, but there were Oldsmobiles and Pontiacs that year. There were only one or two Chevrolet teams. Richard won the 500 in a Buick. Junior did well and by mid-season. Waltrip won 10 or 12 races in 1981 or 1982, and Buick won the manufacturer's championship. Of course, everyone was racing small block V-8s.

Then Chevrolet obviously got interested in returning and with the debut of the Monte Carlo in 1983, the SS signaled their return. Russ Gee, who at the time was the chief engineer of power trains for Chevrolet, was the key. He got that thing done.

The production model had the flat front end, but with the aero package, it was called the SS, the Monte Carlo has been the most successful car in NASCAR history. It has won six consecutive Manufacturer's Championships, three Daytona 500s, four out of six driver's championships. Allison won in 1983 and Elliott won last year (1988), but Monte Carlo drivers won the other four.

I think the significant things in the modern day are the fact that in the 1983-84 time frame, we recognized the importance of off-road truck racing. We started programs in 1984, and by 1987-88, we had become a dominant force in Class 7 and Class 8. Our products are in almost every category and fifty percent of our retail business is in trucks. Chevrolet wide, we target for three million vehicles and half of that is trucks. I am proud of what we did in trucks in a hurry. We got in there, we learned and we made some mistakes. We quickly turned that around, and in the light trucks, we became the dominant Class 7 truck versus Toyota, Ford, Nissan, Mazda, and Dodge. We have done the same thing in Class 8, and we have an unlimited truck that is to debut this next month that could be the overall winner.

It is a Class 2 truck which means the wheel travel and internals can be modified, engine location, you can do a lot of things to make it extremely fast. So, the success of the truck program and the success of the Baretta as a road racer and a drag racing car is significant.

Today, the bulk of our effort is toward electronic controls. The evolution of show room stock racing would be a nice way to conclude your book because it goes full cycle. Originally, the idea was learning from the race cars and applying it to the production cars. Then, in many ways, the production cars became more advanced technically than race cars. We kind of crossed paths. When we got into aerodynamics, the total performance car, it was no longer just brute horsepower. Today, we have come around to the point that you can go into the showroom and buy a Corvette and a Camaro, install a roll bar, fire extinguisher and safety equipment, and drive to the track and go race for a year with them. To me, we have come full cycle. You go back to the mid-50s or early '60s, the things you remember about a Corvette or Camaro or a 454 Chevelle, then here we are in 1989 and have cars that are total performance cars. They do it all. They accelerate, brake, corner, start, stop. They are safe. They are economical.

When you look at what has made that happen, it is the evolution of the affluent young executives, the high income guys that can buy a race car, have someone transport it around the country, and they get on the airplane on Friday and fly to the track. They are not professional and are not going to win Indy or Le Mans, but that is a whole new generation of racers.

One of the things that has made that happen is the availability of the product, then the emergence of driver's schools. It is almost a cult thing, an "in thing" to do among a group of professionals and executives that are economically in a bracket that allows them to do this.

AG: In terms of other technologies, what do you see for the GTP program?

Herb: The key to any program like a GTP car is applying modern day engineering tools and management processes to designing, building and campaigning the car. It has to be a totally integrated, well balanced system.

AG: When do you think the GTP Corvette might be back?

Herb: Sometime in the early 1990s to mid 1990s.

AG: An all together new car?

Herb: I am proud of what we accomplished up until 1987 based on the steep learning curve that we were on and the Hendrick team was on. I am pretty happy with our involvement up to that point in time. To me the big benefit beyond 1987 is that in 1988 we learned an incredible amount of things about why we were not being successful. And more so than any other program. The '88 program in GTP was a catalyst that motivated us to take a little better look at how we do business, so we will benefit tremendously from 1988. The pay-off of that will be sometime in the future, when the team is there again with the GTP Corvette.

AG: How about the ZR-1 Corvette?

Herb: I don't think the GTO or Trans-Am is a reality. I think that takes the Corvette out of the relationship between the race track and the showroom and doesn't mean that much. It is competing against products that it shouldn't be. The ZR-1 with the LT-5 engine, obviously, it will do some dynamite things, but you have to look at where it fits at the engine's potential, in the 600 horsepower range.

The small block V8 is here to stay. It is going to out-live all of us. Since Duntov and Keinath, engines have been done on an approach where there are more "people involved". We haven't really carved out a new performance engine. We have done a 90-degree V-6, which is a spinoff of the V-8, and the 60-degree V-6. We have done the L4 and those kinds of things, but we really haven't done the kinds of things that Duntov did or something as radical as the "Mark" series of engines that Keinath did. The Indy engine was the next engine of those types, and that was done by Ilmor.

World's fastest street driven car, Calloway Sledgehammer Corvette. D. Randy Riggs photo.

232

Sledgehammer was driven to TRC, then became the world's fastest car with a track record 254.76 mph. D. Randy Riggs photo.

Calloway "Sledgehammer" Corvette

World's fastest road car

Among today's remarkable world of exotic super-fast cars, the Corvette ZR-1 stands out as Chevrolet's most spectacular production effort in the history of the marque. As a production car, there is nothing the performance enthusiast could want from the LT-5 engine and nothing more could be expected of the ZR-1 Corvette as a whole. Chevrolet Division Chief Engineer Fred Schaafsma would have it no other way. In December,1986, he became Chevy's Chief Engineer, and the ZR-1 bears his influence. Although the standard 5.7-liter Corvette is a realistic 155 mph cruiser, this new ZR-1 generation Corvette is the fastest production car built in this country, a realistic 170 mph vehicle. This car has excellent comfort, high style and is universally recognized as America's best sports car. It can pull within a whisker of 1 g lateral acceleration. Then there are those impeccable ABS brakes for easy, no-skid stopping in the shortest path on all sorts of road surfaces.

For the performance enthusiast looking for an "ultimate" machine, the Corvette platform provides the basis for Reeves Calloway to build his twin-turbo version. When Callaway's technicians get through with an RPO B2K special order Corvette with the Z51 suspension, it becomes a car capable of beating most of the world's exotic machines. The Calloway isn't the 32-valve LT-5 engine but the pushrod 350: 180+ mph; 0-60 in under five seconds; 60-100 mph in eleven seconds; with all the Corvette's comforts including air conditioning and still gives 20 mpg. Some piece of engineering!

To build not one of the fastest cars in the world, but THE fastest, Calloway did the Sledgehammer. Building upon his Twin-Turbo package, one very special Corvette was built.

When a German magazine called the Twin-Turbo Calloway a "hammer", Reeves & Co. conceived a 250 mph Callaway Corvette that became, appropriately, the "Sledgehammer".

The Sledgehammer story began unfolding in June, 1988. Callaway's team composed of Tim Good, Elmer Coy, Dave Hendricks and Talbot Hack built the car. Callaway was to drive, but drag racer John Lingenfelter of Ft. Wayne, Indiana was tapped for high speeds runs. Aerodynamics assistance by Tony Cicale and chassis work by Carroll Smith proved highly valuable. Otherwise, the platform of the production Corvette was retained.

The project materialized on the huge 7.5-mile highbanked Transportation Research Center (TRC) track in Ohio. The task of taking a fully streetable car from normal traffic conditions to attempt more than 250 mph goes well beyond anything ever achieved before. In itself, it was a bold undertaking for Callaway's small firm composed of just 38 people, but as word got around, existing American technology from outside corporations was made available in a team effort that made the Sledgehammer more than just a high speed test for Callaway. It was a high speed testbed for the finest technology available anywhere.

A highly modified Twin-Turbo Calloway 350 was taken to 1,013 horsepower, then "detuned" to 898 hp. That made the Sledgehammer a docile cruiser when the car was driven 700 miles from Old Lyme, Connecticut to TRC. The return trip was during a sleet storm and uneventful.

The car achieved its objectives when Lingenfelter flashed through TRC's speed traps at 254.76 mph. Not only did that make Sledgehammer the world's fastest Corvette, the run established the absolute record at TRC, faster than Indy cars, faster than NASCARs, faster than GTPrototypes, and faster than Ferraris, Lambos and everything else built for the road.

Into the Future

Smokey Yunick on the future of automobiles

The future of cars in this country? Well, the first time I was in Cole's office, I saw a sign on the wall that read, "The price of progress is trouble." Under there, it had a name, said Kettering. The trouble we got now is part of progress, and we will eventually get the thing solved. But it doesn't make any difference if we had enough oil to last four million years, it's still not solving anything. The more you use, the quicker the trouble comes. What the problem is, you've got to consume all the fuel. What goes on inside the combustion chamber? The real answer is, they don't know. By the time we get there, I think it will be totally different than the road we are on now. When they finally do find a viable solution to the thing, I think it will be a form of magentism.

Dr. Steve Bates

GM Research & Development Scientist

My Project is to use optical diagnostics on a transparent engine. By transparent, I mean that the liner that encases the piston is made out of transparent material. In this case, a single crystal sapphire which is very expensive.

We are also able to look up through the piston using an extended piston. There is a window in the top, an oil containment section in the crankcase and a mirror in between, so with the mirror, you can look through the top of the piston into the combustion chamber. That is important because top-dead-center is where most of the action is, and you can look up through the piston instead of looking through the side, which is only a narrow band at the top. My project is to use various optical diagnostics to look at what the combustion is doing and to look at what the flow is doing. The two of them interact to give different combustion characteristics.

In order to increase fuel efficiency, and eventually to decrease emissions, we want to be able to go to less fuel for a given amount of oxygen. This either amounts to dilution with combustion products or just putting in less fuel. When you do that, the effect of the flow inside of the cylinder becomes much more important.

One of the things that is not very well understood at this time is how engine design geometry effects the flow. When you get to "lean burn" engines, that becomes much more important as far as what happens during the combustion. So my engine is a way to, in detail, study what happens in each cycle and to find out what happens inside the combustion chamber while the inlet conditions stay the same. I'm looking at the generic physical phenomena that causes the flame to grow the way it does or to cause the spark to ignite the flame at all.

When you get very lean, i.e., very little fuel, you can get into a condition where the cycles oscillate between having a flame and good combustion and not having a flame at all, and this is because of the difference in the contribution of the residuals, the left-over gas from the previous cycle. That sort of effect becomes much more important when you talk about EGR (Exhaust Gas Recirculation).

When you do fuel injection, it turns out that the fuel that goes into the cylinder is actually vaporized from the fuel on the walls rather than coming from the fuel injector. The injector sprays out, and it actually piles fuel up on the walls of the intake port. That sort of thing is not so important for the sort of physics that I want to look at which is the more fundamental combustion.

Basically, I am able to look at it essentially for the first time. I have very light-sensitive cameras; the leaner the mixture the less light that comes out of the flame and the less light you have to take a photograph of it. I have light amplification of up to 10,000 on my cameras, so I can look at very lean flames that people haven't been able to study in detail before. Plus, I have various diagnostics that can actually measure flow velocity inside the cylinder.

Ultimately what you want to do is connect the geometry of the engine to what the flow does and to what the flow does to the flame during combustion; the net result being more efficient engines and less pollution. You want to do all those all at once. So it is very complicated, and you always have a variety of conditions. You have different demands to satisfy when you are running at idle and when you are running at high speed. There are all these kinds of questions that you have to try to answer in detail rather than doing what we have done in the past, which are global studies on engines.

Turbulence is not understood in general, and it is more complicated in an engine. It is more complicated still when it is interacting with combustion, and that is basically what we don't understand. Turbulence in the combustion chamber, in general, is really complicated. You start with a moving air-fuel mixture, then you have it all contained and everything is time varying. It all changes with engine speed, so it is just a real mess to sort out.

In the past, people have thought that you could just analyze everything statistically (globally). That turns out not to be true. There are very special things that happen in each particular cycle that may happen repeatably, and somehow you have to learn how to control them by the engine design.

This will be on the road within five years. A lot of people are starting to look at "lean burn" engines. What I am not including in this 5-years is what they can and will do with catalytic convertors.

Index